W9-BUD-598

The Politics of Broadcast Regulation

Third Edition

Third Edition

The Politics of Broadcast Regulation

ERWIN G. KRASNOW
Senior Vice President & General Counsel, National Association of Broadcasters
LAWRENCE D. LONGLEY
Associate Professor of Government, Lawrence University
HERBERT A. TERRY
Assistant Professor of Telecommunications, Indiana University

FOREWORD by NEWTON MINOW

St. Martin's Press • New York

121269

Library of Congress Catalog Card Number: 81-51850
Copyright©1982 by St. Martin's Press, Inc.
All Rights Reserved.
Manufactured in the United States of America.
09
fed
For information, write St. Martin's Press, Inc.,
175 Fifth Avenue, New York, N.Y. 10010

cloth ISBN: 0–312–62653–3
paper ISBN: 0–312–62654–1

cover design: Tom McKeveny
typography: Edward Cone

Contents

Preface to the Third Edition

Those who follow communications developments, even if they do no more than regularly read *TV Guide,* may wonder why this book is still called *The Politics of Broadcast Regulation.* Articles appear regularly in the academic, popular, and trade press describing a "communications revolution," and sometimes suggesting the demise of broadcasting. They could lead one to expect a different title.

We believe that *The Politics of Broadcast Regulation* remains the most appropriate title for our work. The words in the title, however, do not mean the same thing now that they meant when the first edition appeared in 1973. Then, broadcasting was much more of a discrete industry than it is today. There were competitors, notably cable television, but they were politically and economically weak. Some broadcasters tried to use the regulatory process to fight them off.

By 1978, when the second edition was published, it was clear that broadcasting's competitors were not going to go away. With help from the courts, Congress, and the Federal Communications Commission (FCC), cable had ready access to program sources that made its service attractive to consumers, although it remained a struggling industry. Other electronic mass media were little more than drawing-board projects. Broadcasting's old identity was challenged but had by no means disappeared.

With the arrival of the 1980s, however, it is clear that broadcasting can no longer be understood as an industry apart from or unaffected by other electronic mass media. The Broadcaster's Club, the lunchtime rendezvous for Washington, D.C., broadcast executives and professionals, has renamed itself the National Communications Club. Broadcast networks have begun to offer specialized program services for cable television and seek to change FCC restrictions on their ownership of cable systems. Several broadcast station groups have invested heavily in cable. Communications satellites, which largely arrived on the scene between the second and third editions of this book, have been used by cable entrepreneurs to link cable systems that provide religious, sports, news, and pay-per-program or channel services. Broadcasters have used satellites for the delivery of commercials, programming, and news. Direct-to-the-home broadcast satellite service is being proposed. Other challengers to broadcasting for the attention of viewers and listeners include teletext, videotext, multipoint distribution services, video disks and video tapes, video games, and even home computers attached to TV sets. Plainly, the broadcast world has changed.

We will not ignore all these changes in the present edition of this book. Significant as they are, however, they do not justify a totally new framework or even a retitling of the book. Broadcasting remains the central, mature industry surrounded by a host of interesting and potentially quite significant infant or adolescent media. As these media develop, broadcasting will remain the standard for their assessment. Expectations for them are defined by prior experiences with broadcasting. Most importantly, it must be recognized that they are emerging media: their long-term shape and impact remains unclear. It is premature to try to pull everything together now—to write some kind of comprehensive work about the politics of regulation of all the electronic mass media. Much better is a book that focuses on broadcasting and its modified environment but which takes into account that broadcasting is part of the larger field of electronic communications.

Broadcasting, then, as the term is used in our title, has changed much since 1973. So has regulation. It is possible that the peak of political zeal for regulation, left over from the 1930s and the New Deal, came sometime between the first and second editions of this book. Since the second edition, successive FCC Chairmen have latched onto various buzzwords and philosophies critical of regulation. We have gone from Richard E. Wiley, a Chairman whose objective was "reregulation," through Charles D. Ferris, who preferred "deregulation," to Mark S. Fowler, whose theme is "unregulation." What is going on here, of course, is but a reflection of trends also found in other areas—for example, banking and transportation.

Regulation may be criticized, but it is not about to disappear. New questions about its effectiveness and about the unintended, sometimes harmful effects of regulation are being addressed. The tendency is to talk about increased reliance on the unregulated marketplace, but regulation persists and may, in fact, be a hotter topic now than at any other time since the first edition. Regulatory theory—or deregulatory theory—is intertwined with technological change. Many of the new communications technologies expand the number and variety of media sources. They may bring broadcasters new competition, or they may simply become new business opportunities for them. Their development serves as a stimulus for deregulation, for many would like to establish an inverse relationship between media diversity and regulation: the greater the number of media, the less their regulation.

In sum, we do not mean today the same things by regulation or broadcasting that we meant in 1973. Then, broadcasting was the king of the electronic media mountain. In the 1980s it is clear that the mountaintop will have to be shared. In 1973 regulation was a concept that did not include its antithesis, deregulation, to the degree that it does today. Our old title, *The Politics of Broadcast Regulation,* remains appropriate if its key words are treated in their contemporary context.

One key word remains—politics. Whatever happens in the future will certainly be the result of a political process. In our first edition we described the emergence of citizen groups, the courts, and the White House as participants of increasing importance in an interactive, highly political environment previously dominated by Congress, the FCC, and the regulated industries themselves. The second edition noted that although the powers, objectives, and interests of those participants had changed a bit between 1973 and 1978, the basic political model seemed durable. For this edition, we have updated some fine points of that thesis, but as a basic framework for analyzing broadcast regulation, we have found it still satisfactory. We have attempted to make clear, to those more interested in the politics of regulation than in broadcasting, that much of what is described here occurs in other fields.

We have added some new case studies—disputes over how (or whether) to rewrite the Communications Act of 1934 and what role, if any, government should play in regulating formats used by radio stations. These new studies show more clearly than before the role of Congress and the heterogeneity of views existing within participant groups that we previously may have suggested were homogeneous. The new case study on the format change and revisions in the study on commercial time pay increased attention to the problems that arise when the government attempts to regulate broadcast content. We have also retold some of the early historical material on broadcasting to make it clearer that this is the history of the evolution of a political system and its participant groups rather than a general history of broadcasting.

The annotated bibliography has been updated and the notes that follow each chapter substantially expanded. Those with a deeper interest in the topics we discuss can follow up on suggestions and sources they will find there. If any academic purist is upset by our use of trade journals, we would call attention to an observation of former FCC Commissioner Glen O. Robinson, a professor of law both before and after his Commission service: "What there is to tell [about the inside workings of the FCC] is reported reliably in the trade press, from whom little seems to be witheld."*

Countless individuals have influenced both the original and revised versions of this book, including virtually everyone we have dealt with in the course of our work (Krasnow in his Washington, D.C., communications law practice; Longley and Terry in their research and teaching in political science and telecommunications, respectively). However we wish to single out certain individuals for their special willingness to share their insights into various aspects of the politics of broadcast regulation. Among those deserving credit are Norman Blumenthal, Michael Botein, Robert Bruce, Edwina Dowell, Tim Dyk, Lou Frey, Mel Friedman, Henry Geller, Alan Green, Don Gillmor, Doug Ginsburg, Susan Hill, Charles Jackson, Frank Kahn, John Kamp, Frank Lloyd, Mary Jo Manning, Barry Mitnick, Richard Neustadt, Alan Pearce, Karen Possner, Harry Shooshan III, Chris Sterling, Barry Umansky, Lionel Van Deerlin, Donald West, Steve Weinberg, Bernard Wunder, and Richard Wiley. Blame, if any is deserved, is of course not theirs but ours.

We have not mentioned the titles of the persons who have added to our understanding of the inner workings of broadcasting's political system because, in most instances, these individuals have held a variety of positions during the time this book was written. For example, many staff members of the FCC later worked inside Congress, the White House, the broadcast industry, and citizen groups, or in academe, in itself a statement about mobility within the regulatory system.

We would be remiss if we did not acknowledge our debt to Edward B. Cone,

*Glen O. Robinson, "The Federal Communications Commission: An Essay on Regulatory Watchdogs," *Virginia Law Review,* 64 (March 1978), 169, 172.

Elaine Romano, Richard Steins, and Robert L. Woodbury, Jr., of St. Martin's Press, for their encouragement and editorial skill. Finally, we would like to express our appreciation to the members of our families—Judy, Michael, and Catherine Krasnow; Judith and Becky Longley and Susan Richards; and Pamela and Anne Louise Terry. They provided the encouragement, sympathy, and patience necessary for this book's completion.

At the close of the Preface to the second edition we cautioned readers of that book that it represented our "best shot at a moving target." That advice bears repeating, but with the modification that the target is not only a moving one but one that, like the caterpillar and the butterfly (or the alien spaceship in a video game), may be capable of some radical metamorphoses in the not too distant future.

Erwin G. Krasnow, Washington, D.C.
Lawrence D. Longley, Appleton, Wisconsin
Herbert A. Terry, Bloomington, Indiana

Foreword

The Federal Communications Commission is one of the most important and least understood government agencies. Issues of momentous concern to every citizen come to the FCC, but its responsibilities, limitations, and activities are known only to a small segment of the press, the bar, and the engineering fraternities. True, it is accountable directly to Congress and is therefore subject to frequent congressional reviews of its decisions and deliberations. True, the courts are constantly reviewing—and occasionally reversing—Commission cases and regulations. True, the president appoints the Chairman and Commissioners, thereby exercising some supervisory control. But despite these continuing links with all three branches of the federal government, the FCC remains unfamiliar to most citizens.

For a number of years I conducted a seminar at Northwestern University's Medill School of Journalism. Graduate students of journalism and law students participated, and we probed the issues confronted by the FCC from the perspectives of both law and journalism. Guest lecturers included network presidents, commentators, producers, and regulators. We studied why broadcasting is the only medium of expression under direct governmental regulation. Hard, sensitive, baffling problems arise in interpreting the First Amendment in a world of rapid technological changes. I often ended class sessions by asking students to pretend that they had just been appointed to the FCC by the president and had to vote on a particular case or issue. It did not surprise me that often the vote was close.

That is one reason why I welcomed this book on its first publication and was able to use it so effectively in my class. Very few scholars have paid enough attention to the politics of the federal regulatory agencies. Professor William L. Cary of Columbia University Law School, former chairman of the Securities and Exchange Commission, led the way a decade ago with his classic book, *Politics and the Regulatory Agencies.* In that work Cary (who, fortunately for me, was my law professor when I was a student) perceptively analyzed the relationship between regulation and the political process from a scholarly as well as professional perspective. In 1973, Erwin G. Krasnow, an active member of the communications bar who currently serves as Senior Vice President and General Counsel to the National Association of Broadcasters, and Lawrence D. Longley, a political scientist with expertise in interest group politics, pooled their talents to apply this analysis more specifically to the record of one agency—the FCC. Their efforts produced an uncommonly useful book that probed some very hard cases. The authors showed how the regulatory process actually works, how it is influenced by political realities, and how decisions are really made.

The 1973 edition elicited a uniformly enthusiastic response from the critics, as witnessed by the following sampling of book reviews:

... well-documented and easy to read. The book should not be overlooked. We have relatively few on the topic of broadcast regulation, and this is an innovative perspective on the topic. *(Quarterly Journal of Speech)*

Adequate works on the regulation of American broadcasting, and particularly the role of the FCC, are unfortunately scarce. *The Politics of Broadcast Regulation* is a concise, engagingly written and provocative contribution to that sparse literature. ... If the likelihood of stimulating future research and suggesting a framework for such research is any measure of a work's significance, this is an important book indeed. ... The book occupies an important place in broadcast literature as among the first to attempt a systems approach to broadcast policy-making. *(Journal of Broadcasting)*

In producing this work, authors Krasnow and Longley have merged the practical experience of a communications attorney with the thought process of a political scientist well versed in interest-group politics. Their effort has produced a broad overview of the participants and forces which contribute to the aggregate political process known as broadcast regulation. ... Their book is a first in assembling a working knowledge of the components and principles that make up the political process of broadcast regulation. Moreover, they have taken the added effort to flesh out their assertions about interplay among interest groups with actual case studies of these factors in action. This alone should make it required reading for anyone newly arrived in the practice of communications law or broadcast management. *(Federal Communications Bar Journal)*

In this useful book Erwin Krasnow, a member of the FCC bar, and Lawrence Longley, a political scientist, have teamed up to take a hard look at the usually neglected political aspects of the problems of the Federal Communications Commission. This book provides perhaps the hardest look yet taken at the validity of present regulatory approaches. As such it deserves wide use of any course covering regulation or policy-making in the electronic media. *(Educational Broadcasting Review)*

The second edition, published in 1978, received similar praise:

[The second edition] is a seminal overview of competing clout-wielders in the serious game of public policy formulation in radio and television. *(Journal of Broadcasting)*

[The second edition] is a revision of a widely-used and already classic work. ... The book is now more than ever required reading for students of this field as well as broadcasters, as no other work quite pinpoints the players and issues as well as this one. *(Mass Media Booknotes)*

[The second edition] has much to recommend it. Its generally excellent content and its uniqueness in the literature of broadcasting assure that this work will maintain its secure place in the required reading on broadcast regulation.

. . . The Politics of Broadcast Regulation is interesting enough to leave readers wanting to know more and thorough enough to show them where to seek further information. *(COMM/ENT Law Journal)*

The revised and updated third edition is an even better book as a result of the collaboration of Herbert A. Terry. Dr. Terry, a successful telecommunications instructor and researcher, has a unique background that includes employment as editor of *access* magazine (published by the National Citizens Committee on Broadcasting) and as a faculty intern at the National Association of Broadcasters. The third edition significantly broadens and deepens the analysis of the policy-making process, adding insightful observations on regulatory behavior and pointed illustrations of the struggles over the regulation of entertainment programming formats and the rewrite of the Communications Act.

This edition shows that despite current trends at the FCC and Congress toward deregulation and the proliferation of new technologies undercutting earlier notions of scarcity, pressures continue to be intense in the regulation of broadcasting. The industry is strong, vocal, and has many powerful friends. Citizen groups, a relatively recent interested party, have now acquired some muscle and sophistication in dealing with the regulatory world. The White House is becoming increasingly concerned about regulatory decisions because of its newfound awareness that FCC decisions have both national and international implications. And Congress and the courts have the last word.

Let me give but one example from personal experience of the pressures encountered in broadcast regulation. When I was Chairman of the FCC, I was one of a few Commissioners who wanted to place some limits on the amount of commercial time on radio and television. We strongly believed that some rules were long overdue and proposed that the commercial time rules established by the broadcasters themselves through the National Association of Broadcasters be enforced. I finally mustered a majority on the Commission to support this proposal. After I left, my successor, E. William Henry, was besieged by the industry. Congress reacted almost immediately, and as described in detail in chapter seven, the House of Representatives made it clear to the FCC that it regarded the regulation of commercial time as unacceptable. Thus, we remain the only nation in the world with no rules on how many commercials a broadcaster may run, and our best broadcasters are reduced to the law of the jungle. The FCC is blamed as a tool of the broadcasting lobby when in fact its efforts to regulate were, in this case, frustrated by Congress.

Authors Krasnow, Longley, and Terry document other examples in this work. They conclude, quite properly, that although the FCC may initiate policy, the fate of such policy is often determined by others. A good example is the formulation of policy in the early 1960s concerning international communications satellites. We were able to get Comsat launched quickly and thus preserved American leadership in the world. But we succeeded only because the FCC compromised with various competing economic interests and theories and governmental and private agencies and because we turned to the president and Congress for the final word. This required an understanding of the political process, which almost always involves compromise. Sometimes, such compromise does not serve the best interest of the public, but under our system of government, I do not know a better alternative.

The authors have delved beneath the surface to give their readers an accurate understanding of how the regulation of broadcasting really works. The idea of active practitioners like Erwin Krasnow working in harness with academic authorities like Lawrence Longley and Herbert Terry is a good one. The union of their efforts is in the best interests of their readers. *The Politics of Broadcast Regulation*, however, goes far beyond describing the charged political atmosphere in which decisions are made at the FCC. The book is required reading for anyone interested in understanding how government regulation really works.

Newton N. Minow
Chicago, Illinois
Chairman, Federal Communications
    Commission (1961–1963)
Chairman, Public Broadcasting
    Service (1978–1980)

The Politics
of Broadcast
Regulation

Third Edition

Introduction: The Lay of the Land

Broadcasting in America has emerged from its first fifty years as a crucial element of society, shaping values and opinions, providing diversion, and selling goods and services to a degree unrivaled by other media. Unlike print media, however, electronic media are subject to substantial government regulation. Regulation can be viewed as either a static, point-in-time set of enforceable standards, such as the one requiring broadcasters to provide "equal opportunities" for political candidates to use their stations, or as a dynamic process involving many participants, often with different goals, all influencing each other and producing specific policies and standards for broadcasters. Our focus is on regulation as a process rather than as an outcome. Studying the process of regulation can be highly revealing of how our democratic system of government operates, whether the object of regulation is broadcasting, banking, transportation, or some other field. Since communications is vital to democracy, the study of broadcast regulation is particularly significant in understanding how our society works.

Curiously, although many studies exist of the main participants in the broadcast regulatory process—among them, the Federal Communications Commission (FCC)—few works deal analytically with the structure and functioning of the regulatory system; that is, few examine what scholars call the "politics of regulation." More than two decades ago, Professor Marver Bernstein observed that "remarkably little empirical work has been done to describe and analyze the *political* context of particular regulatory programs."[1] Later, Bernstein concluded:

Our thinking about the regulatory process and the independent commissions remains impressionistic, and the need for empirical research is largely unfulfilled. As a consequence, we fall back on our value preferences concerning the role of government in economic life, on the biases of our professional affiliations, and on assertions by others that support our personal conceptions and conclusions.[2]

The picture has improved somewhat since the early days of such regulatory theorists as Bernstein,[3] Robert Cushman,[4] and David Truman.[5] In the mid- and late 1970s, political scientists, economists, sociologists, and other social scientists jumped on the bandwagon and developed theories of regulation of their own.[6] To the dismay of those who seek a tidy, simple understanding of things, however, no single, unified theory of regulation has been accepted. As Professor Barry Mitnick has noted, the theories advanced "have usually been limited in scope though their authors present them as general in character."[7]

It remains useful to attempt at least to develop and analyze models of the politics of regulation. One problem in doing so is establishing a definition of politics. Definitions of the term are so plentiful and varied that its application to broadcast regulation often lacks precision. Harold Lasswell once commented that political science "is the study of influence and the influential," with "the influential" being "those who get the most of what there is to get." He encouraged analysis of political activities focusing on "who gets what, when and how."[8] That focus can be used to provide the following useful operational definition of politics: *politics consists of those activities leading to decisions about the allocation of desired goods.* In the context of broadcast regulation the activities can range from legal briefs prepared by citizen groups to the appointment of a special White House task force on a key communications problem. They also may include an FCC decision not to regulate radio formats or advertising time or a court of appeals decision to strike down Commission standards for the renewal of broadcast licenses when an incumbent broadcaster faces a competing applicant.[9] Such decisions usually result in allocations of desired goods, with some of the participants getting at least some of what they want.

Despite persistent calls for an emphasis on the political aspects of policy making by agencies such as the FCC, most of the literature on broadcast regulation has emphasized instead such topics as the history and development of the FCC and the broadcast industry, the Commission's legal and administrative status, and the legal problems resulting from the combination of rule-making and adjudicative functions in the same body. The political context of particular regulatory programs is generally omitted or mentioned only perfunctorily. Questions such as "Who gets what, when and how" from the process are rarely considered systematically.[10] We propose to deal specifically with these questions. Their answers are central to understanding the politics of broadcast regulation.

The first chapter of this book examines the basic characteristics and the environmental context of the regulatory process, and then traces the historical development of the broadcast regulatory system. Chapters two and three examine the role of the various participants in the making of policy and are followed, in chapter four, by an analysis of the structure and characteristics of the regulatory process and by the development of a model of the process.

Chapters five through nine consist of five case studies of selected broadcast regulatory policies:

1. The dispute, eventually settled in 1981 by the U.S. Supreme Court, over whether the FCC should regulate the choice of programming formats by radio stations
2. The development of the All-Channel Receiver Act of 1962 as a desperate attempt to resolve the decade-old problem of a crippled Ultra High Frequency (UHF) television service and the shifts in policy and technology that took place in the 1970s and 1980s and offer hope for UHF despite the lack of full technological equality
3. The efforts of the FCC over several years to set commercial time limits for broadcast licensees and the eventual decision not to regulate that area
4. The Commission's attempts in the 1970s and into the 1980s to establish a policy on license renewal challenges
5. The efforts of Congress, especially the U.S. House of Representatives, to rewrite the Communications Act of 1934 to cope with the "communications revolution" of the 1970s and 1980s.

We chose the first four of these five case studies because they present clear instances of controversy over what participants in the regulatory process regard as specific, and important, policy options. They also provide diverse examples of the political environment that produces broadcast regulation—examples that, taken together, demonstrate some generalizations and test some hypotheses about the regulatory process. Those cases span a broad range of policy issues, including the regulation of content (both commercial and entertainment), the regulation of technology, and the regulation (at least in part) of the structure of the industry. In addition, the studies involve diverse interests—radio, TV, advertisers, manufacturers, citizen groups, license renewal applicants, and consumers. The comparative analysis of different types of decisions over an extended period allows for a broad overview of parallels in decision-making approaches and serves to minimize the importance of coincidental events, the special tactics of a particular coalition of opponents, or the attitudes of a specific administration.

We selected the fifth case study, Congress's efforts between 1976 and 1980 to rewrite the Communications Act of 1934, to demonstrate the difficulty inherent in any effort to respond simultaneously to many interrelated concerns. The "rewrite" controversy included each of the issues discussed in the four other case studies and many others as well.

Most important, we believe that the politics of broadcast regulation is best understood in the context of actual instances of political conflict.

In the five cases studied here such conflict is evident, and political gains and losses resulting from policy decisions are quite real.

The book concludes with a look at the politics of broadcast regulation. There we analyze the five case studies as a group and identify some conclusions about the regulatory process in broadcasting.

NOTES

1. Marver H. Bernstein, "The Regulatory Process: A Framework for Analysis," *Law and Contemporary Problems,* 26 (Spring 1961), 341 (emphasis added).
2. Bernstein, "Independent Regulatory Agencies: A Perspective on Their Reform," *The Annals,* 400 (March 1972), 21.
3. See also Bernstein, *Regulating Business by Independent Commission* (Princeton, N.J.: Princeton University Press, 1955).
4. Robert E. Cushman, *The Independent Regulatory Commissions* (New York: Oxford University Press, 1941).
5. David B. Truman, *The Governmental Process: Political Interests and Public Opinion,* 2nd ed. (New York: Knopf, 1971).
6. See, for example: Bruce M. Owen and Ronald M. Braeutigam, *The Regulation Game* (Cambridge, Mass: Ballinger, 1978); James A. Wilson (ed.), *The Politics of Regulation* (New York: Basic Books, 1980); Timothy B. Clark, Marvin H. Kosters, and James C. Miller III, *Reforming Regulation* (Washington, D.C.: American Enterprise Institute, 1981); James C. Miller III and Bruce Yandle (eds.), *Benefit-Cost Analyses of Social Regulation* (Washington, D.C.: American Enterprise Institute, 1979); Chris Argyris et al., *Regulating Business: The Search for an Optimum* (San Francisco, Calif.: Institute for Contemporary Studies, 1978); and Peter H. Schuck, *Regulation: Asking the Right Questions* (Washington, D.C.: American Enterprise Institute, 1979). There are also many articles critical of regulation appearing regularly in the magazine *Regulation,* published bimonthly by the American Enterprise Institute for Public Policy Research.
7. Barry M. Mitnick, *The Political Economy of Regulation: Creating, Designing and Removing Regulatory Forms* (New York: Columbia University Press, 1980), p. 153. Among other virtues, *The Political Economy of Regulation* is a clear and masterfully organized summary and critique of the major conflicting theories of regulation. Mitnick develops his own theory, the "bureaucratic theory of regulation," but wisely does not claim to have solved the problem of developing a unified, persuasive, general theory. The book is also commendable for its thoughtful, systematic analysis of one of the most important of current topics, deregulation. See chapter IX, "Deregulation as a Process of Organizational Reduction," pp. 416–447.
8. Harold D. Lasswell, "Politics: Who Gets What, When, How," in *The Political Writings of Harold D. Lasswell* (Glencoe, Ill.: Free Press, 1951), pp. 295, 309.
9. These examples are discussed in detail in chapters five, seven, and eight.
10. A notable exception to this criticism is Vincent Mosco, *Broadcasting in the United States: Innovative Challenge and Organizational Control* (Norwood, N.J.: Ablex, 1979). Mosco's focus is on the FCC and its interaction

with the broadcast industry over policies on changes in broadcast and nonbroadcast technologies (e.g., subscription and cable TV) that threaten the status quo. Mosco's thesis is that, faced with new technologies, the Commission's effect, if not its intent, is to make new services secondary to dominant broadcast services. Many competitors of the dominant services, however, have lost their secondary status today. FM radio is clearly on an economic par with AM, and it is not the "ancillary service" Mosco makes it out to be (see chapter 5 of his work, "FM: Radio's Second Chance"). UHF-TV, while not as healthy as VHF-TV, seems no longer to be in the "decline" portrayed by Mosco (see his chapter 6 "UHF: Television's Second Chance?"). For further discussion, see chapter six of this book, "UHF Television: The Quest for Comparability." The "short-circuiting" of cable television that Mosco describes (in his chapter 7, "Cable Television: The Electronic Revolution Short-Circuited") has largely been undone by the FCC and the courts. Subscription television, which Mosco describes as "going nowhere" (chapter 8, "Subscription Television: Challenge to 'Free' TV"), has become active, at last, in many major television markets. Again, see our chapter six for further discussion.

PART ONE

The Regulatory Process

One

Origins of Broadcast Regulation: Structure and Theory

The Federal Communications Commission is a creature of Congress, with members appointed by the president; it is subject at every moment to judicial review and is faced with daily pressures from the industries it regulates, other branches of government, and the public whose interest it was created to protect. Yet the regulation of American broadcasting is often portrayed as if it takes place within a cozy vacuum of administrative "independence." In reality, the making of broadcast policy by the FCC, an ostensibly independent agency, is an intensely political process—not incidentally, as an aberration, but by its very nature. The FCC, like other regulatory agencies, operates within a political system involving various participants, including the regulated industries, the public, the White House, the courts, Congress and the Commission itself. It should be noted that those participants are neither monolithic nor unchanging entities but rather aggregations of human beings operating in various roles. Too frequently, the participants are viewed in a way that suggests an impersonal mechanical operation. Witness the description of their activities by the term "government regulation." Realistically, there is no such thing as "government regulation"; there is only regulation by government officials.[1] The essence of the politics of broadcast regulation lies in the complex interactions among diverse participants, not only in their day-to-day confrontations, but also in the more enduring adjustments and readjustments they make in their relationships.

To a great extent these relationships are determined by law—by statutes that are themselves the formal heritage of past political disputes. Such laws, however, are seldom crystal clear; the result of earlier political conflict may have been, and often is, statutes and rules drafted with deliberate ambiguity—broad general mandates that permit the politics of today to determine the rules and standards of tomorrow.[2]

Thus a major problem for regulatory agencies like the FCC is not just to conform to the letter of the law but, beyond that, to find ways to attune their behavior to the requirements imposed by its political environment. This process is more subtle than normally suggested by such concepts as "legislative control of administration" or "administrative representation of interests." To achieve its goals in a changing and dynamic milieu, the Commission often must try to gain or sustain political support against opposition. William W. Boyer aptly describes agency policy making as "environmental interaction": for effective policy initiation an administrator must attempt to perceive and anticipate the behavior of participants in the process and the environment in which they operate. Only thus can an administrator hope to assess accurately the political ecology within which policy decisions must be made.[3] Besides making such assessments and adjustments a regulator also may seek to shape that environment by means of public speeches, private meetings, statements, testimony, and the like—as in calls for deregulation of the broadcast industry or condemnation of television programming as a "vast wasteland." Thus "environmental interaction" is a two-way street: an administrator is constrained by his or her perceptions of environmental forces while at the same time influencing or even partially creating those very forces. The broadcast regulatory process has worked this way from its beginning.

The Historical Context of Broadcast Regulation

Broadcast regulation, like broadcasting itself, has a history spanning just over a half-century. There is more constancy, both substantively and structurally, to that history than one might expect for so dynamic a field. For example, the basic statute under which the FCC currently operates, the Communications Act of 1934, is fundamentally identical to the legislative charter given to the Federal Radio Commission in 1927. The process that produced the 1927 and 1934 acts in fact displayed many features that characterize the regulatory process today. Just like today, the creation of the legislative framework involved many parties—indeed, almost the same parties as those of the 1980s. Like today, the result was compromise—compromise that continued to be susceptible to reconsideration and reinterpretation.

The growth of broadcasting in the early 1920s found Congress and the executive branch almost totally unprepared to meet new obligations in this field. Until 1927 Congress had passed only two laws dealing with radio: the Wireless Ship Act of 1910 and the Radio Act of 1912. Both regulated primarily ship-to-shore and ship-to-ship maritime communications. Although these acts were not designed to deal with broadcasting, then Secretary of Commerce Herbert Hoover, faced with the reality of an emerging broadcast service, attempted to use the 1912 act as a statutory basis for regulation of broadcasters' use of frequencies, hours of operation, power, and similar matters. In 1921 Hoover designated 833 kilohertz (kHz) as the frequency for broadcasting, allowing only one station in a reception area or, if more than one station desired to operate, forcing a time-sharing arrangement. In the summer of 1922 he added 750 kHz as a second broadcast frequency. Sensing the real limits of the early radio laws, however, Hoover convened the first of four broadcaster conferences in 1922 to discuss ways of controlling the use of these radio frequencies. The conferences demonstrate that, even early in its evolution, the industry played an important role in the regulatory process. After two months of study the First Radio Conference unanimously decided that regulation by private enterprise alone —self-regulation—would be inadequate and recommended legislation authorizing government control over the allocation, assignment, and use of broadcast frequencies.

Representative Wallace H. White of Maine sponsored a measure designed to put the recommendations of the conference into effect by authorizing Secretary Hoover, assisted by an advisory committee, to act as a "traffic cop of the air." Congress, however, failed to enact this legislation. Hoover then called a Second Radio Conference in 1923 to work out ways of reducing the mounting radio reception interference caused by the crowding of stations. Shortly before the conference Hoover's attempts to regulate were seriously undermined when the U.S. Court of Appeals for the District of Columbia Circuit ruled that the secretary of commerce lacked legal discretion to withhold licenses from broadcast stations.[4] The court concluded that Congress had never intended to delegate such authority to the secretary of commerce.

While Congress continued to study the problem by holding periodic hearings, Hoover convened more industry conferences. At the Third National Radio Conference in 1924, Hoover commented: "I think this is probably the only industry of the United States that is unanimously in favor of having itself regulated."[5] The industry had come to demand such controls as the increase in stations continued unchecked. By November 1925 more than 578 stations were on the air, and applications had been filed for 175 more. With every channel filled in urban areas, most stations were experiencing considerable interference from other stations and had been forced to work out complex time-sharing schemes.

Despite the evident need, Secretary Hoover's regulatory initiatives were repeatedly thwarted. The final blow came in 1926 when a decisive court ruling deprived him of any authority to regulate radio frequencies, power, or hours of operation. Hoover then limited the Department of Commerce to the role of a registration bureau and intensified his pleas for self-regulation.[6]

By 1926 the chaotic conditions resulting from reliance on voluntary measures brought strong demands from the public and the radio industry that Congress take action. Until then, despite having held several hearings, the House and the Senate had been unable to agree on basic points about who would regulate radio. The House, dominated by Republicans, wanted the secretary of commerce to retain the authority to issue licenses, subject to appeal to a new Federal Radio Commission. The Democratic-controlled Senate, distrustful of the views of the Republican House and president, favored the establishment of a permanent and more independent radio commission.

Addressing himself to the pending Federal Radio Act in 1926, Senator Clarence C. Dill of Washington, chairman of the Senate Interstate Commerce Committee, argued that the influence of radio on the social, political, and economic life of the American people and the complex problems of its administration

demand that Congress establish an entirely independent body to take charge of the regulation of radio communications in all its forms. . . . The exercise of this power is fraught with such possibilities that it should not be entrusted to any one man nor to any administrative department of the Government. This regulatory power should be as free from political influence or arbitrary control as possible.[7]

Finally, in March 1926, Representative White's bill to authorize the secretary of commerce to be the "traffic cop of the air"—substantially the same bill he introduced in 1923—passed the House by a vote of 218 to 123. However, the measure soon ran into difficulties in the Senate, which continued to favor a permanent, independent radio commission. Early in 1927 a Senate-House conference committee hammered out a compromise establishing a Federal Radio Commission (FRC) on a temporary basis for one year.

As finally enacted, this legislation, the Radio Act of 1927, reflected an accommodation of interests between the House and Senate by setting up a curious division of responsibilities between the secretary of commerce and the new Federal Radio Commission. The Radio Act provided that applications for station licenses, renewals, and changes in facilities must be referred by the Department of Commerce to the FRC, and gave the Commission broad administrative and quasi-judicial powers over these applications. The secretary of commerce continued to have such powers as fixing the qualifications of operators, inspecting station equipment, and assigning call letters. After one year, however, the secretary of commerce was to take over all powers—except the power to revoke licenses—and the FRC would continue purely as a part-time appellate body, dealing with appeals from the decisions of the secretary. An important feature of the Radio Act (which, however, received little attention at the time) was the requirement in Sections 9 and 11 that "the licensing authority should determine that the public interest, convenience, or necessity would be served by the granting [of a station's license]."

The act created a Radio Commission of five members appointed by the president with the advice and consent of the Senate. The president was required to nominate one Commissioner from each of five geographical zones. One of the Commissioners was to be designated by the president as its initial Chairman, with subsequent Chairmen being elected by the Commission itself. Having structured the FRC so carefully, Congress then launched the infant Commission with one serious handicap: it failed to give it any money! The Commission was nevertheless able to function due to a clause in the Radio Act allowing it to spend the unexpended balance in the appropriation made to the Department of Commerce under the item "wireless communications laws." The original members of the Commission were forced to do their own clerical work, and for the first four years engineers had to be borrowed from other agencies.[8]

The FRC faced other virtually insuperable problems: its temporary status, with powers expiring after one year; the danger of internal strife, because of each Commissioner's appointment from a geographical zone; the great vagueness of the act and the lack of a specific mandate from Congress; the slowness of Senate confirmation of the Commissioners; constant court challenges to its decisions; and the claim of "prior rights" by stations already on the air. Llewellyn White summarized these problems in vivid terms:

The F.R.C. had found the job cut out for it quite literally killing. One hearing alone required 170,000 affidavits. One out of ten decisions had to be fought through the courts. Congress had allowed the Commission a staff of twenty, including engineers and office workers. Two of the five Commissioners were not confirmed for nearly a year, one resigning in disgust after seven months' backbreaking work without pay.[9]

In addition to administrative bottlenecks the FRC faced monumental technical problems. In 1927 there were 732 stations blanketing all 90 radio channels. At least 129 stations were broadcasting off their assigned channels, and 41 were broadcasting on channels reserved for Canadian use. In practice there were no restrictions concerning power or hours of operation. Adding to the confusion was the presence of completely unregulated amateurs on the broadcast band. In an effort to wipe the slate clean, the FRC announced that it would adopt "a

completely new allocation of frequencies, power, and hours of operation for all of the existing 732 broadcast stations." The Radio Act encouraged this attempt at a fresh start by providing that all existing
licenses were to expire sixty days after its enactment. The act further
stated that "no license should be construed to create any right, beyond
the terms, conditions, and periods of the license." The Commission soon
found out, however, that broadcasters who had been on the air for years
had a very strong interest in preserving their favored status and would
fight lengthy court battles to keep their "rights." As a result the FRC
was largely unsuccessful in its attempts to solve radio's problems on a
case-by-case basis.

Throughout its short history the Radio Commission was subjected to
great congressional pressure. Not really accepting the independent
status of this "independent regulatory commission," Congress continually tinkered with the 1927 act. Since the Radio Commission was originally established for a period of only one year, Congress had to renew
the legislation annually (or let the FRC's activities be absorbed by the
Department of Commerce). This annual review gave Congress a conve-
nient opportunity to conduct hearings and add further legislative restrictions.[10]

One of the most limiting congressional mandates was the Davis
Amendment to the 1928 renewal act, requiring the FRC to allocate
licenses, frequencies, times of operation, and power equally among the
five geographic zones and the states therein. This amendment had been
drafted in response to congressional concern that the Commission favored high-power stations in the North and East and discriminated
against stations in the South and West. The Davis Amendment prevented members of the FRC from functioning effectively as a harmoni-
ous group and seriously impeded the development of radio policy. In
his annual message to the Congress on December 2, 1929, President
Hoover criticized the Davis Amendment, warning that "there is a danger that the system will degenerate from a national system into five
regional agencies with varying practices, varying policies, competitive
tendencies, and consequent failure to attain its utmost capacity for
service to the people as a whole."[11] Hoover also recommended that the
Commission be reorganized on a permanent rather than temporary
basis. This recommendation, however, was then ignored by Congress.

There things stood until in 1933 Franklin Roosevelt requested Secretary of Commerce Daniel C. Roper to direct a study of the organization
of radio regulation. The Roper Committee issued a report in January
1934 recommending the consolidation of the communications regulatory activities of the FRC, the Interstate Commerce Commission, the
postmaster general, and the president into "a new or single regulatory
body, to which would be committed any further control of two-way

communications and broadcasting."[12] Although it strongly supported the centralization of regulatory activities, the report did not take a stand on whether the organization should be of the independent commission type.

Spurred by the Roper Committee recommendations and by general dissatisfaction with the existing structure of governmental regulation, Congress enacted the Communications Act of 1934, which established a new, less tentative Federal Communications Commission (FCC). The Communications Act made various organizational changes from the model of the Radio Commission (it called for seven Commissioners instead of five, for example, and stipulated the appointment of the Chairman by the president) and gave the new agency broader authority over all communications, including interstate telephone and telegraph. Title III of the 1934 act, which dealt with radio, was, however, almost identical to the Radio Act of 1927. Most important, the "public interest" criterion in the 1927 legislation was retained.

An innovation in the 1934 law was congressional emphasis on the long-range planning of broad social goals. Section 303(g) specifically called upon the FCC to "study new uses for radio, provide for experimental uses of frequencies, and generally encourage the larger and more effective use of radio in the public interest." Eventually this provision would lead the Commission to study such unearthly subjects as communications satellites for broadcasting to local receivers and the use of laser beams as relay mechanisms. Congress also required the FCC to report on possible new legislation necessary for reaching long-range goals. Throughout the Commission's history, however, Congress has never provided the agency with sufficient funds to make long-range studies. Former Commissioner Nicholas Johnson put the FCC budget in graphic perspective by pointing out in 1968 that "the Federal Aviation Administration spends as much on *communications research* as the FCC's total annual budget; the Navy spends five times the FCC's annual budget doing cost-effectiveness studies of the communications system on one ship type; [and] Bell Labs has a budget over 15 times that of the FCC."[13]

Several aspects of the early history of broadcast regulation deserve emphasis. Five key participants emerged, themselves giving rise to a sixth, the Federal Radio Commission and its successor, the FCC. The broadcast industry was involved in the genesis of broadcast regulation. Self-regulation was attempted but proved inadequate. After that, the industry worked actively with the executive and legislative branches of government to shape what was viewed as legislation required to eliminate audio chaos. Also involved from the beginning were the courts, whose decisions in 1923 and 1926 made it plain that Hoover could not regulate under the outdated 1912 Radio Act and that new legislation was needed. The public was involved as well, its complaints about deteriorating radio service helping advance radio legislation on Congress's agenda by 1927.

Congress and the executive branch of government are the two remaining participant groups. Hoover, of course, acted as secretary of commerce—a cabinet-level officer. Disputes between the president and Congress are reflected in the "temporary" nature of the FRC and the continuing interaction today between the president and Congress whenever an FCC member is nominated and subjected to the confirmation process. When Secretary of Commerce Hoover's regulatory activities were blocked by the courts, the salvation of American broadcasting lay with Congress. When Congress *did* act to establish a regulatory agency, the agency's existence and financing were subjected to yearly congressional consideration.[14] By giving the FRC limited financial and technical resources, Congress effectively ensured the Commission's dependence on congressional good will and kept a firm grip on this "independent" regulatory agency.

A final distinctive feature of the federal government's early regulation of broadcast stations was the focus on licensing as a primary regulatory tool. Although regulatory agencies such as the Federal Power Commission and the Interstate Commerce Commission exert control over entry by requiring proof of usefulness, the certificates of authority they issue are for indefinite terms and the certification process is secondary to the agencies' other functions of regulating profits and prices. The strong emphasis on the FCC's licensing role results in part from the fact that Congress did not expressly give the Commission the power to regulate the rates or profits of broadcast stations.[15] It predetermined that there would be strongly fought battles over several aspects of licensing in the future: Should the "traffic cop" review such things as choices of content in making licensing decisions? What, in general, would be both the process and standards for getting licenses renewed?

The "Public Interest"—Broadcasting Battleground

Taylor Branch has divided government agencies into two categories: "deliver the mail" and "Holy Grail."[16] "Deliver the mail" agencies perform neutral, mechanical, logistical functions; they send out Social Security checks, procure supplies—or deliver the mail. "Holy Grail" agencies, on the other hand, are given the more controversial and difficult role of achieving some grand, moral, civilizing goal. The Federal Radio Commission came into being primarily to "deliver the mail" —to act as a traffic cop of the airwaves. But both the FRC and the FCC had a vague Holy Grail clause written into their charters: the requirement that they uphold the "public interest, convenience and necessity." This vague but also often useful congressional mandate is key to understanding today's conflicts over broadcast regulation.

The concept of a public interest in radio communications was first expressed officially by Secretary Hoover in a speech before the Third Annual Radio Conference in 1924. One commentator wrote shortly after the passage of the Radio Act of 1927 that the inclusion of the phrase "public interest, convenience and necessity" was of enormous consequence since it meant that "licenses are no longer for the asking. The applicant must pass the test of public interest. His wish is not the deciding factor."[17]

Former FCC Chairman Newton Minow has commented that, starting with the Radio Act of 1927, the phrase "public interest, convenience and necessity" has provided the battleground for broadcasting's regulatory debate.[18] Congress's reason for including such a phrase was clear: the courts, interpreting the Radio Act of 1912 as a narrow statute, had said that the secretary of commerce could not create additional rules or regulations beyond that act's terms. This left Hoover unable to control rapidly changing technologies. The public interest notion in the 1927 and 1934 acts was intended to let the regulatory agency create new rules, regulations, and standards as required to meet new conditions. Congress clearly hoped to create an act more durable than the Radio Act of 1912. That plan has been at least somewhat successful as it was not until about 1976 that Congress seriously began to consider a major change in its 1934 handiwork (see chapter nine).

The meaning of the phrase, however, is extremely elusive. Although many scholars have attempted to define the public interest in normative or empirical terms, their definitions have added little to an understanding of the real relevance of this concept to the regulatory process. One scholar, after analyzing the literature on the public interest, created a typology for varying definitions of the term, but in the end he decided not to "argue for adoption of a single definition, preferring instead to categorize ways in which the phrase may be used. Different circumstances . . . may employ different usages."[19]

A pragmatic but somewhat limited view is one offered by Avery Leiserson, who suggests that "a satisfactory criterion of the public interest is the preponderant acceptance of administrative action by politically influential groups." Such acceptance is expressed, in Leiserson's opinion, through groups that, when affected by administrative requirements, regulations, and decisions, comply without seeking legislative revision, amendment, or repeal.[20] Thus, in order for a policy to be accepted by politically influential groups, it must be relevant to, and must not conflict unacceptably with, their expectations and desires. Defining the interest of the entire general public is considerably more difficult, especially when the general public interest is viewed as more than just the sum of special interests.

Besides providing flexibility to adapt to changing conditions, the concept of the public interest is important to the regulation of broadcasting in another sense. A generalized public belief even in an undefined public interest increases the likelihood that policies will be accepted as authoritative. The acceptance of a concept of the public interest may thus become an important support for the regulation of broadcasting and for the making of authoritative rules and policies toward this end.[21] For this reason the courts traditionally have given the FCC wide latitude in determining what constitutes the public interest. As the U.S. Supreme Court noted in 1981:

Our opinions have repeatedly emphasized that the Commission's judgment regarding how the public interest is best served is entitled to substantial judicial deference. . . . The Commission's implementation of the public interest standard, when based on a rational weighing of competing policies, is not to be set aside . . . for "the weighing of policies under the public interest standard is a task that Congress has delegated to the Commission in the first instance."[22]

Judge E. Barrett Prettyman once expanded upon the reasons for such deference:

It is also true that the Commission's view of what is best may change from time to time. Commissions themselves change, underlying philosophies differ, and experience often dictates change. Two diametrically opposite schools of thought in respect to the public welfare may both be rational; e.g., both free trade and protective tariff are rational positions. All such matters are for the Congress and the executive and their agencies. They are political in the high sense of that abused term.[23]

Despite the usefulness of the public interest concept in keeping up with changing means of communications and the general tendency of the courts to defer to the FCC's decisions, conflicts over the meaning of the public interest have been recurrent in broadcast history. On occasion, the vague statutory mandate to look out for the public interest has hampered the development of coherent public policy since Congress (or influential members of Congress) can always declare, "That is not what we meant by the public interest."[24] Few independent regulatory commissions have had to operate under such a broad grant of power with so few substantive guidelines. Rather than encouraging greater freedom of action, vagueness in delegated power may serve to limit an agency's independence and freedom to act as it sees fit. As Pendleton Herring put it, "Administrators cannot be given the responsibilities of statesmen without incurring likewise the tribulations of politicians."[25]

Judge Henry Friendly, in his classic work *The Federal Administrative Agencies,* made the following comment on how the origin of the "public interest, convenience and necessity" standard serves to confuse, not enlighten:

The only guideline supplied by Congress in the Communications Act of 1934 was "public convenience, interest, [and] necessity." The standard of public convenience and necessity, introduced into the federal statute book by [the] Transportation Act, 1920, conveyed a fair degree of meaning when the issue was whether new or duplicating railroad construction should be authorized or an existing line abandoned. It was to convey less when, as under the Motor Carrier Act of 1935, or the Civil Aeronautics Act of 1938, there would be the added issue of selecting the applicant to render a service found to be needed; but under those statutes there would usually be some demonstrable factors, such as, in air route cases, ability to render superior one-plane or one-carrier service because of junction of the new route with existing ones, lower costs due to other operations, or historical connection with the traffic, that ought to have enabled the agency to develop intelligible criteria for selection. The standard was almost drained of meaning under section 307 of the Communications Act, where the issue was almost never the need for broadcasting service but rather who should render it.[26]

Since Congress has found it inadvisable or impossible to define specifically for future situations exactly what constitutes the public interest, the political problem of achieving consensus as to the case-by-case application of this standard has been passed on to the FCC. The flexibility inherent in this elusive public interest concept can be enormously significant to the FCC not only as a means of modifying policies to meet changed conditions and to obtain special support but also as a source of continuing and sometimes hard to resolve controversy.

Unresolved Regulatory Problems

The regulation of American broadcasting is no less controversial today than it was during the unsettled 1920s and 1930s. The list of unresolved regulatory problems is long, varied, and always changing but can, at least in part, be analyzed under two headings: (1) normative ("what should be") controversies and (2) controversies associated with the emergence or growth of electronic communications technologies that are unlike those of traditional broadcasting. Some of these controversies arise from specific economic and technical characteristics of the broadcast industry. Others are the direct legacy of the historical development of regulation—for example, when certain legal prescriptions and requirements, still on the books, are interpreted differently by various participants at different times in the regulatory continuum. Still other problems may be traced to public attitudes toward government regulation. Seldom can the FCC attempt to frame regulations without becoming entangled in this political thicket.[27]

Disputes concerning legal prescriptions imposed by the Communications Act often have centered on recurring value conflicts—assumptions about what ought or ought not to be done. One such question is the extent to which broadcasting should pursue social as well as economic and technical goals. The emphasis on the social responsibilities of licensees rests on the view that "the air belongs to the public, not to the industry" since Congress provided in Section 301 of the Communications Act that "no . . . license shall be construed to create any right, beyond the terms, conditions, and periods of the license." In recent years, for example, the FCC has adopted rules and policies designed to make broadcasters meet social responsibilities by requiring them to implement equal employment opportunity programs for women and minorities and to provide "reasonable opportunities for the expression of opposing views on controversial issues of public importance"—the Fairness Doctrine—and to schedule television programs for children.

Some of these rules and policies require broadcasters to present, or refrain from presenting, content contrary to what they would choose to do on their own. How far the FCC may go in the direct, or indirect, regulation of content without violating either the Communications Act's own prohibition in Section 326 against censorship or the First Amendment to the U.S. Constitution remains unsettled. Section 326 of the Communications Act states:

Nothing in this Act shall be understood or construed to give the Commission the power of censorship over the radio communications or signals transmitted by any radio station, and no regulation or condition shall be promulgated or fixed by the Commission which shall interfere with the right of free speech by means of radio communications.

However, as we noted above, in the same act Congress also directs the Commission to regulate "in the public interest, convenience and necessity."[28] Using that standard, the Commission has promulgated many rules and policies governing broadcast programming that would be regarded by the courts as unlawful censorship of the print media. Early court cases, however, determined that the FCC did not have to ignore content, that it could consider it without necessarily engaging in censorship;[29] later court cases have perpetuated the view that government supervision of broadcast content is somehow more acceptable than review of print.[30] Clearly broadcasting continues to be plagued by divergent views of how to balance freedom with achieving socially desired and responsible service, while still not engaging in censorship.

Complicating this controversy is the conflict between First Amendment provisions guaranteeing the right of broadcasters, like other media owners and operators, to be free of government control over the content of programming and First Amendment theories that have been developed exclusively for broadcasting and that hold the rights of listeners and viewers to receive information to be "paramount" over the rights of broadcasters.[31] The theory is that in the "scarce" medium of broadcasting, some affirmative government intervention concerning content may be needed to ensure that the public hears diverse ideas and viewpoints. J. Skelly Wright, a judge of the U.S. Court of Appeals, has commented:

[In] some areas of the law it is easy to tell the good guys from the bad guys. . . . In the current debate over the broadcast media and the First Amendment . . . each debater claims to be the real protector of the First Amendment, and the analytical problems are much more difficult than in ordinary constitutional adjudication. . . . The answers are not easy.[32]

These colliding statutory ground rules governing the freedom and obligations of broadcasters have been melded into one of the law's most elastic conceptions—the notion of a "public trustee."[33] The FCC views a broadcast license as a "trust," with the public as "beneficiary" and the broadcaster as "public trustee." The public trustee concept is a natural consequence of the conflicting statutory goals of private use and regulated allocation of spectrum space. Congress gave the FCC the right to choose among various candidates for commercial broadcast licenses and left it up to the Commission to find a justification for providing a fortunate few with the use of a valuable scarce resource at no cost. Legal scholar Benno Schmidt, Jr., thinks the public trustee concept was designed to dull the horns of the FCC's dilemma: to give away valuable spectrum space, with no strings attached, would pose stubborn problems of justification.

As has been noted above, however, some of the strings attached—especially those, like the FCC's Fairness Doctrine, that are content-related—are constitutionally suspect.[34] One option exercised by the FCC to reduce controversy over its activities has been to substitute "content-neutral" or "structural" policies for policies that involve direct review of content. The objective of the Fairness Doctrine, for example, is diverse and balanced expression of views on controversial issues of public importance. Under the doctrine, the FCC can order a station to present an underrepresented view, clearly not a content-neutral act. As an alternative to such content regulation, the FCC can attempt to structure the broadcast marketplace so that there are many stations with different owners and assume thereby that diversity of opinion will result naturally and without direct government review. Many FCC rules and policies—for example, the regulation of station ownership patterns—have been of this type. They do not, on their surface, look normative but are in fact examples of content-neutral means of achieving social objectives.

For some years, however, there was hesitation over the substitution of content-neutral "structural" regulations for content regulation. Broadcasting was thought to be a scarce medium in which structural regulation could not accomplish enough. Beginning in the mid-1970s, however, arguments began to be made more forcefully that FCC review of content should be reduced and structural regulation preferred. Broadcasters tended to argue that, at least in some instances, even structural regulation was unjustified due to what they believed was reliance on an invalid premise: scarcity. Behind many of these criticisms and controversies were changes in electronic communications technology.

Although many correctly argue that the 1970s and 1980s have been (and will be) particularly active decades in the development and expansion of communications technology,[35] the fact is that there have long been two complementary and determinative features of American broadcasting: spectrum space scarcity and technological innovation. Scarcity, of course, has always been the underlying *raison d'être* for broadcast regulation. Because one person's transmission is another's interference, Congress concluded that the federal government has the duty both to select who may and who may not broadcast and to regulate the use of the electromagnetic spectrum to serve the public interest.

Scarcity has been a special problem in the case of broadcast television. Whereas an FM broadcast needs a section of the spectrum 20 times wider than an AM broadcast, a TV broadcast requires a channel 600 times wider than an AM broadcast station's signal.[36] Until 1952 the FCC's allocation policy confined television to a twelve-channel Very High Frequency (VHF) system incapable of offering even two or three stations in many cities. Broadcasters with the only television station (or with one of the two) in a market at that time were in an awkward position to be complaining about governmental regulation, given the profits they were receiving from their near monopoly. The All-Channel Receiver Bill of 1962 and many related FCC policies have been aimed at making additional television service available in many areas, with the expectation that greater diversity in programming would result eventually. Only recently have the economic support systems begun to emerge that could make this twenty-year belief of the Commission true (see chapter six).

Scarcity seems to be much less of a problem in radio broadcasting.

Broadcasters argue that there is little justification for rigid government regulation of ten or twenty competing radio stations in a market while monopoly newspapers operate freely. As scarcity decreases, they have argued, so should regulation. In the early 1980s radio broadcasters gained some government support for their argument. When the FCC decided not to regulate radio broadcasters' choice of program formats, the U.S. Supreme Court in 1981 declined "to overturn the Commission's Policy Statement, which prefers reliance on market forces to its own attempt to oversee format changes at the behest of disaffected listeners."[37] Also in 1981, the FCC decided that marketplace competition made it unnecessary for the Commission to supervise amounts of commercials or nonentertainment programming on commercial radio stations.[38] Later, under Chairman Mark S. Fowler, appointed by President Reagan, the FCC proposed to Congress that much of the legislation supporting FCC content regulation be repealed. The Commission argued that "[t]he traditional spectrum scarcity argument which has provided the basis for support of the Fairness Doctrine [and other content regulations] has become increasingly less valid as new technologies and the proliferation of existing broadcast facilities has made the diversity of opinion available to the public via radio as plentiful [sic] as that available via print media."[39] In a speech shortly after these proposals were made, Chairman Fowler noted that "[s]carcity, to my mind, is a condition affecting all industries. Land, capital, labor, and oil, they are all scarce. With other scarce goods in society, we tend to allow the marketplace to allocate them. In this process, consumers' interests and society's interests are well served."[40] From this analysis of the "myth" of scarcity, plus a review of traditional First Amendment theory, Chairman Fowler concluded that in broadcasting, "[e]conomic freedom and freedom of speech go hand in hand," and advocated reliance on minimally regulated marketplace forces rather than content regulation.[41]

Whatever scarcity there is for commercial broadcasting and other private uses of radio is partly a manmade problem whose dimensions are defined by the executive branch. The FCC's jurisdiction over the radio spectrum is limited by Section 305 of the Communications Act, which exempts from the Commission's power all "radio stations belonging to and operated by the United States." The federal government, through its various agencies and departments, operates a host of radio services occupying approximately one-half of the total available frequency space. With the government's total investment in telecommunications running into the hundreds of billions of dollars and its annual expenditure for equipment, research, and development of over $7 billion, the White House is reluctant to turn these frequencies over to the FCC.[42]

The classic pattern of limited broadcast facilities, which has led to government regulation, also has encouraged technological innovations to expand programming possibilities. Throughout its history the FCC has had to wrestle with new problems brought about by such technical developments as network broadcasting, FM broadcasting, VHF and UHF telecasting, color television, cable television, direct broadcast satellites (DBS), multipoint distribution services (MDS), and other new or modified systems. The making of public policy in each of these areas goes far beyond resolving technical issues. Technical issues frequently disguise what actually are economic interests vying for control of some segment of broadcasting and related markets. The politics of broadcasting are thus present in technical as well as social controversies.

The prolonged and not entirely successful effort to reduce scarcity of TV broadcasting through UHF-TV is examined later as a case study of the difficulties the Commission, and the regulatory system in general, has had in dealing with new technologies. It is sufficient to note here that the FCC, like other regulatory bodies, has been subjected to considerable criticism concerning its inability to cope with change—the most common charge being that it is concerned mainly with preserving the status quo and with favoring the well-established broadcast services. From a technological standpoint, for example, it has been said that the television stations constructed in 1952 might have been operating as early as 1937 had the Commission actively supported the development of this new medium.[43]

An agency's ability to respond to and foster technological change is largely a matter of how dependent the agency is on dominant industry factions—the "haves" as opposed to the "have nots." Throughout its history the FCC has lacked sufficient skilled personnel and funds to weigh the merits of new technology and has been forced to rely on outside advice and technical opinion. When faced with complex technical questions, the Commission often has taken the easy road of finding in favor of the "haves" over the "have nots." Frequently, the result is delay in the development of these technologies. A 1975 study of Commission policy concerning the development of FM radio, UHF-TV, and cable and subscription television concluded that each of these technical innovations developed a status ancillary to the dominant AM-radio and VHF-TV commercial broadcast system.[44] Since 1975 most of these industries have moved beyond such an ancillary status. Throughout most of its history, the Commission (usually with the support of the "haves") sought to limit the growth of technology rather than use technological innovations as correctives to problems. Beginning in the late 1970s, however, the FCC has adopted policies designed to foster technological growth as a way of promoting greater competition in the marketplace and a greater diversity of services.

The ability of a regulatory commission to inhibit or to promote a technical innovation that challenges the regulated (and sometimes sheltered) industry is a measure of the vitality and strength of that agency. As will be shown in chapter six, the FCC has not been highly successful at giving birth to new communications services. At times, in fact, it has almost destroyed them. These failures result, at least in part, from the highly political environment in which the FCC operates. The history of the on-again, off-again FCC regulation of cable television provides perhaps the best example of how difficult policy making becomes when traditional commercial broadcasting confronts new competitors.

The maneuverings with respect to cable television between 1968 and 1981 provide a classic illustration of the political environment in action. In 1968, after the Supreme Court affirmed the FCC's authority to regulate cable systems directly, the Commission took the textbook action: it issued a voluminous set of cable policy proposals and invited comments from broadcasters, cable operators, citizen groups, members of the general public, and other interested parties. Three years and several thousand pages of dialogue later, FCC Chairman Dean Burch sent the House and Senate Communications Subcommittees a fifty-five-page summary of the kinds of rules the Commission had tentatively concluded were necessary for the healthy development of the cable industry. Burch assured Congress that the new rules would not be made effective until several months later—March 31, 1972—in order to allow time for congressional review.

The consideration of cable rules, however, was not to be left to the discretion of the FCC and Congress. President Nixon became involved, in July 1971, by appointing a cabinet-level advisory committee on cable, headed by Dr. Clay T. Whitehead, director of the White House Office of Telecommunications Policy.[45] During the fall of 1971, Chairman Burch and Dr. Whitehead met privately with representatives of cable, broadcast, and copyright interests in an effort to reach a compromise agreement. Meanwhile, the Supreme Court was considering an appeal of a lower court ruling that the FCC had no authority to require cable systems to originate programs—a central element in the Commission's regulatory strategy.

All branches of government—legislative, executive, and judicial— were independently considering the future of cable when the FCC, in a 136-page decision in February 1972, adopted new cable rules based on a private agreement among cable operators, broadcasters, and a group of copyright owners after White House prodding. In a biting dissenting opinion, former Commissioner Nicholas Johnson, a liberal Democrat, said:

In future years, when students of law or government wish to study the decision making process at its worst, when they look for examples of industry domination of government, when they look for Presidential interference in the operation of an agency responsible to Congress, they will look to the FCC handling of the never-ending saga of cable television as a classic case study.

Chairman Burch, a former head of the Republican National Committee, accused Johnson in a special concurring opinion of using a "scorched earth" technique to distort an act of creation into a public obscenity. Burch said that there was no conspiracy, no arm twisting, no secret deals. The cable decision, he said, was the result of months of regulatory craftsmanship of the highest order. Commissioner (later Chairman) Richard E. Wiley, quoting Edmund Burke on the need for compromise, defended the decision on the ground that the "choice realistically confronting the Commission, after all, was this particular program—or none at all."[46]

The comprehensive 1972 rules proved to have a short life. Their key feature was that while they allowed cable television to begin to grow by providing some cable system access to "imported" distant TV signals, the cable television industry was required to provide certain public interest tradeoffs in return. Among them were requirements for relatively large channel capacity systems (twenty channels), two-way potential, and provision of "access channels" for use by government, educational, and citizen groups. Two premises underlay the FCC rules. First, the Commission assumed cable television, through its ability to provide alternatives to local broadcast service, would divide the TV audience (a potentially devastating prospect for UHF), reduce revenues, and eventually cause harm to the ability of local broadcasters to serve the public interest. Second, based largely on its 1968 court victory, the FCC believed it could require a number of public interest services of cable operators if whatever was being required was at least related to broadcasting. By the late 1970s both premises had come under vigorous attack—an attack led jointly by the cable TV industry and the courts.

The first major setback for the FCC came in 1977 when the U.S. Court of Appeals for the District of Columbia Circuit overturned complex FCC rules that limited pay-cable access to movies and popular sporting events. The rules originally had been based on the idea that without such limits popular "free" programs would be "siphoned" from broadcast TV to pay-cable systems. The court, in effect, ruled that such cable rules could be justified only if the FCC had a reasonable basis for expecting that harm to broadcasters and the public would in fact happen. The court found that the FCC could not sustain that burden of proof. For good measure, it also observed that cable, unlike broadcasting, was not technologically "scarce" and suggested that for that reason too the pay-cable limits were invalid.[47] In the wake of this decision, the FCC opened an inquiry into the economic relationship between cable television and broadcasting. In 1980 the Commission used the results of that inquiry—in which it concluded it had previously overestimated the impact of cable on broadcasting—to justify repeal of other FCC cable rules designed to "protect" broadcasters.[48]

At about the same time that the "economic impact" theory for cable regulation was weakening, the Commission's "tradeoffs" in the 1972 cable rules were under attack by the cable industry. This dispute, eventually settled by the U.S. Supreme Court, led to the Commission's elimination in 1980 of its access, twenty-channel, and two-way potential requirements.[49]

By 1981 most of the 1972 compromise had unraveled. The FCC had reduced its regulation of cable television, but state and local government regulation of franchises was becoming more important. Broadcasters, who thought they lost most with the collapse of the compromise, continued to fight the trend in a few court cases,[50] but primarily they hoped that Congress could be persuaded to put some limits on cable through amendment or revision of the Communications Act of 1934 and the copyright statutes. Despite this hope, however, broadcasters had to stand in line with others who thought the Communications Act had to be amended to deal with new technologies and new economic theories (see chapter nine).

From this brief example, it is clear that the regulatory process as applied to broadcasting and related fields is laced with an ample dose of political maneuverings, including U-turns. In the next chapter we look more closely at the people and the institutions constituting this political environment.

NOTES

1. See Lee Loevinger, "The Sociology of Bureaucracy," *The Business Lawyer,* 24 (November 1968), 9.
2. Statutes are laws passed by a legislative body—for example, the U.S. Congress. Usually they must be approved by a member of the executive branch, (e.g., the president) before they go into force. Administrative agencies, like the FCC, often have authority to write rules and regulations based on the statutes they enforce. If they are properly adopted and consistent with the appropriate statutes and the Constitution, these rules and regulations have the force of law. A federal statute, the Administrative Procedure Act, governs the procedures administrative agencies must follow when they write rules. See 5 U.S.C., Secs. 500–612.
3. See William H. Boyer, *Bureaucracy on Trial: Policy Making by Government Agencies* (Indianapolis: Bobbs-Merrill, 1964), p. 68. Two useful surveys of the problems of administrative agencies are Richard Stewart, "The Reformation of American Administrative Law," *Harvard Law Review,* 88

(1975), 1667; and James Freeman, "Crises and Legitimacy in the Administrative Process," *Stanford Law Review,* 27 (1975), 1041. Another study which views the politics of broadcast regulation in terms of the "ecology of regulation" is Robert J. Williams, "Politics and the Ecology of Regulation," *Public Administration,* 54 (Autumn 1976), 219–331. Former FCC Commissioner Glen O. Robinson has written perceptively on the Commission and its potential for reform: Glen O. Robinson, "The Federal Communications Commission," in *Communications for Tomorrow: Policy Perspectives for the 1980's,* ed. Glen O. Robinson, (New York: Praeger, 1978), pp. 353–400.

4. *Hoover* v. *Intercity Radio,* 286 F. 1003 (D.C. Cir. 1923).
5. Quoted in Sydney W. Head, *Broadcasting in America: A Survey of Television and Radio,* 3rd ed. (Boston: Houghton Mifflin, 1976), p. 126.
6. *U.S.* v. *Zenith Radio Corp.,* 12 F.2d 614 (N.D. Ill. 1926).
7. *U.S. Senate, Senate Report 772,* 69th Congress, 1st Session, 2 (1926).
8. Years later, in 1976, Congress repeated many of these mistakes when it created the Copyright Royalty Tribunal with a similar lack of funds and staff.
9. Llewellyn White, *The American Radio: A Report on the Broadcasting Industry in the United States from the Commission on Freedom of the Press* (Chicago: University of Chicago Press, 1947), p. 200.
10. Congress made the Federal Communications Commission a permanently authorized agency in 1934 but in 1981 cut back its authorization to just two years. Congress said the short-term authorization would provide for "[r]egular and systematic oversight" to "increase Commission accountability for the implementation of Congressional policy." U.S. House of Representatives, *House Report 97–208, Omnibus Budget Reconciliation Act of 1981, Conference Report,* 97th Congress, 1st Session (July 29, 1981), p. 899.
11. Quoted in Robert S. McMahon, *The Regulation of Broadcasting,* a study made for the U.S. House of Representatives, Committee on Interstate and Foreign Commerce, 85th Congress, 2nd Session (1958), p. 19.
12. *Senate Committee Print, S. Doc. 144, Study of Communications by an Interdepartmental Committee,* 73rd Congress, 2nd Session (1934).
13. Speech before the Federal Communications Bar Association, Washington, D.C., May 10, 1968, p. 9 [mimeo.].
14. Congress followed a similar approach with the Corporation for Public Broadcasting, which initially received funding and authorization only on an annual basis, although it eventually received some advance, multiyear support.
15. See Roger G. Noll, Merton J. Peck, and John J. McGowan, *Economic Aspects of Television Regulation* (Washington, D.C.: Brookings Institution, 1973), p. 98. Section 153(h) of the Communications Act provides that "a person engaged in radio broadcasting shall not, insofar as such a person is so engaged, be deemed a common carrier."
16. Taylor Branch, "We're All Working for the Penn Central," *Washington Monthly,* November 1970, p. 8.
17. Steven Davis, *The Law of Radio Communications* (New York: McGraw-Hill, 1927), p. 61. A less sanguine assessment was made by Ayn Rand, who characterized the "public interest" as the "intellectual knife of collectivism's sacrificial guillotine." "Since there is no such thing as the 'public interest' (other than the sum of the individual interests of individual citizens), since that collectivist catch-phrase has never been and can never be defined, it amounted to a blank check on totalitarian power over the

broadcasting industry, granted to whatever bureaucrats happened to be appointed to the Commission." Ayn Rand, *Capitalism: The Unknown Ideal* (New York: The New American Library, 1966), pp. 121–122.

18. Newton N. Minow, *Equal Time: The Private Broadcaster and the Public Interest* (New York: Atheneum, 1964), p. 8.

19. Barry M. Mitnick, *The Political Economy of Regulation: Creating, Designing and Removing Regulatory Forms* (New York: Columbia University Press, 1980), pp 278–279. See, in general, Mitnick's chapter IV, "The Concept of the Public Interest."

20. Avery Leiserson, *Administrative Regulation: A Study in Representation of Interests* (Chicago: University of Chicago Press, 1942), p. 16.

21. See Virginia Held, *The Public Interest and Individual Interests* (New York: Basic Books, 1970), pp. 163–202.

22. *FCC* v. *WNCN Listeners Guild,*—U.S.—, 101 S. Ct. 1266, 67 L.Ed.2d 521, 535, (1981).

23. *Pinellas Broadcasting Co.* v. *FCC,* 230 F.2d 204, 206 (D.C. Cir. 1956), *certiorari denied,* 350 U.S. 1007 (1956).

24. For example, see the discussion in chapter seven of a Commission initiative to control advertising "in the public interest," which led to a stern rebuke from the House of Representatives.

25. Pendleton Herring, *Public Administration and the Public Interest* (New York: McGraw-Hill, 1936), p. 138. Vagueness, however, may also serve to protect the agency when its decisions are challenged in the courts, since the judiciary may be loath to overturn actions protected by a broad statutory mandate.

26. Henry Friendly, *The Federal Administrative Agencies* (Cambridge, Mass.: Harvard University Press, 1962), pp. 54–55.

27. For a comparative examination of how broadcast policy emerged differently in Europe from the United States, see Roland S. Homet, *Politics, Cultures and Communications: European vs. American Approaches to Communications Policy-making* (New York: Praeger, 1976).

28. Congress did not uniformly use the phrase "public interest" in the Communications Act. For example, the standard of "public interest" is specified in Sections 201(b), 215(a), 221(a), 222(c)(1), 415(a)(4), 319(i) and 315; "public convenience and necessity" in Section 314(f); "interest of public convenience and necessity," Section 214(a); "public interest, convenience and necessity," Sections 307(d), 309(a), and 319(a); and "public interest, convenience or necessity," Sections 307(d), 311(b), and 311(c)(3). On September 17, 1981, the FCC recommended that Congress drop all broadcast-related mentions of "convenience" or "necessity." It called the words "superfluous. . . . To the extent the issues embodied in these terms are relevant to radio regulation, they are subsumed under Commission review of the 'public interest.' " *FCC Legislative Proposal, Track I,* September 17, 1981, p. 25 [mimeo.].

29. See *KFKB Broadcasting Association, Inc.* v. *Federal Radio Commission,* 47 F.2d 670 (D.C. Cir. 1931) and *Trinity Methodist Church, South* v. *Federal Radio Commission,* 62 F.2d 850 (D.C. Cir. 1932).

30. See *Red Lion Broadcasting Co., Inc.* v. *Federal Communications Commission,* 395 U.S. 367, 89 S.Ct. 1794, 23 L.Ed. 2d 371 (1969) and *Federal Communications Commission* v. *Pacifica Foundation,* 438 U.S. 726, 98 S. Ct. 3026, 57 L.Ed.2d 1073 (1978). In *Pacifica,* at 746, the court stated: "We have long recognized that each medium of expression presents special First Amendment problems. . . . And of all forms of communication, it is

broadcasting that has received the most limited First Amendment protection."

31. *Red Lion Broadcasting Co.* v. *FCC,* 395 U.S. 367, 390, 89 S. Ct. 1794, 23 L. Ed.2d 371 (1969). See also *CBS* v. *FCC,*————U.S.————, 101 S.Ct. 2813, 69 L.Ed.2d 706 (1981).

32. Quoted in Fred W. Friendly, *The Good Guys, the Bad Guys and the First Amendment: Free Speech vs. Fairness in Broadcasting* (New York: Random House, 1975), p. ix.

33. This discussion is based on a theme developed by Benno C. Schmidt, Jr., *Freedom of the Press vs. Public Access* (New York: Praeger, 1976), pp. 157–158. The phrase "public trustee," however, does not appear in the Communications Act. Early in his term, and reflecting the regulatory philosophy of the Reagan administration, FCC Chairman Mark S. Fowler began to question this trustee concept. "Put simply," said Fowler, "we are at the end of regulating broadcasting under the trusteeship model. Whether you call it 'paternalism' or 'nannyism,' it is 'Big Brother,' and it must cease. I believe," continued Fowler, "in a marketplace approach to broadcast regulation. The principal difference between the trusteeship model and the marketplace approach is this: Under the trusteeship model, the Commission fashioned rules to dictate how the broadcaster was to serve his community. In return for adhering to its pronouncements, broadcasters could expect Commission policies that protected [sic] protectionism. Under the coming marketplace approach, the Commission should, so far as possible, defer to a broadcaster's judgment about how best to compete for viewers and listeners because this serves the public interest." "The Public's Interest," an address by Mark S. Fowler to the International Radio and Television Society, New York, N.Y., September 23, 1981 [mimeo.], p. 2.

34. See Steven J. Simmons, *The Fairness Doctrine and the Media* (Berkeley: University of California Press, 1978). Under Chairman Fowler, the FCC recommended that Congress repeal the Fairness Doctrine. See *FCC Legislative Proposals, Track II,* September 17, 1981 [mimeo.], pp. 23–24.

35. See Marc U. Porat, "Communication Policy in an Information Society," and William Lucas, "Telecommunications Technologies and Services" in *Communications for Tomorrow,* pp. 3–60, 245–274.

36. See Clare D. McGillem and William P. McLauchlan, *Hermes Bound: The Policy and Technology of Telecommunications* (West Lafayette, Ind.: Purdue Research Foundation, 1978), pp. 27–34. See also William P. McLauchlan, "Telecommunications Policy: An Overview," *Policy Studies Journal,* VII (Winter 1978), 301–310.

37. *FCC* v. *WNCN Listeners Guild,*————U.S.————, 101 S.Ct. 1266, 67 L.Ed.2d 521, 539 (1981).

38. *Deregulation of Radio,* 84 FCC 2d 968 (1981). At the same time the FCC also decided it was no longer necessary for the government to require commercial radio broadcasters to keep detailed program logs or to specify the procedure by which broadcasters decided what problems existed in their communities that should be addressed by news or public affairs programs. See also Lawrence Mosher, "The Approaching Boom on the Tube: The Regulatory Boxes No Longer Fit," *The National Journal,* February 23, 1980, pp. 304–310.

39. *FCC Legislative Proposals, Track II,* September 17, 1981 [mimeo.], p. 23.

40. "The Public's Interest," an address by Mark S. Fowler, International Radio and Television Society, New York, N.Y., September 23, 1981 [mimeo.], p. 5.
41. Ibid, p. 6.
42. Some scholars argue that scarcity is primarily the product of, rather than the justification for, regulation. See Bruce M. Owen, *Economics and Freedom of Expression: Media Structure and the First Amendment* (Cambridge, Mass.: Ballinger, 1975).
43. See Don R. LeDuc, "The *FCC* v. *CATV,* et al.: A Theory of Regulatory Reflex Action," *Federal Communications Bar Journal,* 23 (1969), 93; and Robert H. Stern, "Regulatory Influences Upon Television Development," *American Journal of Economics and Sociology,* 22 (1963), 347.
44. Vincent Mosco, *Broadcasting in the United States: Innovative Challenge and Organizational Control* (Norwood, N.J.: Ablex, 1979), pp. 13–28. See also Don R. LeDuc, *Cable Television and the FCC: A Crisis in Media Control* (Philadelphia: Temple University Press, 1973); Martin H. Seiden, *Cable Television U.S.A.: An Analysis of Government Policy* (New York: Praeger, 1972); and Paul W. MacAvoy (ed.), *Deregulation of Cable Television* (Washington, D.C.: American Enterprise Institute, 1977).
45. The Office of Telecommunications Policy (OTP) was created on September 4, 1970, when President Nixon signed an executive order implementing Reorganization Plan No. 1, as approved by Congress (see chapter three). Located in the Executive Office of the President, the OTP was headed by a director who reported, at least on paper, directly to the president and who was responsible for formulating and implementing the administration's policy on virtually all telecommunications matters. From the outset, the OTP and the FCC were at odds over which agency should have primacy in dealing with the communications industries. The OTP became part of the Department of Commerce and was renamed the National Telecommunications and Information Administration in 1978.
46. *Cable Television Report and Order,* 36 FCC2d 141, 324 (1972). The FCC's policy on the development of cable television has been subject to considerable criticism. See Clair Wilcox and William G. Shepherd, *Public Policies Toward Business,* 5th ed. (Homewood, Ill.: Irwin, 1975); U.S. House of Representatives, House Interstate and Foreign Commerce Committee, Subcommittee on Communications, *Cable Television: Promise Versus Regulatory Performance,* 94th Congress, 2nd Session (January 1976); U.S. House of Representatives, House Interstate and Foreign Commerce Committee, Subcommittee on Oversight and Investigations, *Federal Regulation and Regulatory Reform,* 94th Congress, 2nd Session (October 1976), pp. 257–258; LeDuc, *Cable Television and the FCC;* Seiden, *Cable Television, U.S.A.;* Richard Olin Berner, *Constraints on the Regulatory Process: A Case Study of Regulation of Cable Television* (Cambridge, Mass.: Harvard Program on Information Technologies and Public Policy, 1975); and Monroe E. Price, "Requiem for the Wired Nation: Cable Rulemaking at the FCC," *Virginia Law Review,* 61 (April 1975), 541–578.
47. *Home Box Office, Inc.* v. *FCC,* 567 F.2d 9 (D.C. Cir. 1977), *certiorari denied,* 434 U.S. 829 (1977).

48. Cable Television Channel Capacity and Access Channel Requirements, 45 *Federal Register* 76178 (November 18, 1980).
49. See *Federal Communications Commission* v. *Midwest Video Corp.*, 440 U.S. 689, 99 S.Ct. 1465, 59 L.Ed.2d 733 (1979).
50. For example, *Malrite TV of New York* v. *FCC,* 652 F.2d 1140 (2d Cir. 1981).

Two

Five Determiners of Regulatory Policy

From its creation, the FCC has enjoyed a broad congressional mandate —at least in theory—to frame responsible public policy toward broadcasting. Although the Commission plays a central role in broadcast regulation, it rarely acts alone. Often the crucial decisions come about through the action, interaction, or, indeed, inaction of other persons or institutions. This chapter examines five of the six major participants in the regulatory policy-making process: the FCC, the broadcast industry, citizen groups, the courts, and the White House. The sixth participant in the regulatory policy-making process—Congress—interacts with the other five so frequently that it will be treated separately in chapter three. Additional participants—such as the Corporation for Public Broadcasting, the Equal Employment Opportunity Commission, and the Federal Trade Commission—often affect policy, but these six stand out because of their continued and repeated involvement in the politics of broadcast regulation.

The FCC

Former Chairman Newton Minow once described the FCC as "a vast and sometimes dark forest, where FCC hunters are often required to spend weeks of our time shooting down mosquitoes with elephant guns."[1] Over the course of its history, the Commission has been bombarded with criticism from various quarters, including criticism from former FCC members like Minow. This is not surprising for a body that must regulate diverse activities—from telephones to broadcast stations and from satellites to microwave ovens—and that, like other regulatory agencies, has the dual responsibility to write rules and regulations and then enforce them as well as the express terms of the Communications Act. This combination of executive, quasi-legislative, and judicial functions in a single agency is, in fact, a common characteristic of, and difficulty for, all regulatory commissions.

Like other agencies, the FCC also sometimes comes in for criticism

33

when it is caught between its potentially conflicting obligations both to help develop and promote the industries it regulates and to see to it that consumers are protected. Perhaps as good a summary as was ever written of the sweeping charges leveled against the FCC was included in the Landis Report on Regulatory Agencies to President-elect John F. Kennedy in December 1960:

The Federal Communications Commission presents a somewhat extraordinary spectacle. Despite considerable technical excellence on the part of its staff, the Commission has drifted, vacillated and stalled in almost every major area. It seems incapable of policy planning, of disposing within a reasonable period of time the business before it, of fashioning procedures that are effective to deal with its problems. The available evidence indicates that it, more than any other agency, has been susceptible to *ex parte* presentations, and that it has been subservient, far too subservient, to the subcommittees on communications of the Congress and their members.[2]

The Landis report focused on one of the most often heard criticisms —the Commission's lack of real independence. The law may establish a regulatory agency as independent from the executive branch, but that does not by any means imply independence from congressional or industry pressures or, in practice, from the White House. There is just no insulating the FCC from politics. The agency must deal with the White House over legislative initiatives and budget matters. Commissioners may, at times, seek executive or congressional favor to increase chances for reappointment. In the words of former Commissioner Robert E. Lee (whose twenty-eight-year term on the FCC set an all-time record for regulatory agency service), "I don't care how good a Commissioner you have been, there comes that time when you've got to kiss a certain number of asses up on the Hill."[3]

Indeed, the argument about lack of independence may be naive. While the FCC is often criticized for not being independent enough to fulfill the abstract objectives of "independent regulatory agencies," too much independence from economic, technical, or political support weakens an agency's ability to develop and implement sound policy. Samuel Huntington, in his study of the Interstate Commerce Commission, explains this seeming paradox:

If an agency is to be viable, it must adapt itself to the pressures from [outside] sources so as to maintain a net preponderance of political support over political opposition. It must have sufficient support to maintain and, if necessary, expand its statutory authority, to protect it against attempts to abolish it or subordinate it to other agencies, and to secure for it necessary appropriations. Consequently, to remain viable over a period of time, an agency must adjust its sources of support so as to correspond with changes in the strength of their political pressures. If the agency fails to make this adjustment, its political support decreases relative to its political opposition and it may be said to suffer from administrative marasmus.[4]

THE FCC AS A BUREAUCRACY

The FCC is more than just an independent regulatory commission wrestling with the problem of its political nonindependence; it is also a bureaucracy. As such it exhibits all the classic symptoms of bureaucracies—massive hierarchy, institutional conservatism, professed rationality, parochial professionalism, and entrenched self-interest.[5]

Lee Loevinger, a former FCC Commissioner, has likened the FCC and other administrative agencies to a pyramid. At the apex (the point most visible at a distance) are the seven Commissioners. Professional and middle-level staff members of the agency form the base of the pyramid, which supports the structure and determines whether it stands upright or leans in any direction.[6] The nature of the pyramid becomes clear from the organization chart shown in Figure 1. The Commission is a mixture of organization by profession (e.g., lawyers in the Office of General Counsel, engineers in the Office of Science and Technology) and by function/industry (e.g., the bureaus that oversee broadcasting, cable television, common carriers—that is, telephone and telegraph—and private—for example, citizens band—radio.

Only the Commissioners, their small personal staffs, and the Office of Plans and Policy are expected to take a look at problems from all perspectives—legal to technical to social—and to consider how various industries interact when a particular policy problem arises. As can be seen, however, the more specialized professional and middle-level staff far outnumber the few generalists at the top, as is inevitable in any organization the size of the FCC. Loevinger maintains that no one can understand the agencies and their operation without "some inquiry into the motivating forces that drive agency members and staff, and into the internal relationships by which work information and agency power are divided among and transmitted between persons comprising the institution."[7]

The attitudes of the FCC's middle-level staff are a significant factor in the development of its regulatory policy. First, unlike the Commissioners and their personal aides who are political appointees subject to periodic change, most of the Commission's other staff members are government career employees, many of whom have spent their entire working lives at the Commission. Second, the Commission's middle-level staff exercises considerable influence through its control of the channels of communication to FCC Commissioners. In choosing among various policy alternatives, FCC Commissioners usually must base their decisions on information selected by staff personnel as relevant and

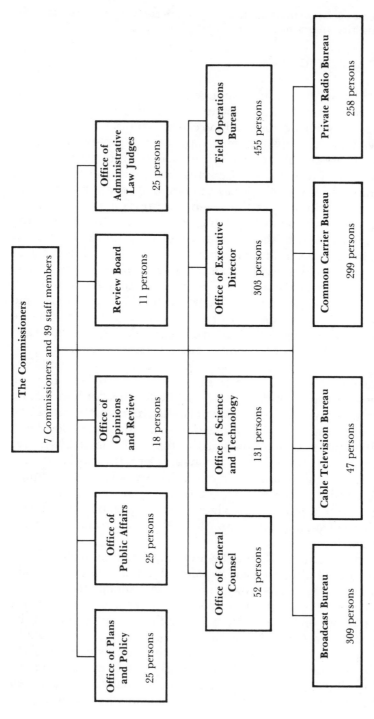

FIGURE 1   Federal Communications Commission Organization Chart (with number of employees authorized for fiscal year 1981)*

*By fiscal year 1982, the Commission, like other federal agencies, was reacting to the impact of Reagan administration budget cuts. The Office of Opinions and Review was abolished, and the number of positions in other bureaus and offices slightly reduced. At the direction of Congress, the FCC eliminated the Office of Executive Director and created a more powerful Office of Managing Director through which the offices and bureaus reported to the Commissioners. Additional changes to streamline the Commission, including elimination or consolidation of bureaus, were under consideration.

significant. It could hardly be otherwise, as former FCC Commissioner Glen Robinson has shown in an analogy:

> Just as, according to Napoleon, an army marches on its stomach, so too an administrative agency "marches" on the information it digests. In contrast to the problem that inspired Napoleon's dictum, however, the administrator's problem is seldom one of quantity. If anything, quite the reverse is true.
> . . .
> No one supposes, of course, that individual agency members themselves digest all, or even a large fraction, of the material submitted to them. That, after all, is what a staff is for—to digest, summarize and make recommendations from this huge volume of information.[8]

The Commissioners are faced with more than just the problems of digesting large quantities of information. Many, including Robinson, have criticized the FCC for relying too heavily on biased information submitted by interested parties, for failing to develop the ability to produce independent research and information, and for gathering information in forms irrelevant for policy making when it is gathered at all.[9] Nor are problems of information quantity or quality the end of the matter. FCC Commissioner Nicholas Johnson perceived the FCC's decision-making process as dominated by entrenched bureau chiefs and agency coordinators who were sometimes reluctant even to present alternatives to the Commissioners for consideration.[10]

Finally, since hundreds of decisions must be made daily by the FCC, the formulation as well as the implementation of policy is frequently delegated to the Commission's middle-level staff. When that happens, another bureaucratic symptom is evident—the struggle for power within the hierarchy. Loevinger contends that the first step toward a realistic understanding of bureaucratic decision making is a recognition that the power motive is to bureaucracy what the profit motive is to business. Government officials and staff members try to maximize the power of their positions. Since they are no exception to this generalization, the FCC Commissioners and staff members seek almost daily to perpetuate and extend their own power. Newly created bureaus and those hired to work in them attempt to justify and prolong their existence, frequently long after their usefulness has ended. Sometimes the power motive is expressed through the assertion of jurisdiction over new industries that are not specifically mentioned in the Communications Act (such as cable television) and the creation of new bureaus (such as the Cable Television Bureau) that have been likened to independent "fiefdoms" within the agency. Under the philosophy of the Reagan administration, and faced with budget cutbacks, some of this behavior changed. Reagan's appointee as Chairman, Mark S. Fowler, seemed to exert power over the agency in a radically different way; namely, to question the Commission's existence—he called it "a New Deal Dinosaur"—and to reduce the size of the staff.[11]

Another characteristic of bureaucracy, related to its concern for survival and power, is a tendency to be inflexible, static, and conservative rather than adaptive, innovative, or creative. As a bureaucracy the FCC is often reluctant to embrace innovative proposals, especially when such actions might mean the abandonment of familiar assumptions and standards. Incremental change—which can be bureaucratically digested in small bits—is often favored over sweeping change.[12] Moreover, a policy that is "rational" in terms of accepted evaluative procedures often is favored over a risky but potentially high-gain policy that demands different criteria for evaluation or may be overturned by the courts. Generally, the FCC has little to gain for pushing a successful technological innovation and much to lose if it fails. Above all, the agency finds that it is best, when in doubt, to demand documentation rather than to make policy. The Commission spent nearly a decade searching for means to encourage development of UHF television, has spent many more years worrying about programming evaluation standards for license renewals and has fretted endlessly about cable television. In other words, the Commission often substitutes evaluating and studying a problem or policy for coming to grips with it. However, during the three and one-half years Charles D. Ferris served as Chairman (1977–1980), the FCC placed special emphasis on pushing successful technological innovations as a means of providing an abundance of communications services to the public. In a retrospective entitled "The *Laissez Faire* Legacy of Charlie Ferris," *Broadcasting* magazine observed that the villain he sought to exorcise was the scarcity of communications services—a scarcity that had been used to justify content regulation of broadcasting.[13] The following long litany of FCC actions underscores the dramatic changes in the regulatory policies of the Commission and the technological structure of the telecommunications and broadcast industries during Ferris's tenure as Chairman:

In one of its most far-reaching moves, the commission literally unscrambled the omelette made up of computer technology and common carrier services, and permitted common carriers, including AT&T, to enter the computer and information services field. It removed most of the remaining shackles from cable television and, by deregulating earth stations and authorizing the use of small ones, facilitated cable's use of satellite service. It advanced the cause of subscription television by repealing the rule limiting such stations to one per market and fostered the growth of multipoint distribution service.

Now, moreover, it is moving toward the authorization of hundreds, possibly thousands, of low-power television stations and has proposed the addition of 140 VHF television drop-ins. In radio, it broke down the remaining 25 clear channels, opening the door to some 125 new AM stations, and voted to reduce AM channel spacing from 10 to 9 khz, an action that could lead to the establishment of another several hundred stations—if other countries in the western hemisphere go along with the plan. . . .

On top of all that, and given the time, it is certain Ferris would have attempted to create a virtually regulation-free environment for direct broadcast satellite service.[14]

DECISION MAKING AT THE COMMISSION

This huge bureaucracy—the FCC—is directed at the top by seven Commissioners with varied social and political backgrounds whose interactions among themselves and with staff members mold Commission policy decisions. Meetings of the Commissioners are held with highly variable frequency but in recent years have averaged about once every ten days. Since 1977 the meetings generally have, by federal law, been open to the press and public. The formal structure of decision making shapes to a significant extent the diverse roles of Commissioners and staff members. Political scientist Bradley Canon has provided an illuminating description of that structure:

Although it varies among individuals, the general level of interaction between Commissioners on policy questions seems low. Thus, only those items considered really important receive any pre-meeting discussion or in-meeting debate. In other cases, the Commissioners vote on the basis of prior judgments and attitudes or follow the recommendations of staff members in whom they have confidence. Commissioners are free to switch their vote between the meeting and the writing of the opinion disposing of the case, but this occurs only occasionally. Opinions are almost always written by staff members and adopted by the Commission, usually with a minimum of supervision and attention. Dissenting opinions, of course, are the responsibility of the dissident, although staff help is not unknown here. About one-fifth of such votes are not accompanied by an opinion.[15]

Publicly displayed controversy is often reduced by premeeting circulation of agenda items among Commissioners. Often an item will not be brought to public vote by the Chairman until such circulation has produced a consensus that avoids a sharp split. Some Chairmen, however, have been less concerned than others with achieving consensus and avoiding such controversy.

Although Section 4(b) of the Communications Act provides that no more than four of the seven Commissioners shall be members of the same political party, the formal political affiliation of Commission appointees who are not members of the president's party is usually of little significance. A study of fifty-one appointments to the FCC and the FTC found that the selections from the president's party typically have been partisan political choices; the others have been "friendly Indians" in sympathy with administration objectives rather than *bona fide* partisans of the opposition.[16] President Truman, for example, placed Republicans on the Commission staff, but because of the Hatch Act his action barred them from further partisan activities. President Nixon appointed a nominal Democratic former broadcaster, James Quello, to the Commission in part as a reward for Quello's support of Nixon during the 1968 campaign. President Reagan later reappointed Quello.

The background of the Commissioners is of some importance in understanding Commission behavior. As is generally true of regulatory bodies, most Commissioners, over time, come from backgrounds in law or prior public service. Lawrence Lichty has analyzed in detail the characteristics of the forty-four FCC and FRC Commissioners between 1927 and 1961.[17] He found that individual Commissioners held office for periods of service of about 4.5 years. These figures were updated by a study done for the Senate Commerce Committee in 1976 covering the period from 1952 to 1976. In that study, the average length of FCC service had grown to 6.7 years, but the figure is distorted by the exceedingly long tenure of Commissioner Robert E. Lee, first appointed by President Eisenhower in 1953, who did not leave the Commission until 1981. A more useful figure is to note that of twenty-four persons appointed to the FCC between 1952 and 1975 whose terms had not yet expired, ten—or about 45 percent—resigned before the end of their terms.[18]

Of the forty-four Commissioners studied by Lichty, twenty-three had legal backgrounds, twenty-four had some prior experience with broadcasting, and all but four had previously held government office on either the federal or state level. In short, the typical Commissioner was trained in law, generally familiar with broadcasting, and quite likely to have had prior government administrative responsibilities. Wenmouth Williams, Jr., updated the Lichty study by analyzing the backgrounds of twenty-two Commissioners who served between 1962 and 1975. Williams found that the typical Commissioner during this period had (1) some government affiliations, (2) strong political affiliations, and (3) some law experience.[19] The previously mentioned 1976 congressional study supported these figures, concluding that of thirty-one appointees to the FCC between 1952 and 1975, twenty, or 65 percent, came immediately from positions in the federal or, more rarely, state government and five, or 16 percent, came from private law practice.[20]

Williams concluded that the political philosophies of the Commissioners had an important impact on regulation during the 1962–1975 period. He noted a strong correlation between "Presidential Commissions" and basic regulatory trends. The Kennedy Commission, concerned with stricter regulation of programming and competition, was typified by Newton Minow's "vast wasteland" speech.[21] Conversely, the

Commission of Lyndon Johnson, a president with conspicuous broadcast interests, preferred to minimize government regulation—as evidenced by Johnson's appointment of Rosel Hyde, a "hands off" Commissioner, as Chairman. More recently, the Commission led by Richard E. Wiley under the Nixon and Ford administrations tended to reflect the probusiness and moderately deregulatory values of those administrations; the Commission headed by Charles D. Ferris, under President Carter, on the other hand began, and in some cases completed, deregulatory initiatives favored by the president while remaining attentive to complaints by consumers and to such social policy issues favored by the Democrats as equal employment opportunity. Chairman Mark S. Fowler, an unabashed supporter of President Reagan ("I'm not a closet Reagan supporter"), announced from the very beginning a deep commitment to follow "the President's philosophy of the least intrusive form of government."[22]

One particularly important result of this common legal and administrative background of many of the Commissioners is the FCC's tendency to see regulatory activities in legal and administrative rather than in social or economic terms. Traditionally the FCC has preferred the administratively and legally sound policy over the controversial or more sweeping alternative. Moreover, the personal background of Commissioners is perhaps not as diverse as suggested by Lichty and Williams. Like other regulatory agencies, the FCC has been stocked by white males, although with the appointment of Freida B. Hennock in 1948, it became the first federal regulatory agency with a female member. From 1927 through 1981, there have been only one Hispanic, two black, and five female appointees to the FCC, with seven of those eight appointments coming since 1970. A closer examination of the Commissioners' backgrounds shows they have tended to be neutral, generalist types, usually knowing little about communications regulation when first appointed. Also, whatever their educational or occupational backgrounds, "consensus" types have predominated over Commissioners with strong personalities or philosophies.

Although we have described the FCC in general terms, it is important to remember that it is not a static institution but one which changes with its cast of characters. Critics frequently attack the Commission as if it were a single, fixed, and unalterable body. Actually, there have been a number of "Commissions" at different times with divergent opinions as to how broadcasting should be regulated. As Lichty concluded:

Changes in the direction and emphasis of the Commission's regulation of broadcasting are a function of the members serving on the Commission at . . . specific times. Further, the personal experience, education, occupational background, and governmental philosophy of the members of the Federal Radio Commission and the Federal Communications Commission directly influence the direction and emphasis of the agency's policy.[23]

In an attempt to show variation within the Commission at different historical periods, Lichty and Williams also analyzed distinctive patterns of Commissioners' backgrounds during various FRC and FCC periods. Their findings, which we have summarized and updated in Table 1, show a modest but clear relationship between Commissioner background patterns and predominant Commission activities concern-

**TABLE 1   Pattern of FRC and FCC Commissioners'
Backgrounds, 1927–1982**

Commission Periods	Background Patterns of Commissioners
1. Establishing technical standards, 1927–1930	Technical experts
2. Important early legal precedents, 1930–1934	Legal background
3. Cleaning-up and vigorous application of the law, 1934–1938	Legal background; prior government experience
4. Trustbusting of broadcast ownership, 1939–1945	Prior government experience, especially public utility and New Deal agency background
5. Public service, new radio facilities, and TV engineering problems, 1946–1952	FCC staff backgrounds as engineers and chief counsels
6. Moderate regulation, 1953–1960	Prior experience on state regulatory commissions and FCC staff background
7. Increased emphasis on programming and competition, 1960–1965	Legal background; prior government experience
8. Moderate regulation, 1966–1969	Legal background; prior government experience
9. Cleaning-up, clarification of exisiting law, 1970–1977	Prior government and political experience
10. Reconsideration of old policies, moderate deregulation, stimulation of new media, 1978–1980	Prior government and political experience; interest in economic aspects of regulation
11. Accelerated deregulation, and interest in marketplace competition, 1981–1982	Prior government and political experience

SOURCE: Adapted and updated from Lawrence Lichty, "The Impact of FRC and FCC Commissioners' Backgrounds on the Regulation of Broadcasting," *Journal of Broadcasting,* 6 (Spring 1962), 97–110; and Wenmouth Williams, Jr., "Impact of Commissioner Background on FCC Decisions: 1962–1975," *Journal of Broadcasting, 20 (Spring 1976) 244–256.*

ing broadcast regulation. Both found that the occupational backgrounds and political philosophies of Commissioners have influenced measurably the regulation of broadcasting. For example, members who had engineering backgrounds dominated the "technical" period while attorneys experienced in governmental regulation were predominant in the "trustbusting" era.[24]

THE INFLUENCE OF INDIVIDUAL COMMISSIONERS

Two other important points about the Commissioners are that (1) they may exhibit factional behavior and that (2) as individuals they often play pivotal roles in decision making. That groups or factions are important in a collegial voting body such as the FCC is certainly not a particularly new or striking idea; the literature on legislative committees and judicial bodies is replete with findings stressing the importance of internal groups and factions. In a study of the FCC as a decision-making group, political scientist Bradley Canon used techniques familiar in analysis of judicial behavior, including bloc analysis and Guttman cumulative scaling. Canon concluded that various voting blocs are important in Commission decisions and are especially present in dissents. He further found that partisan affiliations of Commissioners seem to be related to voting behavior on some issues connected with broad social and economic problems, that appointees of different presidents seem to vote somewhat differently, that the solo dissenter is not an uncommon occurrence, and that there is some consistency among Commissioners in voting patterns.[25]

Canon's conclusion concerning the solo dissenter should be stressed, for throughout the history of the FCC the role of the individual Commissioner has been particularly significant. Lichty observed that "the problems tackled and solutions proposed were due in part to the individual interests of Commissioners and that many important decisions or changes were the result of crusades by one Commissioner."[26] Individual Commissioners' crusades over specific issues—for example, Commissioner Freida Hennock's crusade over educational broadcasting, Commissioner Robert E. Lee's over UHF-TV—have often had considerable impact on the shaping of FCC policy in those areas. It cannot be denied that James Lawrence Fly, Nicholas Johnson, Newton Minow, Kenneth Cox, Dean Burch, Richard Wiley, and Charles Ferris, to name just a few, had significant impact on the Commission beyond the power of their individual votes.

It is significant that five of the seven Commissioners just listed also served as FCC Chairman. Unlike the heads of most regulatory commissions, the Chairman of the FCC has little formal "extra" power. For example, Congress has refused to officially provide the FCC Chairman with general responsibility for staff and management.[27] Still, the Chairman is more than first among equals. The Chairman speaks for the Commission, has a much larger staff, and is visible as the president's "choice" as leader. Former Commissioner Kenneth Cox has pointed out that the Chairman of the FCC has a major impact on the preparation of the agenda at Commission meetings and "has a much more direct relationship with the bureau chiefs as to scheduling, the allocation of priorities, and so on." New or replacement bureau chiefs are proposed to the Commission by the Chairman. The Chairman's influence was increased in 1981 when a "managing director" was created in a position close to the Chairman. According to Cox, a Chairman "definitely has some edge in influence" since "there is some inclination on the part of some individual Commissioners, if they don't feel strongly about a matter, to go along with the Chairman if he wants to say something is a matter of importance to him."[28] This may be particularly true since FCC meetings are now, for the most part, conducted in public. According to Norman Blumenthal, a member of the FCC's Review Board, the Government in Sunshine Act, which requires open meetings, compels absolute loyalty to the Chairman and the "scripting out" of policy discussions beforehand. Unlike earlier times, no staff independence is permitted. Frequently an FCC Chairman can be instrumental in the selection and appointment (or reappointment) of Commissioners, especially if there has been a close relationship with the White House in furtherance of administration goals. A study of appointments showed that twelve of fifty-one Commissioners appointed were selected largely due to the support of the FCC Chairman, and very few of those would have been nominated without such an endorsement.[29]

The extent of the power of a Chairman, however, depends on ability, determination, and on the willingness of colleagues to give needed latitude. Many observers regard Richard E. Wiley as the most powerful Chairman in recent FCC history. Wiley, having served also as general counsel and a Commissioner, played an important role in hiring and promoting Commission staff members.[30] Les Brown, formerly of the *New York Times,* observed that "the Wiley years [were] among the most productive in the agency's history for the handling and disposition of cases and the bureaucratic flow of paper."[31] Wiley made the Commission a more efficient agency by changing various procedures, including instituting a three-month calendar for items that he prepared personally in order to give issues priority and a deadline. He moved issues onto the voting agenda when he perceived a consensus among his colleagues. Compromises in language or modifications of rules were customarily hammered out in his office before Commission meetings. Thus, while the Commission produced approximately four times the number of decisions under Chairman Wiley's leadership as under any previous administration of comparable length, it also produced the fewest dissents.[32] Wiley attributes his success to the fact that the other six Commissioners were "compatible [and] of similar philosophy." During most of his tenure as Chairman, the Commission consisted entirely of Nixon appointees, the first time a president had named all seven members of the FCC since its formation in 1934.[33]

Wiley's impressive record of support from his colleagues seemed for a time undercut by decisions in the federal courts, especially in the U.S. Court of Appeals for the District of Columbia Circuit. In an article entitled "Wiley's FCC: In Danger of Disappearing," *Broadcasting* magazine commented that decisions in lower courts in 1976 and 1977 were stripping the Wiley Commission of its major milestones.[34] Characterizing the record as "grim," the article referred to the following court actions:

1. The finding by a U.S. district court judge that Chairman Wiley's role in the National Association of Broadcasters' adoption of the family viewing concept for TV infringed broadcasters' First Amendment rights
2. The overturning by the court of appeals of media cross-ownership rules permitting the retention of most local newspaper-broadcast combinations (a practice known as "grandfathering")
3. The reversal, on the ground of censorship, of the Commission's declaratory ruling that a George Carlin comedy record broadcast by a New York City radio station was "indecent"
4. The overturning, based on statutory and First Amendment grounds, of FCC rules designed to guard against pay-cable's siphoning of movie and sports programming from regular commercial broadcasting
5. The court's expression of dissatisfaction with the FCC's policy of allowing broadcasters and marketplace forces to determine formats of radio stations

Subsequent higher-court decisions, however, reversed all of those rulings—except for the family viewing controversy, which was remanded to the FCC, and the decision dealing with the limits on cable systems that provide per-program or per-channel pay services. Thus, Wiley's record was largely vindicated about the time that Republicans, under Chairman Mark Fowler, regained control of the Commission in 1981.

Wiley's successor, Charles Ferris, also seemed to aspire to strong leadership, but did not, during most of his tenure, achieve support from Commission colleagues comparable to Wiley's. Ferris attempted to move the Commission in new directions and in doing so faced some staff resistance. He left office trailed by criticisms of inefficiency and of having contributed to low staff morale. Things might have turned out differently had there been a second Carter term to produce more sympathetic colleagues, an advantage Wiley enjoyed under the Nixon and Ford presidencies.

Ferris had his most significant impact on common carrier policy.

While most of his predecessors had concentrated on the more glamorous area of broadcast regulation, Ferris regarded the most important communications issues for the next decade as those in telecommunications—the transmission of voice and data by wire, satellite, and microwave. He predicted that the decreasing costs and increasing capacity of telecommunications systems would revolutionize both home and business environments, and he attempted to move his fellow Commissioners toward favoring increased competition and innovation in this field, which had been dominated by AT&T in the past.

Ferris also determined to deregulate significantly both cable television and radio broadcasting. He achieved those goals by a narrow 4 to 3 vote eliminating restrictions on cable carriage of distant television signals and by substantial Commission majorities for the elimination of (1) satellite earth station licensing, (2) requirements that cable systems obtain "certificates of compliance" from the FCC, and (3) requirements that commercial radio broadcasters broadcast minimum public affairs and news percentages, observe commercial time limitations and program logging rules, and formally ascertain (survey) the problems, needs, and interests of their communities.

Perhaps Ferris's most significant innovation in television broadcasting came through his hiring of economists for a three-year network inquiry and his transforming of the Office of Plans and Policy into, in effect, an office of "Chief Economist." Ferris's introduction of a substantial number of economists into the highest levels of FCC decision making created an atmosphere in which past legal structures for broadcast regulation were challenged by economic models favoring open entry of new technologies such as direct satellite-to-home broadcasting. This swing away from the traditional FCC reliance on lawyers and engineers caused substantial uncertainty both in the agency and among the affected industries. But Ferris argued that it seemed like time for an economic regulatory agency to hire more than a handful of economists to assist in its deliberations.

A fascinating example of the role a Chairman can have in forging a majority in favor of a policy is provided by the events surrounding the FCC's issuance, early in 1966, of proposed rules to regulate cable systems. The following excerpts from a report in *Broadcasting* magazine indicate the importance both of groups within the FCC and of individual Commissioners in the formulation of a consensus:

None of the tough new proposals was adopted for rulemaking by more than a bare majority of the Commission. Thus, a single defection, even the wavering of a formerly committed Commissioner, can kill a proposal or strip it of meaning. Representatives of groups directly affected know this, and are lobbying accordingly, on Capitol Hill as well as at the Commission.

The Commissioners themselves are uncertain and divided in their guesses as to what kind of rules, if any, will emerge. They talk of "shifting coalitions" among their number, of differing weights various Commissioners ascribe to the arguments of different industry figures.

The Commission statement on the CATV [cable TV] issue last week is a case in point, representing as it does a number of compromises on some extremely controversial questions.

. . .

Chairman Henry is credited by his colleagues for the degree of unanimity that was achieved. "It was very close," said one Commissioner in commenting on the Commission's decision. "It could have failed by an eyelash." "The Chairman," he said, "did a very constructive job."

The Chairman moderated his own previously hard line and abandoned the even harder line advocated by the staff. This cost him the support of Commissioner Cox, who favored stricter regulation. But it won the support of Commissioner Loevinger and held the vote of the other Commissioners.[35]

The potential influence of one Commissioner—particularly a Chairman working outside the FCC structure—is shown in Newton Minow's attempt to change, through appeals to public opinion, what he perceived as a "hostile environment" partially paralyzing the Commission. According to Minow:

Very early I decided that of all the routes I might take to the best performance of my job, the most effective and the wisest road in the long run was to speak out in the hope of influencing public opinion about television . . . and so I went to the people with public speeches.[36]

By seeking to draw upon and to encourage active public involvement in American broadcasting, Minow was, in effect, attempting to strengthen his role as Chairman by creating public support for certain types of policies. Like Nicholas Johnson, who also tried to mobilize public opinion, Minow believed that he would gain more from going public than he would lose by antagonizing those interest groups favoring a quieter approach.[37] His characterization of television as a "vast wasteland" electrified, and horrified, a convention of National Association of Broadcasters shortly after he became Chairman and resulted in wide publicity in magazines and newspapers. Minow challenged broadcast executives to sit down in front of their television sets for a full day, assuring them that they would observe a "vast wasteland" of game shows, violence, formula comedies, sadism, commercials, and boredom.[38] After that, broadcasters closed ranks even more tightly to oppose many of Minow's policies. Years later one of Minow's successors, Mark Fowler, would adopt a different approach to the use of the Chairman's speechmaking influence. In an address to broadcasters, Fowler observed that "the FCC has no business trying to influence by raised eyebrow or by raised voice for that matter. I confess that there was a romance bordering on chivalry when a Chairman might declare television to be a wasteland. Those kinds of pronouncements, as I see my job, are not mine to make. You are not my flock, and I am not your shepherd."[39]

The adjustment that the FCC makes to the demands and actions of interested parties is always a rough balance of the forces that affect both its political environment and its internal operations and of the prevailing attitudes of the American public toward regulatory issues. The problem for a regulatory commission is how to respond to these pressures while maintaining some integrity of purpose and freedom of decision. The dilemma is sharp: if a regulatory commission is content to respond to dominant interests, it may lose its meaning, whereas if it defies major forces in its environment, it may risk its existence.

Industry

Introducing the broadcast industry as a second participant in the regulatory process raises the important issue of the purpose of a regulatory commission and its relationship to the industry it was created to oversee. Recognizing the tensions and the pressures routinely applied by industry, Marver Bernstein has characterized regulation as "a two-way process in which the regulatory agency and the regulated interest attempt to control each other."[40]

Much early federal regulatory legislation was motivated by a desire to curb the abuses resulting from concentrated economic power. The Interstate Commerce Act of 1887, the Sherman Act, the Federal Trade Commission Act, and the Clayton Act all reflect this desire. With the passage of the Transportation Act of 1920, the Radio Act of 1927, and the Communications Act of 1934, Congress expanded the mandate of many regulatory commissions to include the broader but less well-defined charge of regulating in the "public interest." As noted in chapter one this ambiguous mandate is made even more so by the obligation imposed on an administrator to meet ill-formed public expectations of the "public interest" as well as more often forcefully stated congressional and industry desires. At least to some degree administrators can legitimately see their charge as including the preservation and encouragement of the regulated industry. The crux of their problem, then, is determining to what degree that goal should be subservient to other considerations, particularly to a larger conception of the public interest.

INDUSTRY-COMMISSION RELATIONSHIPS
—A COMPLEX WEB

On a day-to-day basis Commissioners are forced to immerse themselves in the field they propose to regulate; however, the line between gaining a familiarity with one or several industries' problems and becoming biased thereby in favor of an industry is perilously thin. It is difficult for Commissioners and their staff to work closely with an industry without coming to see regulatory problems in industry terms. As Professor Landis reported to President Kennedy, "It is the daily machine-gun-like impact on both agency and its staff of industry representatives that makes for industry orientation on the part of many honest and capable agency members, as well as agency staffs." Landis also observed, however, that direct contacts by industry representatives "of necessity . . . are frequently productive of intelligent ideas," whereas contacts with the general public "are rare and generally unproductive of anything except complaint."[41] As Robinson put it, the problem is "not that *regulators* have been captured by industry but rather that *regulation* has been captured by industry."[42]

The opinions and demands of the broadcast industry are expressed through consultative groups (such as joint industry-government committees), interchange of personnel, publication of views in the trade press, liaison committees of the Federal Communications Bar Association, social contacts and visits to offices of Commissioners, informal discussions at state broadcaster and trade association meetings, and the formal submission of pleadings and oral argument. The Commission is largely dependent for much of its information about proposed policies, especially about the impact of or potential for technological developments, on industry trade associations, the networks, and broadcast licensees.

Given such numerous opportunities to influence each other, it is hardly surprising that the pattern of industry-Commission relationships is dynamic and ever-changing, with shifting degrees of industry control. To some critics the Federal Communications Commission seems "captured" by the broadcast industry. While there may have been times when that assertion was true, it seems now to be off target. Since a regulatory agency must make enough alliances with effective power centers to retain its vitality, it must necessarily "come to terms" with significant elements in its environment by knowing which ones are powerful and which offer the best hope for continued vitality if an alliance is formed. In the 1980s, as different industries compete with one another, the Commission often receives entreaties not just from broadcast interests but also from their competitors. As Robinson has said:

Because most important controversies involve conflicting industry constituents, the "capture" [by a single industry] explanation would appear to have limited value as a guide to agency behavior. But the "capture" theory is not totally meaningless. Though it cannot fully explain how the agency will choose among competing industry interests, the theory does suggest how the agency will choose between industry and nonindustry interests or between regulated and unregulated interests.[43]

Former FCC Chairman John Doerfer once offered what is probably a classic justification for extensive consultation with the regulated industry: "It is naive to think that it is possible to legislate without conversations and conferences, without people who know problems of the particular industry."[44]

In the intricate and dynamic relationship between the FCC and the industry, the Washington communications lawyer plays a special role—not only in interpreting FCC policies for broadcast licensees but also in shaping the policy direction of the Commission. In a study of Washington lawyers, Joseph Goulden noted that while the lawyer's historic role has been to advise clients on how to comply with the law, the Washington lawyer's present role is to advise clients on how to make laws—and to make the most of them. Goulden described how the Washington lawyer serves as the intermediary that holds together the economic partnership of business and government:

Relations between some Washington lawyers and officials of the regulatory agencies can be so intimate they embarrass an onlooker. The lawyers and the regulators work together in a tight, impenetrable community where an outsider can't understand the language, much less why things are done the way they are. The lawyers and the regulators play together, at trade association meetings, over lunch, on the golf courses around Washington. They frequently swap jobs, the regulator moving to the private bar, the Washington lawyer moving into the Commission.[45]

In the view of economists Bruce Owen and Ronald Braeutigam, "the Washington law firm is essential to success in the regulation game." They advise established firms and industries that "it is useful, at a minimum, to deny potential competitors access to the best firms by keeping them on retainer."[46]

There is constant criticism of a "revolving door" relationship between the FCC and those it regulates. Many Commissioners enter the FCC either from communications-related law practice or, on occasion, from the communications industries themselves. Looking at appointees to the FCC between 1961 and 1975, the House Subcommittee on Oversight and Investigations concluded that of nineteen appointees in that period, five had been directly or indirectly employed by FCC-regulated industries in the five years prior to their appointment and ten had been so employed in the prior fifteen years.[47] Many of these same regulators sought regulated-industry employment at the end of their FCC service:

the same House subcommittee determined that of sixteen FCC Commissioners who left the agency between 1961 and 1975, four accepted subsequent employment in regulated industries.[48] Several efforts have been made to limit the potential for conflict of interest posed by such rapid turnover between the industry and its supervising Commission. Federal criminal law contains restrictions, strengthened under the Carter administration, on the ability of ex-Commissioners and high-level staff to practice before the FCC.[49]

President Carter attempted to control the problem by having prospective high-level appointees state their intention to serve their full terms. The door, however, continues to revolve. After the 1980 presidential elections, the successful Republican forces and the then Democratic Chairman, Charles Ferris, worked out a bargain that allowed Ferris to remain in office long enough to boost his government pension, even though he removed himself from decision making. The *quid pro quo* for the Republicans was Ferris's promise to resign early and create the chance for Reagan appointees to the Commission. He would, perforce, be replaced with a Republican Chairman if he did not resign. For Ferris, in addition to the boost in pension, there was the chance to revolve out of a minor role on the Commission into the private practice of communications law.[50]

The networks also play a special role in lobbying on behalf of industry positions before the FCC, Congress, and the White House. All three television networks maintain offices in Washington, D.C., consisting of several lobbyists.[51] In 1977 the U.S. Court of Appeals for the District of Columbia Circuit, discussing the impact of what it regarded as *ex parte* ("off the record") contacts in the FCC pay-cable proceedings, singled out visits by ABC Chairman Leonard Goldenson and President Elton Rule with key members of Congress, who in turn successfully pressured the Commission to halt relaxation of pay-cable rules. The court also cited the remarks of Everett Erlich, ABC's senior vice-president and general counsel, before the ABC Television Network affiliates on May 10, 1974:

As most of you know, the FCC just prior to Chairman Burch's sudden departure, was on the verge of modifying pay TV rules applicable to movies. . . . We took the leadership in opposing these proposals with the result that key members of Congress made it known in no uncertain terms that they did not expect the Commission to act on such a far-reaching policy matter without guidance. The Commission got the message and has postponed for several months reconsideration of this particular issue.[52]

Former Commissioner Nicholas Johnson characterized as the "subgovernment phenomenon" the domination of an agency's policy making by a coalescence of lobbyists, specialty lawyers, trade associations, trade press, congressional subcommittee staff members, and Commission personnel who cluster around each of the regulated industries—and the bar of the Broadcasters Club (now the National Communications Club). This subgovernment, Johnson maintained, grows around any specialized private interest–government relationship that exists over a long period of time, is self-perpetuating, and endures unaffected by tides of public opinion and efforts for reform. Johnson described the broadcasting industry subgovernment as including

> the networks and multiple station owners, the Federal Communications Bar Association, *Broadcasting* magazine, the National Association of Broadcasters, the communication law firms, and the industry-hired public relations and management consultant firms. It also includes the permanent government staff—regulatory, executive and congressional—which is concerned with [the] day-to-day activities of the broadcasting industry. People in this subgovernment typically spend their lives moving from one organization to another within it.[53]

THE NAB AND OTHER BROADCAST LOBBIES

The leading voice (or trumpet, depending on the occasion) for the broadcast industry is the National Association of Broadcasters (NAB), a trade organization with more than 5,300 member radio and television stations, an annual budget of nearly $8 million, and a staff of over 150 based in a $6 million building situated only three blocks from the FCC.[54] For more than a half-century, the NAB has been remarkably effective in thwarting efforts to place onerous regulatory burdens on broadcasters. One conspicuous instance was the NAB's success in persuading the House of Representatives to block the FCC's proposed adoption of rules on commercial advertising. (This case study is discussed in chapter seven.) The lobbying prowess of the broadcasting industry—especially during the years before 1947—has been described by Murray Edelman as follows:

> At a public hearing it is the "regulated" who appear and offer argument—regularly, forcefully, and with a show of massed strength. The industrial giants in this field have, moreover, shown marked ability and determination to organize pressure on Capitol Hill, on the Commission, in the press, and over the radio whenever it has appeared to them that a proposed or promulgated Commission policy would affect their interests adversely. Groups that represent listeners are rare, and those that do arise have become impotent with impressive regularity.[55]

In recent years, however, the NAB has encountered increasing difficulty in its efforts to fend off congressional and FCC regulation of the broadcast industry. The climate in which broadcast regulation takes place has changed markedly in the last fifteen years. Three trends in particular have been responsible for this change, and all have made the NAB's job more difficult.[56]

First, the organizations represented by the NAB have grown in number and diversity, ranging from the smallest "mom and pop" AM radio stations to the largest television networks and conglomerate owners of multiple communications media. Whereas the broadcast industry is often portrayed as monolithic, fractionalization of views on specific issues is common. For example, networks differ with affiliated stations on retaining FCC rules that limit the amount of network programming, and many daytime radio broadcasters split from others when proposals were under consideration to squeeze stations closer together electronically—a move that might create more full-time stations but also increase competition. Because the NAB's membership is so diverse, smaller, more specialized trade organizations have sprung up over the years to protect the interests of television stations (Association of Maximum Service Telecasters), television translator stations (National Translator Association), UHF television stations (Council for UHF Broadcasting and the National Association of UHF Broadcasters), clear-channel AM radio stations (Clear Channel Broadcasting Service), daytime AM stations (Daytime Broadcasters Association), stations owned by blacks (National Association of Black-Owned Broadcasters), religious stations (National Religious Broadcasters), and AM and FM stations (National Radio Broadcasters Association). Moreover, a separate and perhaps more potent lobbying group is made up of the three national networks, whose Washington representatives work in a kind of loose alliance. Thus the broadcast lobby is not truly monolithic but comprises many associations supporting several different and sometimes conflicting specific interests. These associations have tended to weaken the NAB's lobbying power, since it sometimes cannot present a united front on regulatory questions. Nevertheless, it is still a force to be reckoned with. An example of the formidable strength of the broadcast lobby, when acting as a unified force, is the defeat in June 1977 of a legislative proposal by Senator Ernest Hollings (D-South Carolina) to apply the Fairness Doctrine (a requirement that broadcasters air contrasting viewpoints on controversial issues of public importance) to the broadcast advertising of products containing saccharin. Hollings, then chairman of the Senate Communications Subcommittee, ascribed the defeat of his proposal by the Senate Commerce Committee to the power of broadcasters over their elected representatives, who will "vote anything that the local broadcasters want." Hollings said that "rather than a chairman of a subcommittee, I felt like a foreman of a fixed grand jury."[57]

Second, the broadcast lobby also must contend with the potent lobbying efforts of other industries regulated by the FCC. The American Telephone & Telegraph Company (AT&T), for example, traditionally has had a significant impact on the selection of FCC Commissioners. Three of President Eisenhower's first four appointments to the FCC were state public utility commissioners, and those appointments have been traced to the efforts of AT&T officials.[58] During the 1970s the cable industry, represented by the National Cable Television Association and the Community Antenna Television Association, opposed broadcasters on the cable regulatory issues before the FCC, the courts, and Congress. A powerful adversary of broadcasters on frequency allocation issues is the land mobile industry (whose interests are represented by the manufacturers of two-way radios and various trade associations). Some have predicted that the 1980s will be, for communications corporations, as litigious as were the 1960s and 1970s when, as will be described below, citizen groups often posed legal obstacles to broadcasters. With the crumbling of boundaries that have separated industry elements for years, increased litigation between communications firms over entry to markets may replace battles with citizen groups and keep communications lawyers well employed.

Third, the broadcast industry no longer enjoys the same position within the political system that it did in the early decades of broadcast regulation.[59] Then the regulatory process was dominated by (and largely restricted to) three major participants—Congress, the FCC, and the industry itself. The lines of influence and power were clear, and the industry knew how to work for what it wanted. But this balance of forces, which prevailed for so long, has now been altered by the increased involvement of three other participants in broadcast regulatory policy making: the public, in the form of citizen groups; the White House, by means of special advisory bodies, appointment powers, budgetary control, and the active communication-oriented divisions of cabinet-level agencies; and the courts, in the form of judicial opinions prescribing and precluding FCC policy initiatives. Together, the development of these three active participants in broadcast regulation has modified the Commission's role from one of making peace with Congress and a dominant industry to one of attempting to placate several often antagonistic interests.

Citizen Groups

Commissioner Nicholas Johnson has denied that the FCC responds only to pressure from the broadcast industry: "It responds to pressure from anybody," he declared.[60] Until 1966, however, only those with a demonstrable economic stake in the outcome of a case were permitted to intervene in FCC radio and television licensing proceedings. In a landmark decision adopted in March 1966 the U.S. Court of Appeals for the District of Columbia Circuit forced the FCC to allow the Office of Communication of the United Church of Christ to challenge the license renewal of WLBT-TV, Jackson, Mississippi, on the ground that the station discriminated against its black viewers, who constituted 45 percent of the city of Jackson. The court held that responsible community organizations such as "civic associatons, professional societies, unions, churches, and educational institutions or associations" have the right to contest license renewal applications. In a unanimous opinion written by Judge Warren Burger (now the Chief Justice of the United States), the court of appeals ruled that granting legal standing to those with such an obvious and acute concern with licensing proceedings as the listening audience is essential in order "that the holders of broadcasting licenses be responsive to the needs of the audience without which the broadcaster could not now exist."[61]

The challenge by the Office of Communication appeared to be lost when the FCC concluded its hearings with limited citizen group participation by granting the license renewal to the owners of WLBT. But the court of appeals again encouraged citizen participation in 1969 by overruling the Commission's decision and ordering that the FCC consider new applications for the WLBT license.[62] Because of the court's action the FCC assigned an interim license for the station to a new licensee, pending the outcome of further hearings. The "interim operator" continued to run the station for approximately ten years. It was not until late 1979 that the Commission finally selected a new licensee.

The long-term significance of the WLBT case was well summarized by *Broadcasting* magazine:

The case did more than establish the right of the public to participate in a station's license-renewal hearing. It did even more than encourage minority groups around the country to assert themselves in broadcast matters at a time when unrest was growing and blacks were becoming more activist. It provided practical lessons in how pressure could be brought, in how the broadcast establishment could be challenged.[63]

For a time, roughly 1969 through the mid-1970s, citizen groups emphasized the WLBT strategy—the filing of what are called "petitions to deny"—as the heavy artillery in disputes with broadcasters. As a legal matter the strategy was rarely successful: petitions to deny were rather routinely denied, albeit after much delay, and challenged licenses were renewed. Occasionally, however, the FCC would accompany its denial of a petition with the articulation of a new obligation for broadcasters. For example, the Commission might recognize more overtly than before a broadcaster's obligation to serve a population subgroup (e.g.,

Asian-Pacifics) and at the same time conclude that the challenged broadcaster had met this obligation. Such an FCC statement was often taken to heart by other broadcasters. As a practical matter as well, citizen groups soon discovered that broadcasters, despite the high likelihood they would eventually prevail, were willing to negotiate differences with unhappy listeners and viewers and thereby avoid, they hoped, lengthy, expensive, and at least somewhat uncertain legal proceedings.

In 1969, citizen groups began to enter into agreements with broadcast stations concerning programming and employment practices. A number of black groups in Texarkana, Texas, aided by the United Church of Christ, negotiated an agreement with KTAL-TV for withdrawal of a petition to deny in exchange for a thirteen-point statement of policy by the station covering employment of blacks, minority programming, news coverage, and programs dealing with controversial issues. The FCC endorsed the KTAL-TV negotiations and agreement as a preferred means by which a station could fulfill its obligation to provide service meeting community needs and interests. Other broadcasters subsequently entered into similar agreements, and by September 1971, *Broadcasting* magazine commented, "It is hard to find a community of any size without its organizations of blacks, Chicanos, Latinos, liberated women, activist mothers or other concerned types negotiating for stronger representation in broadcasting."[64]

Broadcasters continued to enter into citizen group agreements throughout the early 1970s. In return for withdrawal of a challenge, broadcasters typically agreed to make changes in station programming and employment practices. An important test case involved an agreement between Los Angeles television station KTTV and a citizen group. KTTV agreed not to televise forty-two cartoons judged to be "unsuitable for young children," to precede eighty-one other programs with a warning to parents that program content might be harmful to children, and to televise a series of special programs designed to encourage local performers. The FCC refused to give force to the agreement on the ground that it infringed on the licensee's responsibility to decide how to serve the public interest.[65] The Commission's concern that licensees had been making promises to citizen groups that undercut the broadcasters' responsibility led to its adoption in 1975 of standards for determining the validity of broadcaster–citizen group agreements.[66] The standards generally allow broadcasters to enter into agreements with citizen groups if the former maintain responsibility at all times for determining how best to serve the public interest.

In the late 1970s and early 1980s, the numbers of petitions to deny declined.[67] There were several reasons for this. First, many of the leaders of the citizen movement were taken into the FCC, FTC, and related agency staffs under the Carter administration, creating a gap in leadership and experience.[68] Second, the continued denial of petitions discouraged some citizen activists. Third, broadcasters became more skilled at negotiation and at other methods of heading off public complaint. Fourth, and finally, by the early 1980s, private sector financial support for the citizen movement was declining and government funding had not been obtained, the basic citizen group philosophy of enlisting the government to cure social ills enjoyed less favor, and, without disappearing, their abilities to mobilize influence declined.[69]

In their heyday, the number and variety of citizen groups were surprising, given their lack of financial and political support. The Office of Communication, United Church of Christ (UCC) and the National Citizens Committee for Broadcasting (NCCB)—headed by former FCC Commissioner Nicholas Johnson—functioned as facilitators for the activities of more locally oriented groups and maintained a citizen group "watch" on national matters pending before the FCC and Congress. The UCC conducted regional workshops and published pamphlets to instruct others in their legal rights in FCC proceedings. The NCCB published *access* magazine as a kind of trade journal for the citizen movement.

In 1977 the NCCB distributed the Citizen Media Directory as a guide to about sixty "media reform groups," a measure of the size of the movement at that time. The groups can be loosely divided into three types: national groups without local chapters, national groups with local chapters, and purely local groups. In addition to the NCCB and UCC, other prominent national groups have included Accuracy in Media (AIM), a conservative watchdog of national print and electronic news media; Media Access Project (MAP), a public interest law firm providing legal counsel for citizen groups; and the National Black Media Coalition (NBMC) and National Latino Media Coalition (NLMC), each representing the interests of their ethnic constituents.

Action for Children's Television (ACT) and, to a lesser extent, the National Parent-Teachers Association (PTA) and the National Organization for Women (NOW) typify national groups that, in part, work through local citizen group chapters. The PTA and NOW typify a few groups, including some labor unions, that formed for other purposes but in the 1970s or 1980s developed special interests in broadcasting.

As the foregoing brief lists indicate, despite the description of these groups by some commentators as guardians of the overall public interest, many citizen groups tend to espouse the cause of a single special interest (e.g., blacks, Chicanos, or children). However, every interest group in this area (including broadcasters) tends to equate the public interst with its self-interest. As the lists suggest, the interests of the groups are not homogeneous, and conflicts among them have occurred. When General Electric proposed to merge its broadcasting interests with those of Cox, the NCCB opposed the merger because, in its view, it would result in an unhealthy concentration of media control. The NBMC, on the other hand, supported the proposal because General Electric and Cox had agreed that some stations would be spun off to black owners.

Citizen groups have not limited their strategies to license challenges through petitions to deny alone. They have tried to force the FCC to enforce specific rules or policies in instances where the citizen groups believed rule or policy violations existed. Under the FCC's Fairness Doctrine, for example, broadcasters are required to spend a reasonable amount of time discussing controversial issues of public importance and, when they do so, provide a reasonable opportunity for opposing views to be heard. Public interest law firms, such as the Citizens Communications Center, MAP, and the Stern Community Law Firm, began in the late 1960s to bring "test" cases before the Commission and the courts. The UCC, together with several other religious groups and the NCCB, filed friend of the court briefs with the court of appeals and the U.S. Supreme Court in the landmark *Red Lion* case, in which the Supreme Court upheld the Fairness Doctrine, stating, "It is the right of the viewers and listeners, not the right of broadcasters, which is paramount."[70]

A few citizen-filed Fairness Doctrine complaints have succeeded. A university law professor, John F. Banzhaf III, successfully used the doctrine in 1968 to obtain free time for the American Cancer Society's anticigarette spot announcements in response to then lawful cigarette ads on TV.[71] In most instances, however, Fairness Doctrine complaints fail, and the courts usually hesitate to overturn the FCC's decisions in such cases. Citizen leaders seem to believe, however, that even an unsuccessful complaint can sensitize broadcasters to their concerns.

Citizen groups have had some successes in lower federal courts but have tended to lose cases on appeal to the U.S. Supreme Court. In 1971, for example, a group called the Business Executives' Move for Vietnam Peace persuaded the U.S. Court of Appeals for the District of Columbia Circuit to rule that members of the public have a First Amendment right to hear diverse viewpoints and that, accordingly, a broadcaster who accepts paid product ads cannot exclude those who want to buy time to present opinions on controversial issues.[72] Major victory turned to major defeat in 1973, however, when the Supreme Court reversed the court of appeals, saying that broadcaster compliance with the Fairness Doctrine was enough; broadcasters could choose how to present opposing views rather than being forced to accept paid opinion advertising.[73] Since then, citizen groups have won before the U.S. Court of

Appeals for the District of Columbia only to lose before the U.S. Supreme Court in other cases—for example, FCC's decision not to break up most co-owned newspaper–broadcast station combinations in the same community[74] and not to regulate radio broadcasters' choice of program formats (a case treated in more depth in chapter five).[75]

Primarily because of the indirect impact and complex nature of most broadcast issues, the general public has been apathetic and uninformed about them. Until the late 1960s the FCC had done little to promote greater participation by the public in its proceedings, both licensing cases and rule-making proceedings, or to encourage a better understanding of the role citizens might play in broadcast regulation. In the late 1960s, however, Commissioner Johnson began to use his considerable persuasive powers toward that end. Through various media Johnson took directly to the public the issues on which he had been defeated by his colleagues on the Commission. At the same time he acted as a gadfly in prompting other Commissioners to take up the cause of greater public participation in broadcast regulation. According to Les Brown, Johnson

campaigned, through speeches, magazine articles, and a book, *How to Talk Back to Your Television Set,* to alert the citizenry to their rights to challenge a broadcast licensee at license renewal time—as it were, to "vote" against or for his continuance as a station operator—which was, within the trade, the most unorthodox and unpopular thing an FCC Commissioner had ever done.[76]

Johnson's efforts to involve the public to a greater degree were somewhat successful. After meeting with a group of Boston housewives from ACT, for example, Chairman Dean Burch persuaded his colleagues to initiate a rule-making proceeding on ACT's proposals to require television stations to carry fourteen hours of children's programming each week and to prohibit the broadcasting of commercials on such programs. More than 100,000 letters were filed in this proceeding by concerned members of the public. The FCC refused to adopt these specific proposals but issued policies and guidelines, rather than rules, on children's programming and commercials.[77] This proceeding reflects another citizen group tactic. Like ACT, other groups have filed petitions for rule making with the FCC asking it to change old rules or adopt new ones. Citizen groups have been active participants in the proceedings by which the FCC conducts studies or formulates new rules by filing comments on the FCC's Notices of Inquiry or Notices of Proposed Rule Making.

The Commission, reacting to pressure from Congress and the public, has taken a number of steps to encourage greater citizen participation.[78] It has published an informational booklet on how to file complaints and intervene in renewal and transfer of license proceedings that occur when broadcast stations are sold. In 1976 the FCC created a Consumer Assistance Office to provide informational services to the public. Until budget cutbacks in 1981, the office distributed a weekly publication, *Actions Alert,* which summarized pending rule makings and announced new Commission inquiries. Under former Chairman Richard Wiley the FCC held a series of mass public meetings at scattered sites across the nation, which, if nothing else, gave the regulators a feeling for what was on the minds of some members of the public. Still, the meetings often left the public convinced that the FCC was a weak agency because it would not respond to their often expressed desire for strong programming regulations.[79]

Citizen groups, in response to encouragement to participate, have been taking a sometimes active role in congressional hearings affecting the FCC. In the early 1970s they influenced the selection of Commissioners, as shown in the appointment of the first black (Benjamin Hooks) to the FCC. Senate Communications Subcommittee Chairman John Pastore (D-Rhode Island) insisted, at the urging of citizen groups, that President Nixon nominate a black for a vacant FCC seat.[80] In 1976 representatives of citizen groups, for the first time, testified at the House Appropriations Subcommittee's hearings on the FCC budget and urged the funding of various consumer group activities.[81] Representatives of citizen groups also played a prominent role in the many congressional activities associated with the efforts to rewrite the Communications Act of 1934 (see chapter nine).

Despite its activism and occasional successes in the 1970s, the liberally oriented citizen movement, by the 1980s, had fallen on hard times. In early 1981 the Citizens Communications Center—one of the "oldline" public interest law firms—virtually disappeared into the clinical law program at Georgetown University Law Center.[82] After some severe financial setbacks, Nicholas Johnson's NCCB was absorbed into the Ralph Nader conglomerate.[83] The broadcast industry has successfully beaten back efforts, both at the FCC and within Congress, to provide some public funding for citizen group activities, and in the 1980s foundations—notably the Ford Foundation—that had supported the movement through the 1970s withdrew much of their support.

Although the liberal citizen movement now seems to be out of vogue, there is an emerging conservative and/or religious citizen movement of considerable wealth and vitality. AIM has been reported to have an annual budget of more than $1 million.[84] Another conservative group, apparently well funded, has resurrected an earlier citizen group tactic and may have discovered that nongovernmental means of influencing broadcaster behavior can be just as important as governmental means, and more consistent with conservative ideology as well. In 1976 the NCCB commissioned studies of prime-time entertainment programming violence and ranked sponsors by the amount of violent content they underwrote. The intent was to encourage consumers to bring pressure to bear on sponsors of violent programs to withdraw sponsorship or, if possible, change program content.[85] In 1981 Reverend Donald Wildmon, head of the National Federation for Decency, announced the formation of a Coalition for Better TV (CBTV) and claimed the support of more than 200 other interest groups, including Reverend Jerry Falwell's Moral Majority. Reflecting a generally conservative outlook toward sex and morality on television, the group announced that it would monitor network TV programs for a three-month period—for "sex scenes, gratuitous violence intended to injure, and abundant profanity"—and, at the end of that period, reveal the results of the monitoring and the sponsors of the most disapproved shows. The coalition initially indicated it would urge a one-year boycott of sponsors of such shows. Like the earlier NCCB strategy, the idea was to influence broadcaster performance through economic rather than government means. Shortly before it would have started the boycott, however, and after one major national advertiser publicly announced policies that seemed to mirror the goals of the coalition, it announced that its campaign was a sufficient success so that it would not reveal the results of its monitoring.[86]

The future of citizen groups and of the citizen movement is murky. Regulatory tools they have used for years may become unavailable in a climate of deregulation. The conservatives' rediscovery of economic pressure may portend one strategy for the future. There is also a chance that citizen group activity may be directed more at local government than at the FCC, Congress, or other Washington-based institutions. Developments in cable television account in part for the shift. Cable systems are built under franchise agreements struck between cable operators and state and local governments. The agreements are no longer deeply subject to federal control, but many citizen groups have emerged to argue for specific provisions (e.g., a community access channel) either in the franchise agreement or in a local cable television ordinance or state law. Some communities have created permanent bodies, including members of the public, to monitor the performance of their cable television systems.

The discussion of cable television is linked to a general sense that the old-line citizen groups may, if they are not careful, miss out on the chance to influence new communications developments if they concentrate too heavily on avoiding "losses" in their oldest area of interest—broadcasting. Emerging technologies may be the ones most subject to citizen group influence exactly because they are new—not yet burdened with old traditions or established interests. As former Congressman Lionel Van Deerlin noted in *access:*

If [the media reform movement] is to remain not only alive but effective, it must expand its vision. This means, quite simply, that the movement must acquire a working knowledge of new telecommunications technology and a broader political base . . . While the media reform movement concentrates its efforts on blocking radio deregulation and imposing new rules on children's television, it is missing an excellent opportunity to shape the new telecommunications industry instead of merely reforming the old; to create policy instead of merely responding to it.[87]

If the citizen movement follows Van Deerlin's advice and attempts to shape communications policies for new technologies, it seems likely —at least on occasion—to meet opposition to its intervention. When that happens, the movement may find itself back in the company of the institution that to a large degree created it in the first place—the courts —in an effort to sort out the role of citizen groups in the policy environment of the 1980s.

The Courts

Even though only a very small proportion of the FCC's actions are reviewed by the courts, the significance of judicial review in the Commission's policy-making and adjudicatory processes cannot be measured by statistical analysis alone. Judicial review, no matter how seldom invoked, hangs as a threatening possibility over each administrative or legislative decision. Although the courts ordinarily allow other arms of government (such as the FCC and Congress) to make policy, the judiciary possesses a crucial veto power. Consequently, the FCC must always keep one eye on the courts to make sure that the policies it adopts can successfully run the judicial gauntlet. The continual threat of judicial review thus tends to have an impact on the policies of the FCC even when these policies are not formally adjudicated. As former FCC Chairman Richard Wiley has noted:

The almost iron-clad guarantee that every major or controversial FCC action will have to pass judicial muster has resulted . . . in more careful and thorough Commission consideration of proposed decisions. . . . [O]ur track record . . . reflects our determination to engage in better legal analysis, increased sensitivity to procedural rights of parties and, finally, greater responsiveness to our ultimate mandate to serve the public interest.[88]

Under Section 402(b) of the Communications Act, appeals from FCC decisions in broadcast licensing matters must be filed with the U.S. Court of Appeals for the District of Columbia Circuit. Appeals involving compliance with FCC rules and orders must be filed with the federal district courts under Section 402(a) of the Communications Act, whereas appeals of FCC rule changes may be filed in any of the eleven

circuit courts of appeals. The Communications Act also provides that
the decisions of the court of appeals shall be final, subject only to review
by the U.S. Supreme Court upon issuance of a discretionary writ of
certiorari. Congress established the writ of *certiorari* in 1925 to enable
the Supreme Court to cut down the volume of its work by declining to
review some cases. As a result most cases are now finally decided by the
courts of appeals, and most of these by the U.S. Court of Appeals for the
District of Columbia Circuit.[89] It is perhaps paradoxical that that court,
certainly the most experienced in broadcast cases, has tended recently
to overturn FCC decisions (e.g., the case of radio format change to be
discussed in chapter five), while the much less schooled—in broadcast
issues—U.S. Supreme Court has the final word and has generally supported the Commission.

The Court of Appeals for the District of Columbia is comprised of
eleven judges, plus senior circuit judges, appointed for life by the president with the advice and consent of the Senate. With few exceptions
the decisions of the courts of appeals are made by panels of three
judges. Since the late 1960s, as we have seen, the Court of Appeals for
the District of Columbia Circuit has played an increasingly important
role as a participant in the shaping of broadcast regulatory policy. The
appellate court has decided a large number of cases involving broadcast
regulatory issues only because citizen groups began raising questions
that had never been subjected to the crucible of judicial review. Since
the Anglo-American judicial system limits judicial review to properly
presented cases and controversies involving real legal disputes, the
courts are basically passive: they cannot reach out to embrace problems
of interest to them but must wait until the problems are brought to
them by other parties. Issues are now being raised before the courts
which previously went unnoticed by the FCC and other parties. No
one, for example, thought to file a Fairness Doctrine complaint against
a nationally broadcast speech by President Eisenhower, whereas Fairness Doctrine complaints were repeatedly filed with the Commission
and the courts when President Nixon delivered major broadcast
speeches.

There are two main ways courts evaluate challenges to FCC decisions: statutory review and constitutional review. Most often, the constitutional challenge to an FCC decision consists of the charge that the
Commission has somehow violated the First Amendment's prohibition
on abridgment of freedom of speech or press. Such an argument, indeed, can be found in most court cases involving challenges to FCC
actions. Those allegations have been remarkably unsuccessful over the
years at the U.S. Supreme Court, partly because the tradition at the
court is to avoid constitutional questions altogether if a decision can be
reached on other grounds. When the court has addressed questions of

constitutionality, it has never ruled that the FCC has violated the First Amendment to the Constitution.[90]

Statutory construction involves the comparisons of, for example, a newly adopted FCC rule or regulation with the standards of a statute like the Communications Act. The objective is to determine whether what has been done is or is not in accord with governing laws. In this area the vague public interest standard embodied in the Communications Act by Congress has offered the courts the opportunity for a significant role in overseeing the FCC. As the Supreme Court observed:

Congress has charged the courts with the responsibility of saying whether the Commission has fairly exercised its discretion within the vaguish, penumbral bounds expressed by the standard of "public interest." It is our responsibility to say whether the Commission has been guided by proper considerations in bringing the deposit of its experience, the disciplined feel of the expert, to bear . . . in the public interest.[91]

The most controversial question here is whether or not the courts actually make communications policy. One school of thought on this issue is reflected by the late Judge Harold Leventhal of the U.S. Court of Appeals for the District of Columbia Circuit, who noted that courts are normally more concerned with how a decision was reached than with the substance of the decision itself:

Its supervisory function calls on the court to intervene not merely in case of procedural inadequacies, or bypassing of the mandate in the legislative charter, but more broadly if the court becomes aware, especially from a combination of danger signals, that the agency has not taken a "hard look" at the salient problems, and has not genuinely engaged in reasoned decision-making. If the agency has not shirked this fundamental task, however, the court exercises restraint even though the court would on its own account have made different findings or adopted different standards.[92]

Things may not be as clear-cut, however, as Leventhal suggests, for it is possible that the courts cannot, in the communications area, avoid making policy. The reason is that the standard of public interest, convenience, and necessity is so imprecise that almost any interpretation of it—by the FCC or by a court—makes policy. As former FCC Commissioner Glen Robinson notes:

The delegation of legislative power [through the Communications Act] ultimately transfers power not only to agencies but also to courts that supervise the exercise of agency power. This may seem contradictory. In theory, as statutory terms of agency power and discretion broaden, the justification for judicial interference, at least on substantive or jurisdictional grounds, becomes more limited. However, when such terms (or their judicial construction) become so broad as to lose all practical significance, an agency and its supervisory courts enjoy ample room to share the power that the legislature has relinquished.[93]

In other words, in Robinson's view it is unavoidable that courts will make and shape policy even though it is not necessarily desirable that they do so.

A third school of thought on the issue, reflected in the views of David Bazelon, former chief judge of the U.S. Court of Appeals for the District of Columbia Circuit, is that it is proper for courts to adopt activist positions toward making communications policy: "We stand on the threshold of a new era in the history of the long and fruitful collaboration of administrative agencies and reviewing courts."[94] It is, he said, no longer enough for the courts to uphold agency actions, "with a nod in the direction of the substantial evidence test and a bow to the mysteries of administrative expertise." Bazelon believes a more positive or activist judicial role is demanded by the changing character of administrative litigation: "[Since] courts are increasingly asked to review administrative litigation that touches on fundamental personal interests in life, health and liberty [and to] protect these interests from administrative arbitrariness, it is necessary to insist on strict judicial scrutiny of administrative action."[95]

A textbook example of activist judicial review of Commission policy making is the March 1977 decision of the Court of Appeals for the District of Columbia Circuit setting aside the Commission's pay-cable programming restrictions.[96] The court conducted its own extensive review of the evidence in the record, going so far as to analyze—and criticize—the methodology of mathematical models contained in broadcaster comments as well as the meaning of the results. The court in this case also lived up to its activist role by expanding the scope of prior judicial prohibitions against so-called *ex parte,* or off-the-record, contacts between FCC decision-making personnel and parties interested in the outcome of informal rule-making proceedings.

The U.S. Supreme Court, however, may have no interest in the "partnership" in shaping policy conceived by Judge Bazelon and his colleagues. In recent years that court has repeatedly overturned decisions of the U.S. Court of Appeals where, in the Supreme Court's eyes, the court of appeals has substituted its policy or judgment for that of the "expert" administrative agency—the FCC. In the format change controversy we describe in chapter five, for example, the court of appeals overturned an FCC decision not to supervise broadcasters' choices of formats under certain conditions despite earlier court of appeals' decisions ordering them to do so. Judge Leventhal's concurring opinion accused the FCC of violating the "court-agency partnership," which "depends on mutuality of respect and understanding."[97] The majority of the *en banc* court rejected arguments by the FCC that the judiciary had substituted its policy on the matter for the FCC's policy rather than just subjecting the FCC's procedures and standards to a straightforward comparison with the Communications Act.[98]

The U.S. Supreme Court, however, overturned the court of appeals. The Supreme Court disagreed with the appellate court's approach to review of FCC decisions:

> Our opinions have repeatedly emphasized that the Commission's judgment regarding how the public interest is best served is entitled to substantial judicial deference. . . . The Commission's implementation of the public interest standard, when based on a rational weighing of competing policies, is not to be set aside by the Court of Appeals, for "the weighing of policies under the 'public interest' standard is a task that Congress has delegated to the Commission in the first instance."[99]

Since the courts play an important role in the FCC policy-making process, it follows that other participants in the process will attempt to influence court action. Obviously, the various interest groups cannot approach the courts through the same methods that would be appropriate in approaching Congress: there are no campaign funds, no ballot boxes, and no lavish lunches with which to influence federal judges.[100] Generally, there are only two methods by which pressure may be exerted on the courts. The first is through the appointment of judges. Here, influence must proceed indirectly through the president and the Senate. The other and more direct means of influencing the courts is through the regular procedure of litigation. Filing a court appeal is largely a defensive maneuver, since by the time a group is forced to resort to judicial review the policy has already been made by the FCC. But whereas the FCC and the Congress are most often affected by politically powerful and wealthy groups, the courts may be influenced almost as easily by a single individual or very small groups as by a large and powerful interest. Even in cases where the outside groups are not parties to the case, a court may allow them to participate in the role of *amici curiae* ("friends of the court"). In litigation the decisions of the court are frequently influenced by factors such as the strategic timing of a bona fide test case, the submission of a well-written brief, the rendition of persuasive oral argument, or the publication of a thoughtful law review article or book on the specific issue.

The White House

Professor William Cary, a former chairman of the Securities and Exchange Commission, has pointed out what should be apparent to any serious observer but is often overlooked or ignored: that the president is a person but the White House is a bureaucracy—a collection of people.[101] The FCC, like most government departments and agencies, does not deal with the president (except on matters of the greatest national or international importance) but with the White House staff.[102] Under most recent administrations the FCC and other regulatory agencies have sent detailed monthly summaries of their principal activities and pending projects to a key presidential aide. Under the Reagan administration, FCC chairman Mark Fowler has met openly with high White House officials. Different presidents, moreover, have varied in their level of interest in the FCC. Franklin D. Roosevelt was very interested in FCC policy decisions (especially the question of ownership of radio stations by newspapers), but his successor, Harry Truman, showed little or no concern about Commission policies. Presidents Kennedy, Nixon, and Carter were actively interested in broadcast matters, whereas President Ford played a relatively passive role on issues of direct concern to broadcasters, and President Johnson, because of family broadcast holdings, tended to exert influence mostly behind the scenes.

A less tangible form of control is the mood set by the president and the White House for the regulatory agency and for regulation in general. Especially at the beginning of an administration, the White House may be able to create a hospitable political climate for the agency. President Kennedy's "New Frontier" theme, for example, created a favorable mood for a more active regulatory role by Newton Minow. Similarly, President Gerald Ford, exercising a leadership role on general regulatory reform complementary to Chairman Wiley's "deregulation" program of eliminating archaic and duplicative FCC regulations, conducted White House "summit conferences" and supported legislation urging regulatory agencies to eliminate rules and paperwork requirements unnecessarily burdensome to businesses. President Reagan provided an appropriate philosophical background for Chairman Fowler's campaign for "unregulation."

THE POWER OF APPOINTMENT

The White House influences communications regulation in many ways. One of its most important formal controls is the power of the president to choose administrative agency commissioners as resignations occur or terms expire and, in most instances, to appoint a chairman. Presidents, of course, also nominate judges—whose decisions are crucial to the development of regulatory policy—and members of the board of such quasi-public corporations as the Corporation for Public Broadcasting and the Communications Satellite Corporation (COMSAT). The appointment power enables the president to set the tone for administrative agencies. Although the Communications Act specifies that only four Commissioners of the FCC may have the same party affiliation, the president has wide latitude in appointing those who he thinks will reflect his own political and administrative ideas. As noted earlier virtually every president has tried to select persons as Commissioners who agree with the administration's philosophy and policy objectives, regardless of party identification. Because few Commissioners serve out their full terms, even a new president may quickly gain control of the FCC. Within six months of taking office, for example, President Reagan had the opportunity to make four FCC appointments.[103]

In making appointments to the FCC, the president is subject to many different pressures from Congress, the industry, the press, and the public. According to the Hoover Report, the Senate's power of confirming Commission appointments has often caused the president to consider not so much his appointees' abilities or qualifications for the job as the probability of their acceptance by the Senate.[104] Furthermore, since appointments to the FCC are closely watched by the regulated industries, the president rarely appoints a Commissioner if the regulated industries are politically aligned in opposition. As Roger Noll points out, "While the appointment process does not necessarily produce Commissioners who are consciously controlled by the industry they regulate, it nearly always succeeds in excluding persons who are regarded as opposed to the interests of the regulated."[105] Trade publications such as *Broadcasting, Television Digest,* and *Variety* play an important role in influencing industry opinion on various candidates and in letting broadcasters know who is opposed to their interests. A study of the manner in which the FCC and FTC Commissioners are appointed noted that *Broadcasting* magazine probably monitors FCC vacancies with greater care than the White House: "There are very few trade journals which are more politically potent than *Broadcasting* magazine: the number of FCC aspirants who have had their ambitions either assisted or quashed as a result of this magazine's coverage defies estimation."[106] In general, those who have studied the White House appointments process have concluded that it has not necessarily produced the best possible appointees, not been approached with sufficient care by White House staff members, and is perhaps, in the words of one presidential adviser, "not quite a random walk."[107] They have not been very hopeful, moreover, about improvement in or reform of the process nor, for that matter, about doing anything to clear up consistent complaints of an overly active revolving door between the regulatory agencies and the regulated industries in terms of pre- or postagency employment of Commissioners and high-level staff members of agencies.

The Communications Act authorizes the president to designate one of the seven Commissioners as Chairman of the FCC. Since the Chairman holds that position subject to the will of the president, not surprisingly the conduct of individuals serving as Chairman is influenced by the expectations and viewpoints which radiate from the White House. Moreover, with respect to both the Chairman and other Commissioners, a sense of loyalty and considerations of reappointment (or appointment to other government posts) may have a subtle influence on the thinking and behavior of those appointed.[108]

The White House also sometimes exercises some informal control over major personnel selections at the FCC, including such positions as general counsel, managing director, and chief of the Broadcast Bureau. Prior to making high-level staff appointments, the Chairmen of the FCC often have checked with the White House to secure a "political clearance."

THE OFFICE OF MANAGEMENT AND BUDGET.

Another powerful form of White House pressure is exerted through the Office of Management and Budget (OMB—formerly the Bureau of the Budget). This office, one of the president's staff agencies, reviews and revises all department and agency budget requests before they are presented to Congress. In addition, agencies such as the FCC must submit their legislative recommendations to OMB before asking for congressional consideration; further action depends on word from the director of OMB that a proposal is consistent with the president's program. OMB also has the power to authorize agencies such as the FCC to add "supergrade" (high-salaried) staff positions. In this connection Professor Cary points out that a regulatory agency is paralyzed unless it is allowed to recruit able staff and fill vacancies at the top.[109] Beginning with the Ford administration presidents have shown increasing interest in general regulatory reform and have given OMB major responsibilities in the area. OMB's Office of Information and Regulatory Affairs has become the center for White House analysis of regulatory policy. In addition, the Paperwork Reduction Act returned to OMB authority to approve or, most importantly, disapprove forms used by regulatory agencies—a power used by the Reagan administration to attempt to reduce the costs and pervasiveness of regulation.

LINE AGENCIES

In addition to influence on broadcast regulation through the FCC and other regulatory agencies and through the White House staff, presidents shape policy through their control of the line agencies headed by members of the president's cabinet. The most significant cabinet departments for communications policy are the Department of Commerce, the Department of Justice, the Department of Defense, and the Department of State.

The influence of the Department of Commerce has been evolving over several administrations and centers on how active the President wishes to be on general communications policy questions and where within all the agencies subject to White House control the president wishes to develop policy positions. The White House also has created leverage in the regulatory process by forming advisory commissions. During his administration President Johnson created a Task Force on Communications Policy. The report of this task force, the result of the work of fifteen departments and agencies of the federal government and a large number of consultants, had the effect of delaying for several years FCC action on the controversial subject of communications satellites. In 1971 President Nixon created a cabinet-level Committee on Cable Television. The possibility of support for cable television served as a weapon for the Nixon administration in its feud against the networks.

The Nixon administration, however, began the transition from the use of ad hoc advisory groups toward more permanent policy-related offices within the executive branch designed to coordinate the operations of the federal government's communications systems and formulate and implement White House telecommunications policy positions. Under President Nixon these functions were kept under the tight supervision of the Executive Office of the President by creation of the Office of Telecommunications Policy (OTP). President Carter allowed slightly less direct supervision through establishment of the National Telecommunications and Information Administration (NTIA) within the Department of Commerce, although he retained direct control of some telecommunications policy functions through the domestic policy staff at the White House.

The OTP was created when President Nixon, in February 1970, submitted to Congress his Reorganization Plan No. 1.[110] The office was to serve as the president's principal adviser on domestic and international telecommunications policy. Initially there was some concern that the new office might dominate the FCC. A legal assistant to Commissioner H. Rex Lee then viewed the OTP as a threatening and improper political encroachment on the independence of the Commission. The FCC, he said, "is easily overwhelmed by the power, prestige and influence of the President."[111] However, then FCC Chairman Dean Burch (a Nixon appointee) assured the House Reorganization Subcommittee that the Commission favored "a strong, centralized entity to deal with telecommunications issues within the executive" and that he had "absolutely no fear of either an actual or possible undue influence by the White House on the Commission by virtue of this office."[112] When neither the Senate nor the House voted to disapprove the Reorganization Plan within sixty days after its submission to Congress, the Office of Telecommunications Policy came into existence on April 20, 1970.

The OTP, especially in its first three years, made a significant impact on broadcast regulatory policy. In the fall of 1971 OTP played a broker's role in bringing together representatives of the broadcasting, cable, and copyright industries and acted as a mediator in getting the parties to accept a compromise agreement on cable rules. It was successful in forging a compromise because of the vacuum created by prior FCC indecisiveness in developing an overall cable policy and the OTP's willingness to exert pressure in private sessions on groups representing broadcasters, cable system owners, and copyright holders. In response to a proposal by the OTP, the FCC initiated an inquiry in 1971 looking toward the deregulation of radio, thus anticipating the later lessening of regulatory controls on radio programming and commercial practices. The OTP also took stands and thereby stimulated debate on a wide number of substantive issues, including standards on license renewals, the substitution of a limited right of paid access in place of the Fairness Doctrine, the role of the Corporation for Public Broadcasting in financing network programming of the Public Broadcasting Service, and spectrum allocations policy. Based on a study prepared by the OTP, the FCC made extensive changes in the Emergency Broadcast System. In the long run, the OTP's most significant contribution may have been its successful advocacy to the FCC of an "open skies" policy toward domestic communications satellites, which allowed any financially qualified party to put up a satellite. Under that policy satellite communications services flourished.

Throughout its life, but particularly as a result of two policies it articulated in 1972, the OTP was the focus of intense criticism by many who saw in the Nixon administration a shift of power from Congress and toward the presidency. In February of that year, Dr. Clay T. Whitehead, OTP's first director, told the House Subcommittee on Communications and Power that the administration opposed, at that time, any permanent financing for the Corporation for Public Broadcasting unless local public stations were given greater power to control programming. In December he suggested that television station owners be held strictly responsible at license renewal time for the content of network-originated programming, particularly news; he then linked increased affiliate pressure on the networks to reduce "ideological plugola" and "elitist gossip" with an extended five-year license term long sought by the broadcast industry. Post-Watergate research on the Nixon administration shows that Dr. Whitehead's attacks on the networks, public broadcasting, and the affiliates were elements of a deliberate assault on the centralized, national media from a White House that had viewed the media as a tormentor.[113]

In July 1977 President Carter sent Congress his plan for executive branch reorganization. In part responding to campaign promises to reduce the size of the direct White House bureaucracy, Carter proposed to abolish the Office of Telecommunications Policy, shift most of its policy advisory functions to the Commerce Department, lodge other duties with the Office of Management and Budget, and retain a small policy staff in the White House.[114] Despite some concern that Carter was "downgrading" telecommunications policy by moving it out of the White House, the Carter plan became law on October 20, 1977, after neither House nor Senate voted to oppose it.

The resulting body in the Department of Commerce, eventually called the National Telecommunications and Information Administration (NTIA), served as the main policy advice arm of the White House on domestic and international telecommunications policy. To head it, Carter selected a thoughtful, Washington communications policy maker—some called him a "guru"—former FCC general counsel Henry Geller.[115] Pursuing a policy heavily oriented toward control of telecommunications industries by structuring their marketplaces rather than by directly regulating their behavior, Geller and his staff actively involved the NTIA in both common carrier and broadcast communications issues. NTIA filed petitions for rule making with the FCC —and comments in other proceedings—aimed at increasing the number of broadcast outlets and, in line with Carter administration policy, increasing minority ownership of those and other communications services. Other areas of interest included rural telecommunications, competition in common carrier communications, and the organization and funding of public broadcasting.[116]

As planned, the NTIA became the principal advocate for the administration at congressional hearings on telecommunications issues.[117] In addition, under Geller's direction, the new organization managed to shed the criticism of overpoliticization that, in the late stages of the OTP's history, was attached to it and hindered its effectiveness and credibility. Like the OTP, however, the NTIA had little direct power to make policy; as Geller noted, "We depend solely on the cogency of our arguments" before Congress, the FCC, and the courts.[118] Although the NTIA introduced several novel notions into the telecommunications policy mill, the Carter administration left office before many of them could be implemented by the FCC or Congress.[119] The fate of many of the ideas championed by the Geller-led NTIA fell to Reagan administration appointees. In such hands their fate seemed likely to be mixed, with the Reagan administration likely to endorse moves toward deregulation begun under Carter appointees but not as likely as Geller and his associates to seek wide-ranging restructuring of the industries by means of stricter multiple ownership rules or to allocate additional stations for minority use.

Under President Carter's reorganization, the President's domestic policy staff remained responsible for providing some advice on telecommunications and information policy, especially on national security, emergency preparedness, and privacy issues. According to a Carter staff aide, the primary responsibilities of the domestic policy staff with respect to communications matters were: (1) to keep the president advised on the small number of communications issues that merited his attention; (2) to participate in the appointments process; and (3) to work with the NTIA and other federal departments and agencies to coordinate the administration's position on communications matters.[120] The Office of Management and Budget was responsible for federal telecommunications procurement and management—becoming, in the process, a major factor in the development of telecommunications technology. In addition, OMB was charged with settling interagency disputes regarding government frequency allocations, although the NTIA was given the "first shot" at government spectrum allocations and in practice few if any disputes reached OMB.[121]

We have included the Department of Justice in the White House since it is the president's legal arm. As the agency generally responsible for the enforcement of federal laws and with the specific responsibility of deciding what FCC cases should be pursued in the courts, the Justice Department exerts a strong influence on the Commission.[122] The Solicitor General's Office in the Justice Department has authority to decide which cases the federal government should ask the Supreme Court to review and what position the government should take in cases before the courts. At times the Justice Department has even challenged FCC decisions by appealing them in the courts. When the Justice Department protested the Commission's approval of a proposed ABC–International Telephone and Telegraph (ITT) merger, the case caption read: *United States* v. *Federal Communications Commission.* The Justice Department's appeal was one of the factors that prompted ABC and ITT to abandon their plans for merger. In another court of appeals proceeding the Justice Department intervened on the side of community groups, which eventually won the right of groups challenging a station's renewal application to be reimbursed for legal fees.

The Justice Department's Antitrust Division has taken an active role in FCC proceedings and was successful in breaking up common ownership of a daily newspaper, cable system, and television station in Cheyenne, Wyoming. In Beaumont, Texas, the Antitrust Division asked the FCC to deny an application to transfer the license of KFDM-TV to the publisher of the only daily newspaper in Beaumont. Faced with such opposition, the parties withdrew the application. The Antitrust Division also played a key role in FCC proceedings that resulted in a ban on cross-ownership of local television stations and cable systems and the prospective prohibition of local cross-ownership of daily newspapers and broadcast stations. In addition, the Justice Department participated in the FCC's proposed "drop in" proceeding, which could lead to more VHF channels, and helped draft the prime-time access rule (which forbids television stations in the top fifty markets to program more than three hours of network offerings during the 7:00 to 11:00 P.M. period). The Antitrust Division also sued the three commercial television networks, charging them with an unlawful monopoly over prime-time programming. The suit was eventually settled by agreements ("consent decrees") between the Justice Department and the three networks in which the networks agreed to reduce their control over the production and distribution of prime-time entertainment shows and the department agreed to drop the case.[123] In 1979 the Justice Department sued the National Association of Broadcasters, alleging that the commercial time limits specified in the NAB Television Code encouraged TV stations to reduce artificially the amount of commercial time, thereby inhibiting competition and driving up the price of TV advertising.[124] An antitrust suit filed in late 1980 against "Premiere," a pay-cable programming joint venture of Getty Oil Company and four major film studios, resulted in a preliminary injunction in early 1981 that killed the project.[125]

Other cabinet-level offices also influence telecommunications policy. The Department of Defense is a major user of spectrum space. Under the Carter administration the amount of space controlled exclusively by the government and not subject to FCC control dropped from more than 50 percent of all space to about 25 percent. Private users control about 35 percent of all space, and about 40 percent is shared between the government and private interests.[126] The Defense Department is involved actively both in managing much of the government's space and in using that part of the spectrum shared with private users. As a major user of privately owned communications services, the Defense Department follows common carrier proceedings and has even opposed the Justice Department's efforts to break up AT&T.[128]

The Department of State plays a technical role in international communications issues, including holding conferences, negotiating treaties, and even becoming involved in day-to-day communications disputes with neighboring nations, especially, in recent years, Canada and Cuba. The substantive interest of the State Department, however, is negligible. As a White House memo put it, "The FCC and NTIA develop communications policy objectives, and State runs the negotiations."[127]

The FCC, the industry, citizen groups, the courts, and the White House, as we have seen, are important participants in the system of broadcast regulation. Even this brief account of their role and sources of authority and power, however, repeatedly has mentioned the U.S. Congress—a participant of such importance that it requires lengthy analysis, to which we turn in the next chapter.

NOTES

1. Newton N. Minow, *Equal Time: The Private Broadcaster and the Public Interest* (New York: Atheneum, 1964), pp. 258–259.
2. James M. Landis, *Report on Regulatory Agencies to the President-Elect*, published as a committee print by the Subcommittee on Administrative Practice and Procedure of the Senate Committee on the Judiciary, 86th Congress, 2nd Session (1960), p. 53. Seventeen years later a major congressional study of the FCC produced a generally similar assessment:

   The Commission's principal handicaps have been (1) insufficient public representation to offset the assiduous attention paid by commercial interests, (2) failure to anticipate or keep pace with technical and commercial developments in communications, (3) a deficiency of technical expertise for analysis of complex issues resulting in failure to develop facts basic to regulation of the broadcasting and telephone industries, and (4) inertial acceptance of prevailing patterns (U.S. House of Representatives, Interstate and Foreign Commerce Committee, Subcommittee on Oversight and Investigations, *Federal Regulation and Regulatory Reform*, 94th Congress, 2nd Session [October 1976], p. 2).

   A useful summary of the major criticisms of the FCC, and of proposals to reform it, is found in Vincent Mosco, *Broadcasting in the United States: Innovative Challenge and Organizational Control* (Norwood, N.J.: Ablex, 1979), pp. 3–27, especially Table 1.1, "Proposals to Reform the FCC," pp. 2–4.
3. "At Large with Robert E. Lee," *Broadcasting*, June 29, 1981, p. 36. To avoid such subservience, Lee recommended that Commissioners serve single fifteen-year terms without possibility for reappointment.
4. Samuel P. Huntington, "The Marasmus of the I.C.C.: The Commissions, the Railroads, and the Public Interest," *Yale Law Journal*, 61 (April 1962), 470. See also The President's Advisory Council on Executive Organization, *A New Regulatory Framework: Report on Selected Independent Regulatory Agencies* (the Ash Report) (Washington, D.C.: Government Printing Office, 1971); and Marver H. Bernstein, *Regulating Business by Independent Commission* (Princeton, N.J.: Princeton University Press, 1955). For a more contemporary example of an agency's marasmus, consider the experience of the Federal Trade Commission under the chairmanship of Michael Pertschuk (1977–1981). See chapter three, "Congress: Powerful Determiner of Regulatory Policy."
5. See Anthony Downs, *Inside Bureaucracy* (Boston: Little, Brown, 1967). The work—especially chapters on "Internal Characteristics Common to All Bureaus," "Officials' Milieu, Motives and Goals," and "Bureaucratic Ideologies"—is an excellent starting point for any assessment of bureaucratic behavior. Some interesting comments on bureaucratic analysis, and

other forms of analysis of the FCC, are found in G. Gail Crotts and Law-
rence M. Mead, "The FCC as an Institution," in *Telecommunications: An
Interdisciplinary Study,* ed. Leonard Lewin, (Dedham, Mass.: Artech
House, 1979), pp. 39–120.

6. The analysis that follows is based primarily on Lee Loevinger's articles
   "The Sociology of Bureaucracy," *The Business Lawyer,* 24 (November
   1968), 7–18 and "The Administrative Agency as a Paradigm of Government—A Survey of the Administrative Process," *Indiana Law Journal,* 40
   (Spring 1965), 1.
7. Lee Loevinger, Review of William L. Cary, *Politics and the Regulatory
   Agencies,* in *Columbia Law Review,* 68 (1968), 382.
8. Glen O. Robinson, "The Federal Communications Commission: An
   Essay on Regulatory Watchdogs," *Virginia Law Review,* 64 (1978), 169,
   216.
9. Ibid., 217–224.
10. See "Lack of Direction is Handcuffing the FCC," *Television/Radio Age,*
    April 3, 1972, p. 61. See also Richard Olin Berner, *Constraints on the
    Regulatory Process: A Case Study of Regulation of Cable Television* (Cam-
    bridge, Mass.: Harvard Program on Information Technologies and Public
    Policy, 1975), pp. 75–76.
11. Quoted in "Fowler on Radio's Wavelength," *Broadcasting,* September 21,
    1981, p. 28.
12. It may occur to some that the FCC's movement, in the late 1970s and early
    1980s, toward deregulation of broadcasting and cable television and reli-
    ance on marketplace forces required an abandonment of such familiar
    assumptions and standards and may not be compatible with this analysis.
    Actually, the FCC's support of broadcast deregulation is incremental in at
    least two senses. First, the Commission had begun much earlier to rely
    increasingly on competition in what was normally thought of as monopoly
    common carrier services. Second, FCC staff members could be viewed as
    climbing aboard the deregulation bandwagon for broadcasting only after
    the path had been blazed by others for other industries, notably the
    deregulation of air transportation.
13. *Broadcasting,* January 19, 1981, pp. 37–42.
14. Ibid., p. 37. Quite a few of these initiatives, notably the move to 9 kHz AM
    channel spacing and the decision to allow AT&T to enter information
    services, were subsequently reversed or questioned by the FCC or the
    Department of Justice after the Reagan administration assumed power in
    1981.
15. Bradley C. Canon, "Voting Behavior on the FCC," *Midwest Journal of
    Political Science,* 13 (November 1969), 593–594. Canon's comments are
    from the "pre-sunshine" days when Commission meetings were not open
    but still seem to characterize even those events. For an interesting de-
    scription of an FCC meeting, see Nicholas Johnson and John Dystel, "A
    Day in the Life: The Federal Communications Commission," *Yale Law
    Journal,* 82 (1973), 1575–1634. The FCC's first open meeting is described
    in "Like a Day with the Sunshine at the FCC," *Broadcasting,* March 28,
    1977, p. 29.
16. James M. Graham and Victor H. Kramer, *Appointments to the Regulatory
    Agencies: The Federal Communications Commission and the Federal
    Trade Commission (1949–1974),* printed for the use of the Committee on
    Commerce, U.S. Senate, 94th Congress, 2nd Session (April 1976), pp. 385–

386. For a general assessment of the effect of political parties, see Stuart S. Nagel "Regulatory Commissioners and Party Politics," in *The Legal Process from a Behavioral Perspective,* ed. Stuart S. Nagel, (Homewood, Ill.: Dorsey Press, 1969), pp. 237–244.

17. Lawrence Lichty, "Members of the Federal Radio Commission and Federal Communications Commission: 1927–1961," *Journal of Broadcasting,* 6 (Winter 1961–1962), 23–24. See generally Ross Eckert, "The Life Cycle of Regulatory Commissioners," *Journal of Law and Economics,* 24 (April 1981), pp. 113–120.

18. Graham and Kramer, *Appointments to the Regulatory Agencies,* p. 422.

19. Wenmouth Williams, Jr., "Impact of Commissioner Background on FCC Decisions: 1962–1975," *Journal of Broadcasting,* 20 (Spring 1976), 239, 244.

20. Graham and Kramer, *Appointments to the Regulatory Agencies,* p. 422.

21. Williams, "Impact of Commissioner Background on FCC Decisions: 1962–1975," p. 256. Williams's claims that there was a Minow Commission is perhaps overstated. Newton Minow rarely could command a majority of his fellow commissioners and was a frequent dissenter in the Commission he chaired. Whatever regulatory philosophy Minow inspired did not really appear until E. William Henry succeeded him as Chairman.

22. Quoted in "What Makes Fowler Tick?" *Broadcasting,* June 22, 1981, p. 23.

23. Lawrence W. Lichty, "The Impact of FRC and FCC Commissioners' Backgrounds on the Regulation of Broadcasting," *Journal of Broadcasting,* 6 (Spring 1962), 97.

24. Ibid., 108. Political scientist William T. Gormley, Jr., has supplemented the Lichty and Williams analyses in an article entitled "A Test of the Revolving Door Hypothesis at the FCC," *American Journal of Political Science,* 23 (November 1979), 665–683. Gormley examined the effect of prior employment and political party on the voting behavior of FCC Commissioners and concluded that while there is some tendency for former broadcasters to be cohesive, differences among Commissioners related to party identification are even more important.

25. Canon, "Voting Behavior on the FCC," 609–611.

26. Lichty, "The Impact of FRC and FCC Commissioners' Backgrounds on the Regulation of Broadcasting," 108–109. However, Roger Noll contends: "Policies of multiheaded bodies such as regulatory commissions tend to be at the median position within the group. The middle-of-the-road individual can always lead a majority against any proposal that he opposes" (Roger G. Noll, *Reforming Regulation* [Washington, D.C.: Brookings Institution, 1971], p. 43).

27. In 1961 President Kennedy submitted Reorganization Plan No. 2, which would have allowed the Chairman of the FCC a greater degree of power to delegate Commission responsibility to individual Commissioners, Commission panels, and staff members. The House of Representatives defeated the FCC reorganization plan by a resounding vote of 323 to 77. The unpopularity of the president's proposal was a direct result of Newton Minow's "vast wasteland" speech, which was delivered five weeks before the House vote. See "Did Minow Scuttle FCC Reorganization?" *Broadcasting,* May 22, 1961, pp. 56–57. On September 17, 1981, the FCC asked Congress to amend the Communications Act to allow "integrated bureaus" to be created on an ad hoc basis such "as the Commission may determine to be necessary to perform its functions." The Commission

noted that "[t]he purpose of this amendment is to permit reorganization of the Commission staff to account for alternations in the nature and distribution of the agency's regulatory responsibilities." *FCC Legislative Proposal, Track I,* September 17, 1981 [mimeo.], pp. 15–16.

28. Kenneth A. Cox, "What It's Like Inside the FCC," *Telephony,* September 5, 1970, pp. 56–57. An excellent overview of internal power within regulatory commissions, including the FCC, is provided in David M. Welborn, *Governance of Federal Regulatory Agencies* (Knoxville: University of Tennessee Press, 1977). For a detailed assessment of this book, see Lawrence D. Longley, Review of *Governance of Federal Regulatory Agencies, The Journal of Politics,* 41 (1979), 278–280.

29. Graham and Kramer, *Appointments to the Regulatory Agencies,* p. 382. For example, Newton Minow, while serving as Chairman of the FCC, played an important role in blocking the reappointment of John Cross as an FCC Commissioner and in selecting Kenneth Cox as Cross's successor. See Graham and Kramer, pp. 185–195.

30. See Scott H. Robb, "Wiley's Impact on FCC Staff Will Still Be Felt as Power Shifts to Carter Administration," *Television/Radio Age,* March 28, 1977, p. 93.

31. Les Brown, "Broadcasting Industry Is Wary over Carter's Choice as Chairman of the F.C.C., Succeeding Wiley," *New York Times,* December 7, 1976, p. 82C.

32. During fiscal year 1975, Wiley's vote was with the majority 98.9 percent of the time. The Commissioner with the most dissents, Benjamin Hooks, voted with the majority 96.3 percent of the time. See "In Search of Dissent at the FCC: The Commission that Sails Together Fails Together," *access 16* (August 11, 1975), 7.

33. See Brown, "Broadcasting Industry Is Wary over Carter's Choice."

34. *Broadcasting,* April 11, 1977, p. 27. In an editorial entitled "Who's in Charge Here?" *Broadcasting* magazine said that "the FCC has suffered one humiliating defeat after another in the U.S. Court of Appeals for the District of Columbia Circuit" (*Broadcasting,* April 4, 1977, p. 106).

35. "How the FCC Takes Control," *Broadcasting,* February 21, 1966, p. 31; and "Heavy Hands on Government Controls," *Broadcasting,* February 21, 1966, p. 50.

36. Minow, *Equal Time,* pp. ix–x.

37. After he left the Commission, Johnson quipped: "When people used to ask me 'Do you work for the FCC' my response typically would be, 'No, I work against the FCC!' " Ronald H. Coase and Nicholas Johnson, "Should the Federal Communications Commission be Abolished?" in *Regulation, Economics and the Law,* ed. Berhard H. Siegan (Lexington, Mass.: Lexington Books, 1979), p. 47.

38. See "Minow Observes a 'Vast Wasteland,'" *Broadcasting,* May 15, 1961, pp. 58–59. Many ad agency persons said Minow used "shock treatment." See "Advertisers and Agencies Minow Fans," *Broadcasting,* May 15, 1961, p. 53.

39. "The Public's Interest," an address to the International Radio and Television Society, New York, N.Y., September 23, 1981 [mimeo.], p. 9.

40. Bernstein, *Regulating Business by Independent Commission,* p. 279. An insightful assessment of industry-agency relations is provided in Paul J. Quick, *Industry Influence in Federal Regulatory Agencies* (Princeton, N.J.: Princeton University Press, 1981).

41. Landis, *Report on Regulatory Agencies,* p. 71.
42. Robinson, "The Federal Communications Commission," 192. "Because economic security is a characteristic of many, if not most, regulatory schemes," Robinson commented, "business interests tend to prefer regulation to the unsettling vicissitudes of competition" (ibid.).
43. Ibid., 190–191.
44. Quoted in Victor G. Rosenblum, "How to Get into TV: The Federal Communications Commission and Miami Channel 10," in *The Uses of Power: 7 Cases in American Politics,* ed. Alan F. Westin (New York: Harcourt Brace Jovanovich, 1962), p. 196. There are legal restrictions on the manner in which interested parties may make known their views to the FCC. These restrictions are known as the *ex parte* rules. Doerfer, ironically, carried his industry "consultations" too far: they were part of what forced his resignation from the Commission. See Bernard Schwartz, *The Professor and the Commissions* (New York: Knopf, 1959).
45. Joseph C. Goulden, *The Superlawyers: The Small and Powerful World of the Great Washington Law Firms* (New York: Weybright and Talley, 1972), p. 6.
46. Bruce M. Owen and Ronald Braeutigam, *The Regulation Game: Strategic Use of the Administrative Process* (Cambridge, Mass.: Ballinger, 1978), p. 7.
47. U.S. House of Representatives, Subcommittee on Oversight and Investigations, Committee on Interstate and Foreign Commerce, *Federal Regulation and Regulatory Reform,* 94th Congress, 2nd Session (1976), pp. 452, 455.
48. Ibid., p. 453.
49. See 18 U.S.C., Sec. 207 (1980).
50. See "Reagan Starts Moving on FCC," *Broadcasting,* March 2, 1981, p. 31. Ferris joined the law firm of Mintz, Levin, Cohn, Ferris, Glovsky, and Popeo. For a further examination of the revolving door thesis, see Gormley, "A Test of the Revolving Door Hypothesis at the FCC."
51. For descriptions of the manner in which the network and other broadcast lobbyists function, see "Moving Muscle to Washington," *Broadcasting,* February 21, 1972, pp. 38–42; Alan Pearce, "The Economic and Political Strength of the Television Networks," in *Network Television and the Public Interest,* eds. Michael Botein and David M. Rice (Lexington, Mass.: Lexington Books, 1980), pp. 3–24; and Barbara Matusow, "When Push Comes to Shove," *Channels of Communication,* August/September 1981, pp. 33–39.
52. *Home Box Office* v. *FCC,* 567 F.2d 9, 52, n. 112 (D.C. Cir. 1979), *certiorari denied,* 434 U.S. 829 (1977).
53. Nicholas Johnson, "A New Fidelity to the Regulatory Ideal," *Georgetown Law Journal,* 59 (March 1971), 883–884. Today the "subgovernment" probably includes even major citizen groups and their present and former leaders.
54. For the NAB budget, see *Television Digest,* February 2, 1981, pp. 2–3; on the estimated 1978 value of the building see "Investment," *Broadcasting,* August 7, 1978, p. 7. A good general article on the NAB is "The New NAB," *Broadcasting,* April 10, 1978, pp. 42ff. Like many trade associations, NAB maintains a political action committee (Television and Radio Political Action Committee—TARPAC) through which contributions are made to political campaigns. Given the size of the NAB and the industry, the

number of candidates supported and the amounts distributed are very modest. See *Television Digest,* October 27, 1980, p. 4. See also Brooke Gladstone, "Making Friends on the Hill . . . For Just Pennies a Day," *Channels of Communication,* August/September 1981, p. 38. This article lists TARPAC's expenditures for 1979 and 1980 as $88,000:

> That puts broadcasting's Political Action Committee on a par with the National Forest Products PAC (roughly $92,000 in total expenditures); the Securities Industry PAC ($92,000), and the United Airlines Good Government Fund (about $79,-000). During the same period, the American Medical Association, the automobile industry, and the realtors each managed to cough up well over a million dollars apiece to help keep their friends in Congress (ibid.).

55. Murray Edelman, *The Licensing of Radio Services in the United States, 1927 to 1947: A Study in Administrative Formulation of Policy* (Urbana: University of Illinois Press, 1950), pp. 220–221.
56. See Bruce Thorp, "Washington Pressures—Radio-TV Lobby Fights Losing Battle Against Rising Federal Control," *National Journal,* August 22, 1970, p. 1807. See also Bill Keller, "Long Faced with Federal Regulation, Broadcasters Turned to Lobbying," *Congressional Quarterly Weekly Report,* August 2, 1980, pp. 2180–2181; and Dick Brown et al., "Media Lobbyists: An Unreported Story," *The Progressive,* July 1979, pp. 37–41.
57. Quoted in "Whistling Dixie," *Broadcasting,* August 15, 1977, p. 66.
58. See Graham and Kramer, *Appointments to the Regulatory Agencies,* p. 373. Graham and Kramer state that from April 1953 until March 1960 the Chairmen of the FCC were men who were fully acceptable to AT&T.
59. Congressman Lionel Van Deerlin has maintained: "Broadcasters have become so predictable they are losing their credibility—and with it, their clout. . . . As a member of Congress who has listened to a chorus of special interest hard sells each time change is proposed, I can tell you it is very, very tedious—and very unpersuasive" (quoted in "NAB 'Utterly Predictable,'" *Television Digest,* March 31, 1980, p. 5).
60. Nicholas Johnson, *How to Talk Back to Your Television Set* (New York: Bantam Books, 1970), p. 163. A 1977 report of the Senate Committee on Governmental Affairs agreed with Johnson's statement when it commented that regulatory agencies, rather than being "captured" by industry interests, simply are responding to the input they receive; the committee recognized, however, that until the recent past the regulated industries were the source of almost all input to the agencies. See U.S. Senate, Committee on Governmental Affairs, *Study on Federal Regulation, Public Participation in Agency Proceedings,* vol. 3, 95th Congress, 1st Session (July 1977), p. 2.
61. *Office of Communication of the United Church of Christ* v. *FCC,* 359 F.2d 994, 1002 (D.C. Cir. 1966).
62. *Office of Communication of the United Church of Christ* v. *FCC,* 425 F.2d 543 (D.C. Cir. 1969).
63. "The Pool of Experts on Access," *Broadcasting,* September 20, 1971, p. 36.
64. Leonard Zeidenberg, "The Struggle over Broadcast Access II," *Broadcasting,* September 27, 1971, p. 24.
65. *National Association for Better Broadcasting,* 55 FCC2d 800 (1975); *reconsideration denied,* 58 FCC2d 966 (1976).
66. *Broadcaster-Citizen Agreements,* 57 FCC2d 42 (1975).
67. Informal statistics kept by the FCC show the following numbers of petitions involving renewal applications for 1970–1980: 1970 = 15, 1971 =

38, 1972 = 68, 1973 = 48, 1974 = 37, 1975 = 94, 1976 = 35, 1976 transition quarter = 14, 1977 = 19, 1978 = 97, 1979 = 19, and 1980 = 17. The trend is downward, except for peaks in 1972, 1975, and 1978. Staff members attribute those peaks to petitions to deny license renewals in California, where the tactic has remained popular and where there are many stations.

68. This movement of citizen group leaders created hope on the part of the groups and fears on the part of broadcasters that citizen "causes" would be advanced within the Commission by these former citizen leaders. Based on the record of the Ferris Commission, both the fears and hopes proved to be exaggerated. See Susan Witty, "The Citizens Movement Takes a Turn," *Channels of Communication,* June/July 1981, pp. 71–72.

69. See ibid., pp. 68–73, for a good review of the state of the citizen movement at the start of the 1980s (which, nevertheless, overestimates its impact on the Communications Act rewrite efforts to be discussed in chapter nine).

70. *Red Lion Broadcasting Co.* v. *FCC,* 395 U.S. 367, 390 (1969).

71. *Banzhaf* v. *FCC,* 405 F.2d 1082 (D.C. Cir. 1968). Since then, the FCC has overturned the Banzhaf cigarette doctrine, holding in its 1974 *Fairness Doctrine Report:*

> We do not believe that the underlying purposes of the Fairness Doctrine would be well served by permitting the cigarette case to stand as a Fairness Doctrine precedent. . . . We do not believe that the usual product commercial can realistically be said to inform the public on any side of a controversial issue of public importance. . . . Accordingly, in the future, we will apply the Fairness Doctrine only to those commercials which are devoted in an obvious and meaningful way to the discussion of public issues (*The Handling of Public Issues Under the Fairness Doctrine and the Public Interest Standards of the Communications Act,* 48 FCC2d 1, 26 [1974]).

> The Commission's *Fairness Doctrine Report* was appealed to the U.S. Court of Appeals for the District of Columbia Circuit by the Friends of the Earth and the National Citizens Committee for Broadcasting. The court affirmed the Commission's decision not to apply the Fairness Doctrine to standard product commercials and advertisements making product efficacy claims about which there is a dispute. *National Citizens Committee for Broadcasting* v. *FCC,* 567 F.2d 1095 (D.C. Cir. 1977). *Certiorari denied,* 436 U.S. 926 (1978).

72. *Business Executives' Move for Vietnam Peace* v. *FCC,* 450 F.2d 642 (D.C. Cir. 1971).

73. *CBS* v. *Democratic National Committee,* 412 U.S. 94 (1973).

74. *FCC* v. *NCCB,* 436 U.S. 775 (1978).

75. *FCC* v. *WNCN Listeners Guild,* ———U.S.———67 L.Ed.2d 521 101 S.Ct. 1266 (1981).

76. Les Brown, *Television: The Bu$iness Behind the Box* (New York: Harcourt Brace Jovanovich, 1971), pp. 256–257.

77. *Children's Television Report and Policy Statement,* 50 FCC2d 1 (1974). This FCC policy statement provides general guidelines urging television stations to reduce the level of commercials on programs designed for children and to devote a reasonable amount of time to children's programs, a significant portion of which should be educational or informative in nature. The U.S. Court of Appeals for the District of Columbia Circuit affirmed the Commission's decision. *Action for Children's Television* v. *FCC,* 564 F.2d 458 (D.C. Cir. 1977). The Commission in 1979 reopened the inquiry to assess the effects of the 1974 decision. Children's Television

Programming and Advertising Practices, 45 *Federal Register* 1976 (January 9, 1980).

78. There is one fascinating instance of massive citizen participation in the face of FCC efforts to halt it—the so-called "Petition Against God." In late 1974 two citizen activists asked the FCC to freeze grants of noncommercial radio and TV licenses to government and religious organizations and to study any restrictions on free speech the groups practiced. On August 1, 1975, the Commission denied the petition. The petition, however, was misconstrued and a national rumor circulated that the FCC planned to ban religious broadcasting. The mail started to arrive—by 1978 a total of more than 7 million pieces of it. The FCC was unable to stop the flow; it has placed articles in *TV Guide*, hired consultants, and even paid $250,000 to try to stop the rumor by answering some of the letters. When the Commission did that, it discovered that some of the letters had been forged—sent without the knowledge of the alleged sender. Mail and phone calls continue to arrive. The FCC, by special agreement with the U.S. Archives, keeps the letters only one month and then buries them in a landfill in suburban Maryland. See "Hell Hath No Fury," *Broadcasting*, February 13, 1978, p. 104; *Television Digest*, August 6, 1979, p. 5; *Television Digest*, October 29, 1979, p. 4. Community radio entrepreneur Lorenzo Milam, under a pseudonym, published a book about the petition and its early reactions: A. W. Allworthy [pseud.], *The Petition Against God* (Dallas, Tex.: Christ the Light Works, 1976). Milam was one of the filers of the 1974 petition.

79. On those meetings, and especially the FCC staff reaction to them, see Barry Cole and Mal Oettinger, *Reluctant Regulators: The FCC and the Broadcast Audience* (Reading, Mass.: Addison-Wesley, 1978), pp. 106–116. Meetings in Washington, D.C. were revived in 1981 by Chairman Fowler.

80. See ibid., pp. 6–7. For more details, see Graham and Kramer, *Appointments to the Regulatory Agencies*, pp. 307–308, 318, 323, and 327–331.

81. See "Outsiders' Ideas of How FCC Can Best Spend Its Budget Aired in House Hearing," *Broadcasting*, March 29, 1976, pp. 22–23.

82. See "Citizens to Merge," *access 111* (December 15, 1980), 4.

83. See "Ralph Nader Joins Nick Johnson in Revitalized NCCB," *access 59* (October 23, 1978), 1.

84. See Witty, "The Citizens Movement Takes a Turn," p. 70. A table including information on the budgets of other citizen groups can be found on p. 71 of this article.

85. On the NCCB tactics and "violence index," see "Statistical Report Provides Up-to-Date TV Violence Analysis," *access 40* (August 9, 1976), 22; "Citizens Groups Shoot It Out with Advertisers on TV Violence," *access 46* (October 1, 1976), 4; "NCCB Violence Index to Use Two Scales," *access 46* (October 1, 1976), 4; and " 'Quest' Tops List," *access 47* (January 1977), 4. For advertiser and broadcast industry reactions, see "NCCB Ties Together Advertisers and Violent Programs," *Broadcasting*, August 2, 1976, p. 26; "PTA, AMA Mount Efforts Against TV Violence," *Broadcasting*, December 6, 1976, p. 40; "Their Own Baby" [editorial], *Broadcasting*, December 20, 1976, p. 66. A most interesting advertising industry reaction—one of cautious support of the NCCB approach—is found in an *Advertising Age* editorial: "A Program Worth Watching," *Advertising Age*, August 9, 1976, p. 14.

86. On the formation of the group, see "Crusade Sets Out to Clean Up TV,"

Broadcasting, February 9, 1981, pp. 27–29. By March 1981, *Advertising Age* reported a "scramble" to clean up TV shows, saying that the networks had passed the word to Hollywood to "tone down risqué or violent program elements" ("Scramble Underway for 'Clean' TV Shows," *Advertising Age,* March 3, 1981, pp. 1, 80). The editorial reaction to the Coalition for Better TV's monitoring and sponsor identification plan was much more hostile than that to the earlier NCCB activities. See, for example, "Morality Boycott" [editorial], *Advertising Age,* February 16, 1981, p. 16.

87. The Van Deerlin quote is from a special edition of *access:* see "Media Reform—Past, Present and Future," *access 100* (June 30, 1980), 4. Fourteen other leaders of government and of the citizen movement also contributed articles. For other perspectives on the future of the movement, see Anne W. Branscomb and Maria Savage, *Broadcast Reform at the Crossroads* (Cambridge, Mass.: Kalba Bowen Associates, 1978). An excellent theoretical treatment of how public interest groups are formed and sustained, and how they decide on their goals and tactics, can be found in Jeffrey M. Berry, *Lobbying for the People* (Princeton, N.J.: Princeton University Press, 1977).

88. Address by Richard E. Wiley, Chairman, FCC, to the American Bar Association Bicentennial Institute Oversight and Review of Agency Decision Making, Washington, D.C., March 18, 1976, p. 11 [mimeo.].

89. On September 17, 1981, the FCC proposed to Congress that this section of the act be amended to allow most appeals of Commission decisions to be taken to the U.S. Court of Appeals for the judicial circuit in which the petitioner resides or has its principal office. As the Commission candidly noted, "[t]his amendment probably would reduce the importance of the D.C. Circuit's role in the interpretation of communications law." *FCC Legislative Proposal, Track I,* September 17, 1981 [mimeo.], at p. 57.

90. A recent example of the tendency not to decide constitutional questions involves the FCC's efforts to "channel" indecent broadcasts into times of the day when children are not in the audience. The FCC's efforts can be traced to a 1975 order of the Commission to Pacifica Foundation's WBAI in New York (see *Pacifica Foundation,* 56 FCC2d 94 [1975]). A three-judge panel of the U.S. Court of Appeals for the District of Columbia Circuit overturned the FCC's actions on a 2 to 1 vote, but of the two judges voting to overturn, only one, Chief Judge David Bazelon, concluded that the FCC's actions violated the First Amendment (see *Pacifica Foundation* v. *FCC,* 556 F.2d 9, 24–30 [D.C. Cir. 1977]). When the U.S. Supreme Court overturned the U.S. Court of Appeals' decision, five members of the high court agreed that the FCC's original order did not violate the First Amendment, although they were unable to support a single opinion to express those views (see *FCC* v. *Pacifica Foundation,* 438 U.S. 726 [1978]). The justices adopting this view were Chief Justice Warren Burger plus Associate Justices John Paul Stevens, William Rehnquist, Harry Blackmun, and Lewis Powell.

91. *FCC* v. *RCA Communications, Inc.,* 346 U.S. 86, 91 (1953).

92. *Greater Boston Television Corp.* v. *FCC,* 444 F.2d 841, 851 (D.C. Cir. 1971), *certiorari denied,* 403 U.S. 923 (1971).

93. Robinson, "The Federal Communications Commission," 169, 176. For a perceptive, if somewhat dated, article on the U.S. Court of Appeals for the District of Columbia Circuit, see Steve Millard, "Broadcasting's Preemptive Court," *Broadcasting,* August 30, 1971, p. 23.

94. *Environmental Defense Fund* v. *Ruckelshaus,* 439 F.2d 584, 597 (D.C. Cir. 1971).
95. Ibid., p. 598.
96. *Home Box Office, Inc.* v. *FCC,* 567 F.2d 9 (D.C. Cir. 1977), *certiorari denied,* 434 U.S. 829 (1977).
97. *WNCN Listeners Guild* v. *FCC,* 610 F.2d 838, 860 (D.C. Cir., 1979).
98. Ibid., 854–858.
99. *FCC* v. *WNCN Listeners Guild,* ———U.S.———, 67 L.Ed.2d 521, 535, 101 S.Ct. 1266 (1981). Quoting *FCC* v. *National Citizens Committee for Broadcasting,* 436 U.S. at 810, 56 L.Ed. 2d 697, 98 S.Ct. 2096 (1978). Perhaps an explanation for such judicial restraint can be found in the views of Chief Justice William Howard Taft, who served on the Supreme Court during broadcasting's early years. When asked to explain his reluctance to review such cases involving radio law, Taft is reported to have said, "Interpreting the law on this subject is something like trying to interpret the law of the occult. It seems like dealing with something supernatural. I want to put it off as long as possible in the hope that it becomes more understandable before the court passes on the questions involved" (cited in Ronald Coase, "The Federal Communications Commission," *Journal of Law & Economics,* 2 [1959], 40).
100. The following discussion is based on Loren P. Beth, *Politics, The Constitution and the Supreme Court* (New York: Harper & Row, 1962), chapter four.
101. William Cary, *Politics and the Regulatory Agencies* (New York: McGraw-Hill, 1967), pp. 6–7.
102. Former FCC Commissioner Glen Robinson has a slightly different interpretation. He agrees that the common belief is that FCC matters are not "important" enough to trouble the president but questions whether or not that should be the case:

> No doubt one major reason for the absence of a clear, strong, and constant voice from the White House is the seemingly obvious fact that most of the concerns confronting the regulatory agencies are simply beneath the notice of a President. After all, a President pondering the fate of nations can scarcely be expected to decide to adopt new regulations governing cable importation of distant broadcast signals. Or can he? I cannot pretend to comprehend the weighty matters that occupy a President's attention, but even a casual survey of newspaper reports suggests that not everything that consumes the President's workday is of higher importance than many of the issues confronting the regulatory commissions. In fact, few regulatory issues are more important than those pertaining to the role of communications in American life—the kind of issues with which the FCC deals routinely (Robinson, "The Federal Communications Commission," 169, 206).

103. The Reagan experience is a bit out of the ordinary, although it is common for several Commissioners (and, typically, the Chairman) to resign shortly after a shift of party at the White House. Usually, because the FCC has seven Commissioners rather than the five typically found on other agencies, it is hard for a president to gain such early control. The ability of the president to influence FCC decisions is also limited by the Commission's regulatory mission, touching as it does on sensitive First Amendment matters.
104. Committee on Independent Regulatory Commissions, *A Report with Recommendations Prepared for the Commission on Organization of the Executive Branches of the Government* (Appendix N) (Washington, D.C.: Government Printing Office, 1949).

105. Noll, *Reforming Regulation,* p. 43.
106. Graham and Kramer, *Appointments to the Regulatory Agencies,* p. 200. For insight into the role played by the trade press in FCC broadcast matters, see Barry G. Cole and Mal Oettinger (once a reporter for *Broadcasting* magazine), *The Reluctant Regulators, the FCC and the Broadcast Audience* (Reading, Mass.: Addison-Wesley, 1978).
107. Quoted in Graham and Kramer, *Appointments to the Regulatory Agencies,* pp. 375–421. See also Robinson, "The Federal Communications Commission," 203–211.
108. Although the Communications Act does not deal with the issue of removal of Commissioners "for cause," the president may remove a Commissioner only upon a showing of extreme inefficiency, neglect of duty, or malfeasance in office. See *Humphrey's Executor* v. *United States,* 295 U.S. 602 (1935); and *Wiener* v. *United States,* 357 U.S. 249 (1958). Although it has never been exercised, Congress has the power of impeachment. During the Eisenhower administration, Richard Mack in 1958 and John Doerfer in 1960 resigned from the FCC at the request of the Eisenhower White House. Neither resisted the request, obviating the need for further actions. See Graham and Kramer, *Appointments to the Regulatory Agencies,* p. 41.
109. Cary, *Politics and the Regulatory Agencies,* p. 12. Thus early in President Reagan's administration, it was important when OMB told the FCC that it would have to reduce its work force by 622 persons within about one year. See "FCC Layoffs Loom," *Television Digest,* October 12, 1981, p. 3.
110. Reorganization Plan No. 1, H.R. Doc. No. 71–222, 91st Congress, 2nd Session (1970).
111. Edwin B. Spievack, "Presidential Assault on Communications," *Federal Communications Bar Journal,* 23 (1969), 157.
112. Hearings before the Subcommittee on Executive and Legislative Reorganization of the House Government Operations Committee, Reorganization Plan No. 1 of 1970, 91st Congress, 2nd Session (1970), p. 50. See also Bruce Thorp, "Agency Report: Office of Telecommunications Policy Speaks for the President and Hears Some Static," *National Journal,* February 13, 1970, p. 343.
113. See William E. Porter, *Assault on the Media: The Nixon Years* (Ann Arbor: University of Michigan Press, 1976), which contains the text of Whitehead's infamous Sigma Delta Chi speech, Vice President Spiro Agnew's Des Moines and Montgomery speeches attacking the media, and White House memoranda between H. R. Haldeman, Jeb Stuart Magruder, Lawrence Higby, and Charles Colson. The Carter administration released a number of Nixon administration documents that supported the theory of an attack on the media and on public broadcasting. See *The Nixon Administration Public Broadcasting Papers: A Summary, 1969–1974* (Washington, D.C.: National Association of Educational Broadcasters, 1979). See also Irwin B. Arieff, "Government Interference in Public Broadcasting Disclosed," *Congressional Quarterly Weekly Report,* March 24, 1979, pp. 533–535.
114. According to Richard Neustadt, a member of President Carter's Domestic Policy Council staff, the president regarded the White House-based OTP as politically dangerous because there might be an irresistible urge for White House staff members to use it to prod the FCC to advance the president's political interests. Assigning responsibility to the Department of Commerce seemed safer: "Thus, if a President's communications policy goals are expressed by NTIA in the Department of Commerce it would

not seem to be as political. Such political distance is an important consideration in matters involving broadcasting and the First Amendment" (interview, Washington, D.C., July 10, 1981).

115. For insights into Geller and the first two years of activity of the NTIA, see "Geller as Guru," *Broadcasting*, February 19, 1979, pp. 35–46.

116. The Public Telecommunications Financing Act of 1978, Pub. L. 95–567 (November 2, 1978), shifted responsibility for the grant program to build public telecommunications facilities from the Department of Health, Education and Welfare to the NTIA. See 47 USC, Secs. 390–395. In time, the dollar amounts involved in this effort would be substantially higher than the rest of the NTIA budget.

117. Many of the NTIA's (and the Carter administration's) interests in telecommunications are summarized in a campaign document entitled "Communications Policy in the Carter Administration," a memorandum by Richard Neustadt, White House Domestic Policy Staff, September 1980.

118. Quoted in "Geller as Guru," p. 36.

119. See Francis E. Rourke and Roger G. Braun, "The President and Telecommunications Policy—The Failure of an Advisory System," Paper prepared for delivery at the 1980 Annual Meeting of the American Political Science Association, Washington, D.C., August 1980.

120. Interview with Richard Neustadt, Washington, D.C., July 10, 1981.

121. See Laura B. Weiss, "Reagan, Congress Planning Regulatory Machine Repair," *Congressional Quarterly Weekly Report*, March 7, 1981, pp. 409–414.

122. On September 17, 1981, the FCC asked Congress to allow it to conduct most of its own litigation, instead of relying on the Department of Justice. *FCC Legislative Proposals, Track II*, September 17, 1981, [mimeo.], p. 6.

123. See "It's Settled: ABC, Justice Come to Terms," *Broadcasting*, August 25, 1980, p. 31.

124. Historically, the Antitrust Division has been even more concerned about common carrier than broadcast competition.

125. The studios are Columbia Pictures Industries, MCA, Inc., Paramount Pictures Corp., and Twentieth Century-Fox Film Corp. See "Justice Dept. Fulfills Prophecy on Premiere," *Broadcasting*, August 11, 1980, pp. 20–24; and "Premiere Won't Take 'No' for an Answer," *Broadcasting*, January 5, 1981, p. 31.

126. Interview with Donald Jansky, National Telecommunications and Information Administration, Washington, D.C., July 3, 1981.

127. See "U.S. Phone Lines Called Vulnerable," *Washington Post*, May 6, 1981, p. B-1. The article maintains that Department of Defense support for Bell Telephone encouraged the Justice Department, in 1956, to accept a consent decree with Bell that, although it imposed limits on Bell's operations, did not achieve Justice's objective of separating Bell from Western Electric or some of its operating divisions. In May 1981, Justice and Defense Department leaders held several meetings in which Defense again stood up for Bell against continued Department of Justice activities, in yet another antitrust case, to split off parts of the Bell system. See "DOD Meets Justice over AT&T Suit," *Washington Star*, May 16, 1981, p. B-5.

128. Richard Neustadt, "Communications Policy in the Carter Administration," White House Domestic Policy Staff [memorandum], September 1980, p. 8.

Three

Congress: Powerful Determiner of Regulatory Policy

The historical enthusiasm of Congress for attempting to direct and oversee broadcast regulatory policy is hard to understate. "When I was Chairman," Newton Minow has written, "I heard from Congress about as frequently as television commercials flash across the screen."[1] Such enthusiasm for making views known to the FCC, however, has not freed Congress from recurring criticism for "its failure to provide guides and standards for the Commission to follow, and for its frequent and often premature interference in the Commission's rare attempts to formulate policy on its own."[2] This chapter focuses on Congress's active but often criticized role as a key participant in the regulatory process. Essentially, there are three main issues: What are we talking about when we speak of Congress? What form does congressional involvement take? What impact does Congress have on the formulation and implementation of broadcast policy?

Congressional Structure and Concerns

When we discuss Congress's role in the regulation of broadcasting we do not intend to refer just to the power of Congress as a whole. Power is distributed quite unevenly in that body, particularly in a specialized area like broadcast regulation. First of all, Congress is divided into the Senate and the House of Representatives. Sometimes the Senate takes the lead in a policy area (as in the FCC's license renewal controversy in 1970); at other times the activity is in the House (as in the 1963 bill to block the FCC's consideration of commercial time limits and most efforts in the 1970s to rewrite the Communications Act of 1934).[3]

It is also true that the House and Senate are not the ultimate subdivisions of power within Congress. The truly vital actors are the committees and subcommittees, where most of Congress's work is really done. In terms of broadcasting (and other communications industries), the most important committees are the House and Senate Committees on Commerce, each of which has, in turn, a subcommittee primarily devoted to telecommunications. The groundwork on most legislation is done in these subcommittees. As legislation moves up the hierarchy in the Congress toward discussion on the floor, there is less and less opportunity to influence its fine points.

Committees and subcommittees, of course, are no more than groups of members of Congress. The attention of members to the activities of their subcommittees and committees varies widely. Rarely do all members have equally intense interest in a matter under consideration. Thus through sustained interest, a single member of a committee or subcommittee frequently exerts more influence on a legislative outcome than one would expect. In most but not all instances, the most influential member of a committee or subcommittee is its chairman, who directs most of the group's activity. A highly placed FCC staff member once said privately that the word of then Senator Warren Magnuson, chairman of the Senate Commerce Committee, was practically law to the FCC: "They bow and scrape for him. He doesn't have to ask for anything. The Commission does what it thinks he wants it to do." This was also true of Oren Harris, former chairman of the House Interstate and Foreign Commerce Committee: "He cracked the whip lots of times down here."[4] The same has been true of nearly every recent chairman of either the Senate or House Commerce Committee and the communications subcommittees. Other committees, especially the Appropriations and Judiciary Committees, take occasional interest in broadcasting and regulatory issues, but the Commerce Committees are undoubtedly the center of congressional influence on broadcasting. The result of all this, in William Boyer's words, is that "an administrator must . . . sensitize his decision-making to the wishes and predilections of committee chairmen primarily and legislators generally."[5]

One reason that Congress has involved itself so closely in broadcast regulatory policy is that it senses special obligations in regard to regulatory agencies. In theory, all such agencies are "an arm of Congress," fleshing out the details of delegated congressional authority. Consequently, many legislators consider review of agency performance an integral part of Congress's mission. To Congress the independence of regulatory commissions such as the FCC means independence from White House domination, not independence from its congressional parent.

The power of Congress over the Commission is both pervasive and multifaceted. Since the FCC lacks the political protection of the president or a cabinet official and has few effective means of appealing for popular support, members of Congress have little fear of political reprisal when dealing with the Commission or other independent agencies.[6]

Newton Minow tells a trenchant story about the day, shortly after his appointment to the Commission, when he called upon House Speaker Sam Rayburn. "Mr. Sam" put his arm around the new FCC Chairman and said, "Just remember one thing, son. Your agency is an arm of the Congress; you belong to us. Remember that and you'll be all right."[7] The Speaker went on to warn him to expect a lot of trouble and pressure, but, as Minow recalls, "what he did not tell me was that most of the pressure would come from the Congress itself."[8]

This pervasive congressional concern with Commission activities makes the FCC extremely wary about possible reactions from Congress —a phenomenon that political scientists call the process of "anticipated reaction," "feedback," or "strategic sensitivity." In this connection Boyer has commented:

What matters here is not that an administrator is forced by a vote or an overt instruction of any legislative committee to initiate a particular policy, for seldom does this happen. More important is an administrator's assessment of the given ecology within which he must make his policy decision. For efficacious policy initiation, he must attempt to perceive and anticipate the behavior of legislative committees and the environment reflected by them.[9]

Congress and the Broadcast Industry

Congressional involvement in regulatory policy and its close supervision of the FCC may also be traced to the fact that many representatives and senators are sympathetic to the broadcast industry. This community of views is subtle, sometimes attributed in part to the financial interests of some members of Congress in broadcasting. Direct or family-related investments of congressional representatives in broadcasting, however, are not as extensive as often thought. In the 95th Congress (1979–1980), six senators and ten representatives had such an interest in broadcast stations.[10]

Congressional support for industry positions is more accurately viewed as just the normal attempt by legislators to satisfy, where possible, the demands of important, prestigious, and useful constituents. That the industry both values and courts such support is clear. "Most of our work," said Paul B. Comstock, former vice president and general counsel of the National Association of Broadcasters, "is done with Congressional committees. We concentrate on Congress. We firmly believe that the FCC will do whatever Congress tells it to do, and will not do anything Congress tells it not to do."[11] Given that Congress only infrequently amends the Communications Act, much broadcaster pressure on Congress is intended to bring about indirect congressional pressure on the FCC. As former Commissioner Glen Robinson put it, "The chief purpose for lobbying Congress today is not so much to obtain legislation but rather to gain Congressional leverage to pressure the agency to take some particular action."[12]

The broadcast industry and Congress have been described as linked by an "umbilical cord."[13] Broadcasters control a very important commodity to politicians—electronic media exposure. While politicians can buy time from broadcasters for campaign advertising, they are particularly concerned about how they are treated in radio and television newscasts and on public affairs programs and about their access to free time, if any, offered by stations.[14] Such appearances, during paid or free time, assist politicians in their efforts both to get reelected and to communicate with their constituents. Broadcasters benefit too, for, at least in the case of TV stations, they regularly report their news and public affairs programming to the FCC at license renewal time. Robert Mac-Neil's analogy describing the "tense mutual interdependence" of Congress and the broadcast industry is apt:

Imagine the situation of a street peddler who sells old-fashioned patent medicines. He needs a license to stay in business, and the city official who issues them is dubious about most of the peddler's wares. Yet it just happens that one product, a magic elixir, is the only thing that will cure the official's rheumatism and keep him in health. So the two coexist in a tense mutual interdependence, the peddler getting his license, the official his magic elixir.[15]

The need for the elixir, however, does not translate into broadcaster freedom from criticism or into an automatic willingness of politicians to trade votes for coverage. National political leaders who are too prominent for the media to ignore can, of course, criticize with impunity. They, however, are rarely interested in communications policy matters. Lesser-known members of Congress often find they can exploit natural differences between local stations, which they usually praise, and "the industry" or "the networks," which they safely and roundly criticize. Similarly, former Vice President Spiro Agnew, often critical of TV news coverage of the Nixon administration, primarily criticized the networks rather than individual stations. Thus the concern that members of Congress will not criticize the broadcast industry or vote against its interests is commonly overstated. If anything, a senator or representative may sometimes be reluctant to criticize local broadcasters directly if he or she believes reelection depends in great measure on the amount and tone of exposure to be obtained from them.

Congress has not, however, totally ignored its self-interest in political broadcasting. Over the years it has incorporated into the Communications Act certain protections for itself. Under the act all candidates for federal office must be provided "reasonable access" to a station, on a paid or free basis at the discretion of the broadcaster. Broadcasters must also provide "equal opportunity"—popularly called "equal time"—for all candidates to use the station, and during certain times just before elections, they must sell candidates time at that station's "lowest unit charge."[16]

A final explanation for congressional interest in broadcasting is that many members of Congress have an intrinsic fascination with communications issues, reflecting their constituents' concerns with the impact of broadcasting on society. Thus they are not hesitant to criticize the industry on specific controversial matters such as sex and violence in programming or the quality of the industry's service to children, although they may display substantially less interest in broader, less controversial communications policy matters (see chapter nine).

Congressional Strategies for Overseeing Broadcast Regulation

Congressional influence on broadcast policy making assumes many forms. The primary ones are control by statute, use of the power of the purse, the spur of the investigations, the power of advice and consent, the continuing watchfulness of standing committees, supervision by multiple committees, pressures of individual members of Congress and staff, and congressional control by legislative inaction.[17] Each of these forms of influence will be examined next, with an emphasis on events in the late 1970s and early 1980s.

CONTROL BY STATUTE

This most obvious and public congressional activity is applied only infrequently to broadcast regulation. Having set basic policy in the acts of 1927 and 1934, Congress has rarely chosen to influence the administration or formulation of policy by the FCC through enacting additional or amendatory legislation.[18] The FCC's annual reports covering an entire decade (fiscal years 1970 through 1979) list only twelve congressional acts affecting the Commission, excluding routine budget authorizations for the FCC and for public broadcasting. Of these twelve acts, just four are of direct concern to broadcasters; the others deal mostly with common carrier aspects of the Communications Act.

As noted earlier, the Radio Act of 1927 and the Communications Act of 1934 give the Commission little more guidance as to its goals, duties, or policies than the vague "public interest, convenience and necessity" standard. Congress granted such a broad mandate to the FCC because it had neither the desire nor the expertise to grapple with the complex and continuing problem of regulating an emerging technology. This task was left to the new agency. The absence of clear guidelines for FCC policy making, however, opens the Commission to other forms of congressional influence and, on rare occasions, to a direct overruling of the Commission by legislative action.[19] As Professor Louis Jaffe observes, the continuing threat of congressional investigation is virtually inevitable when the regulatory area is a "jungle without statutory directives."[20] Thus nonstatutory controls—many of which will be discussed shortly—are key to the FCC's relationship with Congress.

Statutory controls are used occasionally, however. In Congress, hundreds of bills are introduced but few become law. Broadcasting is no exception to this pattern. Those amendments to the Communications Act passed by Congress in the 1970s through early 1982 typified the longstanding tendency of Congress to provide only minor, narrowly focused amendments to the act rather than change its fundamental principles. The one effort to modify fundamental principles, a proposed complete revision of the Communications Act of 1934, did not pass (see chapter nine).

One theme, running through the broad sweep of congressional amendments to the act from 1934 through the early 1980s but especially prominent in actions in the 1970s, is frequent congressional self-interest in tinkering with the act, particularly those parts relating to political broadcasting. The Federal Election Campaign Act of 1971 provided that willful or repeated failure by a broadcast licensee to provide "reasonable access" to a candidate for federal office could result in a loss of license. It also required broadcasters, during periods just prior to elections, to sell all candidates political ad time at the station's "lowest unit rate"—that is, the lowest rate charged to any other user for a similar time slot.[21] Neither the law nor its legislative history specified exactly what Congress had in mind by the phrase "reasonable access." Such details were left to the Commission and the courts.[22] In another, perhaps self-interested act, Congress in 1973 prohibited broadcasters from "blacking out" professional football, baseball, basketball, or hockey games sold out seventy-two hours before their starting time.[23] Some said the primary force behind this act was the congressional desire to watch home games of the Washington Redskins.

Other amendments to the act were less obviously self-interested. In 1970, over the strenuous objection of broadcast and advertising industry groups, Congress prohibited cigarette ads on regulated electronic media effective January 2, 1971.[24] An interesting feature to this legislation was that while it went against the wishes of the communications industry, it was endorsed by the tobacco industry. That industry preferred no broadcast ads at all to a situation where broadcast ads might, because of the FCC's Fairness Doctrine, be opposed by antismoking messages.

Some legislation was actually sought by, or strongly supported by, communications industry interests. In 1976 the act was changed to allow TV translator stations to originate some local information programs and appeal for funds, and to permit unattended operation of FM translators.[25] In 1978, after years of debate, Congress approved legislation (1) increasing to $20,000 the maximum fine the FCC could impose for violation of the act and/or FCC rules, (2) making more parties (including cable systems) subject to such fines, and (3) ordering the FCC to step in and set policies for use of utility poles by cable systems in those states where state law did not cover the subject.[26] The cable industry wanted the "pole attachment" provisions and was willing to accept potential liability to fines in order to get them. Broadcasters did not like the increase in fines but wanted cable operators and others (such as unlicensed CB operators, who sometimes interfered with broadcasters) to be subject to them. In the context of the Senate-House compromise over the fiscal 1982 federal budget, the first to reflect President Ronald Reagan's philosophy of government (and, accordingly, a budget bill with much more substantive legislation included than usual), Congress incorporated several amendments to the Communications Act of importance to broadcasters. Prior to the changes, all broadcast station licenses were for three-year terms. As amended, TV station license terms were extended to five years and radio terms to seven. In addition, the FCC was given the option of using a lottery—if weighted in favor of women, minorities, labor unions, and community organizations "underrepresented in ownership of telecommunications facilities"—to decide among several qualified applicants for new broadcast stations. Congress also amended the act to discourage "payoffs" to groups that filed frivolous competing license applications "in order to harass an incumbent."[27]

During the 1970s there were several congressional enactments important to broadcasters even if they did not amend the Communications Act. The most notable of these was a copyright revision, passed in 1976 after fifteen years of debate, replacing the outdated Copyright Act of 1909. Among other things the act required that in exchange for royalty payments based on the number of nonlocal broadcast signals carried and on the revenues of the system, cable television systems would receive a compulsory license to carry copyrighted TV broadcast programs without the consent of either the broadcaster or the copyright holder.[28] This politically sensitive issue of copyright payments by cable television systems had long delayed congressional revision of copyright law. Then Chairman Dean Burch, in a concurring opinion to the FCC's 1972 *Cable Television Report and Order,* observed that "the obstacle to legislation has long been the ability of any or all of the contending industries—cable, broadcasting, copyright—to block any particular legislative approach with which they might take issue."[29]

Despite enactment of the new copyright law, differences among program copyright owners, cable operators, and broadcasters persist. Many cable operators still harbor considerable distaste for paying any copyright fees, and virtually all segments of that industry regard reporting and accounting requirements created by a Copyright Royalty Tribunal as needlessly onerous. The tribunal's efforts to dispense monies collected have dissatisfied many, who have, in turn, proposed review or even elimination of the tribunal concept—a proposal that would require congressional action. The prospect of broadcaster-initiated infringement suits arising from violations of the FCC's rules governing the carriage of television signals is anything but pleasant for cable operators, but FCC changes in those signal carriage rules making it easier for cable systems to bring in distant stations have displeased broadcasters. Broadcasters remain unhappy about what they view as unreasonably low royalty fees amounting to "unfair competition" from cable. Copyright owners, likewise, contend that the fees paid by cable operators are inadequate and remain concerned about the loss of control over distribution of their product. Performers continue to seek a "performers' royalty" similar to payments currently made to composers, authors, and publishers of music. The issue has been around for more than twenty years, but the broadcast industry, which estimates that the cost of such a royalty would be up to $20 million per year, has consistently and so far successfully opposed proposed congressional solutions.

Under pressure from broadcasters and state governments, the Criminal Code's prohibition on the broadcast of material that might promote lotteries was amended in 1975 to allow broadcasters in states with state-operated lotteries to promote them.[30] State governments became involved after they discovered the state-run lottery as a revenue device in the early 1970s. They found, however, that they could not buy broadcast advertising to promote their lotteries and even that, in some instances, local broadcasters were fearful to treat the lottery as news. State governments, along with broadcasters, worked with their congressional delegations to get the Criminal Code changed.

Another area of congressional interest to broadcasters, one in which they share goals with print media, pertains to laws affecting journalism. In 1980 Congress in effect overturned an earlier U.S. Supreme Court decision by requiring that both federal and state authorities, in most instances, obtain documents from offices of journalistic organizations by subpoena rather than by search warrant.[31] In still another area, in 1978, after years of argument, the House of Representatives agreed to permit TV coverage of activities in the House chambers, using cameras run by House employees rather than by broadcasters.[32] Thus far, despite broadcaster pressure, the Senate has remained camera shy.

Regulatory reform was a final area of concern throughout the 1970s and early 1980s. Although many broad regulatory reform proposals were considered, only a few became law. In some cases, congressional legislation was preceded by similar executive actions or executive orders from the president. In the area of regulatory ethics, Congress, in 1976, approved a "Government in the Sunshine Act" that required regulatory agencies, such as the FCC, to conduct open public meetings.[33] Two years later, it passed a strengthened ethics bill intended to deal with the "revolving door" problem of regulators leaving agencies for private sector jobs in the fields they once regulated. The new law placed tougher limits on the services former Commissioners and high-level staff members could provide upon leaving the Commission.[34]

Two additional new laws dealt with the burdens placed on business by regulation, especially small businesses (a classification into which most broadcast stations fall). On September 19, 1980, Congress approved the Regulatory Flexibility Act, which requires rule-making agencies to prepare an "initial regulatory flexibility analysis" before issuing a notice of proposed rule making. The analysis must identify the burdens the proposed rule might place on small business, show how the proposed rule might overlap or conflict with other rules, and describe significant alternatives, if any, to the proposed rule that might accomplish the same objectives. If an agency issues a final rule adopting its original proposals, then it must show why it did not adopt one of the less burdensome alternatives. Agencies are also required to review and identify existing rules that place especially heavy burdens on small businesses.[35]

Congress passed a companion piece of legislation less than three months later—the Paperwork Reduction Act of 1980—the objective of which is to minimize and rationalize paperwork required by the government. The Act requires that most "information collection" requests of regulatory agencies pass through a new Office of Information and Regulatory Affairs in the White House Office of Management and Budget. Its goal is a 15 percent reduction in federal paperwork by October 1, 1982, with another 10 percent to follow shortly.[36] Together, the two 1980 acts moved Congress some distance toward responding to the complaints of industry, including the broadcast industry, about "excessive" federal regulation. Moreover, they are probably only the first steps in what is likely to be a continuing effort by Congress at regulatory reform.

A perhaps more significant step, although one that did not affect the Federal Communications Commission directly, came in May 1980 when, after more than a three-year fight, Congress at last authorized a regular budget for the Federal Trade Commission. Under Carter-appointed Chairman Michael Pertschuk, the FTC had deeply antagonized business interests through proceedings involving children's television advertising, used car sales, insurance, funeral home practices, and the loss of trademark protection. The congressional response had been, since 1976, a refusal to give the Commission a regular budget. On May 1, 1980, the FTC actually ran out of money and officially shut down for one day—the first federal agency ever to find itself in such a predicament.

After that, Congress, responding to business pressures, tried out on the FTC one of the most controversial proposed regulatory reform measures ever—the legislative veto. Prior to this enactment the only way Congress could undo an FTC regulation it did not like was to pass legislation undoing the rule—a time-consuming and rarely followed practice. The Federal Trade Commission Improvements Act of 1980 requires that the FTC submit all final rules to Congress. The rules automatically go into force unless, within ninety days, both houses of Congress adopt disapproving concurrent resolutions. Such a congressional disapproval procedure seemed, at least to its proponents, to be a quick and easy way for Congress to keep control of a miscreant regulatory agency. Detractors of the law argued, however, that it would create excessive opportunity for political forces to sway the rule-making process and lend uncertainty to the actions of the FTC.[37] In any event, despite President Carter's belief in its unconstitutionality, the legislative veto for FTC rules went into effect, thus opening (depending on eventual court actions) a new means for Congress to influence the actions of regulatory agencies.

THE POWER OF THE PURSE

Like all units of government, regulatory agencies need money to operate. Through its hold on the purse strings—a power shared with the White House Office of Management and Budget—Congress can control not only the total amount of money allocated to regulatory agencies but also the purposes for which funds are to be used.

The "power of the purse" resides primarily within subcommittees of the Appropriations Committee of each house of Congress, although individual members of Congress also try to influence the projects and research of agencies. Both the Senate and House subcommittees hold annual hearings for the purpose of examining the FCC's budget requests and questioning FCC Commissioners and top-level staff members. Many opportunities arise, both at the hearings and on other occasions, for the subcommittees to scrutinize Commission behavior and to communicate legislative desires to regulatory officials.

Appropriations subcommittees, for example, have determined the direction of the FCC by limiting the use of funds for personnel. When

Senator Ernest Hollings (D-South Carolina) served as Chairman of both the Senate Communications Subcommittee and the Appropriations Subcommittee responsible for the FCC budget, he had a unique opportunity to command the attention of the Commission. In June 1977, Hollings wrote then FCC Chairman Richard Wiley stating his objection to the FCC's request to reallocate $350,000 from other FCC projects to fund a special ten-member staff that would begin work on a large-scale inquiry into network television[38]—a wide-ranging study begun by the FCC in January 1977 after the Westinghouse Broadcasting Company petitioned the FCC to reexamine network-affiliate relationships. Hollings virtually acknowledged that his refusal to authorize Republican Wiley's request was politically motivated—in his words, by a "desire to preserve the options of the soon to be named new [Democratic, it was assumed] Chairman of the Commission."[39] The FCC, recognizing the obvious, accepted Senator Hollings's letter as decisive by a 7 to 0 vote. A few months later, with the new FCC Chairman (Charles Ferris) aboard, the funds transfer was approved.

There is at least one instance, unique perhaps in all of government, when Congress has attempted to limit its own power of the purse. Under the Public Broadcasting Act of 1967, Congress provided for only year-by-year funding of public radio and television.[40] During the Nixon administration it became obvious that such hand-to-mouth existence opened the system to political pressure, not just from the president but also from Congress. Thus a search began for a system of guaranteed longer-term funding that would provide some political "insulation" for the system. In 1975 and again in 1978, Congress at last provided for multiyear, advance funding authorizations—the only instance of such spending of federal funds—in order to reduce the potential for subtle budgetary influence on public broadcasting. In exchange for such advance funding, however, Congress imposed special equal employment opportunity and "community participation" obligations (e.g., public meetings of station boards, advisory committees, etc.) on the recipients of these funds.[41] The principle of advance funding was challenged in 1981 when President Reagan proposed severe cutbacks and recisions in already approved funds to cut federal spending. In the end, however, advance funding authorizations remained, although at slightly reduced levels—$130 million annually for fiscal years 1984, 1985, and 1986. Leaders of public broadcasting generally were pleased with the compromise. National Public Radio President Frank Mankiewicz called it a "great victory for public broadcasting" that "gives us time on turnaround for alternative sources of funding"—a recognition that the Reagan administration continued to question the notion of advanced funding and might eliminate it in future budgets. Several changes were also made at the same time to reduce the size of the board of the Corporation for Public Broadcasting and to provide for specific radio and television station representation on it.[42]

Another effective technique of legislative review involves the suggestions, admonitions, and directions conveyed to the FCC by means of committee reports accompanying appropriations bills. Although the reports are not law, the Appropriations Committees expect that they will be regarded almost as seriously as if they were—an expectation agencies usually fulfill. In June 1974 the intense national concern about the alleged presence of violent or sexually explicit material on television—a matter of general congressional interest since 1970—came to a head at hearings before the House Appropriations Committee. The FCC was ordered to "submit a report to the Committee by December 31, 1974 [a deadline subsequently extended], outlining specific positive actions taken or planned by the Commission to protect children from excessive programming of violence and obscenity."[43] Indicating displeasure with what it saw as a dereliction of the FCC's duty, the committee also stated its "reluct[ance] to take punitive action to require the Commission to heed the views of Congress and to carry out its responsibilities," but it added, "if this is what is required to achieve the desired objective such action may be considered."[44]

Responding to instructions in the reports of both the House and Senate Appropriations Committees, Chairman Wiley initiated a series of meetings with the top officials of the networks and the National Association of Broadcasters (NAB). The meetings continued through the fall, and early in 1975 the family viewing policy was born. The family viewing standard, inserted into the NAB Television Code in the spring of 1975, generally provides that the first hour of network prime-time programming and the preceding hour (i.e., 7 through 9 P.M. Eastern Time) consist of programming suitable for viewing by the entire family. Former Senator John Pastore, then chairman of both the Communications Subcommittee and the Appropriations Subcommittee on the FCC budget, applauded family viewing as a responsible answer to the problem of televised violence. On October 30, 1975, however, several individuals and groups engaged in the creation and sale of television programs filed suit, charging that the new code provisions and the efforts of Chairman Wiley to take action violated the First Amendment, the Communications Act, the Administrative Procedure Act, and antitrust laws. On November 4, 1976, U.S. District Court Judge Warren Ferguson issued a decision generally supporting the complaining parties.[45] Just over three years later, however, the U.S. Court of Appeals for the Ninth Circuit vacated Judge Ferguson's decision. The court of appeals concluded that the district court was not the right forum for the family viewing suit and that the FCC should have had the first shot at considering the complaint.[46]

Another very explicit example of Congress using its purse string controls occurred in 1978 when the Senate, largely at the urging of Lowell Weicker (R-Connecticut), added $750,000 and five staff members to the FCC's fiscal year 1979 budget for a study of the comparability of UHF and VHF television. The directions given the Commission were precise:

The [Senate] Committee [on Appropriations] directs that the Commission devise a plan for UHF to reach comparability with VHF in as short a time as practicable. . . . This plan should address all the technical and regulatory aspects of achieving parity and should set a schedule for dealing with each, including dates for achieving specific goals, such as noise level reductions. It should also include indications of the probable need for any legislation necessary to fulfill the plan.[47]

Similarly Senator Hollings added $440,000 to the Commission's fiscal 1980 budget for a study of problems related to reducing AM channel spacing—the dial distance between stations—from 10 kHz to 9 kHz.[48]

In addition to telling regulatory agencies what to do, Congress can tell them not to do something. This has rarely happened at the FCC, but a good example of how far Congress will go with that tactic is the mandated termination of several controversial Federal Trade Commission proceedings in 1980. In May of that year, Congress passed an FTC budget authorization but expressly prohibited the Commission from using appropriated funds to cancel any trademark on the ground that it had become a common descriptive name, to promulgate a proposed rule regarding funeral industry trade practices, or to investigate certain activities of agricultural trade cooperatives.[49] Of particular importance to the broadcast industry, Congress prohibited the FTC from using appropriated funds to use its rule-making powers in order to prohibit "unfair" advertising.[50] This, in effect, killed a longstanding FTC inquiry into children's television advertising. The FTC's proposals to ban or restrict advertising to children had been built on a theory that such advertising was, by its nature, unfair.

Finally, Congress can exercise its power of the purse through the overall level of appropriations approved for an agency. If appropriated funds are below needs or are cut, then the agency must set priorities and often cannot do all that it might want to do. Indeed, some believe that the FCC's initiatives toward deregulation in the 1980s stem as much from a desire to reduce and rearrange its own workload as they do from a desire to provide relief for regulated industries. When ordered by the Reagan administration to cut approximately $4.8 million from its budget and 8 percent in personnel during development of the fiscal year 1982 FCC budget, the Commission responded by cautioning Congress that delays in broadcast license applications would be likely, that there might be less economic-based research useful in common carrier cases, that the Commissioners might participate less in international conferences, and that nine offices outside Washington, D.C. would probably be closed.[51]

Stress on congressional control through exercise of the power of the purse, however, should not be carried too far. Compared to the mountainous total federal budget, the FCC's budget appropriation amounts to but a molehill. In recent years the FCC's budget has equaled just slightly over one-ten thousandth of the total U.S. budget.[52] Congress pays attention to such a budget, but perhaps not quite as much attention as it pays to the budgets for defense or social services. Nevertheless, the budgeting process illustrates, perhaps more vividly than any other, the myth of the FCC's "independent status." One of the clearest indications ever given that Congress understands the lack of independence came in a conference committee report accompanying the fiscal year 1982 federal budget. In that budget Congress switched the status of the FCC from that of a permanently authorized agency to one given only a two-year authorization. As the conference committee explained:

In adopting this provision the conferees believe that Congress is exercising its appropriate role to ensure that the American people benefit from competition and deregulation. It is appropriate, therefore, that Congress be given the opportunity for regular and systematic oversight of the FCC's implementation of Congressional policy. A two-year authorization instead of the prior permanent authorization for the FCC will provide that opportunity.

Regular and systematic oversight will increase Commission accountability for the implementation of Congressional policy. Congress will benefit from greater exposure to the Commission's expertise on the policy implications presented by the new telecommunications services made possible by rapidly changing technologies. The Commission, in turn, will have a better appreciation of Congressional intent.[53]

THE SPUR OF INVESTIGATIONS

Throughout its nearly fifty-year history, perhaps no federal agency has been as frequent a target of vilification and prolonged investigation by Congress as the FCC. From its inception through the early 1960s, the Commission was almost always under a congressional investigation or the threat of one. The frequency and intensity of broad-ranging investigations of the Commission seem to have slackened in the 1970s and early 1980s, but at the same time Congress and related government institutions have hardly abandoned the strategy of an occasional intensive examination.[54] As a former FCC staff member once noted, the FCC is "viewed by its progenitors on Capitol Hill as a delinquent creature, not to be trusted, and requiring frequent discipline."[55]

In its early days there were frequent investigations where the entire operation of the FCC was dissected under klieg lights by hostile committees. One of the most heated of such investigations occurred in the early 1940s, when Representative Eugene Cox of Georgia, a one-time FCC supporter, turned hostile critic. Cox sponsored a resolution calling for the establishment of a select committee to scrutinize the organization, personnel, and activities of the Commission.[56] Just a few years later, between 1957 and 1961, the House Subcommittee on Legislative Oversight, led by Representative Oren Harris (D-Arkansas), conducted a sustained series of investigations into FCC proprieties that, among other things, led to the resignations of Commissioner Richard Mack and Chairman John C. Doerfer. More than twenty years later, the strain of those investigations was vivid in the memory of Commissioner Robert E. Lee:

> I remember Frank Stanton telling me at one time that his research guys reported we were on the front page of the *New York Times* something like 30 days in a row, or some awful figure. It was uncomfortable; you were waiting for the other shoe to drop. And the gumshoes were all over you; they were coming in and wanting to see your phone calls, if you kept a list, and look at your correspondence. They'd come in the office and rifle through stuff.[57]

Despite possible debilitating effects on the Commission, congressional investigations have helped keep the FCC viable by focusing attention on problems posed by new technologies, by eliciting constructive approaches to deficient areas of regulation, or by uncovering areas where new legislation is necessary. The Harris investigations uncovered "payola" in the recording and broadcast industries, rigged television quiz shows, and licensing improprieties. They led to changes in the Communications Act giving the FCC more authority to act against or prevent such practices.

Up until the 1970s most of the labor involved in investigations (and oversight) was performed by the members and staff of congressional committees and subcommittees. In the 1970s, budgets and staff sizes were expanded, increasing Congress's ability to conduct investigations. At the same time Congress created or expanded a number of other organizations, giving them investigatory powers or responsibilities. The Congressional Research Service, expanded in function and strengthened by the Legislative Reorganization Act of 1970, maintains a large staff to assist members of Congress by evaluating legislative proposals, analyzing testimony, and preparing background memoranda. The Congressional Budget Office, created in 1974, provides members of Congress with detailed budgeting and fiscal information. The Office of Technology Assessment (OTA), authorized in 1972, plays a minor role in providing information to Congress on the impacts, both beneficial and adverse, of technological applications. It also identifies policy alternatives for technology-related issues. In 1974 Congress authorized the General Accounting Office (GAO) to provide assistance in congressional investigation and oversight. During the 1970s the GAO prepared several studies of FCC activities. To increase pressure on agencies to act on GAO findings, Congress requires agencies to respond within sixty days of a GAO report, both to congressional committees and the Office of Management and Budget.[58]

Congress has also created independent groups to conduct investigations and studies affecting broadcasting. The most significant of these has been the U.S. Commission on Civil Rights, started by Congress in 1957. The Commission on Civil Rights has been concerned with equal employment opportunity in industries regulated by the Federal Communications Commission and with depiction of minorities and women in broadcast programs.[59]

Investigations conducted by Congress and related agencies between 1970 and 1980 can be divided into four types: (1) fairly narrow investigations of specific FCC actions, (2) broader investigations into controversial industry issues, (3) investigations of FCC structure and operation, and (4) broadcast-related investigations not exclusively, or even primarily, targeted at the FCC. Investigations into specific actions are fairly rare, although criticism of recent FCC actions often works its way into congressional oversight hearings (discussed later in this chapter). In 1970 the House Investigations Subcommittee held a closed-door investigation of the FCC's inquiry into the operations of an Indiana broadcaster who eventually lost several radio station licenses.[60] In 1977 and 1978 the same subcommittee, under a different chairman, concluded that the FCC was lax in enforcing the conflict of interest provisions of the Communications Act that limit communications-related stockholdings by Commissioners and staff.[61] Plans by the FCC, in 1980–1981, to move from Washington, D.C., to nearby Rosslyn, Virginia, were investigated by several congressional subcommittees. In at least two instances, GAO or Congressional Research Service investigations were initiated by congressional committees. One concluded that the FCC could do something it said it could not do—create a fee schedule that would charge broadcasters (and others) for FCC services.[62] The other study advised the FCC that it could not do something it did not particularly want to do—require that cable television systems obtain broadcasters' consent prior to "retransmitting" copyrighted programs, as was being urged by the president's National Telecommunications and Information Administration.[63]

A number of investigations focused on controversial or even scandalous aspects of broadcast station and network operations. Until the mid-1970s, one of the favorite topics of such investigations was television violence. In part the reason was that the chairmen of Senate and House Communications Subcommittees during much of this time, Representative Torbert Macdonald (D-Massachusetts) and Senator John Pastore (D-Rhode Island), both made personal crusades against TV violence. Pastore had been responsible for the creation of the Surgeon General's Advisory Committee on Television and Social Behavior, which concluded a study of television violence in 1972.[64] Violence remained a continual topic at Congressional oversight hearings, in both houses of Congress, until about 1977, when Congressman Lionel Van Deerlin (D-California) replaced Macdonald as Chairman and inherited yet another violence investigation in progress. Van Deerlin wanted to move forward with his planned "rewrite" of the Communications Act of 1934 and saw the violence investigation—which had become a topic of great concern to the broadcast networks and hence controversial within the Subcommittee—as a diversion from his broader objective. In addition, he had First Amendment reservations about government regulation of violent content and quickly brought the investigation to a close.[65]

As far as scandal went, the House Investigations Subcommittee conducted a brief inquiry into payola allegedly associated with guest appearances on late-night talk shows,[66] held hearings into claimed "news staging" by networks,[67] and made the targets of investigation two CBS documentaries—a planned documentary on a never executed invasion of Haiti and a celebrated examination of Defense Department public relations, "The Selling of the Pentagon."[68] During the latter investigation, Representative Harley Staggers (D-West Virginia), chairman of the Subcommittee, demanded "out-takes" (unused film) from CBS so his subcommittee could judge whether the network had distorted the comments of those interviewed. CBS argued the out-takes were analogous to a reporter's private notes and protected by the First Amendment. The battle over a contempt of Congress citation, resulting from CBS President Frank Stanton's refusal to obey a Commerce Committee subpoena, was fought ultimately on the floor of the House largely on the constitutional issue. But a fear was also voiced by some in Congress that the power of television, especially the networks, had gone unchecked for too long. In the end the resolution citing Stanton for contempt was effectively rejected when the House, by a vote of 226 to 181, recommitted it to the Commerce Committee.[69]

Several years later, the House Communications Subcommittee put TV sports under a microscope. It examined winner-take-all CBS tennis tournaments that were not exactly as advertised; allegedly fixed ABC boxing matches; and, for the sake of equanimity, NBC's relationship with the Soviet Union concerning its proposed coverage of the 1980 Olympic Games. For that investigation, the Subcommittee hired an outside special counsel and brought high network officials to Capitol Hill. ABC and CBS promised reforms to prevent future irregularities, while NBC emerged generally unscathed with a subcommittee finding that the Olympics, if covered, would still be under NBC's rather than the Soviet's control.[70] During this time period as well the Senate Subcommittee on Alcoholism and Narcotics investigated TV's depiction of alcohol and alcohol abuse and concluded that more industry self-regulation was needed;[71] the House Select Committee on Aging examined how the elderly were shown in television programs;[72] and Senator Philip Hart's (D-Michigan) Antitrust Subcommittee attempted to determine if the television industry was trying to "warehouse" (purchase without expectation of use) films in order to prevent them from becoming available to cable television.[73]

The FCC has long been criticized for delay, bad management, poor planning, and other organizational or operational sins. It became subject to congressional investigation about such matters in the late 1970s when subcommittees in both the Senate and House focused on general regulatory agency "reform." Examinations of how the FCC has functioned have ranged from the arguably petty—a complaint by Representative Staggers that nine of thirty-four law school graduates hired by the FCC in 1972 failed the bar examination the first time they took it[74] —to much more substantial complaints. In 1975, Congressman John Moss (D-California) assumed control of the House Subcommittee on Oversight and Investigations and immediately began a comprehensive study of several regulatory agencies. The Subcommittee's report, *Federal Regulation and Regulatory Reform,* was the product of nearly two years of investigation that included 28 days of public hearings, some 220 witnesses from both government and the private sector, a hearing record of 3,500 pages, and extensive written submissions from individuals and agencies.[75] The FCC's answer to the subcommittee's 96-question inquiry required 1,800 hours to prepare and nearly 20,000 pages to present, if one counts supporting documents also sought by Moss.[76] The study ranked the agencies by measuring several aspects of their performance, including such criteria as fidelity to Congress's public protection mandate, the quality and quantity of agency activity, the effectiveness of agency enforcement programs, and the quality of public participation. The subcommittee ranked the nine agencies by three grades (top, middle, and bottom) and placed the FCC in the middle grade. Justifying this ranking, the report noted:

The Federal Communications Commission has shown signs only recently of loosening its close relationship with the broadcasting and telephone industries. It has begun to encourage competition in the sale of telephone equipment and has opened more of the television market to cable television.[77]

The Commission has not always fared as well in other congressional investigations of its efficiency or its policies.[78] The House Subcommittee on Administrative Law was so convinced in 1975 that the FCC was a major "sinner" in terms of regulatory delay that it made the Commission the first target of several days of hearings into the causes of delay.[79] In 1977, after an eighteen-month study Senator Abraham Ribicoff's (D-Connecticut) Committee on Governmental Affairs used the FCC's comparative renewal process, discussed further in chapter eight, as a prime example of unnecessary bureaucratic delay and singled out the Commission for a generally poor record of citizen participation in agency proceedings.[80] The Ribicoff committee had the Library of Congress's Congressional Research Service conduct a survey of lawyers practicing before regulatory agencies. Seventy-eight percent of the respondents ranked "undue delay in the regulatory process" as one of the three most important problems facing the FCC. Although confident of the integrity of the Commissioners and of the relationship between Commissioners and staff, the lawyers had more doubts about the technical knowledge of the FCC Commissioners[81] than about that of any other agency's commissioners. The staff of the House Communications Subcommittee investigated coordination among the FCC and related White House agencies, the Office of Telecommunications Policy, and the Office of Telecommunications in the Department of Commerce, and found squabbling, power plays, suspicion, and a lack of coordination quite typical.[82] A 1978 study by the General Accounting Office concluded that the FCC was responsible for more "paperwork"—some 30 million man hours per year—on the part of those regulated, than any other government agency.[83]

The GAO has not restricted itself to criticisms of FCC management and efficiency, although those have been the primary areas of its concern. Two GAO studies of the FCC were released in 1979. One, the more traditional for GAO, noted inadequate planning, poor management tools, and little concern about staff utilization, organization, or development.[84] The less traditional GAO report, begun in 1977 on a "self-generated basis" (i.e., not requested by a member of Congress), was much more broad-ranging, as is indicated by its title—*Selected FCC Regulatory Policies: Their Purpose and Consequences for Commercial Radio and Television.* [85] Much more of a substantive rather than management analysis, the GAO recommended indefinite broadcast license terms, use of lotteries to choose among competitors for new licenses, development of quantitative programming standards that would justify renewal of station licenses, and repeal of portions of the Communications Act dealing with treatment of controversial issues of public importance and candidates for public office by broadcast stations. Two years later, another GAO study expressed substantial doubt about the FCC's ability to regulate and monitor the competitive aspects of telephone companies, and implied strong criticism of the FCC's decisions in the 1970s and 1980s to allow AT&T to enter new fields through separate subsidiary corporations.[85a]

Not all investigations related to broadcasting directly involve the FCC. The GAO has concluded that U.S. government-operated international broadcast services—Radio Free Europe and Radio Liberty—"occasionally" broadcast "inaccurate and inflammatory" content, although they generally present an objective image of the United States.[86] It has also investigated the Copyright Royalty Tribunal, a body created by Congress in 1976 to, among other things, collect and distribute copyright license payments made by cable television systems.[87] Two studies, one by the Congressional Research Service[88] and the other by the Office of Technology Assessment,[89] have examined U.S. participation in and preparedness for the 1979 World Administrative Radio Conference, an international meeting dealing with spectrum allocation policies. These studies cover the FCC but also other participants, mainly the Departments of State and Commerce. Jumping into the fray of a controversy between the House of Representatives, the Senate, and the broadcast industry, another Congressional Research Service investigation concluded that if broadcasters were charged fees they could not exceed the costs of regulation.[90] The study had been requested by Senator Barry Goldwater (R-Arizona). Its findings were generally in accord with his views on spectrum charges and matched broadcaster views of the maximum level of such fees. These views were contrary to those on the subject held by the House Communications Subcommittee and Senate Democrats. Finally, in 1979 the House Small Business Committee conducted an investigation of Small Business Administration loan programs after such loans first became available for broadcast industry investments. The administration's objective had been to stimulate minority ownership of broadcast properties, but it turned out that only seven of the first thirty-two grants went to minority businesses.[91]

As can be seen, investigations related to broadcasting by the Congress are frequent and varied. There seems to be a slight tendency for them to have partisan motivations. Chairman Wiley's Republican-controlled FCC was subjected to more investigations (and tougher oversight hearings, as will be discussed shortly) by a Democratic Congress than was Charles Ferris's FCC under the Carter administration and a Democratic Congress. Whether such investigations are harmful or salutary, partisan or nonpartisan, however, they have one inevitable result. Their specific findings may not all be acted upon, but the general effect of continued congressional investigative activities is to further attune the FCC and other governmental groups involved in broadcasting to the wishes and expectations of Congress.

THE POWER OF ADVICE AND CONSENT

The statutory limitation on the tenure of Commissioners and the requirement that the Senate confirm their appointments provide Congress with another means of controlling the FCC. The late Senator Edwin Johnson, former chairman of the Senate Commerce Committee, believed that "the existing system of giving the Executive the appointive power to the Commissions which are the arms of Congress is basically unsound" since "it is only natural that those who owe their jobs to the Executive would be reluctant to oppose Executive policy and suggestions." He suggested that the appointive power be vested in the Speaker of the House and the confirmation requirement remain with the Senate.[92] Although this suggestion was not adopted, it is indicative of congressional suspicions about executive appointments. In the first three years of the Federal Radio Commission's existence, from 1927 until 1930, a distrustful Congress limited the tenure of Commissioners to one year.

Even with the present seven-year terms (staggered so that the term of only one Commissioner expires in any one year, although additional vacancies may occur through death or resignation), the need for confirmation by the Senate continues to be an important means of congressional control for several reasons. First, before a president makes any nomination requiring Senate approval, there is a custom of consulting senators who are from both the nominee's state and the president's party.[93] Second, if some powerful senator has strong objections to a nomination, opportunities exist to delay or block the appointment.[94] Third, since every presidential appointment or reappointment to the FCC is first passed upon by the Senate Commerce Committee, the opinions on communications matters expressed by individual senators at confirmation hearings are likely to receive careful consideration by new Commissioners. Frequently, in fact, the confirmation process is used by members of Congress to influence the nominee's position on various policy matters. At hearings, senators have tried to extract promises as to the formulation of particular policies or the submission of future reports on specific projects. For example, during the confirmation hearings on the nomination of Glen Robinson, Senator Pastore, a staunch defender of the Fairness Doctrine, expressed concern with a law review article written by Robinson questioning the doctrine's constitutionality. In response to close questioning by Pastore, Robinson promised not to lead a "crusade" to eliminate the doctrine.[95]

A fascinating study, published in 1976 by the Senate Commerce Committee, reviewed the circumstances of appointment of fifty-one members of the FCC and Federal Trade Commission over a twenty-five-year period (1949–1974). The authors, lawyers James Graham and Victor Kramer, recounted the important role played by members of both houses in the appointment process. They found that about one-half of the appointments to the FCC and FTC involved a significant degree of active congressional sponsorship and that fourteen of the Commissioners were appointed—and some subsequently reappointed—almost entirely due to the efforts of a single member of Congress.[96] They concluded that most Commission appointments are the result of "well-stoked campaigns conducted at the right time with the right sponsors, and many selections can be explained in terms of powerful political connections and little else."[97]

In many instances presidents have turned to persons with congressional backgrounds in order to obtain quick confirmations. When one of "their own"—member or staff—is the nominee, Congress will usually not impede confirmation with philosophical inquiries into the individual's views on the relationship between Congress and the regulatory agencies—perhaps because it can be assumed that the nominee is only too aware of what that relationship is and the importance of maintaining it. Thus in 1971, after another nominee proved to be the target of an Internal Revenue Service audit, President Nixon nominated a member of Congress, Charlotte Reid (R-Illinois), as a replacement. Reid was quickly confirmed.[98]

Congressionally related nominations can also be used to solve a problem presidents sometimes have in filling vacancies near the end of their terms. Because control of the White House may shift with the election, Congress, especially when controlled by a party different from that of the president, is usually hesitant to confirm the appointments of what may be an outgoing chief executive. Other political considerations may also block end-of-term appointments. Thus, former broadcaster James Quello, whose term expired in June 1980, was left on the FCC through the end of the Carter administration and into the Reagan administration, which eventually, at the strong urging of broadcasters, reappointed him.[99] Hispanics preferred an appointment from their ranks, but Italian-Americans urged Carter to reappoint Quello. Carter, in order to avoid offending anyone, chose not to act to renominate or replace Quello prior to the election and, after his loss in November 1980, congressional tradition dictated that the vacancy be held open for President Reagan.

The only recent exception to this pattern of inability to make appointments at the end of presidential terms came near the end of the Ford presidency when two vacancies occurred. Ford proposed to appoint Republican Margita White, a member of his White House staff, to a full seven-year term. To make the appointment attractive to congressional Democrats, he planned to name Joseph Fogarty, then counsel to the Senate Communications Subcommittee, to a two-year term created by a resignation. Eventually Ford was forced to switch the terms— White for two years and Fogarty for seven—but the opportunity for two appointments, one of which could be filled in a fashion highly attractive to Congress, permitted Ford to make appointments in a situation other Presidents had found impossible.[100]

President Carter looked to Congress for appointments to the chairmanship of both the Federal Communications Commission and the Federal Trade Commission. Charles Ferris, then counsel to House Speaker Thomas P. O'Neill (D-Massachusetts), was selected for the FCC, while Michael Pertschuk, chief counsel for the Senate Commerce Committee, was named FTC Chairman. As expected, their appointments were easily confirmed.[101] The pattern continued under President Reagan. Although he named a communications lawyer active in his election campaign, Mark S. Fowler, as FCC Chairman, President Reagan almost simultaneously nominated Mary ("Mimi") Weyforth Dawson, an aide to Senator Robert Packwood (D-Oregon), chairman of the Senate Commerce Committee, to an FCC opening.[102]

In the 1970s the Senate's attitude toward the confirmation process underwent significant change. The Senate's failure to confirm two of President Nixon's Supreme Court nominations, Clement Haynsworth and G. Harold Carswell, marked the beginning of a harder look at presidential appointees, even to regulatory agencies. In 1973 Chairman Warren Magnuson (D-Washington) and other Commerce Committee members urged Senate rejection of a nominee to the Federal Power Commission (FPC), Robert H. Morris, on the ground that he had served as counsel to a major oil company subject to FPC jurisdiction for several years. The Senate rejected the Morris nomination by a vote of 49 to 44, the first time in nearly forty years that the Senate had formally voted to reject a nominee to a regulatory agency.[103]

The Senate's increased concern over the quality of regulatory appointments is reflected in Senator Magnuson's remarks to a consumer group in 1973:

We have always given the President—without regard to party—the benefit of the doubt on regulatory appointments—but I must tell you that we have swallowed nominees by [the Nixon administration] who have left a bitter aftertaste, and our tolerance for mediocrity and lack of independence from economic interests is rapidly coming to an end.[104]

President Nixon was forced to withdraw FCC nominations of Sherman Unger, the target of an Internal Revenue Service investigation, and Luther Holcomb, a former vice-chairman of the Equal Employment Opportunity Commission (EEOC). Holcomb had been described as a Democrat, but the discovery of correspondence on EEOC stationery indicating that he had been an active campaigner for Nixon and other Republicans led to withdrawal of his nomination.[105] Partisan politics, however, probably plays a role in Senatorial reaction to White House nominees. Most of the instances just discussed involved nominees by a Republican president examined by a Democratic Congress. Clearly President Reagan, early in his administration, succeeded in gaining confirmation for many appointees with close ties to industries that would be subject to their supervision. In this, he was unquestionably aided by Republican control of the Senate.

One of the major issues surrounding FCC nominations in recent years is the belief by significant interest groups that they should be "represented" on the Commission. Broadcasters were consequently enthusiastic when President Nixon, on September 21, 1973, nominated former broadcaster James Quello for an FCC vacancy. Consumer interest groups, however, objected to Quello—particularly as a replacement for their hero and representative, Nicholas Johnson. The result was an eight-day Senate hearing on Quello's nomination—the longest hearing ever for an FCC nominee—and a seven-month delay in confirmation. When Quello was reappointed by President Reagan, his hearing—combined with that of another FCC nominee—lasted only forty minutes, although there was substantial lag at the White House between announcement of the intention to reappoint and transmittal of necessary papers to Congress.[106]

Feminist and minority groups have also pressured Congress and the president to appoint members of their constituencies as FCC Commissioners. Although the first woman to serve on the FCC was Frieda B. Hennock, appointed in 1948, no tradition of a continuous representation of women on the FCC was established until Nixon's appointment of Congresswoman Reid. Reid was succeeded by Margita White, herself followed by Anne Jones, general counsel for the Federal Home Loan Bank Board, appointed by President Carter. With Dawson's 1981 appointment by President Reagan, the FCC for the first time had two women serving simultaneously.

In 1971 and 1972 Senator Pastore insisted that President Nixon appoint a black to the FCC. He refused to take action on Nixon nominees until a black appointee, who would prove to be Judge Benjamin Hooks, was announced for the next vacancy.[107] After Hooks resigned to assume leadership of the NAACP, President Carter replaced him with a black communications attorney, Tyrone Brown. When Brown resigned, immediately following President Reagan's election, he included the following in his resignation letter to outgoing President Carter:

I hope that your successor will recognize, as you did, that minority representation at the Commissioner level is very important. Such an appointment is
not merely a matter of "tokenism"; it reflects an understanding that minority
representation at the Commissioner level is the most effective way to assure
that minority perspectives are considered during the agency's deliberations.[108]

Brown's language about "minority representation" seems very carefully chosen. Throughout the Carter administration, Hispanic leaders
had urged the White House and Congress to appoint a Hispanic to the
FCC. Hispanics supported Reagan more forcefully than blacks during
the 1980 election, so it was not surprising that with Reagan's inaugura-
tion, the president was under even more pressure to name the first
Hispanic to the FCC. Reagan's staff settled on Henry Rivera, an attorney, as Brown's replacement. Rivera, not coincidentally, was from New
Mexico, home state of Senator Harrison Schmitt, an important Republican member of the Senate Communications Subcommittee facing reelection, whose support Rivera received.[109]

CONTINUING WATCHFULNESS OF
STANDING COMMITTEES

Under the Legislative Reorganization acts of 1946 and 1970, each
standing committee of the Senate and the House "shall review and
study on a continuing basis, the application, administration, and execu-
tion" by administrative agencies of any law within its jurisdiction.[110]
The House Committee on Energy and Commerce and the Senate Committee on Commerce, Science and Transportation make the studies in
communications areas, and those committees have prime responsibility
for the initiation and consideration of legislation affecting broadcasting
and related industries. In practice, most of the responsibilities are exercised by subcommittees; currently the Telecommunications, Consumer
Protection, and Finance Subcommittee in the House and the Communications Subcommittee in the Senate. In theory the watchfulness of
these committees and subcommittees is exercised in two main ways—
by hearings on proposed legislation and by more general oversight
hearings on agency activities. In practice it is sometimes difficult to
distinguish between the two activities. Between 1976 and 1980, while
considering his proposed "rewrites" of the Communications Act of
1934, Congressman Van Deerlin's House Communications Subcommittee all but dispensed with formally designated oversight hearings and
instead performed its oversight functions within the context of hearings
on Van Deerlin's bills. Where once oversight hearings were regularly
scheduled annual activities, during the years when comprehensive
Communications Act rewrites were being considered, they occurred

with unpredictable frequency. Some regularity seemed to return in 1981. As always, such oversight hearings, when held, were all too often either prompted by, or at least dominated by, issues of the moment. As former Commissioner Robinson has noted, formal oversight hearings often are something of a ritual and not always terribly productive:

> To begin with, the attendance of committee members tends to be spotty at best. It is not uncommon for the seven FCC Commissioners, accompanied by twenty or more top staff members, to appear before a subcommittee of one—the chairman. . . . Another problem is that those members who do attend often are not prepared adequately to exercise their oversight function. . . . Thus, agency members and their staff come to the hearings armed with documents and materials that may have taken several man-months to prepare, to be confronted all too often with trivial questions about the closing of a telegraph office in a Congressman's district or the latest "equal time" case or programming complaints. . . . After several hours of such maneuvers, the Congressmen and agency members retire to their respective lairs to resume their previous tasks. The record of the session is then assembled and shipped to the Government Printing Office to be put in a suitable printed form for burial in appropriate libraries and archives.[111]

Things are not always quite as bad as Robinson suggests. One of the potential advantages of frequent contact between an agency and a standing committee is that the members and staff of the committee acquire the substantive knowledge necessary to meet the agency's officials in a battle of the experts. As a result of such a continuing relationship, there develops in some cases "a healthy mutual respect between the committee and administrator, both of whom have a common objective and, in substantial measure, a common fund of information."[112] Congress's decision in 1981 to convert the FCC from a permanently authorized agency to one requiring reauthorization every two years may increase the power of the standing committees, which must approve or disapprove of the reauthorization. This would be on top of the continuing—annual—watchfulness of the appropriations subcommittees that review the agency's requests for funds. (Complaints have sometimes been made about lack of coordination between the appropriations and communications subcommittees.)

Standing committees frequently are able to have a major impact on agency decisions merely by holding hearings. During such sessions committee members can communicate their views to a captive audience of FCC Commissioners, who usually try to portray themselves as flexible, hard-working members of a public-spirited agency.[113] The history of congressional supervision of the FCC is replete with examples where policies of the Commission were shaped by a single committee or its chairman, often without even an official policy directive.

The FCC pays more than passing attention to suggestions made during FCC oversight hearings. At such hearings in 1971, and in a subsequent letter the late Representative Torbert Macdonald (then House Communications Subcommittee Chairman) suggested to FCC Chairman Dean Burch that the Commission establish a Children's Television Bureau to deal with programming and advertising aimed at young people. After several months of private discussion on the matter with Macdonald and his staff, Burch announced on September 14, 1971, that the Commission had decided to establish such an office and planned to staff it with experts in the field who would be prominently involved in advising the Commission on children's programming. After Burch left the FCC and Macdonald died, however, the special office faded into the background, with children's issues being considered by the Office of Plans and Policy and by special "task forces" related to a subsequent children's television inquiry. In a March 1980 budget hearing, that for practical purposes became an oversight hearing, Representative Mark Andrews (R-North Dakota) complained to Chairman Ferris that a November 23, 1979, letter from Andrews had not been acknowledged by the FCC until early February 1980, and that there was still no answer from the Commission. Ferris said he had "no explanation nor . . . an excuse" for the delay.[114] When he returned to the FCC, he ordered that all pending congressional correspondence be answered in one week. There were, it turned out, more than 700 such letters waiting just within the Broadcast Bureau.[115]

As has been noted, congressional interest in broadcasting was, to a very large extent, absorbed in broad efforts to rewrite the Communications Act of 1934, during the years between 1976 and the early 1980s. That process meant that almost every topic related to electronic communications was addressed by the congressional committees during hearings and investigations related to the rewrite process. Looking beyond that process, which is described in detail in chapter nine, the array of topics treated in other hearings is surprisingly limited and predictable. During the 1970s several perennial issues returned to congressional attention repeatedly. One area of frequent interest was that of sexual, violent, or "drug-related" content on broadcast stations and cable television and the somewhat related concern about providing appropriate programming for children.

Also attracting frequent attention was the regulation of cable television and its cognate issue, copyright policy toward cable television systems. Congress also was involved almost continually in supporting (or criticizing) FCC efforts to provide equal employment opportunity in broadcasting for minorities and women and to improve ownership opportunities for those groups in the industry. It dealt occasionally, as well, with advertising issues, especially advertising oriented toward children. And it was concerned with the FCC's spectrum management policies, especially those related to international treaties and conferences; with problems of creating VHF-TV service for New Jersey and Delaware, the only two states without indigenous commercial VHF-TV stations; with the "hardships" faced by UHF-TV stations competing with VHF for audiences and revenues; and with telecommunications services for rural areas of the United States. It also examined FCC treatment of religious broadcasters, the Commission's policies and limitations on ownership and proposals to make more information public about the financial affairs of stations. At the urging of the broadcast industry, oversight hearings repeatedly examined FCC station renewal policy, both in general and, on occasion, with regard to specific stations. In a somewhat self-interested vein, Congress took the Commission to task over rulings interpreting the laws regarding political broadcasting. Finally, the FCC, like many other administrative agencies, was examined for its policies toward public participation in its decision making, its responsiveness to consumers, the open meetings it held, and any delay it caused.

SUPERVISION BY MULTIPLE COMMITTEES

Although the commerce and appropriations committees and subcommittees perform most of the oversight in the communications area, during the past decade the number of other congressional committees which have become involved in the area has increased substantially. As William Cary, who served four years as Chairman of the Securities and Exchange Commission, once commented, such supervision of agency policies "is sometimes wearing, almost unendurable, but is an integral part of the system."[116] Supervision by multiple committees allows more members of Congress, representing a greater range of interests, to have a voice in agency policies, but it often leads to duplication and overlapping legislative review.

Nearly fifty congressional committees and subcommittees attempted to review some aspect of the FCC's regulatory practices and policies between 1970 and 1981. Aspects of the FCC's regulation of cable television, for example, were studied by the committees (or subcommittees) on the judiciary and government operations, as well as by the commerce committees. Copyright was examined by the judiciary committees of both houses, which also considered antitrust implications of FCC activities and several problems related to broadcast journalism (e.g., "shield laws" to protect journalists from being compelled to disclose confidential sources). Committees related to small business in both houses examined issues such as media concentration, so-called all-channel (AM/FM) radio legislation, FCC spectrum allocation policies, and advertising regulation. The Senate Agriculture Committee held hearings on rural telecommunications and committees on science and astronautics examined extraterrestrial communications through hearings into satellite policy. Satellites were also examined by the House Foreign Relations Committee, while it and its Senate counterpart examined international telecommunications treaties. The Senate Select Committee on Alcoholism and Narcotics looked into depiction of alcohol consumption on television, while the House Select Committee on Aging examined how the aged were portrayed. Committees on government operations and government affairs of both houses examined such issues as regulatory reform, fees charged regulated industries, open meetings, and FCC responsiveness to consumer interests.

The FCC is obviously a busy testifier before Congress. In the second session of the 96th Congress in 1980, the FCC testified at twelve committee or subcommittee hearings, ten in the House of Representatives and only two in the Senate. Of these appearances, only three were before a communications subcommittee. The others were before such diverse groups as the Consumer Subcommittee of the Senate Committee on Commerce, Science and Transportation (interested in the activities of FCC administrative law judges) and the Subcommittee on Civil Service, House Committee on Post Office and Civil Service (which wanted to know how the FCC was implementing the Civil Service Reform Act of 1978).[117] Such a schedule places heavy demands on the FCC Chairman. In an interview on the eve of his departure from the Commission after twenty-eight years of service, former FCC Chairman Robert E. Lee observed, "I have no regrets about leaving. I think the thing that made up my mind . . . was my four months as Chairman. It was real pain, particularly in testifying. I made 11 appearances on Capitol Hill."[118]

On broad or complex issues, several committees may be involved simultaneously. When the Communications Satellite Act of 1962 was under consideration, FCC Commissioners testified before nine committees and subcommittees—the House Committee on Science and Astronautics, the House Committee on Interstate and Foreign Commerce, the Communications Subcommittee of the Senate Committee on Commerce, the Senate Committee on Aeronautical and Space Science, the Senate Committee on Commerce, the Senate Committee on Foreign Relations, the Antitrust Subcommittee of the House Judiciary Committee, the Subcommittee on Monopoly of the Senate Select Committee on Small Business, and the Subcommittee on Antitrust and Monopoly of the Senate Judiciary Committee. When the Commission, in late 1980 and early 1981, contemplated an eventually abandoned move from the District of Columbia to Rosslyn, Virginia—just across the Potomac River—it attracted the attention of an incredible number of committees and subcommittees. In addition to being discussed by the House Telecommunications, Consumer Protection, and Finance subcommittees and the Senate Communications Subcommittee, the proposed move was examined by at least five other congressional units—a House appropriations subcommittee, the House District of Columbia Committee, the Senate Environment and Public Works Committee, the House Subcommittee on Public Buildings and Grounds, and the Senate Subcommittee on Limitation of Contracted and Delegated Authority. The FCC's proposed move was also the object of a GAO investigation.

The involvement of committees other than the commerce committees and their subcommittees normally involved in communications issues can pose some difficulties to interest groups seeking to influence congressional behavior. There was substantial concern, for example, when in 1974 it appeared that legislation dealing with license renewal standards, which the broadcast industry strongly desired, might be examined by the Antitrust Subcommittee of the Senate Judiciary Committee. Such a delay would have killed the bill for that session of Congress, and broadcast interests fought to avoid examination of it by additional committees.[119] Activity of other committees can force interest groups to work in unfamiliar surroundings, but they can nonetheless have an influence. After studies suggested that saccharin caused cancer Senator Edward Kennedy (D-Massachusetts) proposed a bill that, among other things, would have required health warnings in radio and TV ads for products containing saccharin. Because the ads would have been hard to do within the time constraints of broadcast advertising, broadcast interest groups fought Kennedy's bill vigorously. In this, they had to deal both with Kennedy's Health Subcommittee of the Senate Commerce Committee and, eventually, with the entire Senate as they attempted to avoid a Senate floor vote. On this issue, broadcast interests prevailed, defeating Kennedy's bill. The episode led Senator Ernest ("Fritz") Hollings, (D-South Carolina), newly named chairman of the Senate Communications Subcommittee and a Kennedy bill supporter, to comment: "Rather than a chairman of a subcommittee, I felt like a foreman of a fixed jury."[120]

PRESSURES OF INDIVIDUAL MEMBERS
OF CONGRESS AND STAFF

Although it is difficult to measure their impact, the actions of individuals in Congress and their staff frequently are influential in shaping the course and direction of FCC policy. Newton Minow pointed out that "it is easy—very easy—to confuse the voice of one congressman, or one congressional committee, with the voice of Congress."[121] More recently, Commissioner Robert E. Lee, in a farewell address to the Federal Communications Bar Association, observed:

Every Commissioner is tested in his or her early days by requests for special attention. Many times these requests are legitimate; they seek redress for unreasonable delay or bureaucratic red tape. Of course one must respond. But, if special favors are granted, the requests never stop and one finds 535 bosses calling the tune.[122]

Professor Kenneth Culp Davis contends that the day-to-day influence of members of Congress may be even more important to agencies than committee hearings and that individual influence seldom comes to public attention. He cites as an example private meetings between the chairman of the House Commerce Committee and the Chairman of the FCC for the purpose of "working over" cable regulations prior to their being issued by the Commission in 1968.[123]

The influence of congressional staff members cannot be overlooked either. The staff members of the relevant congressional committees maintain a close liaison with the FCC and impart committee members' views and expectations to the Commissioners, personnel of the FCC's Legislation Division, and other Commission staff members. A 1975 Senate study found that staff communication with agency personnel was the technique used most frequently by Congress in overseeing the operation of regulatory agencies.[124] Although committee staff members usually have low visibility (with Nicholas Zapple, former counsel to the Senate Communications Subcommittee, and Harry Shooshan III, former counsel to the House Communications Subcommittee, being notable exceptions)[125], many, especially lawyers, play a crucial role both in shaping the body of laws and in overseeing the activities of regulatory agencies.

Individual members of Congress can influence not only the FCC but also the broadcast industry. In April 1970, for example, Representative Paul Rogers (D-Florida) wrote letters to pharmaceutical companies, major television networks, the National Association of Broadcasters, the FTC, and the Food and Drug Administration seeking to restrict television advertisements of mood-altering drugs. Late the following fall Rogers announced that the NAB had adopted guidelines, to become effective February 1, 1971, on advertisements for nonprescription drugs, including stimulants, calmatives, and sleeping aids.

The significance of an individual or group of Congressmen and women to the FCC can be seen in the case of Tennessee Senator Howard Baker, who, when serving as ranking minority member of the Senate Communications Subcommittee, played a key role in a controversial proposal initiated by the United Church of Christ (UCC) to "drop in" (add at less than normal geographic distances) ninety-six VHF television channels. In March 1977 the FCC, by a vote of 4 to 2, proposed to consider assigning short-spaced VHF drop-ins in Knoxville, Tennessee (as strongly urged by Senator Baker), and three other markets. *Broadcasting*, in an editorial entitled "Nobody's Baby," commented:

It's obvious . . . that nobody on the FCC is enthusiastic about this proceeding. Maybe there is something to those reports that the rule-making was forced upon the FCC by the insistence of Senate Minority Leader Howard H. Baker (R-Tenn.) that a V be dropped into Knoxville, Tenn. The assumption is that the commission had to include some other markets to reduce the visibility of the Knoxville accommodation.

At the end the FCC will have to decide whether the public as well as Senator Baker and the interests he represents would be served by these proposals.[126]

In 1980 the Commission approved four short-spaced VHF-TV channels, including one for Knoxville, Tennessee.[127]

During the 1970s individual members of Congress have participated actively in FCC proceedings involving the enforcement of the Fairness Doctrine and Section 315, the equal opportunities provision of the Communications Act. For example, Representative Patsy Mink (D-Hawaii), the sponsor of an anti-strip-mining bill, filed a Fairness Doctrine complaint with the FCC in 1974 against a Clarksburg, West Virginia, radio station that refused to broadcast an eleven-minute program supporting her legislation. In 1976 the FCC cited the station for not covering the local strip-mining controversy at all.[128] The decision was the first Commission ruling that a station, as part of its obligation under the Fairness Doctrine, had to cover a specific controversial issue of public importance because of its extreme significance to the station's community.

Another member of Congress was involved in a court decision that paved the way for the League of Women Voters to sponsor and televise a series of presidential and vice-presidential debates. In 1975 the FCC issued a ruling exempting from the equal opportunities requirement the press conferences of candidates and political debates controlled by third parties.[129] Representative Shirley Chisholm (D-New York), together with the Democratic National Committee and the National Organization for Women, appealed the FCC decision to the U.S. Court of Appeals for the District of Columbia Circuit, which upheld the Commission.[130] Later, during the 1976 presidential campaign, former Senator Eugene McCarthy (D-Minnesota) was unsuccessful in persuading the courts either to block the Carter-Ford debates or to order him included in them.

Individual members of Congress also have participated in the process by which the FCC writes and revises rules and regulations through filing comments with the Commission on proposed rules. Sometimes their participation is actively sought by parties concerned with the outcome of such proceedings. In 1974, for example, advocates of relaxed rules for pay-cable services celebrated when eight members of Congress filed comments in an FCC proceeding that proposed easier access to programming by pay-cable operators.[131]

The creation of the Congressional Black Caucus has added another dimension to the ways in which individual members of Congress can exert pressure on the FCC. The caucus had its genesis in 1970 when black members of the House first began to work together on specific issues. Early in 1972 the caucus created a Task Force on the Media, which has held public hearings, conducted conferences, issued position papers, and participated in FCC rule-making proceedings on issues pertaining to minority ownership, employment, and programming. Also influential has been the Congressional Wives Task Force, a bipartisan group of some fifty wives of U.S. senators and representatives, who in 1977 and 1978 issued two reports on television programming.[132] Although seeming to favor industry self-regulation as the primary way to reduce violence and improve children's programming and advertising, the task force also said it would "actively pursue the appointment of commissioners to the FCC who will represent the interests of viewers rather than those of broadcasters."[133]

Not every approach from members of Congress, however, is successful. For years members of the New Jersey and Delaware congressional delegations have tried to get the FCC to establish commercial VHF-TV stations in their states, the only ones in the United States without such service. They have also attempted to elicit support from their congressional colleagues for legislation to accomplish this end. So far, their efforts have failed both with the FCC and with Congress, although the Commission has responded with several proceedings designed to improve attention to New Jersey by New York and Philadelphia VHF-TV stations and to increase UHF-TV coverage of the state.[134] In 1980 Representative Robert Kastenmeier (D-Wisconsin), then chairman of the House Subcommittee on Courts, Civil Liberties and the Administration of Justice, and Tom Railsback (R-Illinois), ranking minority member of the same subcommittee, both cautioned FCC Chairman Charles Ferris against additional FCC relaxation of rules regarding cable television's use of copyrighted broadcast programs. Kastenmeier wanted the FCC to hold off until his subcommittee could further consider contemplated changes in copyright laws regarding cable systems and video programming. Despite these strong objections, however, the FCC went ahead with its rule changes, although subsequent Congresses have continued to consider related changes in copyright law.[135]

The FCC, then, pays substantial attention to individual members of

Congress but does not always do exactly what they want. Congressional frustration with this state of affairs was expressed vividly by former Senator Birch Bayh (D-Indiana) at a campaign meeting with Indiana broadcasters. After saying that he would "frankly welcome" replacement of FCC Chairman Ferris with a new Chairman, Bayh observed:

I worked with Chairman Ferris when he was employed in the Senate and he is a very personable fellow. But I find now that when I write a letter to him voicing concerns of my constituents, all I get back is a letter explaining why he plans to do exactly what he's already decided to do. I think that's enough said.[136]

CONTROL BY LEGISLATIVE INACTION

Inaction by Congress in many instances may have as great an impact on the Commission and others, and on the making of policy, as the actual enactment of legislation. Professor Louis Jaffe contends that where Congress is unable to determine a policy on issues that demand congressional expression, the failure to act should be viewed as an abdication of its legislative authority and a delegation of power to the agency. Jaffe points out that it is not unusual for a problem to be left to administrative determination "because the issue is politically so acute—so much a matter of conflict that Congress is unable to formulate a policy."[137] Such irresolution, however, has not prevented Congress from later responding to a Commission interpretation with hostility. Even when Congress has been willing to delegate important decisions to the Commission, it has reserved the right to criticize and oppose these decisions subsequently. One of the toughest tasks of the FCC, then, is to make crucial decisions when the *wishes* of Congress are quite unclear, but its *presence* is very real.

Congressional failure to act on the issue of subscription pay television (STV) during the 91st Congress (1969–1970) allowed the FCC to authorize STV on a permanent basis. In the previous Congress the House Committee on Interstate and Foreign Commerce had adopted resolutions requesting that the FCC defer final consideration of rules authorizing STV operations. However, in the 91st Congress the House Commerce Committee was almost evenly divided on the issue. After a dispute between the communications subcommittee, which essentially favored the proposed FCC rules, and opponents of STV on the full committee, the House Commerce Committee, by a vote of 15 to 13, approved a bill that would allow STV operations under much more restrictive regulations than those favored by the subcommittee and the FCC. No further action was taken on the bill, and in August 1970 the FCC authorized the first technical system for STV, granting advance approval to Zenith Radio Corporation's Phonevision System.

There have been persistent pleas in the 1970s by the courts, the affected industries, and the FCC itself for congressional guidelines concerning the development of cable television. For example, in a concurring opinion to the Supreme Court's decision in *United States* v. *Midwest Video Corporation,* Chief Justice Warren Burger said congressional action on cable television was imperative. "The almost explosive development of CATV," according to Burger, "suggests the need of a comprehensive reexamination of the statutory scheme as it relates to this new development so that the basic policies are considered by Congress and not left entirely to the Commission and the Courts."[138] Despite such calls for action, and extensive congressional studies,[139] Congress—by inaction—instead has allowed the FCC to set the standards for cable development and growth. In another area, common carrier policy, years of congressional inattention led to a series of FCC decisions that brought competition to many aspects of common carrier telephone service, previously monopolized by AT&T.[140] Congress also has failed to respond to repeated FCC requests for legislative guidance on such key regulatory issues as obscenity and license renewal standards, with the result being that the Commission simply moves forward (or sometimes sideways) as best it can.

As noted in chapter two, Congress, by its failure to act, permitted the creation of an Office of Telecommunications Policy to serve as the president's principal adviser on domestic and international telecommunications policy. Similarly, in 1977 congressional failure to act allowed that office to be abolished. It is interesting to note that the House Government Operations Committee had issued reports in 1965, 1966, and 1967 urging the president to submit a reorganization plan to Congress "to reconstitute the functions and responsibilities of the Director of Telecommunications Management in a separate office in the Executive Office of the President."[141]

In a field such as communications where the interests of powerful industry forces frequently collide with one another as well as with the interests of the general public, nothing is more unsettling to many lawmakers on Capitol Hill than the prospect of making a law! Thus, rather than enact new laws or amend the Communications Act, Congress has preferred to use a variety of informal techniques in directing and overseeing the activities of the FCC. Such informal controls are rarely subject to review by Congress as a whole and enable legislators to advance personal or constituent interests without the need for a full-scale political battle. Hearings, investigations, and studies provide Congress with an effective means of ensuring that the FCC is constantly aware that it is an "arm of Congress."

NOTES

1. Newton N. Minow, *Equal Time: The Private Broadcaster and the Public Interest* (New York: Atheneum, 1964), p. 36.
2. Robert S. McMahon, *The Regulation of Broadcasting*, Study made for the Committee on Interstate and Foreign Commerce, House of Representatives, 85th Congress, 2nd Session (1958), p. viii. See also Glen O. Robinson, "The Federal Communications Commission: An Essay on Regulatory Watchdogs," *Virginia Law Review*, 64 (March 1978), 172, 173–182, 197–203.
3. These policy controversies are examined in chapters seven, eight, and nine.
4. Louis M. Kohlmeier, Jr., *The Regulators: Watchdog Agencies and the Public Interest* (New York: Harper & Row, 1969), p. 67.
5. William W. Boyer, *Bureaucracy on Trial: Policy Making by Government Agencies* (Indianapolis, Ind.: Bobbs-Merrill, 1964), p. 46.
6. See Roger G. Noll, *Reforming Regulation* (Washington, D.C.: Brookings Institution, 1971), p. 35.
7. Newton N. Minow, Review of William Cary's *Politics and the Regulatory Agencies*, in *Columbia Law Review*, 68 (1968), 383–384.
8. Minow, *Equal Time*, p. 35.
9. Boyer, *Bureaucracy on Trial*, p. 42.
10. See "Broadcaster Kin on Capitol Hill," *Broadcasting*, May 7, 1979, p. 65.
11. Quoted in Bruce Thorp, "Washington Pressures," *National Journal*, August 22, 1970, p. 1809.
12. Robinson, "The Federal Communications Commission," 169, 175.
13. Robert MacNeil, *The People Machine: The Influence of Television on American Politics* (New York: Harper & Row, 1968), p. 243, citing Bernard Rubin.
14. An estimated 70 percent of U.S. senators and 60 percent of representatives regularly use such free time. See ibid., p. 246. Since 1972, radio and television stations have been required by Section 312(a)(7) of the Communications Act to "allow reasonable access to or to permit purchase of reasonable amounts of time for the use of a broadcasting station by a legally qualified candidate for Federal elective office on behalf of his candidacy." Because broadcasters under Section 315 of the act must provide "equal opportunities" for candidates for office to use their stations, the effect of Section 312(a)(7) is that, except for news-related programs, candidates appear almost exclusively in paid advertising time.
15. Ibid., p. 243.
16. See 47 U.S.C., Sec. 312(a)(7) and 315. On September 17, 1981, the FCC recommended that Congress repeal Sections 312(a)(7) and 315 of the Communications Act. The Commission maintained that "[o]ne step toward restoring broadcasting to First Amendment parity with the print media is to eliminate arbitrary and mechanical restrictions on both the coverage of political candidates and the sale of broadcast time to them. . . . Repeal should permit greater opportunity for presentation of significant candidates' views to the public." *FCC Legislative Proposals, Track II*, September 17, 1981 [mimeo.], pp. 18–20, 22. The quotation is from p. 22.
17. For an excellent review of the various forms of congressional review of the FCC and other regulatory agencies, see U.S. Senate, *Study on Federal Regulation*, vol. II, *Congressional Oversight of Regulatory Agencies*,

Committee on Government Operations, 95th Congress, 1st Session (1975).
18. Exceptions to this generalization are examined in chapter six, which discusses the All-Channel Receiver law, and in chapters seven and eight, which probe unsuccessful attempts by Congress to pass bills dealing with commercials and license renewal procedures but that nonetheless gave signals to the FCC.
19. An example of Congress's quickly and directly overruling the FCC began when, on February 19, 1959, the FCC ruled that news film clips of Mayor Richard J. Daley entitled a perennial minor candidate, Lar "America First" Daly, to equal opportunities. See *CBS, Inc. (WBBM-TV)*, 18 R.R. 238 (1959). Less than seven months later (September 14, 1959), Congress amended Section 315 to exempt certain news programming from the equal opportunity obligation. See 73 *Stat.* 557 (1959).
20. Louis Jaffe, *Judicial Control of Administrative Action* (Boston: Little, Brown, 1965), p. 48.
21. Federal Election Campaign Act of 1971, Pub. L. 92-225 (February 7, 1972), 86 *Stat.* 3, codified at 47 U.S.C., Secs. 312(a)(7) and 315(b)(1).
22. See *CBS, Inc.* v. *FCC*, _____U.S._____, 101 S.Ct. 2813, 69 L.Ed. 2d 706 (1981) and associated lower court and FCC decisions. In this case, the U.S. Supreme Court strengthened the hand of the FCC and politicians in controlling political uses of broadcasting, and weakened the position of broadcasters.
23. Pub. L. 93-107 (September 14, 1978), 87 *Stat.* 350. By its own terms this law expired December 31, 1975. Congress considered renewing it but never did so. Instead, it decided to rely on the word (and political good sense) of leaders of professional sports that they would continue to operate in the spirit of the law.
24. Public Health Cigarette Smoking Act of 1969, Pub. L. 91-222 (April 1, 1970), 84 *Stat.* 87.
25. Pub. L. 94-553 (July 1, 1976), 90 *Stat.* 794.
26. Communications Act Amendments of 1978, Pub. L. 95-234 (February 21, 1978), 92 *Stat.* 33. In September 1981 the Commission asked Congress to increase the maximum forfeiture for a single offense from $20,000 to $100,000 and to improve FCC methods for collecting the forfeitures when licensees refused to pay. See *FCC Legislative Proposals, Track II*, September 17, 1981 [mimeo.], pp. 27–29.
27. See Omnibus Budget Reconciliation Act of 1981, Pub. L. 97-35 (August 13,1981) especially Section 1243. See also *House Report 97-208, Omnibus Budget Reconciliation Act of 1981, Conference Report to Accompany H.R. 3982*, 97th Congress, 1st Session (July 29, 1981), p. 898. Trade press accounts of the politics of the broadcast sections of the budget bill are found in "Broadcasters Win Big on License Terms," *Broadcasting*, August 3, 1981, pp. 27–28, and "Congress Okays Longer Licenses, Lottery," *Television Digest*, August 3, 1981, pp. 2–3.
28. Copyrights Act, Pub. L. 94-553 (October 19, 1976), 90 *Stat.* 2541, codified at 17 U.S.C.
29. *Cable Television Report and Order*, 36 FCC2d 141, 290 (1972).
30. Pub. L. 93-583 (January 2, 1975), 88 *Stat.* 1916.
31. Privacy Protection Act of 1980, Pub. L. 96-440 (October 13, 1980), 94 *Stat.* 1879. The Supreme Court case that provoked the law was *Zurcher* v. *Stanford Daily*, 436 U.S. 547 (1978).
32. H.R. 866, 95th Congress, 2nd Session (June 12, 1978).

33. Government in the Sunshine Act, Pub. L. 94-409 (September 13, 1976), 90 *Stat.* 1241.

34. Ethics in Government Act of 1978, Pub. L. 95-521 (October 26, 1978), 92 *Stat.* 1824.

35. Regulatory Flexibility Act of 1980, Pub. L. 96-354 (September 18, 1980), 94 *Stat.* 1164, codified at 5 U.S.C., Secs. 601–612. Partly on the basis of this legislation, Chairman Mark S. Fowler, in 1981, created a special task force to review all FCC rules and recommend changes and/or deletions.

36. Paperwork Reduction Act of 1980, Pub. L. 96-511 (December 11, 1980), 94 *Stat.* 2812, codified at 44 U.S.C., Secs. 3501–3520.

37. Federal Trade Commission Improvements Act of 1980, Pub. L. 96-252 (May 28, 1980), 94 *Stat.* 374. Provisions for the congressional veto are codified at 15 U.S.C., Sec. 57(a)(1). A similar requirement to transmit rules to Congress is placed on the Federal Election Commission (FEC). It gives Congress thirty days to object, by one-house veto, to FEC rules. See 2 U.S.C., Sec. 438(d). In early 1980, under pressure from broadcasters, Congress almost vetoed an FEC rule dealing with funding and sponsorship of candidate debates. See *Congressional Record,* March 21, 1980, p. S2812 (remarks of Senator Claighborn Pell); March 12, 1980, p. H1821 (remarks of Representatives Bill Frenzel and Lionel Van Deerlin).

38. The House Appropriations Subcommittee had approved the FCC's request.

39. Quoted in "FCC Gives Up on Investigation of TV Networks," *Broadcasting,* July 4, 1977, p. 23.

40. Public Broadcasting Act of 1967, Pub. L. 90-129 (November 7, 1967), 81 *Stat.* 365.

41. See Public Broadcasting Financing Act of 1975, Pub. L. 94-192 (December 31, 1975), 89 *Stat.* 1098; Public Telecommunications Financing Act of 1978, Pub. L. 95-567 (November 2, 1978), 92 *Stat.* 2405. A classic example of the need to insulate public broadcasting occurred during a hearing in 1976 of the House Communications Subcommittee. After Commissioner Benjamin Hooks said he had a letter in which WETA-TV (D.C.) justified not carrying "Black Journal" in prime time because it drew less than 1 percent of the audience, Representative Torbert MacDonald asked for a copy of the letter and said, "I'll be happy to take care of that in five minutes. They haven't got their full appropriation" (quoted in "All Fairly Quiet on House Oversight Front," *Broadcasting,* March 8, 1976, p. 23).

42. See Omnibus Budget Reconciliation Act of 1981, Pub. L. 97–35 (August 13, 1981), Secs. 1221–1234. The Mankiewicz quote is from "Broadcasters Win Big on License Terms," *Broadcasting,* August 3, 1981, pp. 27–28.

43. *House Report 1139,* 93rd Congress, 2nd Session (1974), p. 15; see also *Senate Report 1056,* 93rd Congress, 2nd Session (1974), p. 17.

44. *House Report,* ibid.

45. *Writers Guild of America, West, Inc. et al.* v. *FCC et al.,* 423 F. Supp. 1064 (1976).

46. *Writers Guild of America, West, Inc. et al.* v. *American Broadcasting Co., Inc.,* 609 F.2d 355 (1979), *certiorari denied,* 101 S.Ct. 85 (1981). For an interesting insight into the motives and strategy of those who approved and those who disapproved of family viewing, see Geoffrey Cowan, *See No Evil: The Backstage Battle Over Sex and Violence in Television* (New York: Simon & Schuster, 1979).

47. *Senate Report 95-1043, Departments of State, Justice and Commerce, the Judiciary, and Related Agencies Appropriations Bill, 1979,* 95th Congress, 2nd Session (July 28, 1978), pp. 71–72. The Commission responded to the congressional mandate by creating a UHF Comparability Task Force and issuing three related Notices of Inquiry: Gen. Doc. 78-391, Gen. Doc. 78-392, and Gen. Doc. 78-393. See chapter six, "UHF Television: The Quest for Comparability." On Senator Weicker's interest, see *Hearings, Senate Committee on Appropriations, State, Justice, Commerce, the Judiciary and Related Agencies, Fiscal Year 1979,* Part 5, 95th Congress, 2nd Session (Washington, D.C.: Government Printing Office, 1978), pp. 1606–1610.

48. See *Television Digest,* August 6, 1979, p. 4.

49. Federal Trade Commission Improvements Act of 1980, Pub. L. 96-252 (May 28, 1980), 94 *Stat.* 374, Secs. 18–20.

50. Ibid., Sec. 11.

51. See "Trimmer Look for the FCC," *Broadcasting,* March 2, 1981, p. 38; and "Revised FCC Budget to Cause Further Backlogs, Testifies Lee," *Broadcasting,* March 16, 1981, p. 52. These warnings, and the decision to absorb cuts "across the board" rather than by selectively eliminating activities, were made under Acting FCC Chairman Robert E. Lee during the time prior to confirmation by the Senate of Lee's replacement, Mark Fowler. It was up to Fowler, of course, to implement or modify the FCC's planned reaction to the reduced Reagan budget. By late 1981 it was apparent that budget reductions, whatever their eventual level, would force abolition of some parts of the FCC and reduction in size and service from others. "FCC Beset by Budget Cuts," *Broadcasting,* October 19, 1981, pp. 31–32.

52. In fiscal year 1980 the total federal budget was over $759.6 billion, of which the FCC received $75.8 million or 0.013 percent. According to Reagan administration budget proposals, by fiscal year 1982 the federal budget should be $695.3 billion while the FCC is slated to receive $72.2 million. This drops the FCC's "share" to 0.010 percent of the total budget.

53. *House Report 97-208, Omnibus Budget Reconciliation Act of 1981, Conference Report to Accompany H.R. 3982,* 97th Congress, 1st Session (July 29, 1981), p. 899.

54. This may be due to nothing more than changes in congressional subcommittee leadership. When Representative John Dingell (D-Michigan) took over the House Oversight and Investigations Subcommittee, *Television Digest* speculated he would be more active than Representative Bob Eckhardt (D-Texas), who had run the subcommittee for two years. Dingell was compared to active investigators Oren Harris (D-Arkansas) and John Moss (D-California), who had previously chaired the subcommittee. See *Television Digest,* December 15, 1980, p. 4.

55. Walter B. Emery, *Broadcasting and Government,* rev. ed. (East Lansing: Michigan State University Press, 1971), p. 396.

56. The lasting impression left by the Cox investigation on an FCC insider is recounted in ibid., pp. 347–398.

57. "At Large with Robert E. Lee," *Broadcasting,* June 29, 1981, p. 38.

58. See 31 U.S.C., Sec. 1176.

59. See U.S. Commission on Civil Rights, *The Federal Civil Rights Enforcement Effort—1974, vol. I, To Regulate in the Public Interest* (Washing-

ton, D.C.: Government Printing Office, November 1974), especially pp. 1–89; U.S. Commission on Civil Rights, *Window Dressing on the Set: Women and Minorities in Television* (Washington, D.C.: Government Printing Office, August 1977); and U.S. Commission on Civil Rights, *Window Dressing on the Set: An Update* (Washington, D.C.: Government Printing Office, January 1979).

60. The broadcaster was Don Burden. See "Hill Goes into Spring Training," *Broadcasting*, January 26, 1970, pp. 52–54.

61. The Commissioner was James Quello, who owned $23,500 worth of technically forbidden stock, which he quickly sold. See "FCC Berated for Policy on Stock Holdings of Its Employees," *Broadcasting*, May 30, 1977, p. 28. See also *Television Digest*, May 30, 1977, p. 4. Further investigation found forty-five FCC employees of GS-13 rank or above in violation. See "Moss Unit Hits FCC for Lax Enforcement of Stock Conflicts," *Broadcasting*, February 27, 1978, pp. 68, 70.

62. The study was by GAO at the request of Senator Ernest Hollings (D-South Carolina). See "GAO Tells FCC to Set Up New Fee Schedule," *Broadcasting*, May 16, 1977, pp. 34–36; and "GAO Says FCC Should Refigure Fee Schedule, Make Partial Refund," *Broadcasting*, August 15, 1977, pp. 42–43. In 1979, at the request of Senator Barry Goldwater (R-Arizona), the Congressional Research Service declared that any fees charged broadcasters could not exceed the costs of the administration of regulation—that is, there could not be a "spectrum use" fee. See David R. Siddal, "Legal Analysis of Radio Spectrum Use Charges" (Washington, D.C.: Library of Congress, Congressional Research Service, April 20, 1979).

63. This Congressional Research Service study had been initiated by Congressman Van Deerlin (D-California), himself an opponent of "retransmission consent." See *Television Digest*, December 3, 1979, p. 6.

64. Surgeon General's Scientific Advisory Committee on Television and Social Behavior, *Television and Growing Up: The Impact of Televised Violence* (Washington, D.C.: Government Printing Office, 1972).

65. After hearings were held, Van Deerlin had great difficulty getting a final report out of the subcommittee. Initial drafts of the report placed most of the blame for violence on the TV networks and went so far as to encourage their restructuring as a remedy. Supporters of the networks on the subcommittee insisted on repeated versions to spread the blame. The report went through at least six drafts and was only finally issued after Van Deerlin took more control, settled for a version that spread blame widely, and allowed dissenting statements by several members of the subcommittee. See "Congress's Turn on TV Violence," *Broadcasting*, February 28, 1977, p. 20; "Stand-off at Van Deerlin's Session on TV Violence," *Broadcasting*, March 7, 1977, pp. 52–56; "House Mulls Strong Violence Statement," *Television Digest*, May 9, 1977, p. 2; "TV Networks Can Expect Less Whip in Upcoming Hill Violence Report," *Broadcasting*, May 23, 1977, pp. 50–51; "Networks Still the Villains in Van Deerlin Staff Report on TV Violence," *Broadcasting*, July 25, 1977, pp. 19ff.; "Van Deerlin Takes Firmer Control of Violence Report," *Broadcasting*, August 1, 1977, p. 23; and "Spreading the Blame for TV Violence," *Broadcasting*, October 3, 1977, p. 29. The final report is *Violence on Television*, put out by the House Committee on Interstate and

Foreign Commerce, Subcommittee on Communications, 95th Congress, 1st Session (September 29, 1977).

66. See "Government Probes TV Kickbacks," *Television Digest,* March 2, 1970, p. 4.

67. See "Staggers on News Staging," *Broadcasting,* May 22, 1972, pp. 51–52; and "Staggers Wants to Pass the Buck on News Staging to the FCC," *Broadcasting,* May 29, 1972, p. 42.

68. On Haiti, see *House Report 91-7319, Network News Documentary Practices—CBS "Project Nassau,"* Report of the Special Subcommittee on Interstate and Foreign Commerce, U.S. House of Representatives, 91st Congress, 2nd Session (1970). On "Selling of the Pentagon," see *Subpoenaed Material Re Certain TV Documentary Programs,* Hearings before the Special Subcommittee on Investigations, Committee on Interstate and Foreign Commerce, U.S. House of Representatives, 92nd Congress, 1st Session (1971) and *Proceeding against Frank Stanton and CBS, Inc.,* H.R. Doc. No. 349, 92nd Congress, 1st Session (1971).

69. Also in the news area, the House Ethics Committee investigated how CBS correspondent Daniel Schorr obtained, and funneled to the *Village Voice,* a secret House Intelligence Committee report on the CIA. See "White Hat or Black for CBS's Dan Schorr?" *Broadcasting,* March 15, 1976, pp. 22–23; and "Epilogue on Schorr," *Broadcasting,* October 11, 1976, p. 43.

70. See "Hill Sports Probe: Slow Crank-up May Be Cover for a Fastball," *Broadcasting,* June 27, 1977, pp. 57–58; "Network Sports Probe Broadened," *Television Digest,* July 4, 1977, pp. 3–4; "Van Deerlin Will Reluctantly Let Networks Go on Sports Probe," *Broadcasting,* November 14, 1977, pp. 48–49. For an interesting insight into the relationship between Van Deerlin and his staff on this study, see "Coach Van Deerlin Calls Plays," *Television Digest,* November 28, 1977, pp 2–3.

71. U.S. Senate, Committee on Government Operations, Subcommittee on Alcoholism and Narcotics, *Hearings on Media Images of Alcohol, the Effects of Advertising and Other Media on Alcohol Abuse,* 94th Congress, 2nd Session (1976).

72. See "Plenty of Work Awaits Congress on Its Return," *Broadcasting,* September 25, 1977, pp. 28, 32.

73. See "House Staff Asking TV, Pay Cable about Movie Tug-of-War," *Broadcasting,* September 9, 1974, p. 63.

74. See "Staggers' Detectives Give Low Marks to FCC's Newly Hired Lawyers," *Broadcasting,* September 3, 1973, p. 23.

75. U.S. House of Representatives, Interstate and Foreign Commerce Committee, Subcommittee on Oversight and Investigations, *Federal Regulation and Regulatory Reform,* 94th Congress, 1st Session (1976), p. iii.

76. See "FCC Activity Burst This Week," *Television Digest,* July 28, 1975, p. 2.

77. Quoted in ibid., pp. 12–13.

78. For early criticisms of the FCC's behavior, see Charles S. Hyneman, *Bureaucracy in a Democracy* (New York: Harper & Brothers, 1950); Committee on Independent Regulatory Commissions [the Hoover Commission], *A Report with Recommendations Prepared for the Commission on Organization of the Executive Branch of the Government,* (Appendix N), Washington, D.C.: U.S. Government Printing Office, 1949; and James M.

Landis, *Report on Regulatory Agencies to the President-Elect,* Subcommittee on Administrative Practice and Procedure, Committee on the Judiciary, U.S. Senate, 86th Congress, 2d Session (December 1960).

79. See "Hill Hearing Told FCC Drags Its Feet," *Broadcasting,* December 1, 1975, p. 30.

80. These findings are contained in Volume III, *Public Participation in Regulatory Agency Proceedings,* and Volume IV, *Delay in the Regulatory Process* of what was ultimately a six-volume study released between January 1977 and December 1978. See U.S. Senate, Committees on Government Operations/Government Affairs, *Study on Federal Regulation,* vols. I–VI plus Appendix to Volume VI, 95th Congress, 1st and 2nd Sessions (1977–1978).

81. The Congressional Research Service study is reported as Appendix B, pp. 267–396, of *Study on Federal Regulation,* vol. I, *The Regulatory Appointments Process,* (1977).

82. See "Congressional Unit Cites Inefficiencies among FCC, OTP, OT," *Broadcasting,* January 5, 1976, p. 30.

83. See "Top Rating for FCC as Generator of Paperwork," *Broadcasting,* December 4, 1978, pp. 24–26. Of the 30 million hours, 18 million were due to logging rules that the FCC eliminated for commercial radio in 1981. Some believe that FCC elimination of commercial radio logging rules was partly or largely motivated by the Commission's desire to get out from under the charge of being the top paperwork-generating agency.

84. U.S. General Accounting Office, CED-79-107, *Organizing the Federal Communications Commission for Greater Management and Regulatory Effectiveness,* July 30, 1979. For the FCC's response, see "FCC Responds to GAO's Criticisms," *Broadcasting,* October 8, 1979, pp. 76ff. The fiscal year 1982 federal budget reacted to these and other criticisms by mandating that the Commission create a position of managing director charged with reporting annually to Congress on the "goals, objectives, and priorities of the Commission." See Omnibus Budget Reconciliation Act of 1981, Pub. L. 97–35 (August 13 1981), Sec. 1252.

85. U.S. General Accounting Office, CED-79-62, June 4, 1979. For the FCC's response, see "FCC to GAO, No. 1: You're Right," *Broadcasting,* August 13, 1979, p. 57.

85a. U.S. General Accounting Office, CED–81–136, *Legislative and Regulatory Actions Needed to Deal with a Changing Domestic Telecommunications Industry,* September 24, 1981.

86. Cited in *Television Digest,* March 23, 1981, p. 7.

87. This was at the request of the House Copyright Subcommittee. See *Television Digest,* May 18, 1981, p. 4.

88. Reported in *Television Digest,* February 12, 1979, p. 5.

89. Reported in *Television Digest,* November 10, 1980, p. 7; and *Television Digest,* March 23, 1981, p. 8.

90. David R. Siddell, *Legal Analysis of Radio Spectrum Use Charges,* Library of Congress, Congressional Research Service, April 20, 1979.

91. Reported in *Television Digest,* January 8, 1979, p. 3.

92. Edwin G. Johnson, "Carrying Coals to Newcastle," *Federal Communications Bar Journal,* 10 (1949), 183.

93. The views of key senators are given great weight in the president's selection of a nominee. In response to a question posed at the confirmation

hearing of Judge Benjamin Hooks concerning the steps that led to his appointment, Senator Howard Baker (R-Tennessee), ranking minority member on the Senate Communications Committee, said that the idea of naming a black originated with Senator John Pastore and that the two of them later found a "sympathetic ear" for the proposal at the White House. Baker looked for a candidate in Tennessee who was not a Republican (the FCC had its full statutory complement of four Republicans) and who would not be "a special-interest commissioner." He selected Judge Hooks, whom he had known for a long time, and discussed his nomination with Senator Pastore and then the White House. See "Road Looks Clear for Hooks, Wiley," *Broadcasting*, May 29, 1972, pp. 28, 29.

94. Senator Charles Tobey (R-New Hampshire) launched a one-man crusade against a favorable report on the renomination of Colonel Thad Brown in 1940 and used the hearings to condemn Brown for his handling of charges of monopoly against the networks. Commissioner Brown's renomination was rejected by the Senate. See Carl J. Friedrich and Evelyn Sternberg, "Congress and the Control of Radio-Broadcasting," *American Political Science Review*, 37 (December 1943), 806–807.

95. See "FCC Nominees Breeze Through Senate Hearing," *Broadcasting*, July 1, 1974, pp. 22–23.

96. James M. Graham and Victor H. Kramer, *Appointments to the Regulatory Agencies, the Federal Communications Commission and the Federal Trade Commission (1949–1974)*, printed for the use of the Committee on Commerce, U.S. Senate, 94th Congress, 2nd Session (April 1976), pp. 381–382.

97. Ibid., p. 391.

98. See "Senate Confirms Reid Appointment," *Broadcasting*, March 6, 1972, p. 27. Reid's congressional district was about to be eliminated through redistricting.

99. See "Quello, Rivera Get Reagan Nods," *Broadcasting*, June 8, 1981, p. 35.

100. See "Exchange of Terms Clears Way to FCC for White, Fogarty," *Broadcasting*, September 6, 1976, p. 3.

101. See "Clear Sailing for First Days of Ferris FCC," *Broadcasting*, October 17, 1977, pp. 21–22. Normally, Senate approval is by a simple voice vote. In Ferris's case, he requested a roll-call vote and was supported by 85 to 0, an effort to put extra Senate support behind his chairmanship. See "Pertschuk Gains Senate Approval," *Broadcasting*, April 11, 1977, p. 41.

102. See "No Discouraging Words for Dawson," *Broadcasting*, May 25, 1981, p. 25.

103. See Graham and Kramer, *Appointments to the Regulatory Agencies*, pp. 353–354.

104. *Washington Post*, February 14, 1973, p. 6D.

105. See Graham and Kramer, *Appointments to the Regulatory Agencies*, pp. 364–368.

106. See "Quello, Rivera Sail Through Hearing," *Broadcasting*, July 27, 1981, pp. 32–33.

107. See Graham and Kramer, *Appointments to the Regulatory Agencies*, pp. 327–330.

108. Reported in "Brown Goes, Quello, Ferris to Stay," *Television Digest*, January 12, 1981, pp. 1–2.

109. See "Rivera Nomination on Way," *Television Digest*, April 27, 1981, pp.

1–2; and "Quello, Rivera Get Reagan Nods," *Broadcasting,* June 8, 1981, p. 35.

110. Congress thought the phrase "continuous watchfulness" contained in the 1946 Legislative Reorganization Act was too vague and renamed the oversight function in the 1970 act "legislative review." Legislative Reorganization Act of 1970, Pub. L. 91–510 (October 26, 1970), 84 *Stat.,* 1140, Title I, Sec. 118(a)(1), codified at 2 U.S.C., Sec. 190(d).

111. Robinson, "The Federal Communications Commission," 180–181.

112. Nathaniel L. Nathanson, "Some Comments on the Administrative Procedure Act," *Northwestern University Law Review,* 41 (1946), 421–422.

113. See William L. Morrow, *Congressional Committees* (New York: Scribner's, 1969), p. 162.

114. U.S. House of Representatives Committee on Appropriations, *Hearings Concerning Departments of State, Justice, and Commerce, the Judiciary, and Related Agencies Appropriations for 1981,* Part 4, 96th Congress, 2nd Session (1980), p. 397.

115. See "Early, Ferris Clash on RKO," *Television Digest,* March 10, 1980, pp. 1–2.

116. William L. Cary, *Politics and the Regulatory Agencies* (New York: McGraw-Hill), 1967, p. 137.

117. Information provided by the Legislation Unit, Office of the Executive Director, Federal Communications Commission, May 14, 1981. The FCC staff commented that this was probably fewer appearances than normal because 1980 was an election year.

118. "At Large with Robert E. Lee," p. 37. Frequent trips to Capitol Hill quickly disturbed Lee's successor, Chairman Mark S. Fowler. Asked during an oversight hearing in September 1981 "if there's anything Congress could do for FCC, Fowler said committees could coordinate their oversight hearings, so FCC could spend less time preparing testimony and more time working for public. FCC is 'seriously impaired in going about our work,' said Fowler, because of numerous requests to testify." "In Brief," *Broadcasting,* September 21, 1981, p. 104.

119. See "Renewal Relief Hits Major Obstacles as Pastore Submits Mild Bill and Hart Waits to Queer Anything Stronger," *Broadcasting,* September 16, 1974, p. 4. As we note in chapter eight, the bill eventually died but for other reasons.

120. See *Television Digest,* June 27, 1977, p. 3; July 11, 1977, p. 5; July 25, 1977, p. 5; August 1, 1977, p. 1; August 8, 1977, pp. 5–6 (includes the Hollings quote); and August 15, 1977, p. 5.

121. Minow, *Equal Time,* p. 35.

122. "Requiem for a Regulator," Speech by Commissioner Robert E. Lee to the Federal Communications Bar Association, Washington, D.C., June 10, 1981 [mimeo.], p. 8.

123. Kenneth Culp Davis, *Discretionary Justice* (Baton Rouge: University of Louisiana Press, 1969), p. 148.

124. *Study on Federal Regulation,* vol. II, *Congressional Oversight of Regulatory Agencies* (1975), p. 81.

125. For a blistering criticism of Zapple, published on the eve of his retirement, see Thomas Redburn, "Wedding Presents, Cigars and Deference," *Washington Monthly,* June 1975, pp. 4–10.

126. *Broadcasting,* March 14, 1977, p. 86.

127. *VHF-TV Top 100 Market,* 81 FCC2d 233 (1980).

128. *Rep. Patsy Mink,* 59 FCC2d 987 (1976).
129. *Aspen Institute Program on Communications,* 55 FCC2d 697 (1975).
130. *Chisholm* v. *FCC,* 538 F.2d 349 (D.C. Cir. 1976), *certiorari denied,* 429 U.S. 880 (1976).
131. See "Pay-Cable Lobbying Pays Off," *Television Digest,* October 7, 1974, p. 3.
132. A summary of the first report can be found in "Congressional Wives Enlist in Crusade Against TV Violence," *Broadcasting,* October 17, 1977, p. 46. See also *A Report on Television Programming by the Congressional Wives Task Force,* Washington, D.C., September 1977 [mimeo.]; and *Addendum to Report on Television Programming,* Washington, D.C., June 1978 [mimeo.].
133. *A Report on Television Programming by the Congressional Wives Task Force,* ibid., p. 5.
134. See "Little Oversight Goes a Long Way," *Broadcasting,* May 17, 1976, pp. 26, 27; *Television Digest,* May 30, 1977, p. 3; "Varied Menu for S. 611, 622 Hearings," *Broadcasting,* June 25, 1974, pp. 67–68; and "N.J. Senators Covet WOR-TV, New York," *Broadcasting,* June 2, 1980, p. 57. See also FCC BC Docket No. 79–270 (March 5, 1980), BC Docket No. 79-269 (March 6, 1980), and BC Docket No. 80-719 (January 13, 1981)— all pertaining to New Jersey TV service. In early October 1981, the U.S. Senate approved a bill, S. 898, which while mostly devoted to common carrier issues required the FCC to assign the next available VHF-TV station to New Jersey. See "Bell Gets Its Bill Out of Senate," *Broadcasting,* October 12, 1981, pp. 27–28.
135. See "Ferris Rejects Hill on Cable Dereg," *Television Digest,* March 31, 1980, pp. 2–3. The FCC was upheld on appeal in *Malrite TV of New York* v. *FCC,* 652 F.2d 1140 (2d Cir. 1981). Signals from Congress on this question were mixed. House Communications Subcommittee Chairman Lionel Van Deerlin (D-California) urged the FCC to proceed with its cable deregulation. The U.S. Supreme Court refused to review *Malrite.*
136. Quoted in *Television Digest,* October 6, 1980, p. 5.
137. Jaffe, *Judicial Control of Administrative Action,* p. 41.
138. 406 U.S. 649, 676 (1972).
139. The House Communications Subcommittee conducted extensive cable television hearings in 1975 and 1976 and, in connection with that study, produced a lengthy report on the subject. After the cable hearings were over, however, the subcommittee never prepared cable television legislation. Instead, it moved to the general Communications Act rewrite process described in chapter nine. See U.S. House of Representatives, Committee on Commerce, *Cable Television: Promise versus Regulatory Performance,* 94th Congress, 2nd Session (1976).
140. See *In the Matter of Use of the Carterfone Device in Message Toll Service,* 13 FCC2d 420 (1968) (competition in phone equipment); and *In re Applications of Microwave Communications, Inc.,* 18 FCC2d 953 (1969) (competition through so-called specialized common carriers). See also *Second Computer Inquiry,* 77 FCC2d 385 (1980) as modified by *Second Computer Inquiry,* 84 FCC2d 50 (1980) (which permits AT&T to respond to its new competitive environment by offering certain computer-enhanced (data processing) communications services through separate subsidiary corporations.) For a GAO study skeptical of the FCC's ability to police this new scheme for telecommunications, see U.S. General Ac-

counting Office, CED–81–136, *Legislative and Regulatory Actions Needed to Deal with a Changing Domestic Telecommunications Industry,* September 24, 1981.

141. House Report 91-930, *Approving Reorganization Plan No. 1 of 1970 (Telecommunications),* 91st Congress, 2nd Session (March 19, 1970), p. 5.

Four

Broadcast Regulation: An Analytic View

Broadcast regulation, we have seen, is shaped by six primary determiners—the FCC, the industry, citizen groups, the courts, the White House, and Congress. In addition there are miscellaneous participants —the Federal Trade Commission or the Commission on Civil Rights, for example—sometimes involved in specific broadcast-related issues but whose participation in the regulatory process, while important, is less constant. We have also seen that the six primary determiners rarely can accomplish much by unilateral action. The president, for example, names members of the FCC but checks out potential appointees in advance with significant interest groups (the industry and, infrequently, citizen groups). In the end, the Senate must formally approve nominations. The determiners, in other words, interact with each other in a complex fashion. Often those interactions are as important as, or more important than, what the determiners do on their own. Any attempt to understand what goes on in broadcast regulation must explain regulation as the outcome of complex interaction patterns within a dynamic system—what we will term the "broadcast policy-making system."

It is remarkable that so little effort has been devoted to the systematic understanding of broad-scale regulatory systems such as those affecting broadcasting. That is not to say that people have not attempted to understand broadcasting regulation. It is to point out that they have tended to shy away from attempts to explain it in analytic systems terms. There is a significant research literature surrounding each of the determiner groups we have identified. That literature is often interdisciplinary because political scientists, economists, historians, sociologists, and even psychologists have something to say about each of these groups. On occasion, the perspectives of one field are used to criticize or enlighten research that approaches the subject from another perspective. We have a body of literature about judicial behavior, relevant to an understanding of the role of the courts in broadcast regulation,[1] and interest group behavior, relevant to understanding both the industry and citizen groups.[2] Presidential[3] and congressional[4] decision making has occupied the attention of scholars for decades. Many persons have delved deeply into theories of regulatory agency behavior, with at least some of that attention being devoted to the FCC.[5] Rarely do these scholars make the error of assuming that one group exists in a vacuum; there is always some recognition that other groups influence the behavior of the participant being most directly studied. Often, however, that single group of greatest interest becomes the focus of attention.

The problem with such an approach is that it does not conform to reality. The moment one has understood and perhaps even predicted an administrative agency's act, for example, one finds that that action can be undone by the judiciary. It is possible to reach a finely detailed understanding of how and why Congress produced a particular law, but unless it is also understood that the consequences of that law will be profoundly influenced by how an administrative agency implements it or how courts interpret it or how affected industries behave under it, the perspective will be too narrow to result in real understanding of policy making.

It would be marvelous if there were an agreed upon general theory of the politics of regulation that incorporated the behavior of all the significant determiner groups.[6] Unfortunately, as yet no such accepted theory exists. Theories are easier to develop and test for simple laboratory-like phenomena than for more complex events and systems. Scholars have not yet even achieved consensus about which of several competing theories of regulatory agency behavior should be used for the analysis of an organization such as the FCC.[7]

This lack of agreement on a general theory, however, does not mean that the attempt to gain at least some systematic understanding of the broadcast regulatory process is futile. It simply means that the objective is not quite what it would be if there were a unified theory. With such a theory, at its most refined state, the objective would be to predict the behavior of the entire system. Lacking such a general theory, present goals must be more modest. We shall propose here a generalized model and develop some statements about its behavior. The model will help explain things and perhaps even allow some "retrodiction": it assists in understanding what has gone on even if it is not, like many models, developed to a stage where it permits prediction. In part two of this book, we will present five case studies of the broadcast regulatory system in action. The model and the generalizations proposed here can then be seen in action.

A Systems Approach to Broadcast Regulation

The politics of broadcast regulation can be seen in terms of an analytical framework or model we term the "broadcast policy-making system." Such a framework can be used both to understand the regulatory process and to suggest to scholars a conceptual orientation for work in this area.

As is the case with any model, the one we are suggesting is a simplification of reality. Yet to simplify is to streamline, to strip off surface complexities in order to show the essential elements of a system. Because virtually any economic or political process may be analyzed graphically in terms of such a systems approach, it also affords a uniform way to evaluate and compare a variety of situations or processes. A model directs attention to, and focuses on, key relationships and activities. By doing this, it helps define order in a real political world with many subtleties. An analytic system of this type is, in the words of political scientist Robert A. Dahl, "an aspect of things in some degree abstracted from reality for purposes of analysis."[8] Its primary test is not whether it is elegant or neat but whether it fosters an understanding of the political process or processes being studied.

Figure 2 represents the broadcast policy-making system. The six recurring participants in the regulatory process—those identified and discussed in chapters two and three—are the authoritative decision-making agencies at the heart of the model. The figure also charts various channels of influence among these six participants. It is significant that there is no one pathway through the core of the broadcast policy-making system, and any one of the various routes necessarily involves many participants. The key to understanding the politics of broadcast regulation lies in simultaneously analyzing the individual participants and their interactions. As Gary Wamsley and Mayer Zaid point out, "Policy is as much or more a product of factors within the interstices of the system's 'black box' . . . as it is of pressures or inputs from outside."[9] Although outside pressure, or "inputs," and the internal politics of each of the decision-making bodies can raise issues and define alternatives, it is the political relationships of, and interactions among, the six key determiners that are truly crucial to broadcast regulation.

Three of the principals (the White House, the courts, and citizen groups) usually play a less immediate, sustained, and direct role than the other three (the FCC, Congress, and the regulated industries). Thus, the primary channels of influence, information, and contact are traced

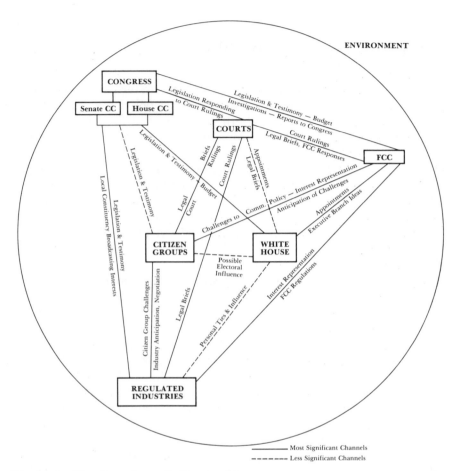

Legislation & Testimony — Budget
Investigations — Reports to Congress
Legislation & Testimony
Legislation Responding to Court Rulings

Court Rulings
Legal Briefs, FCC Responses

Briefs
Rulings
Court Rulings
Appointments
Legal Briefs

Legal Court
Budget

Policy — Interest Representation
Anticipation of Challenges
Appointments
Executive Branch Ideas

Interest Representation
FCC Regulations

Challenges to Comm.

Possible
Electoral
Influence

Personal Ties & Influence

Citizen Group Challenges
Industry Anticipation, Negotiation

Legal Briefs

Local Constituency Broadcasting Interests

CONGRESS

Senate CC | House CC

COURTS

FCC

CITIZEN GROUPS

WHITE HOUSE

REGULATED INDUSTRIES

ENVIRONMENT

———— Most Significant Channels
- - - - - - Less Significant Channels

Figure 2   The Broadcast Policy-Making System

among these three most significant determiners as the outer triangle in Figure 2.

The system produces policy dynamically. Policy decisions—which might be called "outputs"—emerge from the interaction of some or all of the participants. Although the need for policy decisions may sometimes be stimulated by parties outside the system—for example, by an action of the Federal Trade Commission—in most instances, the functioning of the system itself generates the need for still more policy decisions. In other words, although some policy decisions may have long lives, many remain accepted and unchanged only briefly: one day's policy outputs in this system commonly become the inputs for the next day's policy making.

The policy outputs of this system are varied. They include "public" policies such as FCC rules and regulations, final court actions, laws enacted by Congress, and executive orders. An example of legislation would be the statutory requirement, discussed in chapter six, that all television sets sold after a certain date have UHF as well as VHF receiving capacity; an example of an agency decision would be the FCC's desire that incumbent broadcast station licensees should have preferred status, in renewal proceedings, over challengers for their licenses, a topic to be discussed in chapter eight. Outputs may even take the form of decisions not to do something, exemplified by recent trends in "deregulation" such as the FCC decision not to supervise the number of commercials radio stations carry (see chapter seven), or its decision not to concern itself with the entertainment programming format those stations use (see chapter five). In our model, policy outputs may even include many of the actions of the regulated industries, whose implementation of or operation under FCC rules and regulations or the Communications Act of 1934 is, in many instances, authoritative because it is unchallenged.

In most instances, such policy outputs (or authoritative decisions) bestow rewards or impose penalties on other affected interests. Reactions of those interests—or, occasionally, outside interests—stimulate the system to generate further policy output. They become, in effect, input back into the system. Some inputs are specific, such as a demand by a citizen group that a broadcast station not be permitted to change its format. Other inputs are exceedingly general, such as the mood that can be cast over an independent regulatory commission by a president or by the current public image of the agency. It is important to realize, too, that the system does more than merely respond to demands; it also molds political demands and policy preferences.

The system, of course, does not function in a vacuum. It operates in the context of an environment consisting of many factors, some identified in chapter one, including the historical development of broadcast regulation, the basic technical and economic characteristics of broadcasting, and broad legal prescriptions. The environment outside the system also encompasses other factors, such as public attitudes toward broadcasting and government regulation and the actions of related systems—the Federal Trade Commission, for example—which may at times inspire and influence the broadcast policy-making system. It even includes actions and groups beyond the United States, for the spectrum is an international resource and U.S. broadcast networks and programs have a worldwide effect. In recent years, for example, U.S. policies toward spectrum allocation for radio and toward the location and function of communications satellites have had to be reconciled with the desires of our international neighbors. The United Nations Educational, Scientific and Cultural Organization (UNESCO) has debated policies toward a "new world information order" that, although perceived by third world nations to be important to their development, are seen by Western nations as antithetical to notions of press freedom. The major demands and supports—outputs and inputs—that determine what the system does, however, generally originate from within.

Policy outputs—the immediate short-range policy decisions—should be distinguished from policy outcomes—the longer-range consequences of such decisions. As David Easton puts it:

> An output is the stone tossed into the pond and its first splash; the outcomes are the ever widening and vanishing pattern of concentric ripples. The actual decisions and implementing actions are the outputs; the consequences traceable to them, however long the discernible claim of causation, are the outcomes.[10]

From the perspective of the participant groups, there are often clear "winners" and "losers" only when it comes to momentary outputs. It is harder to determine a winner or loser in looking at long-range outcomes. The "success" of an individual output ought to be measured by means other than the degree to which it meets immediate needs— either social ones or those of the participant groups. Success also includes the effect of the outputs on patterns of present and future inputs, and, of course, its relationship to outcomes.

When a policy output—or a long-range outcome—fails to meet the expectations of affected parties or is seen as an inappropriate or inadequate solution to the problems that gave rise to those expectations, that output is likely to be overturned by subsequent actions as frustrated demands arise anew. Indeed, if the system is perceived as being unresponsive to the expectations of key participants over a substantial period of time, then even its most basic features may prove vulnerable (see chapter nine). So far, however, the broadcast policy-making system has, as a system, proved very durable.

Some Generalizations About Policy Making

One important feature of the broadcast policy-making system is that it is highly turbulent. Largely because communications is influenced by rapidly changing technology, few specific policy decisions are stable and long-lasting. The system is always responding to new or changed conditions, with consequent incessant interaction among its participants. The operation of the policy-making system in specific instances is inherently unique; each policy-making problem is likely to differ in important respects from all others. However, certain recurring patterns about the politics of broadcast regulation can be identified:[11]

1. *Participants seek conflicting goals from the process.* Pluralism and dispersion of power in policy making do not by themselves sug-

gest that the process is inevitably a struggle for control or influence. Conceivably the participants in such a process could share certain perspectives concerning what is to be done. Such is rarely the case, however, in the broadcast policy-making process. As the case studies in chapters five through nine show, the gains of one set of participants are usually made at the cost of the interests of another. The policy demands of different groups often conflict; they must usually compete for scarce rewards.

2. *Participants have limited resources insufficient to continually dominate the policy-making process.* In a pluralistic complex such as that outlined in Figure 2, policy-making power tends to be divided. Although the FCC frequently initiates policy proposals, it lacks the ability to implement most of them single-handedly. To prevail, it must win significant support from other participants. Similarly, none of the other five participants has hierarchical control over the policy making process, which is simply to say that nobody dominates the process consistently. In such a system policy making results from the agreement—or at least the acquiescence—of multiple participants, not from the domination of one. Coalitions of diverse participants work together and reward those belonging to them.

3. *Participants have unequal strengths in the struggle for control or influence.* Inequality among participants can arise because one party is inherently stronger, cares more, or develops its potential more effectively. In the 1970s, for example, citizen groups had considerably less strength than the Federal Communications Commission and the broadcast industry in their ability to influence policy concerning radio station format changes. Even when one federal court agreed with the views of a citizen group, another federal court—supported by the FCC and by broadcasters—prevailed. Favorable public opinion, legal symbols, congressional allies, and the like are all potential sources of strength that participants have access to in differing degrees and that they may use with varying success on different issues.

4. *The component subgroups of participant groups do not automatically agree on policy options.* Each of the six groups we have identified consists of many subgroups: citizen groups range from liberal to conservative; the FCC is organized into bureaus representing interests that may conflict, such as cable television and broadcasting; there is not one single court but, instead, a hierarchy of courts, and it is common for a superior court to overturn the actions of an inferior court; radio broadcasters may sometimes view issues differently than television broadcasters. Thus, while it is useful to refer to the six principal participants as if each was one, it is important to recognize that each group may be unable—or find it very difficult—to agree on a common objective or course of action.

5. *The process tends toward policy progression by small or incremental steps rather than massive change.* One means of minimizing opposition to a policy initiative is to show its close relationship to existing and generally accepted policy. Frequently, earlier actions are cited to prove that the desired change is not unprecedented but only a logical continuation of past concerns and policies. One of the beauties of administrative law is that precedents usually can be found for almost any initiative. Although agencies are not as bound by precedent as are courts, they still hesitate to turn their backs on the past when it is pointed out to them. Such slow and gradual shifts in policy are not only strategic but probably inevitable, given the multiplicity of participants with conflicting goals, unequal strengths, and limited resources. Incrementalism tends to be at least a safe, if not necessarily the safest, course of action. As a result, however, the system is rarely bold or innovative and has a hard time responding to environmental pressures for massive change. The five case studies that follow show that the political resources necessary to accomplish significant policy innovations are greater than those necessary to achieve more incremental change or to preserve the status quo.

6. *Legal and ideological symbols play a significant role in the process.* Throughout the evolution of policy a recurring theme of participants is the legal and ideological symbolism they may attach to a discussion of alternatives. In many instances policies are seen as threatening or protecting the "rights" of broadcasters or the "rights" of listeners and viewers, without refined and, most importantly, commonly agreed upon specification of the meaning of those concepts. Broadcast policy-making discussions can also become embroiled in arguments over stock, symbolic rhetoric such as "localism," the "public interest," "access to broadcasting," or "free broadcasting." The terms become symbols cherished by participants in and of themselves without careful thought, or they are not commonly understood, so that ideological rhetoric sometimes supersedes real issues and actions in importance.

7. *The process is usually characterized by mutual accommodation among participants.* Customarily, participants in broadcast policy making do not attempt to destroy one or more of their opponents. Rather, the process is characterized by consensual, majority-seeking activities. Mutual adjustment among participants may occur in a variety of ways, including negotiation, the creation and discharge of obligations, direct manipulation of the immediate circumstances in which events are occurring, the use of third parties or political brokers capable of developing consensual solutions, or partial deferral to others in order to effect a compromise. To some participants, on some issues, however, accom-

modation is difficult if not impossible, and on these issues policy debate is intense and the perceived stakes the greatest.

The five case studies that follow provide an opportunity to examine the politics of broadcast regulation in actual instances of struggle over policy alternatives. We will see the six key participants in the regulatory process using their varying (sometimes insufficient) financial, political, and social resources to attempt to obtain their desires in the face of probable or actual opposition from other participants. We will also see that, if they wish to be even incrementally successful, the participants must be relatively moderate in their goals, must respect legal and ideological symbols, must organize their resources (and the resources of their supporters) carefully, and must exhibit a willingness to adjust their positions in light not only of the positions of others and the resources available to them, but also the presence of potential or very real opponents. The politics of broadcast regulation is not dominated by a single group or interest; rather, the politics of broadcasting consists of complex interactions among multiple determiners of regulatory policy.

NOTES

1. See, for example, Henry J. Abraham, *The Judicial Process*, 4th ed. (New York: Oxford University Press, 1980); Joel B. Grossman and Richard S. Wells, *Constitutional Law and Judicial Policy Making*, 2nd ed. (New York: Wiley, 1980); Glendon Schubert, *Judicial Behavior: A Reader in Theory and Research* (Chicago: Rand McNally, 1964); Sheldon Goldman and Austin Sarat, eds., *American Court Systems: Readings in Judicial Process and Behavior* (San Francisco: W. H. Freeman, 1978); and especially Louis Jaffe, *Judicial Control of Administrative Action* (Boston: Little, Brown, 1965).
2. See, for example, David B. Truman, *The Governmental Process: Political Interests and Public Opinion*, 2nd ed. (New York: Knopf, 1971); Norman J. Ornstein and Shirley Elder, *Interest Groups, Lobbying and Policymaking* (Washington, D.C.: Congressional Quarterly Press, 1978); Congressional Quarterly, *The Washington Lobby*, 3rd ed. (Washington, D.C.: Congressional Quarterly Press, 1979); and especially Jeffrey M. Berry, *Lobbying for the People* (Princeton, N.J.: Princeton University Press, 1977); Andrew S. McFarland, *Public Interest Lobbies* (Washington, D.C.: American Enterprise Institute for Public Policy Research, 1976); and Timothy B. Clark, "After a Decade of Doing Battle, Political Interest Groups Show Their Age," *The National Journal*, July 12, 1980, pp. 1136–1141.
3. See, for example, Richard M. Pious, *The American Presidency* (New York: Basic Books, 1979), especially chapter seven; Richard E. Neustadt, *Presidential Power: The Politics of Leadership from FDR to Carter* (New York: Wiley, 1980); Thomas A. Timberg, *The Federal Executive: The Pres-*

ident and the Bureaucracy (New York: Irvington, 1978); and Richard P. Nathan, *The Plot That Failed: Nixon and the Administrative Presidency* (New York: Wiley, 1975).

4. See, for example, Lawrence C. Dodd and Bruce I. Oppenheimer, *Congress Reconsidered,* 2nd ed. (Washington, D.C.: Congressional Quarterly Press, 1981); Congressional Quarterly, *Inside Congress,* 2nd ed. (Washington, D.C.: Congressional Quarterly Press, 1979); and especially John W. Kingdon, *Congressmen's Voting Decisions,* 2nd ed. (New York: Harper & Row, 1981); Aage R. Clausen, *How Congressmen Decide: A Policy Focus* (New York: St. Martin's Press, 1973); Randall B. Ripley and Grace A. Frankin, *Congress, the Bureaucracy and Public Policy,* rev. ed. (Homewood, Ill.: Dorsey Press, 1980); and Lawrence C. Dodd and Richard L. Schott, *Congress and the Administrative State* (New York: Wiley, 1979).

5. See, for example, Marver Bernstein, *Regulating Business by Independent Commission* (Princeton, N.J.: Princeton University Press, 1955); Sam Peltzman, "Toward a More General Theory of Regulation," *Journal of Law and Economics,* 19 (August 1976), 211–240; Michael Porter and Jeffrey Sagansky, "Information, Politics, and Economic Analysis: The Regulatory Decision Process in the Air Freight Case," *Public Policy,* 2 (Spring 1976), 263–307; Richard A. Posner, "Taxation by Regulation," *Bell Journal of Economics and Management Science,* 2 (Spring 1971), 22–50; and George J. Stigler, *The Citizen and the State: Essays on Regulation* (Chicago: University of Chicago Press, 1975). See also various additional works on regulation cited in the annotated bibliography of this book.

6. For an example of what such a theory might have to include, see James Q. Wilson, "The Politics of Regulation," in *The Politics of Regulation,* ed. James Q. Wilson (New York: Basic Books, 1980), pp. 357–394.

7. Compare, for example, Wilson's work, ibid., with Bruce M. Owen and Ronald Braeutigam, *The Regulation Game* (Cambridge, Mass.: Ballinger, 1978), pp. 1–36. An excellent review of several theoretical ways of looking at the FCC is found in G. Gail Crotts and Lawrence M. Mead, "The FCC as an Institution," in *Telecommunications: An Interdisciplinary Survey,* ed. Leonard Lewin (Dedham, Mass.: Artech House, 1979), pp. 39–119. See also Glen O. Robinson, "The Federal Communications Commission: An Essay on Regulatory Watchdogs," *Virginia Law Review,* 64 (March 1978), 169.

8. Robert A. Dahl, *Modern Political Analysis,* 2nd ed. (Englewood Cliffs, N.J.: Prentice-Hall, 1970), p. 9.

9. Gary Wamsley and Mayer Zaid, *The Political Economy of Public Organizations* (Lexington, Mass.: Heath, 1973), p. 89.

10. David Easton, *A Systems Analysis of Political Life* (New York: Wiley, 1965), p. 352.

11. The generalizations that follow were suggested in part by Charles E. Lindblom, *The Policy-Making Process* (Englewood Cliffs, N.J.: Prentice-Hall, 1968).

PART TWO

Five
Case
Studies

Five

Format Changes: The Case of the Strained Partnership

For more than thirteen years, broadcasters, citizen groups, the FCC, and two federal courts argued over the government's role in regulating the choice of formats by radio stations. Although one might expect such a controversy to turn on questions of lofty rights and noble principles —for example, the strongly pressed First Amendment right of broadcasters to be free from government interference concerning content or the also firmly asserted First Amendment right of listeners to receive diverse programming—in the end, this long-running dispute was mostly about the politics of broadcast regulation. When the U.S. Supreme Court settled the controversy in 1981, it had much more to say about who should play what role in the development of format policy than about what the substance of that policy should be. In short, it defined the politics of policy making in this area rather than deciding the policy questions themselves.

It is tempting to give much of the credit (or blame) for starting this dispute to one man, Dick Grey, who was the television and radio editor of the *Atlanta Journal* in 1968. On March 5, 1968 Glenkaren Associates, Inc., filed an application with the Commission seeking the FCC's approval to sell its Atlanta stations, WGKA-AM and WGKA-FM, to Straus Broadcasting Company. Initially unnoticed was the different format Straus proposed from the one under which WGKA had operated for ten years. Under Glenkaren, WGKA had been programmed as the "Voice of the Arts in Atlanta"—a classical music station. The prospective new owner, Straus, proposed, instead, a "pleasant blending of popular favorites, Broadway hits, musical standards, and light classics"—beautiful music.[1]

The proposed change did not long escape community notice. Under the headline "Listeners Mourn WGKA Change," Dick Grey's May 6, 1968, "Grey Matter" column contrasted the emerging cultural sophistication of Atlanta—highlighted by an upcoming visit of the Metropolitan Opera Company and a successfully completed Atlanta Symphony season—with the prospect that Atlanta's only classical music radio stations might become mere "background music."[2] Between May and August, Grey continued to devote occasional columns to the controversy, often including letters to the paper from unhappy WGKA listeners. Grey contacted FCC sources to keep up with developments and, in early August, complained that the whole problem had come to his attention too late for anyone to be able to file a formal challenge to the sale in the form of a "petition to deny" asking the FCC to stop the transaction. He noted that a letter writing campaign might be the only effective action. On August 21, in response to reader requests, Grey printed the mailing address of the FCC and advised readers that complaints could be sent to "Rosel Hyde, Chairman."[3]

Chairman Hyde's mailbox began to fill with citizen complaints about the *WGKA* case. According to a subsequent Commission talley, the FCC received "about 1,150 letters and an informal petition with approximately 1,024 names protesting the proposed change in format."[4] Many of the letters were highly personal, one writer saying, for example, that the stations were "the reason I don't leave the city."[5] The Commission's problem was to figure out what to do with the transfer request in the face of such informally presented public protest. Its preference was probably to ignore the complaints and grant the transfer without comment, but the FCC had been scolded by the U.S. Court of Appeals for the District of Columbia Circuit only a few months earlier when it approved another radio station license transfer in the face of public complaints without giving some statement of its reasons.[6] In the face of this court rebuke, the FCC decided it had to say something. Its strategy was to be as brief as possible.

On August 28, 1968, the Commission adopted an eight-paragraph order granting the transfer application. Noting that "more than two thousand persons informally asked the Commission not to permit a change in the music format" of the stations, the FCC stated that the selection of format "is one for [the] judgment of the broadcaster, not the Commission." Because the Commission believed "the informal objections to the transferee's proposal raise no substantial question which requires a hearing," it granted the transfer request.[7]

While the FCC was acting in Washington, the unhappy listeners in Atlanta were getting better organized. They formed a group, the Citizens Committee to Preserve the Present Programming of WGKA and WGKA-FM. On September 25, 1968, the group asked the FCC to reconsider the August 28 sale approval. Now things were getting serious, and as often happens with serious FCC matters, the result was delay.

The delay lasted almost a year while the FCC tried to figure out how to respond to the citizen group's complaint and while it asked Straus for additional information about how the station would be programmed and why that program plan had been selected. Finally, on August 13, 1969—almost a year after its original action in the case—the Commission rejected the citizen group complaints and again approved the transfer. The FCC's basic position was, as before, that the "choice of program formats . . . is one for the judgment of the licensee," but this time the decision was more elaborately argued and supported. In addition, there were a few new wrinkles. Straus had modified the program proposals for the FM station, pledging "to meet the needs and interests of the minority audience interested in classical music by presenting . . . from 8 P.M. until 11 or 11:30 P.M. . . . classical music 6 days a week and on Sunday night starting at 8 P.M. a complete opera." In a footnote the Commission noted that in addition to this classical music on WGKA-FM, a daytime AM station, "WOMN . . . Decatur, Ga., broadcasts an all classical music format. The station is located 10 miles from Atlanta and a large portion of the city of Atlanta receives service from WOMN." Given all this, the FCC once again approved the transfer without granting the requested hearing.[8]

It did so, however, over the objections of Commissioner Kenneth Cox. Cox was unsure that WOMN, a 500-watt daytime station in Decatur, really provided much of a substitute for WGKA's coverage of Atlanta. He argued that since surveys done by Straus showed "nearly 100,000 people in Metropolitan Atlanta" preferred a classical format over Straus's proposal, they deserved at least some service. He wondered about the economic motives for the sale, observing that "the stations were profitable" under the classical format and suggested that the objective of the sale seemed to be to "make more money with a popular format having broader appeal." He concluded, "The private interests of the transferor and the transferees have been served; only the interests of the one-sixth of the public to whom classical music is the preferred service have suffered." The only way to have determined that the transfer was in the public interest, Cox maintained, would have been through an FCC hearing.[9]

Key continuing elements of the format change controversy are contained in this early case. The Commission was confronted with a license transfer together with a proposed change of format. Public protest resulted in a petition submitted to the FCC. Questions arose as to the financial necessity of a format change, the seller maintaining that the existing programming would make it impossible to generate additional capital needed for the new owner to make changes in the AM station but Commissioner Cox insisting that the stations, as run, had been profitable. There was the question of what, exactly, the citizens of Atlanta would lose or gain by the change. The Citizens Committee was concerned with the loss of what they perceived as the city's only classical stations, but the FCC viewed the classical music programming of a nearby low-power AM station (plus some to be retained on WGKA-FM) as a reasonable substitute. Straus claimed that no other station in Atlanta then provided a comparable service of "light classics" or "Broadway hits." Each side, in other words, claimed a unique format was involved; the Citizens Committee believed one would be lost, while the buyer asserted one would be added. As we shall see, these three issues —the economic viability of the existing format, its uniqueness, and the amount of public support for that format and protest over its possible abandonment—became the key ones in a long-running dispute between the U.S. Court of Appeals for the District of Columbia Circuit and the FCC. Overarching those issues was the question of whether it was proper under the First Amendment for a government agency to intervene in content decisions regarding station formats. The dispute was watched over and, for a time, successfully exploited by citizen groups. Eventually it would have to be settled by the U.S. Supreme Court.

Enter the Courts

Judicial involvement in this dispute began in earnest in 1970. Unsatisfied with continued FCC rejection of its position, the Atlanta Citizens Committee sought review of the FCC's decisions by the U.S. Court of Appeals for the District of Columbia Circuit. That court heard oral arguments on May 15, 1970, and decided for the Citizens Committee on October 30.

In order to understand the nature of the court-FCC disagreement, a brief review of how the Communications Act of 1934 treats FCC review of license transfers is required. Under the act, the FCC cannot approve a license transfer unless it concludes "that the public interest, convenience, and necessity will be served thereby."[10] The Commission normally makes this decision based on documents filed by the parties to the transfer. It does not have to hold a hearing simply because one is requested by, for example, a citizen group. The act requires, however, that the Commission "shall formally designate the application for hearing" if—and this would include citizen complaints—"a substantial and material question of fact is presented or the Commission for any reason is unable to" find that the transfer would serve the public interest.[11] The FCC claimed to have followed these sections of the act in its WGKA decisions. The court of appeals, however, disagreed.

Judge Carl McGowan wrote the opinion for a unanimous three-judge panel, which also included Judges Edward A. Tamm and Roger Robb. McGowan began by admitting that it was normally up to the FCC to decide what constitutes a "substantial and material question of fact" relevant to a licensing decision. But he observed further that his concern was "whether that discretion in this particular case was required, prior to its exercise, to be informed as accurately as possible by reliable facts relevant to that exercise"[12]—in this case, more facts about the format change. The rest of McGowan's opinion can be interpreted two different ways. One way is to say that McGowan reversed the FCC because it had not exercised its discretion in an informed fashion: it had looked at the right things, but not hard enough. The other way is to say that McGowan reversed the FCC because it did not look at the right things the right way. The first of these interpretations is a normal one for reviewing courts; it simply examines whether the FCC has been thorough and diligent in its use of its discretion. The second interpretation runs the risk of substituting the court's view of the "right" way to approach a problem for the FCC's view; it may involve the courts in something they are not supposed to do—make policy.

McGowan, of course, admitted only to conducting a traditional review of the FCC's exercise of discretion. The Citizens Committee, in its appeal, focused on the same two points that the FCC had analyzed in its decision: the uniqueness of the classical format in the Atlanta market and its financial viability. McGowan accepted that characterization of what was important. He believed, however, that the FCC had not looked carefully at those issues because of the Commission's hesitancy to intrude upon the licensee's freedom to make programming judgments. He noted that the Commission was not "devoid of any responsibility whatsoever for programming" and cautioned that the Commission's responsibility did not "stop whenever 51% of the people in the area are shown to favor a particular format."[13] In essence, McGowan concluded that at least when challenged, the Commission had to consider proposed programming in a licensing context. He feared that the program preferences of a minority of listeners—here possibly 16 percent of Atlanta's population—would not necessarily be satisfied if licensees had unrestricted discretion to program for large audiences and majority tastes.[14] In light of these considerations, he reanalyzed the complaints of the Citizens Committee and the FCC's handling of them. He concluded that the FCC had been too hasty in its evaluation of Glenkaren's assertions that financial losses associated with the classical music format necessitated the format change: the Commission had relied on "flat assumptions" that required a "closer look."[15] He found that the FCC's conclusion that WOMN was an acceptable substitute for WGKA's classical music had been made without sufficient knowledge of how much of Atlanta its signal really served.[16] Finally, he faulted the FCC for not fully investigating whether or not Straus had misrepresented things to the Commission about the surveys it had done to develop and justify its programming plans. "The truth," noted McGowan, "is most likely to be refined and discovered in the crucible of an evidentiary hearing," and that was what he ordered the FCC to conduct.[17]

Despite the importance of this decision, what Judge McGowan said was transcended in importance by how it was interpreted. To the industry and to the FCC, one important point was the Judge's ordering of a hearing. Both the industry and the Commission have historical aversions to hearings. For the Commission they are a drain on economic resources and personnel since they tend to drag on for years. Broadcasters likewise dread hearings for, at best, they tie up for years investment funds and run up interest charges and attorneys' fees. A hearing is, in the words of one broadcast industry spokesperson, "a code word for killing a transfer. Once you've got a hearing and the necessity of the legal fees and the delay, nobody is going to want to go through with [the transaction]."[18] For practical reasons, there was profound FCC and industry concern about Judge McGowan's opinion, regardless of the rationale he provided for it.

There were also, however, more philosophical objections to what was going on. One objection went to the heart of the politics of regulation. *Broadcasting* magazine picked up the theme in an editorial, "The Take-over": "The principal power to make and execute federal policy in broadcast regulation is being captured from the Congress and the FCC by the United States Court of Appeals for the District of Columbia."[19] Despite Judge McGowan's statement that he had respected the FCC's discretion in deciding how to handle transfer applications, *Broadcasting* and other industry institutions were accusing him of substituting his view of proper policy for that of the FCC. Legal scholars and critics have argued since this 1970 case over whether such a "take-over" was occurring. The Supreme Court ultimately would rule, in effect, that it was. The important point for an understanding of subsequent events is that at the time it was widely believed to be happening. In addition, broadcasters and the FCC both believed that the philosophy of the First Amendment was being violated by the supervision of content ordered by the court.

More Citizen Complaints

The outcome of the *WGKA* case piqued citizen group interest in what they could do when radio stations, or at least those being sold, changed their formats. In the last half of 1972 the FCC decided three more cases, two brought to it by complaining citizen groups, involving radio station format changes. In each instance the Commission decided without a hearing that the transfer and associated format change could be approved as being in the public interest. In each case the Commission said it was following, as it understood the opinion, the mandate of the court of appeals in the *WGKA* case. In each instance losing protestors of the format change took the FCC back to that court by appealing the FCC decisions. In two of the three cases, the Commission lost. By the time these three cases were over, the court and the FCC had reached what the Commission accurately described as "a point of fundamental disagreement."[20]

When WGLN in Sylvania, Ohio, was sold in 1972, and the new owner proposed to substitute "middle-of-the-road (MOR) music" for the station's newly adopted, and newly successful, "youth-oriented progressive rock" format, opposition emerged in the form of a local Citizens Committee to Keep Progressive Rock. In response to a Citizens Committee complaint, the FCC concluded that financial losses had been associated with previous formats and refused to conduct a hearing "to determine the numbers in the community which would prefer a 'Progressive Rock' musical format over a 'MOR' format or the measure of advertiser support for such formats." The Commission said broadcasters had the right to select formats and that it would only intervene if "it is shown or appears to the Commission that the format change is not reasonably attuned to the tastes and general interest of the community of license."[21]

One month later another protest over format change surfaced, although this time the protest was lodged by a competing broadcaster as well as by a citizen group. In a complex sales arrangement, KBTR in Denver, Colorado, after transfer to new owners, proposed to drop its all-news format, and become a country and western station. This new format would compete with the format of KLAK in nearby Lakewood, Colorado. Lakewood Broadcasting Service, owner of KLAK, objected to the transfer and the associated format change. So did a group of complaining citizens. The Commission, however, concluded that KBTR's news format was not unique. It might be the area's only twenty-four-hour news format, but news was available from other Denver area stations and, indeed, some had increased their news offerings when KBTR proposed to drop the all-news format. In addition, the Commission was convinced that substantial financial losses could be attributed to running the all-news operation. Over Commissioner Johnson's dissent, the FCC approved the transfer.[22]

Both of the last two format cases were taken in due—and by now routine—course to the court of appeals, which announced its decisions in the two cases on May 4, 1973. Both opinions were written by Judge Edward Tamm, who had voted with Judge McGowan in the *WGKA* case. In the *Lakewood Broadcasting* case, Judge Tamm upheld the FCC's decision supporting KBTR's decision to drop its all-news for-

mat.[23] In the *Citizens Committee to Keep Progressive Rock* case, however, he concluded that a hearing was required over WGLN's programming plans.[24] The issue in both cases, for Judge Tamm, was whether the
FCC had correctly understood and applied the court of appeals interpretation of the Communications Act in the landmark 1970 Atlanta
(WGKA) case. In *Lakewood,* Judge Tamm endorsed the Commission's
"painstakingly thorough" analysis, in which it had properly concluded
from substantial evidence that there were alternative news sources in
Denver and that the all-news format was not viable for KBTR.[25]

Judge Tamm was much less sympathetic to the way the FCC had
treated the Citizens Committee to Keep Progressive Rock. He interpreted the *WGKA* case as holding that "the public has an interest in
diversity of entertainment formats and . . . format changes can be
detrimental to the public interest. . . . The Commission must consider
format changes and their effect upon the desired diversity."[26] Judge
Tamm then began the process of further clarifying *WGKA.* He decided
that the FCC had failed to "recognize its obligation[s]" under that
case.[27] He focused on two issues the Commission had discussed—the
viability of the progressive rock format and the availability of substitutes for it. As to the viability of the format, Judge Tamm suggested that
the issue needed to be examined somewhat independently of the history of prior failed formats the station said had contributed to losses.
WGLN had begun to make money when it adopted the progressive
rock format, a point Judge Tamm believed the FCC had ignored. After
noting that advertising rates and audience figures had gone up under
the rock format, he advised the Commission as to how it should look at
the finances of formats proposed to be abandoned:

> The question is not whether the licensee is in such dire financial straits that an
> assignment should be granted, but whether the *format* is so economically
> unfeasible that an assignment encompassing a *format change* should be
> granted. . . . The question . . . is not whether WGLN (FM)'s prior format was
> profitable in the past, but whether progressive rock as a format has been, and
> is now, "economically feasible."[28]

As to the issue of availability of an alternative progressive rock format,
Judge Tamm concluded that, at best, all the FCC had determined was
that other stations offered "occasional duplication of selections." More
inquiry was required, he believed, into whether or not a unique progressive rock format would be lost.[29]

Judge Tamm suggested the Commission was, improperly, reading
the *WGKA* (Atlanta) case as automatically requiring a hearing if anybody questioned the availability of substitute formats or the financial
viability of a format to be dropped. He attempted to assure the FCC and
the industry by noting that "if none of the issues pertaining to the

format change are *substantially* in dispute, . . . no hearing need be held."[30] At the same time, he recognized that the FCC was unhappy with the format change issue as it was being developed by the court:

> It is our distinct impression . . . that the Commission desires as limiting an interpretation [of *WGKA*] as possible. We suspect, not altogether facetiously, that the Commission would be more than willing to limit the precedential effect of Citizens Committee to cases involving Atlanta classical music stations.[31]

From the standpoint of the FCC or the industry, there was ambiguity as to what to make of these two cases. Both clearly stood for the proposition that if there were public opposition to a format change, there might have to be detailed FCC review. *Lakewood* proved that the *WGKA* case did not always mean hearings were inevitable but *Citizens Committee to Keep Progressive Rock* showed that the court of appeals stood willing to order the FCC to conduct hearings on format changes in situations where the Commission, on its own, had concluded they were unnecessary.[32] It would take one more case to convince the FCC of the folly of the court's directives to the Commission and stimulate it to find a way out from under those directives. This case involved the sale of WEFM-FM, a classical music station in Chicago, Illinois.

From the standpoint of citizen groups, protesting the transfer of WEFM should not have looked very promising. For one thing, at least early in the case, nobody disputed that there were two other stations besides WEFM programming classical music in Chicago. For another, the past finances of WEFM suggested that arguing about the viability of the format might be difficult. WEFM had been put on the air by Zenith Radio Corporation in 1940, largely as a laboratory for the development of FM broadcast technology. Although operating on a commercial FM channel, Zenith ran the station with a noncommercial classical music format until 1966, when it began to run a limited amount of advertising. Zenith claimed losses even under this arrangement, but the local citizen group involved believed that Zenith had not been aggressive in its selling strategies and had benefitted indirectly from its continuing ability to use the station as an FM broadcasting lab. Ambiguity, then, surrounded both the viability of the format and its uniqueness, two of three criteria the court of appeals had been looking at in format change cases. One thing was clear however: when GCC Communications proposed to buy the station and convert its programming to "contemporary music"—that is, rock—there was a substantial citizen protest and the formation of a Citizens Committee to Save WEFM.[33] There could be no doubt about the existence of local protest.

The first step of the committee was to file a petition with the FCC to deny the transfer. It argued that Chicago required service by three classical stations and that court cases forced the FCC to hold a hearing on the proposed transfer. On December 13, 1972, however, the FCC rejected the petition to deny. It concluded that "the existence of other classical music programming in Chicago coupled with the established long continuing losses experienced by the present licensee" obviated any need for a hearing.[34]

On January 23, 1973, the Citizens Committee asked the FCC to reconsider its decision. On March 22, the FCC rejected that request, noting that the Citizens Committee had raised no new issues. The Commission observed, however, that the Citizens Committee was now arguing that there was no substitute for WEFM's classical music service. It accused the Citizens Committee of ignoring WFMT, which the FCC characterized as "a third Chicago station providing classical music programming." The Commission attached coverage maps showing that while WFMT did not cover all the area reached by WEFM, it did cover all of the city of license—Chicago. With these comments, the Commission rejected the petition for reconsideration.[35]

Attached to the Memorandum Opinion and Order denying reconsideration, however, was a short document labeled "Additional Views of Chairman Burch in Which Commissioners Robert E. Lee, H. Rex Lee, Reid, Wiley and Hooks Join." The document, which as the list of names shows, had the support of all FCC Commissioners except Nicholas Johnson, was an odd one, considering that the Commission had just denied reconsideration. The attachment attempted to explain the Commissioners' view of what "the appropriate relationship between this agency [the FCC] and radio broadcasters should be in the entertainment program format area." After stating once again its belief that broadcasters generally should make programming decisions influenced by "competitive marketplace forces," the six Commissioners stated their understanding of when thorough FCC review of format changes might be required:

If and when there is a showing of facts before the Commission indicating that the format is not reasonably attuned to community tastes or that the format change will eliminate a service to the public not otherwise available, a survey of entertainment tastes or a hearing may be required.

Despite this rather narrow view (compared to prior court decisions) of when hearings might be required, the Commissioners promised to "take an extra hard look at the reasonableness of any proposal which would deprive a community of its only source of a particular type of programming."[36] As most observers expected would happen, the Citizens Committee went to the court of appeals to see what that court thought of this latest FCC format change case.

Confident of its victory at the Commission, GCC prepared to switch the station's format. It moved out most of the classical albums and prepared for a midnight, April 7 switch. Meanwhile the Citizens Committee filed the necessary documents with the Court of Appeals for the District of Columbia Circuit to appeal the FCC's decision. On April 6, at about 5:00 P.M. and as GCC employees were "throwing a party for newsmen and staff to celebrate the initiation of the new rock station beginning at midnight," the court issued a stay order that, in effect, forced GCC to retain the classical format pending court review.[37]

During that further review the court of appeals was initially satisfied —or more precisely, two of the members of a three-judge panel, David Bazelon and Roger Robb, were mostly satisfied—with the FCC's actions. They believed that the Citizens Committee did not deserve a hearing because of other classical music programming available in Chicago. They supported the Commission as having acted properly in concluding that WEFM had incurred losses after 1965 when trying to run the classical station commercially. For the first time in this line of cases, one of the judges, Bazelon, considered the constitutionality of what the court was saying. He was unable to resolve all the First Amendment issues but concluded that "the current approach of minimizing regulation except when diversity is most seriously threatened appears to be reasonably in accord with the goals of the Federal Communications Act and the First Amendment." Judge Charles Fahy dissented, feeling a hearing was required to answer questions about Zenith's financial losses.[38]

Undaunted by the setback with the three-judge panel, a decision hereafter called *WEFM I*, the Citizens Committee sought a rehearing of the case by the court of appeals *en banc*, that is, by all the judges of the court. Such requests are rarely granted, but this one surprisingly was. Oral argument were held on June 13, 1974. A decision favorable to the Citizens Committee, hereafter called *WEFM II*, was issued October 4, 1974. Judge McGowan wrote the court's opinion this time, for himself and six other members of the court. Judge Bazelon wrote a lengthy separate concurrence. Only Judges George MacKinnon and Robb dissented. Judge McGowan, author of the opinion in the *WGKA* case that had started development of the format change controversy, used *WEFM II* as a chance to explain (and expand on) the court of appeals view of how the FCC should handle disputed format changes.[39]

Judge McGowan took several exceptions to the FCC's handiwork. After reviewing the FCC's disposition of the case, and the earlier court of appeals format change decisions, he noted some of the ways in which the *WEFM* case differed from its predecessors. In the Chicago case the Citizens Committee had not tried to say that WEFM had a significantly unique format. The FCC had relied on this admission as a principal basis for denying the hearing sought by the Citizens Committee. The judge said the Commission had made too much of the distinction.

Judge McGowan now was concerned, in part, that one of the alleged substitutes for WEFM, WNIB, did not reach all of the WEFM service area although it did thoroughly cover the city of Chicago. After citing court cases holding that licensees had responsibilities to all of their service areas, he announced, "We now hold that the public interest implicated in a format change is the interest of the public in the service area, not just the city of license."[40] So much for the substitutability of WNIB—the one admitted classical station. What, now, to do with the other alleged substitute, WFMT? To some extent, Judge McGowan could have avoided dealing with this question for he had, earlier in the opinion, included some interesting language in a summary of the prior holdings of the court of appeals on format changes:

The disappearance of a *distinctive* format may deprive a significant segment of the public of the benefits of radio, at least at their first-preference level. When faced with a proposed license assignment encompassing a format change, the FCC is obliged to determine whether the format to be lost is unique or *otherwise serves a specialized audience that would feel its loss.*[41]

This language could have been used by Judge McGowan to define WFMT's program service as "distinctive" through "serving a specialized audience that would feel its loss" even though it was not unique. Having set up these conditions, however, he apparently decided instead to try and show that WFMT's programming might be unique. Looking through the court's own records of earlier cases, he found that in a 1968 case involving WFMT, the station had described itself as an "award winning fine arts station," and not as a classical music station.[42] "Against this background," said Judge McGowan, the FCC had "an affirmative obligation to establish that WFMT is in fact a *reasonable* substitute for the service . . . offered by WEFM" before granting the transfer.[43]

Thus Judge McGowan had undercut the FCC's argument that the WEFM transfer did not require a hearing because no unique format was being lost. Still remaining were the issue of Zenith's claim that the format was not viable and some related questions about the Commission's approach to format economics. McGowan concluded that the FCC was being unfair to the Citizens Committee concerning Zenith's claim of losses associated with the format. If Zenith wanted to base the abandonment of its format on such a claim, Judge McGowan reasoned, then Zenith would have to come out in the open with the facts and figures to prove its claims.[44] The related issue, how to approach the philosophy with which the Commission handled regulation of formats, led him to criticize the "additional views" Chairman Dean Burch and five other Commissioners had attached to their second WEFM decision.

Judge McGowan noted that those "additional views" had been intended to explain the "policy considerations" underlying the FCC's format cases. He went on to accuse the Commission of "an apparent error" that had to be, in his mind, corrected in order to avoid continued repetition of other "errors" like the *WEFM* case. His criticism focused on the Commission's reliance on marketplace economics to regulate formats and fill voids if stations made changes. Arguing that "there is . . . no free market in radio entertainment because over-the-air broadcasters do not deal directly with their listeners" but instead sell listeners to advertisers, Judge McGowan concluded that radio broadcasters will attempt to maximize profits—an action that would not necessarily, because of demographic differences and their differential attractiveness to advertisers, lead to "securing the maximum benefits of radio to all the people of the United States" as the Communications Act requires.[45] This analysis led to his most direct attack on the FCC's reluctance to regulate formats. Said the judge, "There is no longer any room for doubt that, if the FCC is to pursue the public interest, it may not be able at the same time to pursue a policy of free competition."[46]

Reactions to the court's decision were sharp and varied. Citizen group leaders, of course, were very pleased. Harry Booth, the WEFM citizen group's attorney, said the decision would "dampen" efforts to convert "quality" AM and FM stations to "rock and roll" and would "give heart" to groups "throughout the country" concerned about station sales and format changes.[47] Broadcasters had several concerns. Stations began to wonder if the issue of format change, always examined before only in the context of station sales and license transfers, could be constrained within those bounds; the language of Judge McGowan's opinion suggested that format changes not associated with sales could also be challenged. Station brokers feared that the prices of stations would decline as stations with poorly performing formats could not be reprogrammed to produce more revenue. Broadcasters and FCC staff members expressed concern that the decision would chill experimentation with new and possibly unsuccessful formats because no broadcaster would want to be locked into a format that did not work out well. They also worried about the implications of the format decisions for more pervasive FCC regulation of broadcast content.

In addition to sharing these First Amendment concerns about content regulation with broadcasters, the FCC had two further reservations about the court's decisions. First, it was obviously concerned about the practicality of the format policy. Could it implement the court's *WEFM* decision? Could it identify sufficient public protest, determine intrinsic financial viability, or figure out when a format was or was not

unique? Second, the FCC was concerned about the broader implications of all these cases—not just *WEFM* but its predecessors as well. The
court, it seemed to some, had defined a new role for itself vis-à-vis the
FCC. Had the court gone too far? Had it made policy rather than just
interpreting the law? Could the FCC, in the future, make policy without being second-guessed by the U.S. Court of Appeals?

New Strategy from the FCC

At this point, the Commission faced a strategic decision. There was
immediate trade journal speculation that the FCC would "take the case
to [the U.S.] Supreme Court."[48] Internally, however, the Commission
settled on a different course of action. Apparently the FCC went as far
as preparing drafts of the papers that would be needed to seek Supreme
Court review, but then, on the advice of the Department of Justice,
decided against filing a petition for *certiorari* (review). Reportedly the
Justice Department advised the FCC that it stood a good chance of
losing.[49] The Commission decided instead on an unorthodox tactic. It
would let the *WEFM* decision stand—and it would hold the hearings
demanded by the U.S. Court of Appeals.[50] Instead of continuing to
battle the court of appeals on a case-by-case basis, the Commission
would open a general inquiry into what its policies toward format
change regulation should be. It would take the risk of offending the U.S.
Court of Appeals, which thought it had already decided what the law
was in the area. The FCC, however, would be in a stronger position to
take to the U.S. Supreme Court the results of an unfavorable court of
appeals decision regarding the outcome of a broad inquiry than to
argue the entire format issue in the context of a single case. If nothing
else, it was an aggressive strategy.

For citizen activists the fourteen months between *WEFM II* and the
implementation of the FCC's strategy to circumvent or overturn it was
the high point of citizen influence over radio format changes. Unlike
some of the more esoteric topics of interest to some citizen group
leaders—topics like the cross-ownership of media, which some pre-
sumed to have an indirect effect on the diversity of media content—a
format change was something that could get citizens worked up. Raising money or getting signatures on petitions, although never easy, was
sometimes fun. The Citizens Committee to Save WEFM, for example,
"picket[ed] Orchestra Hall, home of the Chicago Symphony Orchestra,
to call attention" to their cause.[51] Literature urging that protest letters
be sent to the FCC was distributed outside auditoriums where Chicago
music school graduations were in progress.[52] A book published by the
University of Chicago about the classical music radio audience in Chicago helped defray expenses.[53]

Those who participated in format change controversies often developed a close affinity among themselves and with the station they were attempting to "save." Tanya Bickley, a New Canaan, Connecticut, resident who collected protest letters over a New York City format change while riding the commuter trains caught the spirit in remarking about her favorite station: "I listen to it whenever I can. I love it and so do my friends who fought alongside me."[54] Sometimes those participating in citizen format protest rallies could whip themselves up into a crusading, off-to-do-battle spirit, as is evident in the following description of a rally concerning a round-the-clock jazz station that had changed its format:

To the strains of "Straight, No Chaser," a sealed box containing petitions with 80,000 signatures was loaded into a van yesterday in front of City Hall for delivery to the Federal Communications Commission in Washington. . . .

During a noontime news conference, the trumpet and saxophone duo of Ted Curzon and Harold Ousley played choruses from jazz classics, elected officials promised support and the citizens' group's lawyer vowed a battle up to the United States Supreme Court to get jazz back on commercial radio in New York on a 24-hour-a-day basis.[55]

While the citizen groups enjoyed their few months of victory, documents were being slowly drafted at the FCC to set in motion the Commission's strategy for getting out from under the dictates of the court of appeals. On December 22, 1975, the Commission unanimously adopted the language of a Notice of Inquiry, Docket No. 20682, "to examine whether the Commission should play any role in dictating the selection of entertainment formats."[56] Supporters of the U.S. Court of Appeals viewed that question as having already been answered by the court, but the FCC, here and in other language in the order, was in a challenging mood.

It is obvious from the language of the Notice of Inquiry that the Commission did not intend to be conciliatory toward the court's views. For example, the Commission expressed its deep concern,

that, by rejecting the programming choices of individual broadcasters in favor of a system of pervasive governmental regulation, the Commission would embark on a course which may have serious adverse consequences for the public interest. At the same time, we are concerned that such a course may involve an overly optimistic view of what can realistically be achieved through government regulation.[57]

Recognizing that the court had cautioned the Commission that it might not be able to pursue a policy of free competition and still serve the public interest, the Commission criticized the court for its implicit . . . notion that the Commission, if it tried hard enough, can come up with a measure of collective welfare which is superior to the advertisers' marketplace. There are excellent reasons for supposing, however, that the search for the public interest in entertainment formats may be a difficult and ultimately futile exercise.[58]

The FCC went on and on in this vein. When done, there was hardly an assumption, assertion, or "test" contained in the court's format change cases that the Commission had not argued against or at least expressed doubts about. Although the Notice of Inquiry contained about twenty specific questions on which the FCC sought comment, the proceeding was, in fact, a very wide-sweeping one. The Commission had brought out into the open its disagreement with the court of appeals and hoped that those commenting in the proceeding would help it build a record either leading the appeals court to change its views or resulting in those views being overturned by the U.S. Supreme Court.

The comments soon began to flow in, and were as predictable as the Commission surely expected. Broadcast interests applauded the Commission's challenge to the court of appeals and seconded its desire to refrain from regulation and allow marketplace controls to dominate the format selection process.[59] The National Association of Broadcasters, recognizing the name of the FCC's game, noted:

If the Commission decides, on the basis of the more complete record being compiled in this proceeding, that the court erred in deciding WEFM and other license-assignment cases involving format changes, it is the Commission's duty to adopt a statement of policy to that effect and, upon any judicial review, to invite the court to overrule its decisions in those cases for the compelling reasons present.[60]

Citizen groups interpreted the Commission's inquiry as an "attempt to end run the Court of Appeals"[61] and tried various means to block it. On February 6, 1976, for example, the Citizens Communications Center, a public interest law firm, filed a "Petition to Reconsider, Rescind, Suspend, or Redirect" the format inquiry. Citizens argued that the Notice of Inquiry was only "designed to elicit legal opinions on issues which have already been decided by the courts" and called it a "misguided appeal of the . . . opinion of the U.S. Court of Appeals for the D.C. Circuit in *Citizens Committee to Save WEFM* v. *FCC* . . . not to the Supreme Court—or to Congress—but to broadcasters."[62] The FCC swiftly, on March 9, 1976, denied the petition.[63] Although some citizen groups filed comments reiterating support for the views of the court of appeals on format change cases, for many citizen groups, "The Inquiry itself [was] the problem," not the court of appeals' decisions as the Commission and its supporters intimated.[64]

On July 30, 1976, the FCC released its Memorandum Opinion and

Order in the format change inquiry. The proceeding had been a fast one, a little over twenty-seven weeks from release of the Notice of Inquiry to the release of the final order. Considering that many inquiries languish for months or years, this was prompt indeed and reflected the Commission's desire to move swiftly on a well-understood scenario.

Rarely has an FCC decision been released with such surety that it would not be the final word on the subject. Here, however, there was a game plan known to almost everybody involved in the controversy. The FCC would release its decision, which, given the language of the Notice of Inquiry, would argue that the court of appeals was wrong in forcing the Commission into the format change evaluation business. One or more of the citizen groups that had participated in the proceeding would seek review of the FCC's action in the court of appeals. The court of appeals, most likely *en banc*, would stick to its prior positions and would overturn the FCC decision. The FCC would seek review by the U.S. Supreme Court and finally resolve the controversy unless, of course, the resolution from the court was one that stimulated Congress to amend the Communications Act.[65]

When it released its Memorandum Opinion and Order on July 30, the Commission played its role to the hilt. Given that the Commission had, in effect, gone on the offensive, it could build a complete attack on the decisions of the court of appeals. The FCC could develop the best possible articulation of its position—a better articulation, most likely, than what it could accomplish in any appeal of a single case. When released, the Commission's decision did indeed attack the court of appeals from every imaginable angle. It was hoped that one or more of these arguments would satisfy the court of appeals or, failing that, convince the U.S. Supreme Court should the case go that far.

The Commission was blunt about how it proposed to implement the commands of the court of appeals: it wouldn't. "We must," said the FCC, "refrain from the detailed supervision of entertainment formats which the Court of Appeals holds to be a part of the Commission's statutory responsibilities."[66] The Commission's reasons were summed up near the end of the decision:

Any such regulatory scheme would be flatly inconsistent with our understanding of congressional policy as manifested in the Communications Act, contraproductive in terms of maximizing the welfare of the radio-listening public, administratively a fearful and comprehensive nightmare, and unconstitutional as impermissibly chilling innovation and experimentation in radio programming.[67]

After throwing all these brickbats at the U.S. Court of Appeals, the Commission attempted near the end of the opinion to hold out a small olive branch—the olive branch known as the "partnership doctrine."

The doctrine had first been advanced by Judge Harold Leventhal in the course of a court of appeals review of an FCC licensing case in 1970.[68] In the doctrine, Judge Leventhal propounded the conception of a cooperative relationship between administrative agencies and reviewing courts. The FCC decided to remind the court of appeals of the partnership doctrine in the hopes that it might apply the doctrine as a balm to the wounds inflicted by the Commission on the court in the FCC's format inquiry. The FCC also might have hope that the partnership doctrine would encourage toleration when the court of appeals, as all expected, reviewed the Commission's action. The Commission's appeal was phrased as follows:

The administrative process "combines judicial supervision with a salutary principle of judicial restraint, an awareness that agencies and courts together constitute a 'partnership' in furtherance of the public interest, and are collaborative instrumentalities of justice." . . . When such "partners" come to a point of fundamental disagreement, it is incumbent upon us to take a step back and rethink our entire position if this relationship is to be creative rather than destructive. This Docket is the occasion for the Commission to reconsider its policy on entertainment formats.[69]

The Commission held at least a slight hope that the court of appeals would itself step back and examine the court-FCC relationship in light of the Commission's adoption of what it called a "noninterference policy" in broadcast formats as contrasted with the court's policy, sometimes called the "endangered format" doctrine.

The next step in the process was the FCC's denial of the almost ritualistic petition for FCC reconsideration from citizen groups.[70] The most notable aspect of the handling of the petition for reconsideration was a separate statement by Commissioner Joseph R. Fogarty, who had not participated in the first FCC decision in the format inquiry. Fogarty shared the concerns of the Commission about complying with the court of appeals but was also troubled by the Commission's criticism of the court. The purpose of his statement was to "concur specially . . . to the extent it [the order] respectfully seeks further judicial guidance as to the implementation of the mandate of the format change decisions."[71]

A Court of Appeals Reprise

As one former FCC Chairman noted in a trade magazine column, "The ball is back in the U.S. Court of Appeals' court (no pun intended)."[72] Unlike the FCC, the court of appeals was in no great hurry to review the format issue. Although the FCC's reconsideration order was released on August 25, 1977, making the case ready for judicial review, oral arguments were not held before the U.S. Court of Appeals for the

District of Columbia Circuit until February 7, 1979. It was a case of interest to many parties: eleven citizen groups sought review by the U.S. Court of Appeals, and five more joined through friend-of-the-court briefs. Twenty-one broadcast organizations, including the ABC and CBS networks, joined in support of the FCC. When the court decided the case on June 29, 1979, it returned some of the invective the FCC had heaped upon it almost three years earlier.

In an opinion written by Judge McGowan, author of the *WGKA* and *WEFM II* decisions, the FCC came in for harsh criticism. Recognizing that the Commission had urged the court to reconsider its past format cases, he declined "the Commission's invitation" and instead reminded the FCC that it had "to accept and carry out in good faith its legal duties as interpreted by the court."[73] The Commission, the court believed, had "cast serious doubt on the rationality and impartiality of its action."[74] According to Judge McGowan:

Throughout the format controversy, the Commission has displayed a deep-seated aversion to the decisions of this court . . . while at the same time misinterpreting and exaggerating their meaning. Perhaps as a result of these inter-related defects, the Commission failed to take affirmative steps to minimize what it perceived as the intrusive features of the format decisions while preserving their essence.[75]

. . .

. . . It instituted the present proceeding in the nature of rulemaking with the apparent purpose of overruling the *WEFM* case. Whatever its power generally to proceed by rulemaking rather than adjudication, we think it a somewhat different matter when the seeming purpose of the rulemaking is the circumvention of a recent court decision reached in an adjudicatory context.[76]

According to the court, the Commission's tendency to misread the court's earlier decisions led to the FCC's fears about "administrative quagmires," violations of the First Amendment, and perceived imposition of "common carrier" duties on broadcasters. The court went to considerable length to demonstrate that more modest or moderate, or as the court pointedly put it, "sympathetic and accurate," readings of the cases were possible that would have made the format change principles practical if the Commission had only tried.[77] The court suggested that earlier interpretations of the cases had assumed there would be many hearings when, in fact, the court believed most format disputes could be resolved without one.[78] It stressed that FCC intervention under *WEFM II* was intended to take place not routinely, as a substitute for marketplace action, but only infrequently, when there was evidence the marketplace had failed to provide proper programming incentives. Concluding that the Commission's policy statement was based on such a flawed and antagonistic approach to the court's earlier cases, and also that it had been adopted in a procedurally unsound way, Judge McGowan declared it to be "unavailing and of no force and effect."[79]

As in the FCC's now discounted policy statement, much of the discussion in the court of appeals' opinion, as well as in concurring and dissenting statements, focused on the proper relationship of the court and the Commission. In Judge McGowan's view, the errors in understanding the court-FCC relationship were the Commission's:

> The Commission repeatedly referred to *WEFM* as representing the "policy" of the Court of Appeals, and contrasted it unfavorably with the "policy" of the Commission. . . .
> We should have thought that *WEFM* represents, not a *policy*, but rather a *law* of the land as enacted by Congress and interpreted by the Court of Appeals, and as it is to be administered by the Commission. This court has neither the expertise nor the constitutional authority to make "policy" as that word is commonly understood. . . . That role is reserved to the Congress, and, within the bounds of delegated authority, to the Commission. But in matters interpreting the "law" the final say is constitutionally committed to the judiciary. . . . *WEFM* was an interpretation of a statute applicable to an adjudicatory proceeding and, to this extent, was a decision in which the judicial word is final.[80]

Judge Leventhal, "as sponsor of the court-agency partnership concept and 'hard look' doctrine", added his view that the court "does not view itself as cast in the role of policymaker." He continued:

> In a working partnership, there may be differences between partners, but there is a mutuality of recognition and respect far removed from the approach taken with any stranger or intruder.
> The relationship of court and agency emerges from the functions assigned by Congress to each. Congress has delegated to the agency, here the FCC, the function of making policy. It has given the court the role of review to ensure that an agency decision stays within the intent of the law. . . .
> . . . The court-agency partnership depends on mutuality of respect and understanding.[81]

Seven judges had held that under the court-FCC "partnership," the court had behaved properly in interpreting the law, while the FCC had misbehaved by trying to characterize as "policy making" what was entirely the duty of the court, namely, statutory interpretation.

Three judges, however—Tamm, MacKinnon, and Bazelon—tended to be on the FCC's side on this issue. The most important opinion here is Judge Tamm's. His is also the most interesting vote. Of the five major previous court of appeals format change cases *(WGKA, Lakewood, Progressive Rock, WEFM I,* and *WEFM II),* he had served on panels or in *en banc* reviews four times—more often, in fact, than Judge McGowan although the latter had written the two most important decisions *(WGKA* and *WEFM II).* Judge Tamm himself had authored the court's decisions in *Lakewood* and *Progressive Rock.* In all four prior decisions, he had supported the court's development of format case law. Three of the four times, he had joined Judge McGowan and once *(Lakewood),* he had joined Judge Bazelon.

In this case, however, Judge Tamm would split from his frequent ally, Judge McGowan. The reason appeared to be that he was won over by the FCC's analysis of the court-FCC partnership issue:

I respectfully dissent. The majority's decision, I fear, usurps the proper role of the Federal Communications Commission in the formulation of communications policy. In my view, the Commission's determination that application of [*WEFM II*] will not measurably increase diversity of entertainment formats is neither arbitrary nor capricious. Although I understand the frustration of reexamining an issue purportedly resolved, I believe that the much touted agency-court partnership is well served by continuing dialogue between administrator and judge. I am persuaded that the Commission, which Congress has entrusted with the duty to regulate broadcasting in the public interest, has advanced a reasoned position which this court should uphold.[82]

Judge MacKinnon joined Judge Tamm's dissenting opinion. Judge Bazelon concurred in the majority's decision, on procedural grounds, but he added that he felt

compelled to note [his] agreement with much of Judge Tamm's thoughtful dissent. Implementing the public interest standard calls for a strong dose of policy judgment, a responsibility entrusted by Congress to the FCC. Yet the majority virtually confines the FCC to a spectator's role in formulating policies that will promote and preserve diversity while minimizing the hazards of government intrusion into the content of broadcasting.[83]

The decision of the court of appeals in its review of the FCC's Format Policy Statement, then, turned out to have two main components. First, it overturned the FCC's statement formally as being contrary to the Communications Act as construed and applied in the court's prior format change decisions. Second, the decision, responding to the brief discussion of the court-agency "partnership" in the FCC's original order, substantially criticized the Commission's view of that relationship and its opinion that the court had made policy in earlier cases. One portion of the argument over that issue, from Judge Tamm's dissent, is now more relevant than it at first seemed:

The Supreme Court has often reminded this court of the appropriate relationship between administrative agency and reviewing court. Only last year, the Court, reversing our finding that the Commission had acted improperly in "grandfathering" certain newspaper–broadcast station combinations, noted that the Commission's decision to adopt a general policy of prospective divestiture was primarily judgmental or predictive. . . . In the present case, the majority disregards the Commission's expert knowledge and, in so doing, violates the mandate of *FCC* v. *National Citizens Committee for Broadcasting* [the newspaper-broadcast cross-ownership case].

The majority has lost sight of our role as a reviewing court whose proper function is to uphold an agency's reasonable judgment.[84]

The Supreme Court Decides

Judge Tamm's mention of the Supreme Court was, of course, important because that was where most people expected the case to go next. That had been the understood scenario for years, but since the court of appeals had taken three years to decide the case, it was not immediately apparent whether or not the plan would be carried out. The FCC's policy statement on format change had been strongly associated with Chairman Wiley. During the three years following its adoption, Wiley had been replaced as Chairman by Charles Ferris and three other new Commissioners—Joseph Fogarty, Tyrone Brown, and Anne Jones had come aboard. Thus a majority of the Commission at the time of the court of appeals decision in 1979 had not voted on the original policy statement in 1976.

It was not clear whether, philosophically, the new Commission supported the old policy statement. Generally, the Ferris Commission was, at least in 1979, regarded as more pro–citizen group and anti-industry than the Wiley Commission had been. Ferris's legal assistant, Frank W. Lloyd III, had been an attorney at the Citizens Communications Center and had, in fact, appeared on behalf of the WNCN Listeners Guild in the challenge to the FCC's policy statement at the court of appeals (though he had not participated in it while at the FCC). When the court of appeals' decision overturning the FCC's policy statement was first announced, there was some speculation that Ferris might allow the decision to stand, since it would clearly strengthen the rights of citizen groups in license challenges.

Commission attorneys, however, urged an appeal to the Supreme Court for two reasons. First, this had been the game plan all along—to appeal a case involving a general policy statement rather than a specific licensing situation. Second, many Commission attorneys agreed with Judge Bazelon's dissent that the majority's opinion at the court of appeals level confined the FCC to a "spectator's role in formulating policy." *Broadcasting* magazine discussed this political problem for the Commission in an editorial:

Broadcasters are hoping that the FCC will seek Supreme Court review, knowing, however, that the Commission has undergone radical changes in personnel and attitude since the policy statement of 1976, now overturned, was issued. Perhaps the first inclination of newer arrivals at the FCC will be to disengage from a battle on behalf of the works of predecessors whose philosophies departed with them. In their own interest, however, incumbents must protect the independence that this decision would deny them.

The latest word from the appellate court goes beyond the format issue to mean that the public interest is what the court says it is, not as the FCC construes it. Under those conditions, nothing the FCC does will be immune to the second-guessing of the self-appointed regulators on the court.[85]

On August 24, 1979, the Commission voted 5 to 2 to ask the U.S. Supreme Court to review the decision of the court of appeals. Chairman Ferris along with new Commissioner Jones joined Commissioners Robert E. Lee, James Quello, and Abbott Washburn (all of whom had voted for the 1976 policy statement) in supporting the request for review. Commissioners Fogarty and Brown, who had not voted on the 1976 statement, voted against seeking review.[86] On March 3, 1980, the court decided it would review the court of appeals' decision.[87] The case was argued November 3, 1980, and decided March 24, 1981.

Like the lower court decision in the case, *FCC* v. *WNCN Listeners Guild* attracted many parties when it reached the U.S. Supreme Court. The Commission—still defending its 1976 format policy statement— had the support of all three commercial television networks, the National Radio Broadcasters Association, and the National Association of Broadcasters. Those seeking to support the court of appeals, and overturn the 1976 policy statement, included the WNCN Listeners Guild and ten other citizen groups plus the attorneys general of eight states.[88]

Dick Grey, who had urged his readers in 1968 to write to FCC Chairman Rosel Hyde to protest the format change of WGKA in Atlanta, would have been surprised at the way the case was treated by the U.S. Supreme Court. When Grey urged his listeners to write the FCC, he assumed the government, or at least the FCC, would want to do something about format changes. Actually, of course, the Commission had always wanted to leave those choices up to broadcasters, subject to marketplace influence. For years, the court of appeals had tried to drag an unwilling FCC into the regulation of certain kinds of changes of radio station formats. At last the U.S. Supreme Court was going to decide whether the Commission, if it wanted to do so, could depend on the marketplace or whether the court of appeals could force the Commission to hold hearings into at least some of the transfers and format changes.

The court sided with the FCC, 7 to 2. Justice Byron White wrote the court's majority opinion. White spent very little time discussing whether the Commission's noninterference policy was wise or unsound. First, he concluded that the Communications Act of 1934 did not compel the FCC to hold hearings on format changes:[89] "Congress did not unequivocally express its disfavor of entertainment format review by the Commission, but neither is there substantial indication that Congress expected the public-interest standard to *require* format regulation by the Commission."[90]

Thus whether there was or was not going to be format regulation was subject to the Commission's discretion. While the Commission's historical view had been that it did not want to engage in format change regulation, the court of appeals had always disagreed with that position. Justice White, implying that the politics of broadcast regulation had implications much beyond the format issue alone, held that the U.S. Court of Appeals had improperly overturned a legitimate Commission choice to rely on marketplace forces rather than to regulate.

White outlined the conditions the FCC had to meet in order to make discretionary decisions that the U.S. Court of Appeals should not overturn. It turned out that Judge Tamm had been correct when he had pinpointed the Supreme Court's earlier newspaper-broadcast cross-ownership case *(FCC* v. *NCCB)* as an indication that the Supreme Court was getting tired of excessive overturning of administrative agency decisions by the U.S. Courts of Appeals. White used several phrases and words to explain what the FCC had to do to survive judicial review of its policy making. Quoting from *FCC* v. *NCCB,* White noted that a Commission action should be upheld "so long as that view is based on consideration of permissible factors and is otherwise reasonable."[91] The Commission must provide a "rational explanation" for its conclusions.[92] If it makes predictions of what may happen because of its decisions, those predictions must be "within the institutional competence of the Commission."[93] Finally, White provided the following general analysis of why the Supreme Court supported the FCC and not the U.S. Court of Appeals:

Our opinions have repeatedly emphasized that the Commission's judgment regarding how the public interest is best served is entitled to substantial judicial deference. *See, e.g., FCC* v. *National Citizens Committee for Broadcasting.* . . . The Commission's implementation of the public interest standard, when based on a rational weighing of competing policies is not to be set aside by the Court of Appeals, for "the weighing of policies under the 'public interest' standard is a task that Congress has delegated to the Commission in the first instance." *FCC* v. *National Citizens Committee for Broadcasting.*[94]

Thus, after more than ten years, the Commission finally vindicated its right, if it chose to do so, to leave the selection of broadcast station formats up to broadcasters and marketplace forces. The decision makes no mention of whether or not the FCC's format policies might violate the First Amendment rights of broadcasters, although the policy of noninterference was held to be consistent with the First Amendment rights of listeners and viewers.[95] The case that some believed would set clear guidelines for the FCC's regulation of content turned out, instead, to be mostly about providing better guidelines for the supervision of the FCC by the U.S. Court of Appeals for the District of Columbia Circuit.

Indeed, that is the way *Broadcasting* magazine editorially celebrated the joint FCC-industry victory:

More is to be read into the U.S. Supreme Court's decision of last week in the radio format case than an affirmation of the FCC's authority to defer to the marketplace in program regulation. That alone, of course, would be reason enough for broadcasters to welcome the decision.

But the high court also sent a message to the District of Columbia Circuit Court of Appeals which for years has been insinuating itself in[to] the formulation of regulatory policy. The message was polite but firm: The appellate court is to mind its own business, reviewing the legality of FCC decisions when asked, and to let the FCC mind its making and administering the rules.[96]

NOTES

1. See *Glenkaren Associates, Inc.,* 19 FCC2d 13 (1969).
2. "Listeners Mourn WGKA Change," *Atlanta Journal,* May 6, 1968, p. B13. Grey had been alerted to the change by viewer letters.
3. "FCC Postpones WGKA Action," *Atlanta Journal,* August 21, 1968, p. D9.
4. *Glenkaren Associates, Inc.,* 19 FCC2d 13, 14 (1969).
5. "Atlantans Sound Off as WGKA Changes Tune," *Broadcasting,* May 20, 1968, p. 54.
6. *Joseph* v. *FCC,* 404 F.2d 207 (D.C. Cir. 1968). The Joseph case was decided July 30, 1968.
7. *Glenkaren Associates, Inc.,* 14 RR2d 104 (1968). This FCC order was never published in the official FCC reports and is exceedingly short. It cites no other case or authorities, although the FCC could have relied on the earliest of its format change cases, *The Good Music Station, Inc.,* 23 FCC 611 (1957).
8. *Glenkaren Associates, Inc.,* 19 FCC2d 13 (1969).
9. Ibid., dissenting statement of Commissioner Cox, at 18–19.
10. 47 U.S.C., Sec. 310(b).
11. 47 U.S.C., Sec. 309 (e).
12. *Citizens Committee to Preserve the Present Programming on WGKA-AM and FM* v. *FCC,* 436 F.2d 263, 269 (1970).
13. Ibid., at 272.
14. Broadcasters continually objected to use of abstract format preference surveys. They argued that the best evidence of whether or not the audience wanted a format was actual listenership data, and WGKA attracted far less than 16 percent of the Atlanta audience.
15. *Citizens Committee to Preserve the Present Programming on WGKA-AM and FM* v. *FCC,* 436 F.2d 270 (1970).
16. Ibid., at 271–272.
17. Ibid., at 272.
18. Erwin G. Krasnow, senior vice-president and general counsel, National Association of Broadcasters, quoted in Mel Friedman, "Supreme Court

Test of Format-Change Issue: FCC's On-Off Switch in Radio Deregulation?" *Television/Radio Age*, October 20, 1980, p. 42.

19. "The Take-Over" [editorial], *Broadcasting*, November 9, 1970, p. 78.
20. *Entertainment Formats*, 60 FCC2d 858, 865 (1976). There are three earlier radio format cases and one TV format case that merit brief comment. In *WCAB, Inc.*, 27 FCC2d 743 (1971) the Commission approved the transfer of WCAB, which involved a change in the station's format from a "progressive rock" to a "good music" or "easy listening" formula. Only thirty-four listeners, none from the community of license, complained—not enough, said the FCC. In addition, the Commission concluded that the station had incurred substantial financial losses under the format and that other Milwaukee area stations provided "progressive rock" music. Commissioner Nicholas Johnson dissented. In *Sentinel Heights FM Broadcasters, Inc.*, 29 FCC2d 83 (1971), the Commission approved a transfer of an AM-FM combination. The purchaser originally had proposed to reduce the twenty-four-hour-per-day classical music on both stations to six hours per day and to program approximately 59 percent good music. Later the assignee decided to program 100 percent classical music on the FM station, although the citizen group alleged that the selections proposed would be "unadventurous" and "incongruous works." Commissioner Johnson dissented. See *Order in Citizens Committee to Preserve the Present Programming of WONO(FM)* v. *FCC*, Docket No. 71-1336 (D.C. Cir. 1971). In *Keyes Corporation*, 31 FCC2d 32 (1971) the FCC approved the transfer of a station whose new owner proposed to change from a "quiet pool of instrumental music" to "contemporary popular music and standard popular music from the past." The Commission concluded that the "proposed change of format will not result in the elimination of the only station providing 'quiet pool' entertainment fare." Commissioner Johnson was absent, but Commissioner Robert Bartley dissented. Finally, in *RKO General, Inc.*, 33 FCC2d 664 (1972), the Commission allowed RKO General to give its former experimental pay-TV station, which it had briefly attempted to run as a nonpay operation, to Faith Center. Faith Center proposed a service that would be 48.3 percent religious. The Commission concluded that the station, under RKO's stewardship, was a financial disaster and that other television stations near Hartford, Connecticut, would make up for whatever might not be done by Faith Center's heavy emphasis on religious service. In this instance the FCC was upheld by the U.S. Court of Appeals for the District of Columbia Circuit. See *Hartford Communications Committee* v. *FCC*, 467 F.2d 408 (D.C. Cir. 1972). The court of appeals attributed RKO's generosity to the company's finding itself in "economic quicksand." Charles M. Firestone, who subsequently became an attorney for the Citizens Communications Center, a public interest law firm that represented citizen groups in format change cases, argued the case for the FCC at the court of appeals.
21. *Twin States Broadcasting, Inc.*, 35 FCC2d 969 (1972). Commissioner Johnson dissented. He believed that this case raised "questions identical to" the *WGKA* case, and that it required a hearing: "Our refusal to hold one [a factual hearing] is in clear and direct violation of the law as interpreted by the Court of Appeals" (ibid., at 974).
22. *Charles A. Haskell*, 36 FCC2d 78 (1972).
23. *Lakewood Broadcasting Service, Inc.* v. *FCC*, 478 F.2d 919 (D.C. Cir. 1973).

24. *Citizens Committee to Keep Progressive Rock* v. *FCC,* 478 F.2d 926 (D.C. Cir. 1973).
25. *Lakewood Broadcasting Service, Inc.* v. *FCC,* 478 F.2d 919 (D.C. Cir. 1973).
26. *Citizens Committee to Keep Progressive Rock* v. *FCC,* 478 F.2d 928–929 (D.C. Cir. 1973).
27. Ibid., at 933.
28. Ibid., at 931–932. Emphasis in the original.
29. Ibid., at 932.
30. Ibid., at 931. Emphasis added.
31. Ibid., at 930.
32. After the court ordered the FCC to hold a hearing in the *Progressive Rock* case, the citizen group and the station tried to strike a bargain and avoid the hearing. Buyers of the station agreed that if WIOT-FM, a nearby station that had changed to progressive rock while the *Lakewood* case was pending, decided to drop its format, then the new owners of WGLN would conduct a survey of format preferences in the area. If 20 percent of those surveyed preferred progressive rock, and if the licensee decided a return to the format was economically feasible, then the buyer agreed that he would restore the progressive rock format. The FCC, however, threw out the agreement, holding that in striking this bargain the buyer had abdicated a licensee's responsibility to retain control over programming decisions. See *Midwestern Broadcasting Co.,* 42 FCC2d 1091 (1973).
33. For some details of WEFM's early history and economics, see *Zenith Radio Corp.,* 38 FCC2d 838 (1972), at paragraphs 3–12. Interesting insiders' details of the case are provided in articles by Professor Sammy R. Danna, who served as secretary and historian of the Citizens Committee. See Sammy R. Danna, "The Six-Year Fight to Save WEFM," *Journal of Broadcasting,* 22 (Fall 1978), 425–437; "The Long Fight to Save a Classical Radio Station," *Public Telecommunications Review,* May/June 1976, pp. 38–39; and "The Save-WEFM Case Ends: An Update," *Public Telecommunications Review,* May/June 1978, pp. 48–49. See also John H. Pennybacker, "The Format Change Issue: FCC vs. U.S. Court of Appeals," *Journal of Broadcasting,* 22 (Fall 1978), 411–424, especially 415–421.
34. *Zenith Radio Corp.,* 38 FCC2d 838, 846 (1972). Commissioner Johnson once again dissented, arguing that doubt existed about whether the other FM stations provided a substitute service and about the losses claimed by Zenith. Johnson believed a hearing was required.
35. *Zenith Radio Corp.,* 40 FCC2d 223 (1973).
36. Ibid., at 230–232.
37. See Danna, "The Six-Year Fight to Save WEFM," 429; and "The Long Fight to Save a Classical Radio Station," p. 38.
38. *Citizens Committee to Save WEFM* v. *FCC,* 506 F.2d 246 (D.C. Cir. 1974), at 249–252.
39. Ibid. Judge McGowan's opinion for the court is at 253–268. Judge Bazelon's concurring opinion is at 268–284. Robb's dissent is at 284–285, and Judge MacKinnon's dissent follows on 285–286.
40. Ibid., at 263.
41. Ibid., at 262. Emphasis added.
42. In footnote 28 of the case, McGowan, quoting from WEFM's 1970

renewal application, suggested that at least then the station itself believed its programming added something unique to Chicago's radio diversity. Ibid., at 263.

43. Ibid., at 263–264. Emphasis added.
44. Ibid., at 265–266.
45. Ibid., at 267–268.
46. Ibid., at 267. The remaining opinions are interesting but not as significant to understanding the impact of the case as Judge McGowan's. Judge Bazelon's concurrence was a long, sometimes troubled, discussion of the difficulties of reconciling the First Amendment with many of the regulatory theories for broadcasting the court of appeals had developed over the years. Judge Robb's dissent was a reinterpretation of his earlier view that WEFM required no hearing because WFMT provided a substitute classical music service and no unique format would be lost if WEFM changed its format. Judge MacKinnon generally agreed with Judge Robb.
47. Quoted in "How Wide the Wake of WEFM?" *Broadcasting,* October 14, 1974, p. 30.
48. "Court Activity," *Television Digest,* October 14, 1974, p. 4.
49. See Friedman, "Supreme Court Test of Format-Change Issue," p. 66.
50. FCC Administrative Law Judge Benjamin Harrison conducted the hearings, in both Washington, D.C., and Chicago, in early 1976. He found for GCC and against the Citizens Committee. GCC eventually paid the citizen group's legal fees, contributed the record library to other stations, and helped improve the broadcast facilities of the other classical stations. On February 17, 1978, the station at last changed its format. See Danna, "The Six-Year Fight to Save WEFM," 431–436.
51. Ibid., 428.
52. Danna, "The Long Fight to Save a Classical Radio Station," p. 38.
53. Donald J. Bogue, *The Radio Audience for Classical Music: The Case of Station WEFM, Chicago* (Chicago: Community and Family Study Center, University of Chicago, 1973). The link between the book and the expenses of the Citizens Committee is discussed in Danna, "The Long Fight to Save a Classical Radio Station," p. 39.
54. Quoted in "Classical Music on WNCN-FM Sooths the Savage Breasts," *New York Times,* April 2, 1978, sec. 1, p. 53.
55. "WRVR Group Petitions to Restore Jazz," *New York Times,* December 31, 1980, p. C16.
56. *Entertainment Formats,* 57 FCC2d 580, 584 (1975).
57. Ibid., at p. 582.
58. Ibid. Chairman Richard Wiley issued a separate statement in which he said:

The Court, it appears, believes that FCC Commissioners are capable of doing a better job of distributing formats than that presently performed by the marketplace. While I appreciate this judicial vote of confidence in our ability and expertise, I cannot honestly say that I share the Court's optimism (*ibid.,* at p. 586).

Commissioner Benjamin Hooks concurred, the only one among the Commissioners to indicate that the court's *WEFM* decisions might be workable:

To determine whether a format is unique . . . I would use only a threshold test of conspicuous generic equivalence. . . . To determine whether there is "significant grumbling" about a proposed format change, I would compare the magnitude of the protest to the magnitude of the service area using a zone of reasonableness concept. I would interpret economic feasibility as consistent with a profit comparable to the average station in the market . . . since I don't believe the court expects anybody to labor for less than fair recompense (*ibid.,* at p. 589).

Commissioner Robinson also concurred in a long statement examining what he believed to be the futility or perhaps even self-defeating nature of the court's notions of format regulation. (*ibid.,* at pp. 589–601).

59. See "Broadcasters See FCC as Big Brother in Format Review," *Broadcasting,* April 26, 1976, pp. 30–31.
60. "Comments of the National Association of Broadcasters," Docket No. 20682, April 20, 1976, pp. 1–2. As a measure of the seriousness with which the NAB approached this inquiry, it is interesting to note that its comments were prepared by outside counsel rather than the NAB staff— an extraordinary and expensive step not taken in most FCC proceedings —and included a commissioned study by an economist previously with the Office of Telecommunications Policy.
61. "FCC's End Run on Radio Station Format Change," *access 25* (January 12, 1976), 23.
62. "Petition to Reconsider, Rescind, Suspend or Redirect," Docket No. 20682, February 6, 1976. While the format change inquiry was starting up, the FCC applied the *WEFM* standards to two proposed transfers associated with format changes. In *Post-Newsweek Stations Florida, Inc.,* 57 FCC2d 326 (1975), the Commission approved the transfer of WCKY-AM (Cincinnati), despite 1,200 protest letters over WCKY's "loss" of beautiful music. The Commission said beautiful music could be found on the FM dial. In *Republic Broadcasting Corp.,* 57 FCC2d 336 (1975), the Commission approved the transfer and format change of KEXT-FM because (1) it found other good music stations were available to replace KEXT-FM, and (2) aside from a protest by another broadcaster who would receive more competition because of the new "progressive contemporary soul" format, there was no public protest. When the Citizens Communications Center complained to the FCC that it had prejudged the outcome of the inquiry and had not followed the *WEFM* decision, the Commission pointed to these cases to demonstrate that it had followed the law. They had been decided the same day the Commission had decided to initiate the format inquiry.
63. *Entertainment Formats,* 58 FCC2d 617 (1976).
64. "Comments Filed in FCC Radio Format Inquiry," *access 36* (June 14, 1976), 6. The article is a good summary of citizen comments filed in the proceeding and an adequate review of broadcaster positions.
65. For a hint of the degree to which this was scripted in advance, see "FCC Defends Licensee Right to Choose Radio Formats," *Broadcasting,* August 2, 1976, p. 21ff.
66. *Entertainment Formats,* 60 FCC2d 858, 861 (1976).
67. Ibid., pp. 865–866.
68. *Greater Boston Television Corp.* v. *FCC,* 444 F.2d 841, 851–852 (D.C. Cir. 1970).
69. *Entertainment Formats,* 60 FCC2d 858, 865 (1976). Quoting *Greater Boston Television Corp.* v. *FCC,* 444 F.2d 841, 851-52 (D.C. Cir. 1970).
70. *Entertainment Formats of Broadcast Stations,* 66 FCC2d 78 (1977).
71. Ibid., at 86.
72. Frederick W. Ford and Lee G. Lovett, "The Commission Balks at Entertainment Format Regulation," *BM/E,* [*Broadcast Management/Engi-*

neering] November 1977, p. 76. See also Richard E. Wiley, "FCC Program Format Regulation Back in Court," *Legal Times of Washington,* September 4, 1978, pp. 9, 10.

73. *WNCN Listeners Guild* v. *FCC,* 610 F.2d 839, 855 (D.C. Cir. 1979).
74. Ibid., at 846.
75. Ibid., at 849.
76. Ibid., at 850.
77. Ibid., at 852–854.
78. Ibid., at 843, 854.
79. Ibid., at 858. The procedural problem for Judge McGowan was the FCC's tardy disclosure of a staff study of format diversity. Since this point was not subsequently of much concern to the U.S. Supreme Court, it is not discussed further here. Citizen groups, however, considered it an effort by the Commission to frustrate their interests.
80. Ibid., at 854–855. Emphasis in the original.
81. Ibid., at 860.
82. Ibid.
83. Ibid., at 858–859.
84. Ibid., at 864–865.
85. "Father Knows Best" [editorial], *Broadcasting,* July 9, 1979, p. 74.
86. See "FCC to Seek Supreme Court Review in Entertainment Format Change Case," FCC Press Release No. 20773, August 24, 1979. Fogarty explained four reasons for his vote: (1) he believed the Commission made a mistake when, in 1976, it allowed a study of format diversity that was not made available to parties to the inquiry to influence its decision; (2) he believed the Commission could figure out ways to conduct the kinds of format reviews the court had in mind; (3) he believed the court of appeals decision had not undercut the rationale for radio deregulation; and (4) "an overwhelming majority of the Court of Appeals . . . views the Commission's course of conduct with respect to the format change decisions as obstreperous, disrespectful, and in flagrant disregard of the constitutional principle of judicial supremacy. I wish to have no part in this needless and unseemly confrontation."
87. *Certiorari granted, FCC* v. *WNCN Listeners Guild,* 445 U.S. 914 (1980), p. 3.
88. The initiative for the brief by the attorneys general came from New York, where Attorney General Robert Abrams was personally interested in the issue and where staff members were active in the WNCN Listeners Guild. The staff surveyed the attorneys general of all states, several of whom joined in drafting the brief. In addition to an interest in avoiding the loss of unique formats, the attorneys general were particularly interested that the U.S. Supreme Court not include language in its opinion limiting inadvertently the ability of states and localities to regulate cable television. Partly because of this brief, the U.S. Supreme Court included language suggesting that the FCC may still have a role to play when foreign language news and public affairs programming are involved in a format change.
89. *FCC* v. *WNCN Listeners Guild,* 67 L.Ed. 2d 521, 533,__U.S.__, 101 S. Ct. 1266 (1981).
90. Ibid., at 536. Emphasis in the original.
91. Ibid., at 534.
92. Ibid.

93. Ibid., at 535.
94. Ibid.
95. Ibid., at 540.
96. "Good Fight Well Fought" [editorial], *Broadcasting,* March 30, 1981, p. 106. In the long run, of course, the important question is the influence of the U.S. Supreme Court's decision on future review of the FCC by the court of appeals. Early indications are that the impact of the case may not be immediate. On April 17, 1981—less than a month after the Supreme Court's format change decision—the court of appeals decided *Gottfried* v. *FCC,* 655 F.2d 297 (D.C. Cir. 1981). There the court remanded to the FCC a decision not to apply the Rehabilitation Act of 1973, Pub. L. 93-1112, 87 *Stat.* 357, to either public or commercial television stations. The FCC had been asked to do so through petitions to deny filed by hearing-impaired viewers seeking more programming for them—including captioning. The court agreed with the FCC that the act did not apply directly to commercial stations but held that it placed special obligations on public stations because of their receipt of federal funds. In addition, it suggested—anyway—that all stations had obligations to serve the special needs of hearing-impaired citizens. This led *Regulation,* a generally conservative journal, to suggest that the court of appeals had not learned its lesson from the Supreme Court's format change decision and was again substituting its policy judgment for that of the Commission. See "Reversing the D.C. Circuit at the FCC," *Regulation,* May/June 1981, pp. 11–14. In addition, the issue of format change may not automatically go away. After the Supreme Court's decision, citizen groups began to characterize as "misrepresentations" decisions by stations to change from formats promised to the FCC at the time of approval of a sale or renewal of licenses. Misrepresentation has long been considered a serious matter by the FCC, and citizen activists hoped to use it as another means of involving the FCC in format regulation. In January 1982 the U.S. Supreme Court announced it would review the Gottfried case, setting the stage, perhaps, for yet another criticism of the Court of Appeals' approach to the review of FCC policy decisions. See *Community Television of Southern California v. Gottfried,* U.S. Supreme Court, Doc. No. 81–298.

Six

UHF Television: The Quest for Comparability

To the U.S. Court of Appeals for the District of Columbia Circuit, it is "the ugly stepsister of television broadcasting."[1] To one industry trade journal, it has become "religious broadcaster heaven."[2] To a competing journal, it is "TV's last frontier."[3] To many television viewers, it—UHF television—was for years just an unused dial on the TV set.

Getting viewers to use that dial has been an objective of broadcasters and the government for at least thirty years.[4] Introduced in 1952 on an intermixed basis with VHF (Very High Frequency) stations (Channels 2 to 13) in the same markets, UHF (Ultra High Frequency) television (Channels 14 and above) was, until very recently, unable to compete with VHF for advertisers or audience. Although the FCC repeatedly has expressed its concern about the development of UHF broadcasting, it has not implemented any reliable, systematic plan for strengthening the service. A number of its sporadic attempts to aid UHF television have been helpful, but whatever success the service enjoys today is plainly just as attributable to entrepreneurial ingenuity and changed marketplace conditions as it is to government actions. One action, however, stands out as an exception to the general pattern of ineffectiveness. This is the requirement, enacted into law by Congress in 1962, that all television sets sold in the United States be able to receive both UHF and VHF signals.

The roots of UHF's problems go back to 1945, when the Commission allocated only thirteen VHF channels (subsequently cut to twelve) to serve all the needs of television. This decision rested on two assumptions: (1) that twelve VHF channels would fill TV's immediate needs, and (2) that when UHF broadcasting became technically feasible, it could be introduced as either a supplement to, or a replacement for, VHF television. Neither of these assumptions, however, proved to be true. In 1952 the Commission issued its *Sixth Report and Order* on television allocations, which rejected "all-UHF" television—either nationally or regionally—as economically disastrous for existing broadcasting. As a result, although UHF television was authorized in the same report as a supplement to VHF television, it faced, from the moment of its introduction, crippling competition from established, economically secure VHF stations.

Throughout the 1950s the FCC spent much time dealing with the consequences of this 1952 decision. UHF broadcasting did not prove economically feasible during that period, and the Commission pursued a series of controversial, inconclusive, and ultimately unsuccessful moves to remedy the situation. Among them were:

1. The consideration and rejection, in 1954, of proposals for the "deintermixture"[5] of seven markets then assigned both VHF and UHF television—each to be made all UHF
2. The reconsideration, in March 1955, of five of these deintermixture proposals
3. The decision, in November of that year, not to undertake deintermixture in these five cases—or in any of the thirty other proceedings that meanwhile had been initiated
4. The statement, on January 20, 1956, that deintermixture was a very real possibility and that the FCC was still considering it
5. The announcement, on June 25, 1956, of plans to deintermix thirteen markets (including five that were rejected twice before)
6. The failure, during the period from 1956 through the 1960s, to implement deintermixture in even the majority of these thirteen cases

Only five of the thirteen deintermixtures proposed in 1956 actually were carried out, and they did little to help the UHF industry generally. It is likely, moreover, that the lengthy debates and disputes over UHF during the 1950s served more to point out its sickness to advertisers and viewers than to relieve its problems.

By 1961 the condition of UHF had deteriorated so much that some new initiative seemed required. The production of all-channel television sets—capable of receiving UHF as well as VHF channels—had fallen to a record low of 5.5 percent of all new sets, thus giving the eighty-three commercial UHF stations still on the air little hope of increasing their already tiny audiences.[6] Lack of audience made UHF unattractive to advertisers, and lack of advertising revenue ended the operation of many UHF broadcasters. In the Kennedy years these conditions greatly concerned the FCC, especially the Commission's new Chairman, Newton N. Minow, who had been outspoken about the need to counter the "vast wasteland" of TV's standardized programming fare through the development of additional channels offering program variety and diversity—channels that it then appeared could come only through an unprecedented utilization of the UHF band.

Stimulated by these concerns and hope for the future of UHF television, the Commission announced, on July 27, 1961, a package proposal, including such varied items as: (1) deintermixture of UHF and VHF in eight markets, (2) a "shoe-horning in" of new VHF assignments at less than the standard mileage separation in eight other cities, and (3) a request for congressional action on legislation authorizing the FCC to require that all new sets be capable of receiving both VHF and UHF signals.[7] The idea of dealing with UHF problems by attacking the low level of all-channel receiver penetration was not new. Proposals had been made by the House Judiciary Committee during the 1950s for a legislative requirement that all new television sets be capable of receiving both VHF and UHF channels, and in 1957 Congressman Emanuel Celler (D-New York) had suggested that the heart of the problem was in the limited sales of TV sets with UHF receiving capability.[8]

If the combination of the FCC's three different plans seems unwieldy and somewhat contradictory, it was because on specific proposals, such as that calling for renewed efforts at deintermixture, the Commission was split 4 to 3 and obtained a final unanimous vote on the package only by combining several items.[9] Such a combination of diverse proposals had one advantage, which may have been anticipated by some FCC Commissioners and staff members: one part of the package could be jettisoned at a later time to aid the prospects of other parts of the package. Such is, in fact, what happened. The FCC was, however, unanimous in deciding to request all-channel television legislation.[10]

The two most important elements of the 1961 package were the plans for renewed efforts at deintermixture and the request for all-channel television legislation. This combination created considerable industry fear that the FCC was moving toward an all-UHF television system. Dr. Frank Stanton, president of CBS, confessed to feeling "nervous when the Commission talks about deintermixture at the same time it talks about all-channel sets."[11] Chairman Minow tried to calm such fears by pointing out that Robert E. Lee was the only Commissioner who favored a shift of all television to UHF—a possibility that Commissioner Lee himself later described as "an exercise in futility."[12]

While the combination of deintermixture and all-channel television made broadcasters nervous, deintermixture by itself distinctly alarmed them. Unlike the 1955 and 1956 proposals that would, in most cases, have eliminated VHF assignments unfilled as of 1956, by 1961 the proposals would move existing VHF stations to the UHF band. In an editorial on the new deintermixture proposals, *Broadcasting* magazine warned:

There was a time—before the new VHF stations were built in single station markets—when deintermixture would have been workable with minimal injury to the public and broadcasters. Any change now may be a major wrench and we have the notion that the public will make itself heard.[13]

All eight members of the congressional delegation for the state of Connecticut, for example, opposed the proposal to shift Hartford's only VHF station to the UHF band.[14] By early 1962 *Broadcasting* reported that almost all senators and representatives from markets slated for deintermixture were against the plan.[15] Those industry groups opposed to deintermixture were to make good use of such congressional opposition.

During much of 1961, while controversy developed over deintermixture, little action occurred on all-channel television legislation. In late September 1961, however, Chairman Minow suggested that such a bill might resolve many of the same problems as deintermixture.[16] In January 1962 Minow announced that an all-channel television bill was the FCC's "chief legislative proposal" for that year.[17]

Bills designed to grant the Commission the desired all-channel authority were introduced by Senator John Pastore (D-Rhode Island), chairman of the Senate Communications Subcommittee, and Representative Oren Harris (D-Arkansas), chairman of the House Interstate and Foreign Commerce Committee. Both bills gave the FCC authority to make rules requiring that television sets shipped in interstate commerce have the capacity to receive all channels—UHF as well as VHF—allotted to television. Hearings on this legislation were held by the House Committee on Interstate and Foreign Commerce in February 1962 and by the Senate Commerce Committee in March of the same year.

Much of the testimony at these hearings focused on the topic of deintermixture rather than all-channel television. Many bills had been introduced to halt deintermixture, and strong sentiment existed in both commerce committees for a rider to any all-channel television bill that would specifically prohibit changes in existing VHF assignments designed to achieve the deintermixture of television markets. As *Broadcasting* concluded, "It was made clear in both the Senate and House Committee proceedings that there will be no all-channel bill without a commitment to forgo deintermixture now."[18]

In an attempt to head off such a legislative prohibition, Chairman Minow testified against any statutory moratorium on deintermixture proceedings: "Unless Congress wants to go into the frequency allocation business, we [the FCC] should be left free to make such decisions."[19] It soon became clear, however, that unless the Commission abandoned its deintermixture plans, any all-channel receiver legislation that might pass would be certain to contain a provision prohibiting further deintermixture proceedings. Consequently, the Commission, on March 16, sent Chairman Harris a letter stating:

> If the all-channel receiver television legislation is enacted by this Congress, it is the judgment of the Commission . . . that it would be inappropriate, in the light of this important new development, to proceed with the eight deintermixture proceedings initiated on July 27, 1961, and that, on the contrary, a sufficient period of time should be allowed to indicate whether the all-channel receiver authority would in fact achieve the Commission's overall allocations goals. . . . Before undertaking the implementation of any policy concerning deintermixture, the Commission would advise the Committee of its plans and give it an appropriate period of time to consider the Commission's proposals.[20]

Thus, in the words of Commissioner Robert E. Lee, "Congress in effect made a deal with the Commission—drop deintermixture, and we get the all-channel television bill."[21] Legislative support for the bill increased and included a number of Representative Harris's committee members representing districts threatened by the Commission's deintermixture proposal.[22] The linking of deintermixture and all-channel television in the original 1961 package greatly enhanced the prospects of an all-channel television bill in 1962.

With the support of those opposing deintermixture, the all-channel bill faced comparatively little opposition. Some members of Congress had reservations about the "loss of freedom" involved in requiring people to purchase television sets equipped a certain way, and the Electronic Industries Association (EIA) expressed vocal but isolated concern about the rise in set costs—variously estimated from $25 to $40 retail—which would result from having to include a UHF tuner on each set.[23] This opposition, however, was minor compared to the support for the bill by the president, industry groups such as the three networks, major manufacturers (including General Electric and RCA, despite the EIA stand), and several industry trade organizations (including the National Association of Broadcasters).

There was another theme to EIA's opposition that, however, turned out to be more significant than its arguments about price increases for consumers or limitations on consumer choice. As originally proposed in the House of Representatives, the bill would have given the Commission the authority to set "minimum performance standards" for all television receivers shipped in interstate commerce.[24] EIA characterized the bill as giving "the Federal Communications Commission blank check power to regulate the television receiver manufacturing industry."[25] This the EIA found intolerable. While never conceding that all-channel legislation was a good idea, manufacturers' representatives worked on the language of the bill until, as finally adopted, it no longer gave quite such broad powers to the FCC. The House Committee on Interstate and Foreign Commerce substituted language empowering the FCC to require that television sets "be capable of receiving all frequencies allocated by the Commission to television broadcasting" for the prior language about performance standards.[26] After complaints by the FCC, expressed formally in a letter by Chairman Minow to Senator Pastore, that the House version might leave the FCC "powerless to prevent the shipment in interstate commerce . . . of all-channel sets having only the barest capability for receiving UHF signals,"[27] the Senate subcommittee amended the crucial language to give the Commission power to require that television receivers "be capable of *adequately* receiving all frequencies" allocated for television broadcasting.[28] The question for future years, of course, was what the Commission could do to define adequate reception, short of adopting minimum performance standards.

Favorably reported out of the House Committee on Interstate and Foreign Commerce on April 9, the bill passed the House by a vote of 279 to 90 on May 2. The Senate version was favorably reported by the Senate Commerce Committee on May 24 and was approved by the Senate by a voice vote on June 14. Minor differences between the Senate and House bills were settled in the House by a voice vote on June 29, and on July 10, 1962, President Kennedy signed the legislation into law. As the last stage in this process the FCC availed itself of its newly conferred authority on September 13, 1962, by instituting rule making to require that all television sets shipped in interstate commerce be all-channel television receivers.[29] This rule was adopted on November 23, 1962, to go into effect on April 30, 1964.

The politics of this controversy were rather curious for, as has been suggested, the threat of deintermixture was the major reason that the All-Channel Receiver bill passed in 1962. The opposition to deintermixture was particularly strong since, in every geographic area considered for deintermixture in 1961, existing VHF stations would have been affected. This strong resistance to deintermixture was transformed into positive support for an alternative policy—the All-Channel Receiver bill. Combining a highly unpopular measure with a proposal acceptable to VHF interests ensured sufficient support for passage of the bill by Congress and its implementation by the Commission—once the unpopular idea had been publicly dropped. In this controversy the interests of the broadcast industry converged with those of the FCC. Broadcasters sought to avoid a repugnant policy at almost any cost, while the Commission wanted to provide for diversity and additional competition in TV broadcasting. The result was that enough forces favoring the

All-Channel Receiver bill were aligned to ensure its adoption as public policy.

The initiation of the request for action on all-channel receiver legislation came from the Commission itself—although, as earlier noted, the idea of such legislation derived from a suggestion contained in the 1957 House Judiciary Committee report, "The Television Broadcasting Industry." The FCC, fresh from berating the television industry's "vast wasteland," took a renewed interest in UHF as a means of broadening program choice for viewers. In addition, the Commission had been under pressure from the Senate Commerce Committee for more than five years to find some means of alleviating UHF's woes. The result of Commission interest and congressional pressure was the package of proposals on July 27, 1961. The subsequent focus on all-channel legislation as the chief means of UHF development, however, came about largely because it alone, of the various proposals, did not face immediate overwhelming opposition. To obtain congressional support for all-channel set requirements, the Commission gave up only a proposal on deintermixture, which was limited in applicability and backed by a slim majority of Commissioners. In return, the FCC received authority to implement a policy that had favorable results beyond all expectations. In this sense those UHF investors and operators who had so long suffered financially "really won," for in the successful FCC initiative to obtain the manufacture and sale of all-channel sets, the means were found for at least the potential realization of long-held hopes for UHF television.

FCC Implementation of the Act

Attempts to achieve UHF's potential, since 1962, have involved cautious FCC steps to exercise its authority under the All-Channel Receiver Act. Between 1969 and 1973 the Commission adopted standards for comparable tuning of UHF and VHF channels. These rules required that UHF and VHF tuning devices be comparable in size, location, legibility, special features (if any), and tuning accuracy, and, eventually, they specified requirements for a seventy-channel, "click-stop" (detent) UHF tuner.[30] They were all efforts to make VHF and UHF tuning equally easy for the consumer. The Commission mostly began these proceedings on its own initiative, responding only to general concerns that the All-Channel Receiver Act, limited to the FCC's 1962 implementing rules, was still not accomplishing all it could to promote UHF broadcasting. In 1976 the Commission responded to a new organization attempting to influence UHF policy—the Council for UHF Broadcasting (CUB). CUB filed a simple petition for rule making, pointing out that set manufacturers, while usually attaching a VHF antenna at least to portable sets, rarely attached UHF antennas and sometimes did not include them at all. In response to this complaint, the FCC required that manufacturers, by 1978, include a UHF antenna if they included a VHF antenna and specified that if one antenna was attached at the factory the other would have to be attached as well.[31]

In the eyes of UHF broadcasters, however, there was another pressing problem beyond ease of tuning for consumers or antenna concerns —namely, noise. Noise is interference degrading picture or sound quality. In terms of the picture, it is what viewers often call "snow." The tuner used in the set has much to do with how much noise a picture will have. In order to select among stations, tuners must also be able to reject unwanted signals. This is known as tuner selectivity. Any interference resulting from poorly rejected signals—low selectivity—creates noise, clouding the picture. More noise may come from the tuner circuits themselves, as a by-product of their operation. A tuner's "noise figure" is basically a measure of how much interference the tuner circuits contribute. It is measured in decibels (dB). The lower the decibel level, the better the tuner. VHF tuners typically range from 6 to 8 dB. UHF tuners present electronic design problems not found in VHF tuners and have not until recently achieved comparable noise figures.[32] In 1962 the FCC set the noise level for UHF tuners manufactured under the All-Channel Receiver Act at 18 dB. In recent years, UHF tuners have ranged from 14 to 18 dB, a much higher figure than for VHF and a matter of concern to UHF broadcasters since it means that UHF picture quality may be inferior to VHF.

In 1975 CUB proposed that the FCC adopt sharp reductions in the UHF noise figures: to 14 dB within six months, 12 dB within eighteen months and 10 dB within thirty months.[33] More than one year later, the FCC issued a Notice of Proposed Rulemaking on CUB's petition,[34] and a year after that it adopted lower noise standards. In a typical compromise the Commission did not go as far, or as fast, as CUB proposed, but it did lower significantly the noise figure standards. The Commission reduced the standard from 18 dB to 14 dB for all new models effective October 1, 1979, and for all sets—new or old models—sold starting October 1, 1981. In a more controversial move, it proposed still lower future standards: 12 dB effective October 1, 1982, for new models and October 1, 1984, for all set sales. The Commission concluded that many UHF television viewers would perceive a significant improvement in picture quality under these new standards.[35]

The problem was that when the Commission set the new standards nobody was positive if or how they could be reached or whether doing so might have unexpected side effects. As Commissioner Robert E. Lee, the FCC's most dependable UHF supporter, noted in an unexpected dissenting statement:

During all the years I have advocated UHF parity, I have learned that wishful thinking does not make it happen. I am dissenting here because I think the 12 dB standard represents more wishful thinking. For all we know now, lowering the noise figure from 14 to 12 dB could create other problems which might make the picture on the TV set worse for those who have good reception now. . . . The 12 dB standard may not be the best we can do for UHF. Indeed, if compliance with this rule diverts research attention from designing the best receiver possible, we may not have done UHF any real good at all.[36]

In support of his position, Lee had the company of Commissioner Margita White and the EIA, whose TV set manufacturer members had opposed all along FCC changes in the noise figure standards.

While the EIA accepted the 14 dB limit for 1979 and 1981, it opposed the 1982 and 1984 12 dB standards. Consequently, it sought to block the standards by action in the U.S. Court of Appeals for the District of Columbia Circuit. The EIA's position was that the FCC could not regulate in advance of electronic developments: it could not, to borrow from Lee, regulate by wishful thinking. In September 1980 the court of appeals found in favor of the EIA. The question, essentially, was how far the Commission could go under the 1962 All-Channel Receiver Act in order to make sets "capable of adequately receiving all frequencies" allocated to television broadcasting. The answer from the court was that the 12 dB standard was not presently feasible, that the FCC knew that when it adopted the requirement, and that "the Commission may not prescribe noise regulations that go beyond the present state of the art."[37]

Providentially, the court decision coincided with release of a major FCC study of UHF television that "concluded that stricter UHF noise figure standards, beyond the 12 dB requirement, are not required in order to achieve comparability in this aspect of television receiver design."[38] The Commission's UHF Comparability Task Force report, released in September 1980, came to a number of other quite modest conclusions about what could be done to improve UHF comparability with VHF broadcasting: it decided, for example, that the most significant improvement would result if consumers would install adequate home UHF receiving antennas.[39] The most interesting aspect of events in the area of UHF, however, involves how the task force came into existence in the first place.

The UHF Comparability Task Force was established when Senator Lowell Weicker (R-Connecticut) managed to get an additional $750,-000 added to the FCC's 1979 budget.[40] Weicker's action suggests one of the important characteristics of the UHF controversy—the degree to which it unites many commercial and noncommercial broadcasters. Approximately 40 percent of UHF stations are noncommercial and 57 percent of noncommercial stations are UHF. Congress thought the

All-Channel Receiver Act probably would be of substantial benefit to public broadcasters since so many of their stations were UHF, and public broadcasters have remained actively interested in UHF policy. Both the Corporation for Public Broadcasting and the National Association of Public Television Stations, for example, are active in CUB and public broadcasters were clearly behind the congressional action that led to funding the UHF Comparability Task Force. According to several persons active in the area at the time, the way for Weicker's action was prepared on Capitol Hill largely by public broadcast representatives, especially Hartford Gunn, then vice-chairman of the Public Broadcasting Service. It was probably earlier advances to Weicker by public broadcast interests that led him, in the Senate hearing, to closely link his interest in UHF with improved public broadcast service. At the FCC's April 26, 1978, Senate Appropriations hearing, Weicker indicated that he wanted to explore

an issue that I feel is crying out for FCC support. We all recognize the great potential that television offers to educat[e], entertain, and communicate. . . . In an effort to offer meaningful alternatives the Congress established the Public Broadcasting Service but most PBS stations are forced to operate on the UHF band. Frankly, people don't get a fair chance to select a Public Broadcasting program largely for technical reasons. . . .

Why can't the FCC take the lead in putting UHF stations on a technical par with VHF?

. . .

Let me just make this point for the record. If you [FCC Chairman Ferris] are not prepared to give me figures right now, I would like to know what it is that would be required to accelerate this effort in a technical sense insofar as the FCC is concerned.[41]

The Commission responded, shortly, to Weicker's questions. In part, the FCC said:

While certainly more resources help, the major problem [with quickly achieving comparability] is that mandating such significant changes in the structure of the television industry requires that the public be given adequate opportunity to consider and comment upon any proposed changes. . . . It simply would be unwise for this Commission to mandate dramatic shifts in the structure of television broadcasting without careful and searching consideration."[42]

The Commission's response was a carefully worded invitation to Weicker, if he chose to do so, to help provide "more resources" to perform that "careful and searching consideration." Of course, he did, leading to the FCC's two-year study and its modest September 1980 conclusions, as already noted.[43]

As one report put it in 1979, UHF broadcasters have finally come into their own: "They have turned that proverbial corner, and they have done it largely alone, with little help from others and over tremendous obstacles placed in their way."[44] There are a number of signs of UHF's success: 406 stations—244 commercial, and 162 noncommercial ones—were on the air in late 1981. Instead of reporting the number of UHF stations on the air the trend is, in fact, to report the ever-decreasing number of "vacant" (unused), UHF channels.[45] FCC financial figures covering 1979 showed that 66.3 percent of all UHF stations reported a profit for that year. In 1970 only 32 percent of UHF stations could claim such a distinction. Prices paid to purchase UHF television stations, and advertising rates on those stations, are climbing. While many UHF stations—particularly independent stations—continued to show poor economic records, the picture represents a solid improvement over the doldrums of the 1960s and early 1970s.

There are many reasons for the turnaround, a number of which have little to do with the FCC's efforts to achieve UHF comparability. As an investment opportunity, VHF television is no longer readily open to companies; stations sell at very high prices or are not for sale at all.[46] Broadcast group owners with substantial financial backing are moving into UHF. UHF also benefits from the high demand for television advertising time: it gets a certain spillover from tight competition to buy time of sometimes sold-out VHF stations. UHF may even benefit from the 1952 table of allocations, which put stations where the people were then. Many successful UHF stations are now flourishing in "sunbelt" communities not given VHF stations in the 1950s.

Programming has improved, both because of a general flow of more money into UHF stations but also because UHF broadcasters have learned specialization techniques they can use to attract audiences. In the early days some UHF stations specialized in sports or movies, and a few in foreign language broadcasts in larger markets. Now more and more stations specialize in pay (subscription) television or religious broadcasting. All U.S. pay-TV channels currently operate on UHF, although they could operate on VHF, and in many markets where UHF stations remain unassigned by the FCC there is competition for licenses between pay and religious broadcast interests. Satellites have been effectively used by UHF stations to distribute programming inexpensively, and some UHF stations have combined resources to produce programs comparable to network productions. At least one UHF station, WTBS in Atlanta, Georgia, has found the ultimate solution to the UHF handicap: it has used satellite distribution of its signal to cable television systems in order to become a national "superstation."[47] PBS has accustomed some viewers to watching UHF and, of course, the transmitting and receiving technology has improved.[48]

All this does not automatically guarantee the future for UHF television. UHF still suffers technological handicaps, and nobody expects it to ever achieve full "parity" with VHF-TV. Comparability is all that is sought. New regulatory issues will continue to affect UHF's future. Cable television still seems a mixed blessing for UHF stations, extending the reach of some stations (and converting them to more readily tuned signals) but, in other instances, providing more competition for the UHF broadcaster through imported television signals. FCC proposals to drop in more VHF television stations, to set up "low-power" TV stations, or to authorize direct broadcast satellites are a matter of grave concern to UHF broadcasters. Because so many UHF channels are still unused, other users of the electromagnetic spectrum—notably land mobile radio—look covetously at UHF's spectrum space. This is a problem that even emerges at international conferences since other Western Hemisphere nations, including our Canadian and Mexican neighbors, would like to put to use what they see as wasted UHF spectrum space. The quest for technical comparability for UHF has been long, hard-fought, and unending. The All-Channel Receiver Act has, after nearly twenty years, resulted in 95 percent of American homes having television sets that can receive UHF.[49] The service has, in many instances, become profitable. The durability of its present success, however, is likely to turn for years to come not just on the business skills of those involved in it but also on their political skills in influencing the outcome of UHF's likely future regulatory battles.

NOTES

1. *Electronic Industries Association Consumer Electronics Group* v. *FCC* 636 F.2d 689, 691 (D.C. Cir. 1980).
2. Edmond M. Rosenthal, "UHF Becomes Religious Broadcaster Heaven," *Television/Radio Age,* January 16, 1978, pp. 27–30ff.
3. "UHF: TV's Last Frontier," *Broadcasting,* February 26, 1979, pp. 43–80.
4. The first commercial UHF-TV station went on the air on September 20, 1952, as KPTV, Channel 27, in Portland, Oregon. KPTV was owned by Empire Coil Co., New Rochelle, New York, an electronic parts manufacturing firm. Indicative of difficulties to come, Empire Coil's president, Herbert Mayer, said at the time that he had no idea of the number of TV sets in Portland capable of picking up his signal ("First Commercial UHF, KPTV (TV) Portland, Ore., on Air," *Broadcasting,* September 22, 1952, pp. 25, 82). Mayer sold the station, and the rest of his company, to Storer Broadcasting Co. in 1954 as a package worth a reported $10 million ("Storer Buys Empire Coil Co. for $10,000,000," *Television Digest,* January 9, 1954, pp. 3–4). The deal was approved by the FCC on October 27, 1954, in one of the first applications of an FCC policy that limited a single owner to seven TV stations, no more than five of which could be VHFs ("Many Station Sales, Lots of Dickering," *Television Digest,* October 30, 1954, pp. 3–4). Detroit attorney and oilman George Haggarty purchased

independent Portland TV station KLOR, a Channel 12 VHF, in March 1957, for $1,794,865 (*Television Digest,* March 9, 1957, p. 8). It soon turned out that he had a ninety-day option, from February 11, 1957, to purchase Storer's KPTV as well, then an NBC affiliate (*Television Digest,* April 20, 1957, p. 4). Haggarty exercised the option and purchased KPTV for $1,183,921, plus assumption of certain contracts. He then switched the call letters, and the NBC affiliation, to Channel 12 and took the first commercial UHF-TV station off the air (*Television Digest,* May 4, 1957, p. 4). Oddly, by 1963 this VHF station had gone through a change of ownership, briefly been an ABC affiliate, and, finally, lost its network affiliation and reverted to being an independent television station. Thus, the call letters of the nation's first commercial UHF station now belong to a VHF operation.

5. "Deintermixture" involves the reallocation of television channel assignments so that each community would have either VHF or UHF stations but would not have both. Hence viewers wanting to tune in the popular network programs in UHF markets would be forced to buy UHF converters; in "intermixed" markets (where both UHF and VHF channels were allocated), networks chose to affiliate first with VHF stations, and many viewers settled just for those signals rather than going to the additional expense of adding a UHF converter.

6. It was claimed that there were 120 commercial UHF's on the air in 1953 ("Statistical Analysis, 1946–63: The Television Industry," *TV Factbook No. 34 for 1964* [Washington, D.C.: Television Factbook, 1964], p. 38a). It should be noted that this all-channel receiver production figure of 5.5 percent was a national average, and in some areas, such as central Illinois, where major network service was provided largely or entirely by UHF stations, the all-channel set "penetration rate" was much higher—even up to 65 to 70 percent. Viewers in those areas, however, were outnumbered by viewers in markets where network service was supplied by VHF stations. UHF stations in those other markets, if they existed at all, had but second-rate programs to broadcast to an audience largely unequipped to receive their signals.

7. FCC Public Notice, "Comprehensive Actions to Foster Expansion of UHF TV Broadcasting," July 28, 1961 [mimeo.]. See also *Broadcasting,* August 7, 1961, p. 54. Since the Communications Act did not explicitly provide the FCC with authority to adopt uniform receiver standards, legislation appeared necessary to require the manufacture of all-channel receivers.

8. U.S. House of Representatives, House Judiciary Committee, *Report of the Antitrust Subcommittee Pursuant to House Resolution 107 on the Television Broadcasting Industry,* 85th Congress, 1st Session (March 15, 1957), p. 9.

9. Interviews with Commissioner Robert E. Lee, Washington, D.C., October 25, 1965, and Phil Cross, legal assistant to Commissioner Robert T. Bartley, Washington, D.C., October 25, 1965.

10. U.S. Senate, Senate Commerce Committee, *Hearings on All-Channel Television Receivers,* 87th Congress, 2nd Session (February 20, 21, and 22, 1962), p. 31.

11. Quoted in "Is the FCC Ready to Take Half a Loaf?" *Broadcasting,* March 12, 1962, p. 44.

12. Interview with Commissioner Lee, Washington, D.C., October 25, 1965.

13. "Too Much Too Late" [editorial], *Broadcasting,* August 7, 1961, p. 114.

14. See "Hill Rallies to Save V's," *Broadcasting*, August 21, 1961, p. 50.
15. "Richards Urges NAB Focus on Hill," *Broadcasting*, February 26, 1962, p. 56.
16. See "Parting Shot," *Broadcasting*, October 2, 1961, p. 4.
17. This speech to the National Press Club on January 11, 1962, can be found in Newton N. Minow, *Equal Time: The Private Broadcaster and the Public Interest* (New York: Atheneum, 1964), chapter VI.
18. "Wedding of the U's and V's" [editorial], *Broadcasting*, March 12, 1962, p. 106.
19. Quoted in "FCC's All-Channel Set Bill Falters," *Broadcasting*, February 26, 1962, p. 100.
20. U.S. House of Representatives, House Committee on Interstate and Foreign Commerce, *House Report 1559, All-Channel Television Receivers*, 87th Congress, 2nd Session (April 9, 1962), pp. 19–20. The deintermixture proceedings were terminated officially on September 12, 1962.
21. Interview with Commissioner Lee, Washington, D.C., October 25, 1965. One might ask why Congress and the broadcast industry felt a "deal" was necessary—why, for example, a prohibition of deintermixture was not considered in the absence of an all-channel receiver bill. The answer seems to be that the events of the early 1960s—including the quiz show scandals, reports of improper industry-commission contacts, and the general stir over Chairman Minow's criticisms of television—had put the broadcast industry and its congressional allies on the defensive. Thus a purely negative response to the Commission's attempts to alleviate the problems of UHF television seemed politically untenable.
22. See "House Passes Set Bill," *Broadcasting*, May 7, 1962, p. 50.
23. See "All-Channel Sets Minow's Goal," *Broadcasting*, January 15, 1962, p. 28. Contrary to these predictions, however, retail prices did not increase at all or increased only $5 or $7 per set. Interview with Jack Wyman, staff director of Consumer Products Division, EIA, Washington, D.C., October 20, 1965.
24. H.R. 8031, 87th Congress, 2nd Session (1962).
25. U.S. House of Representatives, House Committee on Commerce, *Hearings on All-Channel Television Receivers*, 87th Congress, 2nd Session (February 20, 21, and 22, 1962), p. 202, Statement of L. M. Sandwick, EIA.
26. *H.R. Report 1559, All-Channel Television Receiver*, 87th Congress, 2nd Session (April 9, 1962), p. 1.
27. Letter from Newton Minow to Senator John Pastore, reprinted in *Senate Report 1526, All-Channel Television Receivers*, (Appendix C), 87th Congress, 2nd Session (May 24, 1962) pp. 20–23.
28. Ibid., p. 8. Emphasis added.
29. Notice of Proposed Rule Making, Docket No. 14769, 27 *Federal Register* 9222 (September 18, 1962).
30. *All-Channel Television Broadcast Receivers*, 21 FCC2d 245 (1970); *All-Channel Television Broadcast Receivers*, 23 FCC2d 793 (1970); *Television Tuning*, 32 FCC2d 612 (1971); and *Comparable Television Tuning*, 43 FCC2d 395 (1973).
31. *Television Broadcast Receiver Antennas*, 62 FCC2d 164 (1976). CUB is an association of public and commercial broadcast groups seeking to promote the technical comparability of UHF and VHF television. Its members, in 1981, were the Corporation for Public Broadcasting, the National Association of Public Television Stations, the Association of Maximum Service

Telecasters, Inc., the National Association of Broadcasters, the Association of Independent Television Stations, Inc., and the Joint Council on Educational Telecommunications. The FCC has done a few other things as well. In 1976 the Commission contracted with Texas Instruments, Inc., to develop a high-performance UHF receiver. It has been sensitive to the "UHF impact" of any proposed changes in the 1952 Table of Allocations of TV channels (i.e., a proposal to move a VHF station into a UHF market); it has provided special consideration when UHF stations have run into problems with construction or modification of facilities and has been concerned when VHF engineering changes might affect UHF. The Commission has special UHF policies under its ownership rules and programming expectations. It considered, until recently, the impact of the development of cable systems on UHF television.

32. In mid-1980 it was reported that Matsushita Electric Industrial Co., Ltd., in Japan had developed an electronically tuned tuner with 5 dB noise levels for Channel 14 and 3 dB noise for Channel 83.

33. RM-2577, filed August 11, 1975.

34. Notice of Inquiry and Proposed Rulemaking, Docket 21010, 41 *Federal Register* 56210 (1976).

35. *UHF Television Receiver,* 69 FCC2d 1866 (1978).

36. Ibid., at 1885.

37. *Electronic Industries Association Consumer Electronics Group* v. *FCC,* 636 F.2d 689 (D.C. Cir. 1980). The quote is from p. 696. The "state of the art" seems to have improved since then (see note 32 above).

38. *Comparability for UHF Television: Final Report,* UHF Comparability Task Force, Office of Plans and Policy, Federal Communications Commission, Washington, D.C., September 1980, p. 89.

39. In addition to recommending an information campaign to get consumers to use better UHF home antennas, the task force made four other suggestions that might involve changes in FCC rules: (1) expand current rules about tuning and reception aids so that if aids such as coaxial input connectors are included for VHF, they should be there for UHF; (2) make some changes in channel selector rules to achieve more accurate tuning and better labeling of channel numbers; (3) clarify rules so that TV transmitters need not be capable of operating at 110 percent of authorized power (a change that could reduce UHF power bills); and (4) specify that manufacturers could delete from receivers UHF Channels 70 to 83, which have been reallocated to land mobile radio services. The FCC initiated an inquiry based on the task force report. (Further Notice of Inquiry and Notice of Proposed Rulemaking, Gen. Docket 78–391, 45 *Federal Register* 70023 [1980].)

40. See *Television Digest,* June 12, 1978, p. 7.

41. U.S. Senate, Committee on Appropriations, *Hearings on H.R. 12934, Departments of State, Justice, and Commerce, the Judiciary, and related agencies appropriations for Fiscal Year 1979,* Part 5, 95th Congress, 2nd Session (1978), pp. 1606–1607, 1609.

42. Ibid. Emphasis added.

43. Some UHF interests are displeased with the final report of the UHF Comparability Task Force. They believe that the task force could have paid more attention to UHF transmitter issues and assisted in the development of more efficient UHF transmission systems through sponsorship of research and development projects. In operation, UHF television stations

often consume two to ten times the power of similar VHF stations, a major factor affecting their profitability. In addition, some UHF interests continue to hope for government action to induce competition in the business of providing Klystron tubes, a crucial and very expensive part of UHF broadcast transmission systems now produced by only one manufacturer for U.S. use.

44. "UHF, TV's Last Frontier," p. 93.
45. According to FCC figures as of June 30, 1981, vacant and unapplied for commercial UHF channels are relatively scarce. In the top 100 TV markets, only 55 of 341 allocations (16.1 percent) are vacant. In the entire country, 206 of 664 (31.0 percent) remain unused. Noncommercial UHF allocations are less completely used: in the top 100 markets, 78 of 176 allocations (44.3 percent) are vacant; the national figure is 377 of 575 (65.6 percent).
46. In July 1981, WCVB-TV, a VHF, network-affiliated station in Boston, Massachusetts, sold for a record $220 million. This high price was rationalized, in part, by the fact that very few VHF stations in major markets had changed owners in previous years. It is interesting to note that the station had been obtained by its sellers through the comparative hearing process for legal fees of "about $2 million"—the only TV license ever to change hands because of a competing application ("Metromedia, WCVB-TV, Boston, $220 Million," *Broadcasting*, July 27, 1981, pp. 27–28). See also chapter 8.
47. One need not, of course, have a TV station license in order to distribute programming by satellite, but it helps. One of the reasons that the "superstation" idea has worked is that copyright policies toward "imported TV signals" mean they can be used by cable television systems with substantially fewer copyright problems than a signal containing the same programming but not originating from a broadcast station could be.
48. In the United States the Public Broadcasting Service has been a leader in the improvement of UHF broadcast technology. In August 1980, PBS issued a progress report claiming that changes likely to cost stations from $30,000 to $120,000 could produce "a reduction of greater than 50 percent in average transmitter power input." Public Broadcasting Service, "Public Television Demonstrates Means for Reducing UHF Transmission Costs by Half," Washington, D.C., August 7, 1980 [mimeo.].
49. *Television Factbook No. 49 (Services Volume)*, Washington, D.C.: Television Digest, Inc. (1980), p. 112a.

Seven

Commercials: How Many Are Too Many? Who Says?

For nearly nine in ten broadcasters—those who run commercial rather than noncommercial stations—advertising is the lifeblood of existence.[1] Except for trivial sources of additional revenue, such as space they may lease to others in buildings they own, commercial broadcasters depend on advertising sales as their only source of revenue to support station operation. However much audiences may criticize commercials, the fact is that advertisers, audiences, and broadcasters exist in a symbiotic relationship with one another, and commercials are essential. When all goes according to plan, broadcasters offer programs (and, for that matter, ads) that attract audiences. If they do that, advertisers are willing to pay broadcasters to include commercial messages in the programming that reaches audiences. If everything is as expected, what advertisers are willing to pay covers the cost of the programs and other expenses and returns a profit to the broadcaster. To advertisers, audiences, and broadcasters, the quantity of advertising is an important issue, about which two key questions can be asked. First, how much is enough? When, if ever, is a boundary crossed into overcommercialization? Second, who should decide the question—broadcasters, listeners and viewers, the government, or perhaps some other organization?[2]

The issue is one that has attracted the interest of many government bodies—the Federal Communications Commission and its predecessor the Federal Radio Commission, the Federal Trade Commission, Congress, the courts, and even, to some extent, the White House. Over most of the history of broadcasting, it has not been a key or burning issue—just a modestly important, persistent one. As former FCC Commissioner Robert E. Lee once noted, "The history of electronic communication reflects a frustration with the need to rely on commercialism to support a broadcasting system that wishful thinkers had hoped would be guided more by high cultural and moral standards than by the profit motive."[3] One such "wishful thinker" was Herbert Hoover who, as secretary of commerce, oversaw the first years of the development of broadcasting and who told the First Annual Radio Industry Conference in 1922 that, to him, "it is inconceivable that we should allow so great a possibility for service . . . to be drowned in advertising chatter." The industry representatives at the conference responded with a resolution "that advertising . . . be absolutely prohibited and that indirect advertising be limited to the announcement of the call letters of the station and the name of the concern responsible for the matter broadcasted."[4]

That, indeed, was the position of the Federal Radio Commission the first time it dealt with the issue in 1927. The Commission observed that "where the station is used for the broadcasting of a considerable amount of what is called 'direct advertising,' including the quoting of merchandise prices, the advertising is usually offensive to the listening public." The Commission did not ban the practice, but it certainly indicated it did not look upon advertising with great favor. Similar skepticism about advertising cropped up in a number of other FRC and FCC cases and policy statements, but generally, until the early 1960s, the Commission stayed away from very direct efforts to regulate the quantity of advertising.[5]

On March 28, 1963, however, the FCC announced it was contemplating policies designed to control the number and frequency of advertisements broadcast by radio and television stations. Although later conceded by Chairman E. William Henry to have been "a radical departure from previous regulation in terms of procedure,"[6] the Commission's concern about advertising abuses was obviously not new in substance. There were the old cases from the 1920s, and more recent pronouncements had been made too. In its 1946 statement entitled *Public Service Responsibility of Broadcast Licensees* (popularly known as the "Blue Book"), the FCC stated that in issuing and in renewing the licenses of broadcast stations, particular consideration would be given to program service factors relevant to the public interest, including the elimination of excessive ratios of advertising to program time. In fact, it expected broadcasters to present at least some "sustaining"—that is, unsponsored—programs.[7] The Commission recognized the broadcast industry's efforts at self-regulation; however, it found "abundant evidence" that the codes of the National Association of Broadcasters were being flouted by some stations and networks.[8] In 1960, less than three years before the FCC's announcement, the Commission had backed off on its expectations for "sustaining" programming but still indicated that regarding advertising

the licensee has the additional responsibility to take all reasonable measures to eliminate any false, misleading, or deceptive matter and to avoid abuses with respect to the total amount of time devoted to advertising continuity as well as the frequency with which regular programs are interrupted for advertising messages.[9]

Beyond this general statement, however, the FCC had, until 1963, hesitated to tread. The Commission had not pursued these early interests actively or specifically in advertising practices,[10] so its 1963 decision was widely considered an unprecedented involvement by the government in an area traditionally left to broadcasters.

The Commission, in its public notice of March 28, 1963, did not indicate a specific approach to the problem of overcommercialization. Although all seven Commissioners agreed on the need for action, they were split on whether to regulate advertising on a case-by-case basis or to institute rule-making proceedings.[11] They did try to reach agreement on "a program for action to be taken before [initiating] a more bloodthirsty approach";[12] however, their attempts at reaching a consensus failed. Consequently, in May 1963 the Commission proposed (by a narrow vote of 4 to 3) the adoption of rules requiring all broadcast stations to observe the limitations on advertising time contained in the NAB Radio and Television Codes.[13] The Commission announced that it wanted to receive a broad cross-section of comments and specifically invited the comments of all organizations and members of the public concerned about the broadcasting of commercial advertising.

The Commission's decision to adopt existing industry codes rather than set its own standards was an interesting one. By proposing standards that the industry claimed to be following, the Commission could argue that it was only trying to do the industry a favor. As reported by *Broadcasting:* "One of the appeals the NAB Codes have for Chairman Minow and some others in the agency is that they were drafted and adopted by the broadcasting industry, not imposed by the government."[14] The incorporation of private industry standards should have made the Commission's task easier; instead, it led to an industry attack on the adoption of any code standards for advertising time. One of the major advantages of the code, in the eyes of the industry, was the flexibility it provided broadcasters who could not live with the time standards; they could just stay out.[15] If the FCC made these standards universal, such flexibility would be lost. In attacking the code *Broadcasting* magazine editorialized that "no fixed rules can successfully be written to cover all kinds of time periods on all kinds of stations."[16] Both *Broadcasting* and its then companion, *Television* magazine, called upon the NAB to scrap all code time standards on advertising.[17] By proposing to regulate advertising time and suggesting the adoption of NAB Code standards, the Commission had, in the words of one broadcaster, "opened a hell of a big can of worms."[18]

Opposition to the Commission's plans continued to increase. In late June 1963 the NAB voted to oppose commercial time limitations and formed committees of broadcasters in each state to contact members of Congress.[19] The Commission scheduled hearings on its proposals for December 9 and 10; however, the Subcommittee on Communications and Power of the House Committee on Interstate and Foreign Commerce anticipated the hearings by holding its own on November 6, 7, and 8 on a bill, introduced by Subcommittee Chairman Walter Rogers (D-Texas), to prohibit the Commission from adopting any rules governing the length or frequency of broadcast ads.[20] Testimony highly critical of the FCC was offered at these hearings by some thirty broadcast and four congressional witnesses. Their objections, briefly summarized, were: (1) the Commission was not empowered to make such rules; (2) the proposed rules would entail an undesirable increase in regulation; and (3) uniform standards for all stations would be undesirable. Support for the Commission came mainly from poorly organized sources such as the League Against Obnoxious TV Commercials and the National Association for Better Radio and Television.

The Rogers bill, H.R. 8316, was approved unanimously by the House Interstate and Foreign Commerce Committee on November 18, in the absence of one committee member who opposed it. Earlier in November the Appropriations Subcommittee of the Senate Appropriations Committee had added injury to insult by cutting $400,000 from the Commission's fiscal 1964 budget request, while criticizing the FCC for straying into policy areas not intended by Congress.[21] The Rogers bill was then sent to the floor of the House, where it waited while the FCC held its planned hearings on December 9 and 10. These events prompted *Broadcasting* to report on December 16 that "the FCC's controversial commercial-time standards reached the end of the road last week, battered and all but friendless."[22]

The membership of the FCC had shifted during this time. Lee Loevinger joined the Commission on June 10, 1963, filling the spot made vacant when Commissioner Henry was made Chairman after Newton Minow's resignation. Without Minow, the Commissioners were deadlocked 3 to 3, and Commissioner Loevinger held the deciding vote. "I knew I had the votes, but Henry kept it bottled up," he said. Because the Chairman kept the proposal from coming to a vote, Loevinger explained, "the false impression was given that the withdrawal [of the FCC proposal] was due to the Rogers bill."[23] Without Loevinger's support for the proposals of March and May 1963, however, there was no hope for their adoption, and, on January 15, 1964, when the commercial proposal was finally voted on, the FCC unanimously terminated the rule-making proceedings.[24]

The House continued its deliberations on the Rogers bill in order to make sure the Commission fully understood its feelings. On February 24, 1964, the NAB dispatched memos to all broadcast stations marked "URGENT URGENT URGENT: Broadcasters should immediately urge their Congressmen by phone or wire to vote for H.R. 8316. . . . [A] vote for the bill is a vote of confidence in the broadcasters in his district. A vote against the bill would open the door to unlimited governmental control of broadcasting."[25] Three days later the House passed the Rogers bill by a resounding vote of 317 to 43.

No actions occurred on this bill in the Senate, and, in fact, it has been suggested that the Senate Commerce Committee would not have favored it.[26] Nevertheless, the episode was conclusive for the FCC at least for a while. As Commissioner Lee summarized it in 1965, "For all practical purposes we will not attempt anything such as this in the conceivable future."[27] The adoption of rules limiting advertising, then, seemed unfeasible, but the question remained: Could the Commission still regulate ads on a case-by-case basis? In its action of January 15, 1964, terminating the rule making, the Commission had expressed its intention to examine new and renewal applications for advertising excesses, and Chairman Henry, in a speech early in February, promised that the Commission would build policy in this area case by case "so that you will know and we will know what the rules of the game are to be."[28] By July 1964, however, Chairman Henry had lost the control of the Commission on this issue to Loevinger (by 4 to 3), and *Broadcasting* reported: "Indications are that only the most extreme cases of overcommercialization will be brought to the Commission's attention."[29] According to Chairman Henry, the campaign against excessive advertising "almost came to a halt . . . until Ford was replaced by [James] Wadsworth [in February 1965]. . . . Now we are questioning new applicants and renewals."[30] The departure of Chairman Henry from the Commission in May 1966 made Nicholas Johnson, a newly appointed Commissioner in June 1966, the possible swing man between Robert Lee, Kenneth Cox, and James Wadsworth, who favored case-by-case scrutiny of excessive commercialization, and Chairman Rosel Hyde, Robert Bartley, and Lee Loevinger, who opposed such activity.

Regulating without Rules

During the late 1960s and early 1970s, the Commission, for all practical purposes, revived its use of NAB standards on a case-by-case basis. The Commission had learned its lesson all right; no FCC rule expressly limited the amount of commercials a broadcaster could carry. Instead, the Commission handled the problem through instructions to its staff. With thousands of applications to be reviewed annually it is obvious that not all of them can be brought to the attention of the seven FCC

Commissioners. Thus, the Commissioners had long delegated to the staff the authority to process routine license applications. Delegated authority has to be controlled, however, and in 1970 the Commission handled the commercial time matter by issuing specific guidelines, based on the NAB code, to the staff. It did not do so, however, in the most public or official of fashions. Years later, the Commission explained what happened:

The Chief of the Broadcast Bureau, with Commission approval, sent a letter to Peoria Valley Broadcasting, Inc., licensee of WXCL. The letter, *although never published,* became a processing standard for the staff. It stated that the licensee's commercial policy "would obviate any problem with the commercial aspects of your operations at the next renewal period." That commercial policy specified "a normal commercial content of 18 minutes in each hour with specified exceptions."[31]

Thus, with an unpublished letter, and only seven years after its battle with Congress, the Commission in effect established the specific standards on commercial time that had been blocked in 1964. Similar standards for delegated authority in processing licensing applications were eventually developed for television.[32] Since broadcasters wanted their licenses renewed easily, they routinely limited their stated commercial policies to correspond with the understood limits. For years, at broadcaster conventions, FCC staff members would explain that there are "no rules" about the number of commercials one could carry but then go on to explain "what the Commission expects"—the limits set out above for staff action!

That is the way matters stood at the end of the 1970s. There were no formal FCC rules limiting the amount of commercial matter. Two factors beyond the economic marketplace, however, influenced what broadcasters did. Radio and television advertising was influenced by the FCC's staff processing guidelines. In addition, it continued to be guided by the self-regulatory codes—separate ones for radio and television—of the National Association of Broadcasters. Although the Code provisions were similar to the FCC staff processing guidelines, they were not identical. Broadcasters considered both in making commercial plans.

The situation began to change in 1975, however. In that year the U.S. Supreme Court gave some protection to advertising under the First Amendment to the Constitution. Previously the court's view had been that advertising content was unprotected, but now, in the name of the rights of consumers to receive truthful information about proposed commercial transactions, the court began to invalidate some government actions that banned certain kinds of ads. By and large, these decisions did not seem to affect the FCC's approach to advertising. The cases continued to allow some regulation of time, place, and manner of commercial speech; prohibited false or misleading advertising or ads proposing illegal transactions; and expressly excluded the "special problems of the electronic mass media."[33]

Between 1971 and 1981, both the FCC and the Federal Trade Commission had toyed with various rules regulating advertising in children's programs or limiting its amount. The notion of doing that—in fact, perhaps even banning advertising to children—had been pressed upon the commissions by Action for Children's Television (ACT), a Boston-based citizen group. During the three years (1971–1974) the FCC deliberated on an ACT proposal, the National Association of Broadcasters, not unmindful of the pressure on the Commission to "do something" to reduce children's TV ads, amended the NAB Television Code to diminish the number of children's ads. In 1974 the FCC decided that it would rely on the industry's codes and that it would expect all television broadcasters to hold children's advertising to those limits.[34] When ACT appealed that action, the FCC's reliance on the code, rather than the adoption of rules, was approved by the U.S. Court of Appeals for the District of Columbia Circuit.[35]

At the Federal Trade Commission, in February 1978, the staff recommended—partly at the urging of ACT—that TV advertising for children under eight years of age be banned, as well as advertising of products that pose serious health risks to children under twelve. The staff also suggested that advertisers of products such as sugared cereals be required to counter their pitches with nutritional and health disclosures.[36] The FTC Commissioners unanimously adopted the suggestions as proposed rules on March 1, 1978, a move that drew immediate and vigorous opposition from the broadcast, candy, cereal, toy, and advertising industries.[37] Opponents of the FTC proposals concentrated their activities at both the FTC and Congress. The children's proceeding, along with other controversial FTC actions, resulted in continual congressional pressure on the FTC from 1978 into 1981 and eventually led to legislation that effectively killed the FTC inquiry.[38]

Thus, the response of the FCC and, to a much lesser degree, FTC, to the children's advertising issue was similar to its earlier response to advertising on radio and television in general: rely primarily on industry self-regulation, staff processing guidelines, and what former Commissioner Robert E. Lee has characterized as occasional public and private "nagging."[39] The Commission's reliance on industry self-regulatory codes seemed to be jeopardized, however, when the U.S. Department of Justice filed an antitrust lawsuit in June 1979 against the NAB because of the limits on advertising time in the television code.[40]

The Justice Department's position was that the code's limits on the amount of "nonprogram" time reflected a conspiracy between the NAB and other unnamed "co-conspirators" to restrain trade and commerce in violation of Section 1 of the Sherman Antitrust Act. The department argued that this conspiracy restricted the amount and format of advertising, restrained price competition, and deprived purchasers of TV advertising time of "the benefits of free and open competition among television broadcasters."[41] Within a few months, the National Citizens Committee for Broadcasting (NCCB) petitioned the FCC for precise rules on television advertising time. The NCCB advised the FCC of what it believed to be the importance of having rules "in place before the Justice Department suit makes an impact on commercial practices."[42] While the NAB code was being attacked, at least indirectly, by citizen groups, broadcasters were strongly supporting it. Even the FCC expressed some support for the code by sending a letter to Congressman Lionel Van Deerlin (D-California), chairman of the House Communications Subcommittee, in which the Commission noted its prior reliance on the code, particularly in the children's TV area, and its general preference for "voluntary industry self-regulation in First Amendment sensitive areas, such as TV commercial practices."[43] As is often true of antitrust cases, however, this one bogged down, and, as of early 1982, the judge hearing the case had taken no action on petitions from both the NAB and the Justice Department seeking immediate resolution of the case in their favor.

It is interesting to note that the Justice Department's suit involved only the NAB Television Code. A Justice Department spokesperson said that the department had not moved against similar provisions in the NAB Radio Code because it did not raise as serious a problem as the television code.[44] Apparently the Justice Department believed that competition, more than the code or FCC oversight, determined radio advertising practices (or that the Radio Code was less binding than the Television Code). By 1978 the FCC seemed to be coming to that conclusion too, and in 1981 it stepped out of the regulation of radio advertising almost completely.

Late in 1978, FCC Chairman Charles Ferris began to suggest some kind of experiment at reducing radio regulation in large markets, where there were many competing radio stations. Exploiting that theme, and deciding at last that radio might have to be regulated differently from television, NAB President Vincent Wasilewski addressed NAB members in New Orleans in November 1978. He sought a declaration of independence for radio, proposing the elimination of FCC rules and policies dealing with amounts of commercial matter and amounts of noncommercial and nonentertainment programming (e.g., news and public affairs) as well as the elimination of requirements that broadcasters formally ascertain the problems, needs, and interests of their communities.[45]

Continuing ongoing industry-government interaction, FCC Commissioner Tyrone Brown acknowledged Wasilewski's speech and told the Southern California Broadcasters Association on December 8, 1978 that he was prepared to accept such deregulation of radio, plus the elimination of FCC requirements that radio stations keep program logs. He believed, however, that the Commission should require commercial radio stations to program a set amount of local content.[46] Picking up on Brown's speech just three days later the NAB presented to the FCC a petition seeking deregulation of radio along the lines Brown had suggested.[47] After several months of staff work, the FCC, on September 6, 1979, adopted a Notice of Inquiry and Notice of Proposed Rulemaking looking toward major deregulation of commercial radio.[48]

The Commission's proposal attracted substantial interest and comment. The Commission held panel discussions, an unusual procedure, on September 15 and 16, 1980, and invited both opponents and supporters of the proposals to participate.[49] In the course of the proceeding, the Commission received 3,247 formal comments on its ideas and more than 16,000 informal comments (i.e., letters). As might be expected, broadcasters strongly supported deregulation (1,125 for, 5 against, and 9 "mixed" according to an FCC tabulation of formal comments), while most other commentors—a mixture of individuals and religious groups—filed opposing remarks (290 for, 1,802 against, and 9 "mixed").[50] Several Carter administration agencies—the Justice Department, the National Telecommunications and Information Administration, the Council on Wage and Price Stability, and the Office of Consumer Affairs—offered general, if sometimes qualified, support for the FCC's proposals.[51] Despite the substantial opposition in a statistical sense, the FCC, on January 14, 1981, voted 6 to 1 to go ahead with radio deregulation. Oddly, Commissioner Brown was the only dissenter. As he had proposed, the FCC eliminated ascertainment and logging requirements for commercial radio broadcasters. The Commission said it would no longer, through staff delegation, supervise amounts of "non-commercial, non-entertainment" program time, and it also eliminated the supervision of the amount of commercial matter. Since the FCC did not, in exchange, require a set amount of local public service programming—"bedrock programming" he called it—Brown dissented.

Basically the FCC concluded that reliance on the competitive radio marketplace to hold down commercials and encourage desired programming worked at least as well and perhaps better than FCC regulation to further the public interest in radio. Stating that "no government regulation should continue unless it achieves some public interest objective that cannot be achieved without the regulation,"[52] the Commission decided that competitive marketplace forces in radio created "a largely self-regulating system and one wherein correction of commercial abuses by the system's own forces may be more swift and more efficient than those ordinarily imposed by the Commission." With that, it eliminated the staff processing guidelines on commercial matter that it had so carefully fashioned beginning in 1970.[53]

The outcome is plainly what broadcasters want it to be on this, the bottom-most of bottom-line issues. Instead of government, broadcasters and, if one accepts the FCC's basis for deregulation, listeners and viewers primarily determine levels of commercial content. For now, television broadcasters remain subject to some FCC supervision of their commercial levels, through staff delegation of authority rules, although they too will probably press for Commission deregulation in this area. For both television and radio, additional guidance comes from the marketplace and, assuming subscription, from the NAB Radio and Television Codes. Even if the codes should be successfully overturned by the Department of Justice, it will be broadcasters—individually rather than collectively—who will decide how many commercials are too many.

NOTES

1. As of September 30, 1981, there were a total of 10,122 radio and TV stations on the air. Of these 8,737 were commercial stations, equal to 86.3 percent of total stations. Noncommercial stations, too, depend on support from business, but not quite in the same way as commercial stations—although there are fewer and fewer differences between acknowledgments for funding support and normal advertisements.
2. One can also, of course, raise questions about the content of ads. When are they false or deceptive? How, if at all, does the Fairness Doctrine apply to them? What are the limits of commercial free speech? Although these questions have been controversial ones in recent years, they are not the subject of this chapter, which is limited to quantitative regulation of television and radio advertising.
3. Robert E. Lee, "The Federal Communications Commission's Impact on Product Advertising," *Brooklyn Law Review*, 46 (1980), 464.
4. Quoted in Murray Edelman, *The Licensing of Radio Stations in the United States, 1927 to 1947: A Study in Administrative Formulation of Policy* (Urbana: University of Illinois Press, 1950), pp. 83–84. Historian Eric Barnouw writes that Herbert Hoover, when he was secretary of commerce, said that " 'if a presidential message ever became the meat in a sandwich of two patent medicine advertisements, it would destroy broadcasting.' When Hoover died on October 20, 1964, NBC broadcast a tribute that was at once followed at its key station by a beer commercial, a political commercial, and a cigarette commercial. The ex-President was triple-spotted into eternity" (*Tube of Plenty, The Evolution of American Television* [New York: Oxford University Press, 1975], p. 357).
5. In *Great Lakes Broadcasting Company*, 3 FRC Ann. Rep. 32, 35 (1929), affirmed in 37 F.2d 993 (D.C. Cir. 1930), *certiorari denied*, 281 U.S. 706

(1930), the FRC stated: "Advertising must be accepted for the present as the sole means of support for broadcasting, and regulation must be relied upon to prevent abuse or overuse of the privilege."

6. Interview with Chairman E. William Henry, Washington, D.C., October 22, 1965. The initiation of the policy within the Commission came from Commissioner Robert E. Lee, who said that the idea for the proposed regulations came from a broadcaster (personal letter from Commissioner Lee, June 14, 1967). In a broader view, however, the policy grew out of a perceived need—especially vivid to New Frontier Commissioners such as Minow and Henry—to meet the problems of advertising excesses.

7. Federal Communications Commission, *Public Service Responsibility of Broadcast Licensees* (Washington, D.C.: Government Printing Office, 1946), p. 55.

8. Ibid., p. 43.

9. *En banc Programming Inquiry,* 44 FCC2d 2303, 2313 (1960).

10. For a brief history of these early days, see paragraphs 1–8 of Appendix G of *Deregulation of Radio,* 84 FCC2d 968, 1091–1093 (1981). See also Richard J. Meyer, "Reaction to the 'Blue Book,' " *Journal of Broadcasting,* 6 (Fall 1962), 295–312; and his " 'The Blue Book,' " *Journal of Broadcasting,* 6 (Summer 1962), 197–207.

11. Interview with Chairman Henry, Washington, D.C., October 2, 1965.

12. Personal letter from former FCC Commissioner Frederick Ford, June 16, 1967.

13. In 1962 a similar proposal to adopt the NAB Codes had been rejected by a 4-to-3 vote. Chairman Newton Minow and Commissioners E. William Henry and Robert E. Lee voted in the minority, while Commissioners Rosel Hyde, Robert Bartley, Frederick Ford, and T.A.M. Craven made up the majority. The replacement of Commissioner Craven by Kenneth Cox in late March 1963 swung the vote in May the other way with Minow, Henry, Lee, and Cox now constituting the majority. Not all broadcast stations belonged then to the NAB, nor do they today. It is possible to belong to the NAB and not subscribe to the code, and also possible to subscribe to the code without being an NAB member. In late 1981, about 46 percent of all radio stations subscribed to the code; for television, the figure was about 49 percent. According to a Code Authority study based on May 1981 ratings, 88.3 percent of all commercial television viewing took place on stations or networks that subscribe to the Television Code. In 1963, fewer than half of all radio stations and fewer than three-quarters of all television stations were code subscribers (Newton N. Minow, *Equal Time: The Private Broadcaster and the Public Interest* [New York: Atheneum, 1964], p. 25).

14. "Commission May Put Ceiling on Commercials," *Broadcasting,* April 1, 1963, p. 84. However, Commissioner Ford contended that the FCC's adoption of the NAB Code would undermine the desire for self-regulation: "What would be the use of trying if Government is going to move in and make the industry's efforts at self-regulation a matter of law? There would be no incentive, self-regulation would be destroyed, and the benefits of a very valuable regulatory tool would be lost" (speech before the Convention of the National Religious Broadcasters, January 23, 1963).

15. *Broadcasting* stated that "some stations are known to have stayed out of the code because they cannot command high enough rates to make a living from the number of commercials now permitted per program pe-

riod" ("Is This the Way Out of the Trap?" *Broadcasting,* June 17, 1963, p. 34).

16. "Time to Quit the Kidding" [editorial], *Broadcasting,* December 23, 1963, p. 78.

17. See "Facts of Life—or Death" [editorial], *Broadcasting,* June 3, 1963, p. 100; "The Haves and Have-Nots" [editorial], *Broadcasting,* July 1, 1963, p. 86; and "Since When Was 'Let's Pretend' a Game for Big Boys?" [editorial], *Television,* January 1964, p. 84.

18. Quoted in "Now a Crisis in the Radio-TV Codes," *Broadcasting,* May 27, 1963, p. 27.

19. See "NAB Boards Resolve to Fight Back," *Broadcasting,* July 1, 1963, p. 44.

20. U.S. House of Representatives, House Committee on Interstate and Foreign Commerce, *Hearings on Broadcast Advertisements,* 88th Congress, 1st Session (November 6, 7, and 8, 1963). Robert Lewis Shayon of the *Saturday Review* noted: "Congressmen who want the FCC to handle limitation of commercials on a case-by-case basis know that the Commission is made least effective this way. Its standards become loose and lack uniformity" ("Forecast for the FCC," *Saturday Review,* January 11, 1964, p. 51).

21. See "Where It Hurts," *Broadcasting,* November 11, 1963, p. 5.

22. "FCC Unhorsed in Commercial Crusade," *Broadcasting,* December 16, 1963, p. 38.

23. Interview with Commissioner Lee Loevinger, Washington, D.C., October 25, 1965. Chairman Henry agrees with him that "the shift in personnel shifted the policy by a shift in votes—not Congressional action" (interview with Chairman Henry, Washington, D.C., October 22, 1965.)

24. *Commercial Advertising,* 36 FCC45 (1965). The Commission attached to its Report and Order, however, a memorandum by the FCC general counsel—longer, in fact, than the Report and Order itself—which continued to maintain that under the Communications Act the Commission had the legal authority to adopt a rule prescribing maximum broadcast time to be devoted to commercial advertising. See Ibid., at 50–61. Although the official vote was unanimous, it must be remembered that the sentiment of the Commissioners was split 4 to 3 (interview with Phil Cross, legal assistant to Commissioner Robert T. Bartley, Washington, D.C., October 25, 1965).

25. Quoted in Eric Barnouw, *The Image Empire: A History of Broadcasting in the United States,* vol. III, *From 1953* (New York: Oxford University Press, 1970), p. 251.

26. Interviews with Nicholas Zapple, counsel to the Senate Commerce Committee, Washington, D.C., October 21, 1965; and FCC Chairman Henry, Washington, D.C., October 22, 1965.

27. Interview with Commissioner Robert E. Lee, Washington, D.C., October 25, 1965.

28. Remarks of Chairman E. William Henry before The Advertising Federation of America, February 4, 1964 [mimeo.], p. 4.

29. "FCC Again Rebuffs Chairman," *Broadcasting,* July 27, 1964, p. 34.

30. Interview with Chairman Henry, Washington, D.C., October 22, 1965.

31. *Deregulation of Radio,* 84 FCC2d 968, 1092 (1981). Emphasis added.

32. These standards were eventually incorporated into the FCC's rules. In early 1981, prior to deregulation, commercial AM and FM stations were

generally limited to eighteen minutes of commercial matter per hour, with "exceptions permitting in excess of 20 minutes of commercial matter per hour during no more than 10 percent of the station's total weekly hours of operation." In seasonal (i.e., resort) markets, the normal expectation was no more than twenty minutes per hour, with exceptions up to twenty-two minutes. There was the chance for up to four minutes per hour more to deal with high demands for political advertising time. For television, the normal standard was sixteen minutes per hour, which could increase to twenty minutes per hour during no more than 10 percent of the station's total hours to provide for political ads. See 47 CFR Sec. 0.281(a)(7), [1979], but remember that the radio provisions have since been deleted.

33. The most important cases are *Bigelow* v. *Virginia*, 421 U.S. 809 (1975) and *Virginia State Board of Pharmacy* v. *Virginia Citizens Consumer Council, Inc.*, 425 U.S. 748 (1976). The reservation as to broadcasting is from *Virginia State Board of Pharmacy*, at 773.

34. *Children's Television Report and Policy Statement* 50, FCC2d 1, 12–13 (1974), *reconsideration denied*, 55 FCC2d 691 (1975). In 1978 the FCC reopened the proceeding, partly to determine if reliance on self-regulation had been effective (*Children's Programming and Advertising*, 68 FCC2d 1344 [1978]). The general expectation was that changes in the FCC's composition following President Reagan's election suggested little likelihood of increased regulation of children's programming or advertising by the Commission.

35. *Action for Children's Television* v. *FCC*, 564 F.2d 458 (D.C. Cir. 1977).

36. See "FTC Takes Dead Aim at Kid Ads," *Broadcasting*, February 27, 1978, pp. 27–28.

37. See "The FTC Moves Toward Killing Commercials on Children's TV," *Broadcasting*, March 6, 1978, pp. 86–92; "FTC Ad Proposal Draws Instant Fire," *Broadcasting*, March 6, 1978, pp. 92–94; and "NAB Rallies the Troops Against Ad Ban," *Broadcasting*, March 6, 1978, p. 42.

38. See "FTC Staff Would Pull the Plug on Kidvid Inquiry," *Broadcasting*, April 6, 1981, p. 39. In October 1981 the FTC officially terminated the proceeding.

39. Lee, "The Federal Communications Commission's Impact on Product Advertising," 473.

40. *U.S.* v. *National Association of Broadcasters*, Civil Action No. 79-1549, complaint filed June 14, 1979. See "Another Hand of Government Strikes at NAB TV Code," *Broadcasting*, June 18, 1979, p. 27.

41. Complaint, ibid., pp. 5–7.

42. "NCCB Asks FCC to Step in with Ad Limitations," *Broadcasting*, August 13, 1979, p. 26. The NCCB proposed a limit of ten minutes per hour for adult programs and five minutes per hour for children, with elimination of advertising to children as soon as possible.

43. See "NAB Code Helps Public—FCC," *Television Digest*, October 29, 1979, p. 2.

44. See "Another Hand of Government Strikes at NAB TV Code," p. 27.

45. See "NAB to the FCC: Set Radio Free," *Broadcasting*, November 13, 1978, p. 25.

46. See "Brown Declares Sentiment for Radio and Cable Emancipation," *Broadcasting*, December 11, 1978, p. 31.

47. RM-3273, filed December 11, 1978. See "NAB Heartily Seconds Brown's

Call for Radio Deregulation," *Broadcasting,* December 18, 1978, p. 48.

48. *Deregulation of Radio,* 73 FCC2d 457 (1979). A perhaps important intervening event was President Carter's speech to the NAB in March 1979, in which he promised regulatory reform. See "Carter's Pledge of Deregulation to NAB Falls on Welcome Ears," *Broadcasting,* April 12, 1979, pp. 38–41. Chairman Ferris was pressured on the issue during the convention. See "Ferris's Q & A a Progress Report on Deregulation," *Broadcasting,* September 22, 1980, pp. 28–30.

49. See "Airing Out Deregulation at the FCC," *Broadcasting,* September 22, 1980, pp. 28–30.

50. Derived from Appendix C, *Deregulation of Radio,* 84 FCC2d 968, 1021 (1981).

51. See "Deregulation Filings Swamp FCC with Wide Range of Ideas," *Broadcasting,* March 31, 1980, pp. 25–27.

52. *Deregulation of Radio,* 84 FCC2d 968, 1006 (1981).

53. Ibid. At this time, the Commission decided to keep its options open to move back in if deregulation of advertising did not work: "Should events demonstrate that these competitive forces are not effective for all markets and instances, we can revisit this issue in detail in a general inquiry or rulemaking procedure at a later date" (ibid., at 1008). Eighteen months later, however, the Republican-dominated FCC led by Chairman Mark Fowler asked Congress to add language to the Communications Act that, in effect, would "codify [write into the statute] the Commission's recent radio deregulation order. This codification would resolve questions concerning the Commission's legal authority to take such action and may render moot certain cases now subject to court litigation." *FCC Legislative Proposals, Track II,* September 17, 1981 [mimeo.], pp. 13–14. Among these court cases was an appeal of the FCC's radio deregulation order filed with the U.S. Court of Appeals, D.C. Circuit. See *Office of Communication, United Church of Christ et al. v. FCC,* Nos. 81–1034, 81–1463, 81–2127, and 81–2134.

Eight

Comparative License Renewal Policies: The Nonindependence of an Independent Regulatory Agency

Few broadcast policy areas have been as intractable in recent years as that involving comparative broadcast renewal proceedings.[1] Such proceedings may occur when, at the end of a license term, an established broadcaster asks the FCC to renew the station's license but faces competition from an applicant for the same facility.[2] The result is, almost inevitably, a comparative renewal hearing before the FCC, a most unwelcome prospect for the incumbent broadcaster especially since uncontested renewals are nearly always granted without a hearing. The hearing, or even the prospect of it, throws a cloud over the operation, and means years of delay and substantial legal expenses. Since only one party can broadcast on a given frequency, the FCC must make a difficult choice between an incumbent broadcaster and a hopeful challenger. Two FCC Commissioners, borrowing from Sir Winston Churchill, referred to this choice as

a riddle within an enigma within a conundrum. The riddle: by what standards is a renewal applicant to be measured. The enigma: by what standards is a renewal challenger to be measured. The ultimate conundrum of course is, even assuming the measurement of such respective standards, how can there be constructed a matrix which can be used to rationally measure and compare two largely unrelatable properties: an empirical property (an existing record) and an a priori property (a set of applicant pledges)?[3]

Prior to 1969 the riddle, enigma, or conundrum was not a major problem. There were, of course, judicial and FCC precedents governing the procedures for dealing with competing applications. In 1945 the U.S. Supreme Court, in *Ashbacker Radio Corp.* v. *FCC,* held that constitutional due process requires an opportunity for all competing applicants for a *new* broadcast station to have a full comparative hearing before the FCC.[4] Then in 1949, in *Johnston Broadcasting Co.* v. *FCC,* the U.S. Court of Appeals for the District of Columbia Circuit ruled that the FCC must consider every material difference between two applicants in such a comparative hearing.[5] These court cases, however, did not involve competing applicants for existing licenses.

One of the earliest FCC policy statements governing competing applicants for an *existing* station was issued in 1951, when the Commission voted to renew the license of WBAL, Baltimore. In the WBAL case the FCC reaffirmed its position that in a comparative hearing for an existing station, the past performance of a broadcaster is the most reliable indicator of future performance.[6] A good record merited renewal, the FCC found, despite a newcomer's promise of a better showing on factors such as integration of ownership with management, local residence, or increased diversification of media ownership—all criteria used in comparisons among applicants for new stations to predict which would provide the best service.

In 1965 the Commission issued its 1965 policy statement covering comparative hearings that involved applications for *new* stations.[7] This statement stressed the importance of such factors as diversification, integration of ownership and management, and local residence. The FCC also stated that the past record of performance of a broadcast station applicant in a comparative hearing for a new station would be of interest to the Commission only if it was either "unusually good" or "unusually bad." Several months later the Commission expanded this policy statement in a case in which two applicants had challenged the incumbent licensee. In *Seven League Productions, Inc.,* the FCC decided that its policy statement on competing applicants for a *new* station should govern the introduction of evidence, but not the weight to be given particular factors, in proceedings involving a competitive challenge to an existing licensee.[8]

This reliance on the incumbent's record of performance erected a barrier so formidable to potential competing applicants that the Commission was forced to decide just one comparative renewal case between 1952 and 1969. In that case, involving the Wabash Valley Broadcasting Corp. (WTHI-TV), the Commission did not even try to factor the incumbent's past performance into the overall comparative decision. Instead, the Commission compared Wabash with its challenger using standard criteria but disregarded those criteria showing shortcomings in Wabash created by FCC policy shifts since Wabash had been licensed originally. Wabash won renewal largely on its past broadcast record.[9]

The wall protecting incumbent broadcasters from successful challenges by newcomers seemed as solid as ever.

That barrier was shaken, however, on January 22, 1969, when the FCC, by a vote of 3 to 1, refused to renew the license of Boston's WHDH-TV and instead gave the license to a competing applicant.[10] The decision aroused great anxiety in the broadcast industry. For the first time in its history the FCC had refused to renew the license of a broadcast station that had an "average" record of performance; and instead it awarded the license to an applicant that, reportedly, would be more actively involved in the station's operation and would add to the diversity of control over mass communications media in the area.

On appeal three years later the Herald-Traveler Corporation, WHDH's owner, asserted before the U.S. Supreme Court that loss of its authority to operate the station would jeopardize the jobs of 2,600 employees of the Boston *Herald-Traveler* and would mean the death of the newspaper. In March 1972, after all legal appeals had been exhausted, the Herald-Traveler Corporation was forced to relinquish control of the station. A few months later the newspaper ceased publication, and its assets were sold to a competitor.

The FCC's action was obviously of great consequence to the communications media in the Boston area, yet for the broadcast industry in general it portended something far more threatening: broadcasters holding immensely valuable licenses might lose them in competitive hearings at renewal time. The initial industry reaction to the FCC's *WHDH* decision in 1969 was one of confusion and shock. The FCC vote itself—involving only four of the seven Commissioners—was described by the trade press as "strange" and "weird."[11] The three-man majority included Commissioners Robert Bartley, Nicholas Johnson, and James Wadsworth (who was generally regarded as a moderate or a conservative). Commissioner Kenneth Cox, on the other hand, did not participate because he had dealt with the case when he was chief of the Broadcast Bureau. Commissioner H. Rex Lee was absent, visiting El Salvador on an educational television matter. Chairman Rosel Hyde abstained, issuing an unusual statement to the effect that he could not make up his mind![12] The position of Commissioner Robert E. Lee, however, was clear: he had provided the lone dissenting vote. Some industry observers, seeking a bright side to the decision, felt that the voting lineup was unique: "Hyde normally will vote to let [a] satisfactory operator keep [his] station; Wadsworth may revert to [a] similar view in other cases; no one knows which way Rex Lee might go; even Cox isn't absolutely rigid on this front—though he likes to keep pressure on licensees."[13]

Confusion resulted from both the majority and the various concurring and dissenting statements in the *WHDH* case. The majority decision noted that the case was an unusual one, involving a challenge by three applicants against WHDH. Although the station had been on the air for years, it had never received a regular three-year license because of charges by the Department of Justice in the late 1950s and early 1960s of improper conferences between the station's former president and the then Chairman of the FCC. In his dissenting opinion, however, Commissioner Robert E. Lee commented that he was "very much afraid that this decision will be widely interpreted as an absolute disqualification for license renewal of a newspaper-owned facility in the same market. Competing applications can be anticipated against most of these owners at renewal time."[14] In a similar vein (but from the opposing viewpoint) Commissioner Johnson's concurring statement concluded: "The door is thus opened for local citizens to challenge media giants in their local community at renewal time with some hope for success before the licensing agency where previously the only response had been a blind reaffirmation of the present license holder."[15]

The *WHDH* decision was immediately attacked by those who feared that the stability of the broadcast industry would be threatened by license renewal challenges. Professor Louis L. Jaffe of Harvard Law School, for example, characterized the decision as a "desperate and spasmodic lurch toward 'the left' " which "overrules an administrative practice of at least eighteen years standing" and probably places "all licensees at hazard every three years, a proposition which would work a revolution in the industry and cause serious problems of financing."[16] In an article entitled "$3 Billion in Stations Down the Drain?" *Broadcasting* magazine asserted that the potential impact of the *WHDH* decision and related FCC proposals aimed at promoting greater diversity of control of mass media "could jeopardize broadcast holdings that, in the top 50 markets alone, are valued at more than $3 billion. . . . The shockwaves of the losses would be felt by thousands of big and small stockholders alike, threatening the financial underpinnings of the broadcast industry and possibly swamping many small broadcast groups."[17] In an accompanying editorial *Broadcasting* commented that "Congress has become the broadcasters' only real hope for a restoration of order in an FCC that has clearly gone out of control."[18]

Whether the FCC had intended its decision with respect to WHDH to be a special case or the initiation of a broad new policy on license renewal challenges will not be discussed here. The importance of the precedent-shattering *WHDH* decision lies in the sequence of political events it triggered. It stimulated widespread controversy in the broadcast industry, Congress, the White House, and among citizen groups. A year later it led to the FCC's adoption, under pressure from Congress and the broadcast industry, of a policy statement on license renewal challenges. Seventeen months later that statement itself would be over-

turned by the courts. More than ten years later the basic policy controversy would remain unresolved. Immediately, the *WHDH* decision
provoked a whirlwind of lobbying and legislative activity intended to
safeguard the interests of broadcast licensees.

Pressure for Congressional Action

Shortly after the release of the *WHDH* decision the National Association of Broadcasters began a lobbying campaign for congressional passage of a bill that would prevent the FCC from considering competing
applications when acting on the renewal applications of a licensee.
Senator John Pastore (D-Rhode Island), chairman of the communications subcommittee and one of the most influential members of Congress in broadcasting matters, delighted broadcasters at the NAB convention in March 1969 by his remarks on harassment at license renewal
time:

It is my deep-seated conviction that public service is not encouraged nor pro-
moted by placing the sword of Damocles over the heads of broadcasters at
renewal time. The broadcaster must have reasonable assurance that if he does
his job—and does it well—he's going to remain in business and not have his
investment go down the drain.[19]

At the same convention broadcasters met with Clay Whitehead and
Abbott Washburn, then White House staff aides, and urged them to
push for legislation on license renewal challenges and to encourage the
appointment of sympathetic Commissioners to replace Rosel Hyde and
Kenneth Cox.[20]

On April 29, 1969, Senator Pastore introduced S. 2004, which would
amend Section 309 of the Communications Act to provide that the FCC
could not consider competing applications for a license at renewal time
unless it had first found, based on the licensee's renewal application,
"that a grant of the application of a renewal applicant would not be in
the public interest, convenience and necessity."[21] Such a two-step approach—decide on renewal first and subsequently consider competitors
if renewal was denied—has been a commonly proposed solution ever
since.

By the time that the Commission acted on requests for rehearing by
the parties in the *WHDH* case, over fifty-five representatives in the
House had introduced bills identical or similar to S. 2004.[22] In a decision
on May 19, 1969, the FCC denied the rehearing requests but again
emphasized that the *WHDH* case was unique since, for reasons stemming from circumstances surrounding the original grant, the existing
licensee of WHDH was "in a substantially different posture from the
conventional applicant for renewal of [a] broadcast license."[23]

In June 1969 *Television Digest* reported that, as a result of a massive lobbying campaign by the industry following the *WHDH* case, the prospects were bright for congressional passage of S. 2004.[24] In addition to Pastore, sponsors of S. 2004 included Senators Mike Mansfield (D-Montana), majority leader; Warren Magnuson (D-Washington), chairman of the Senate Commerce Committee; Norris Cotton (R-New Hampshire), ranking minority member on that committee; and Hugh Scott (R-Pennsylvania), ranking minority member on the Senate Communications Subcommittee.

Hearings on S. 2004 were held by the Senate Communications Subcommittee on August 5, 6, and 7, 1969. During the three days of hearings all but one of the witnesses testified in favor of S. 2004. Those supporting the bill included broadcasters from Rhode Island, Nebraska, Utah, and Pennsylvania, the president of the Federal Communications Bar Association, the general manager of the American Newspaper Publishers Association, and the dean of Temple University's School of Communications. Testifying in opposition was Earle K. Moore, counsel for the National Citizens Committee for Broadcasting.

At this point, however, a combination of events and circumstances slowed the momentum of the broadcasters' campaign and raised doubts among many members of Congress, including several sponsors of S. 2004, about the wisdom of the bill. During August the hearings were cut short because of a lengthy Senate antiballistic missile debate and the Senate's late summer recess. Other pressing business subsequently forced postponement of the resumption of hearings (which had been tentatively rescheduled for the middle of September),[25] and they were not finally reconvened until December. During the intervening months minority groups were increasingly active in protesting the grant of license renewals of television stations that, they contended, catered almost exclusively to white, middle-class viewers. Also, articles critical of S. 2004 appeared in the *New York Times, Harper's,* and *Time* magazine. An unsigned billboard on Sunset Boulevard in Los Angeles proclaimed:

> Watch for this coming subtraction!
> S. 2004
> Freedom's closing number brought
> to you by
> ABC, CBS & NBC Television.[26]

At the time of the initial Pastore hearings in August 1969 six of the seven FCC Commissioners were opposed to S. 2004. However, in October 1969 President Nixon appointed Dean Burch, a former administrative assistant to Senator Barry Goldwater (R-Arizona), as FCC Chairman and also named Robert Wells, a Kansas broadcaster, to the Commission. Both favored legislation like S. 2004. At the confirmation hearings for Burch and Wells, Senator Pastore said he was irked by the "cliché" that S. 2004 was tantamount to giving licensees a license in perpetuity. This cliché, he said, "sounds good, very dramatic, but I am surprised so many people are beginning to believe it. It was never intended as that."[27]

When congressional hearings resumed on December 1, 1969, members of Black Efforts for Soul in Television (BEST) were picketing NAB offices in Washington, New York, and Los Angeles and network-owned stations in Boston, Chicago, Philadelphia, and San Francisco to protest S. 2004 as a form of "backdoor racism," a "congressional charade." The picketers read the following statement:

This bill represents backdoor racism because it is a subtle, and therefore more vicious, attempt to limit the efforts of the black community to challenge the prevailing racist practices of the vast majority of TV stations. . . . The Pastore bill . . . attempts to keep the media safely in the grips of monopolistic and politically selfish private white owners. It would deny black citizens the opportunity to demonstrate their ability to manage a TV station in a manner more consistent with the public interest than the station's present white owners. . . . Sen. Pastore seeks to protect the media barons who operate to satisfy their personal economic greed.[28]

The mood of the December hearings is perhaps best illustrated by one heated exchange between Senator Pastore and the audience. "When you say I introduced a racist bill you offend me," the senator shouted. "The one thing I don't want you people to do is go away and say this is a racist bill!" Blacks in the audience shouted back: "It is, it is!"[29] Senator Pastore was shocked and cited his strong civil rights record whenever a witness intimated that S. 2004 was a racist bill. "I'm not a patsy for the broadcasting industry. I'm nobody's patsy." Pastore also got into a shouting match with John Banzhaf, head of Action on Smoking and Health, who charged: "The bill which bears your name is unnecessary, unfair and unworthy of the support of any Senator . . . and even its consideration at this time is a waste of the Committee's time and a gross misallocation of its resources."[30] The lack of interest and support by other members of the subcommittee was clear since Pastore was often the only senator present at the December hearings.

On December 1, 1969, the FCC testified in opposition to S. 2004. Commissioner Robert Bartley, as the senior Commissioner voting for the FCC's majority position, presented the majority statement, noting that although it was originally adopted by a vote of 6 to 1 (before Burch and Wells succeeded Hyde and Wadsworth), it now could claim only a

4-to-3 majority. Bartley said that the Commission did not support the bill because it "is unnecessary and would, in our opinion, have significant disadvantages to the public interest."[31] The majority statement emphasized that "the spur to a lagging broadcaster posed by the threat of competitors at renewal time is an important factor in securing operation in the public interest."

Concurring statements were delivered by Commissioners Cox, H. Rex Lee, and Johnson. In a forty-nine-page attack on S. 2004, Commissioner Johnson accused the "hear-no-evil-see-no-evil-speak-no-evil" leaders of the NAB of "taking the broadcasters themselves—jovial, prosperous, and martini in hand—down a jungle road into the longest ambush from an outraged citizenry ever unleashed upon an unsuspecting American industry." He questioned whether S. 2004 was constitutional since it would place "restrictions upon the ease with which individuals or groups could enter the field of broadcasting." Johnson contended that "S. 2004 may easily do more to continue racism in this country than any other single piece of legislation now pending before the Congress" and warned that "its passage will leave a frustrated people with no recourse except perhaps to engage in more violent protests and other actions that serve the interests of no one."

Dissenting statements were given to the subcommittee by Chairman Burch and Commissioners Robert E. Lee and Wells. Burch's testimony was significant because he suggested the substitute language for the Pastore bill:

In any comparative hearing within the same community for the frequency or channel of an applicant for renewal of a broadcast license, the applicant for renewal of license shall be awarded the grant if such applicant shows that its program service during the preceding license term has been substantially, rather than minimally, attuned to meeting the needs and interests of its area, and the operation of the station has not otherwise been characterized by serious deficiencies.

The FCC Tries a Policy Statement

At the conclusion of the hearings the chances for passage of S. 2004 seemed remote. The FCC was pressured to devise a way of avoiding legislative defeat for Senator Pastore, the twenty-two Senate co-sponsors of S. 2004, and the more than one hundred sponsors in the House. The first hint of possible FCC action along this line was seen in the December 29, 1969, issue of *Broadcasting*, which predicted that the FCC's first action in January would be a "breakthrough in station licensing policy to alleviate [the] . . . chaos triggered by WHDH-TV Boston revocation case."[32] *Broadcasting* indicated that the Commission would adopt a policy whereby an applicant's license would be renewed following a comparative hearing if the applicant demonstrated in that hearing that the station's program service was substantially attuned to the needs and interests of the area it served.

Stimulated by these predictions in the trade press, the Citizens Communications Center (CCC) and Black Efforts for Soul in Television (BEST) filed a complaint on January 7, 1970, with the U.S. District Court for the District of Columbia. The complaint sought to enjoin the Chairman and members of the FCC from "promulgating any policy, rule or interpretation or making any other change in the standards applicable to comparative broadcast license renewal proceedings without first giving all interested parties notice and an opportunity to be heard." On the same day the complaint was filed, the court denied their request for a temporary restraining order and, shortly thereafter, dismissed the action for lack of jurisdiction.[33] The FCC's attorney told District Court Judge Matthew McGuire that the two groups were simply "guessing" that the Commission would take an action to which they would object and that they had no complaint until it did. The court also agreed with the FCC's contention that exclusive judicial review jurisdiction of the Commission's action is vested in the courts of appeal under Section 402(a) of the Communications Act.

In another effort to dissuade the FCC from issuing a new policy statement on license renewal challenges, the CCC and BEST, on January 9, filed a petition for rule making with the Commission, urging that the issue of comparative hearings be dealt with through a formal rule-making proceeding. In addition, even though the FCC had not yet publicly announced any new policy, the United Church of Christ and the National Citizens Committee for Broadcasting issued statements opposing the adoption of a revised policy on license renewal challenges.[34]

These attempts to forestall FCC action failed. On January 15, 1970, the Commission, by a vote of 6 to 1, issued its *Policy Statement on Comparative Hearings Involving Regular Renewal Applicants.* Under the policy statement the renewal hearing was to be divided into two stages. In the first stage, the past performance of the applicant for renewal of a license would be examined. If the renewal applicant "shows that its program service during the preceding license term has been substantially attuned to meeting the needs and interests of its area and that the operation of the station has not otherwise been characterized by serious deficiencies . . . [its] application for renewal will be granted." If the examiner did not agree that the applicant's service had been so attuned, the hearing would continue into the second state, a direct comparison with the challenger, in which the incumbent licensee would be deprived of any preference due to incumbency. At about the same time the FCC opened an inquiry, Docket 19154, seeking to define the kind of "substantial service" it had in mind. This was, obviously, a somewhat modified two-step process. The Commission stressed its belief that the policy of preferring an incumbent that had compiled a good broadcast record over a rival applicant that offered only untested promises was firmly grounded in administrative precedent and was necessary to preserve industry stability.

In a dissenting opinion Commissioner Johnson said that the American people had been deprived of substantial rights by the Commission's action. It would have been much wiser, he observed, for the Commission to have used traditional rule-making procedures on such a controversial issue, but "there are legal and public relations considerations involved in issuing this statement as *fait accompli* rather than as proposed rule making for public comment." Johnson, in the closing paragraphs of his dissent, said that he could not avoid reference to the "significance of this necessary kind of compromise with broadcasting's power":

The record of Congress and the Commission over the years shows their relative powerlessness to do anything more than spar with America's "other government," represented by the mass media. Effective reform, more and more, rests with self-help measures taken by the public. Recognizing this, the broadcasters now seek to curtail the procedural remedies of the people themselves. The industry's power is such that it will succeed, one way or another. This is sad, because—unlike the substantive concessions it has obtained from Government from time to time—there is no turning back a procedural concession of this kind once granted. Not only can the industry win every ball game, it is now in a position to change the rules.[35]

On the same day it adopted the policy statement, the FCC, by a vote of 6 to 1, denied the petition submitted by the CCC and BEST requesting a rule-making proceeding to codify standards for all comparative proceedings.[36] According to the Commission the policy statement did not change existing law, and this area was simply not conducive to a formal rule. The Commission also observed:

Parties may seek revision of the policy as cases come before the Commission, and may do so in the context of specific factual situations. Interested persons, such as petitioners, may seek to present their views in such cases as *amicus curiae.* If the requested policy changes are rejected, resort may be had to the courts if such rejection is believed unlawful or to the Congress, if it is regarded as unsound policy. While, for all these reasons, we believe that further proceedings would not be helpful, it does serve the public interest to insure that our present policies, based largely on established precedents, are clearly stated. The policy statement does that.[37]

Senator Pastore praised the policy statement and stated that his subcommittee would not take any further action on S. 2004 until the FCC's policy had a fair test:

I think the Commission ought to be given a chance. It's a step in the right direction. All I ever wanted to do right along was to make sure that a good licensee had a reasonable chance to stay in business, without harassment. The FCC policy doesn't eliminate competing applications, but in large measure it eliminates the element of harassment. It will have a salutary effect. It will discourage those engaged in piracy.[38]

Television Digest observed that the FCC's policy statement "has something for every Commissioner (except Johnson, who dissented)— and [the] truth is that implementation will be everything." Thus, in the future, both the toughest and most lenient Commissioners would be able to rest their decisions solidly on material in the policy statement. *Television Digest* further observed that the document had received almost unanimous approval because most of the industry's critics on the Commission infinitely "prefer this easily modified, flexibly interpretable policy—rather than imbedding into law the Pastore bill."[39]

On February 16, 1970, the CCC and BEST filed with the FCC petitions for reconsideration and for repeal of the policy statement and a petition for reconsideration of the Commission's denial of their petition for rule making. Other groups also seeking reconsideration of the policy statement were Hampton Roads Television Corporation and Community Broadcasting of Boston, Inc., two competitors for the television channels of renewal applicants in Norfolk, Virginia, and Boston.

On July 21, 1970, by a vote of 5 to 1 (with Commissioner Bartley absent), the FCC denied the various petitions for reconsideration, emphasizing that the policy statement was not a rule and was not intended to have the effect of one.[40] Again, only Commissioner Johnson dissented. He contended that adoption of the policy statement violated the Administrative Procedure Act, was an abuse of agency discretion, violated the hearing requirement specified by the Communications Act, and violated the First Amendment.[41] In view of the "political events" surrounding the adoption of the policy statement, he believed that the Commission's position could not be considered reasonable or fair:

The impact of citizen outrage measurably slowed the progress of S. 2004, and many Senate observers began to predict the Bill would never pass. Then, without formal rulemaking hearings, or even submission of written arguments, the Commission suddenly issued its January 15, 1970 Policy

Statement—achieving much of what Congress had been unable or reluctant to adopt.

There were many parties who had invested substantial time and money fighting the threatened diminution of their rights, and who no doubt would have opposed our January 15, 1970 Policy Statement on numerous grounds. In challenging S. 2004, many of these parties claimed to represent the interests of important segments of our population: the minorities, the poor, and the disadvantaged. By refusing even to listen to their counsel this Commission reached a new low in its self-imposed isolation from the people; once again we closed our ears and minds to their pleas.[42]

The Court Throws a Monkey Wrench

On April 1, 1970, the CCC and BEST submitted an appeal to the U.S. Court of Appeals for the District of Columbia Circuit challenging the legality of the policy statement. The two broadcasters who filed a petition for reconsideration of the policy statement (Hampton Roads and Community Broadcasting) joined the CCC and BEST in the appeal. RKO General, Inc., and WTAR Radio-TV Corporation, the challenged incumbent licensees in the Boston and Norfolk renewal proceedings, also intervened and filed briefs defending the policy statement. The CCC and BEST argued that the policy statement deprived a new, qualified applicant of the right to a comparative hearing and deprived emerging minority groups of equal protection of the laws:

Since the beginnings of broadcasting, Congress has repeatedly and expressly declared that a broadcast license shall not be a monopoly in perpetuity. Broadcasters for their part have sought to maintain in perpetuity the exceedingly valuable monopoly that is the exclusive privilege to broadcast on one of the limited number of radio or TV frequencies. The intent of the Congress remains in the silent statute books; the broadcasters daily whisper in the corridors of the Commission. The Policy Statement challenged in this appeal represents the FCC's final capitulation to the industry.[43]

During the summer of 1970, when the appeal was pending before the court, the FCC's policy statement became the subject of a study by the staff of the Special Subcommittee on Investigations of the House Committee on Interstate and Foreign Commerce. In a report released in late November 1970, the staff study charged that the policy statement "is not a policy but a flagrant attempt to repeal the statutory requirements and to substitute the FCC's own legislative proposal that a hearing is not required when it involves a license renewal proceeding having several competing applicants." The study further asserted that it "was not until now that any agency has had the temerity to usurp Congressional power and by way of a 'policy statement' repeal a constitutional and statutory requirement in the interest of easing Commission workload requirements." The policy statement, the study concluded, "exemplifies both an unwarranted solicitude for the economic well-being of the licensee who enjoys a wealth-producing permit to use the public's precious airwaves and an indifference to the public interest including the right of viewers and listeners to have access to viewpoints and programs from diversified sources."[44]

The staff study was not endorsed by members of the subcommittee or its chairman, Harley Staggers (D-West Virginia), who merely forwarded the document to the FCC with a request that the Commission submit a detailed legal opinion on the staff's conclusions by December 21, 1970. Acting with unaccustomed haste, the Commission submitted a detailed response three days in advance of the deadline, declaring its innocence of the study's charges.[45]

On June 11, 1971, a three-judge panel of the court of appeals found the FCC's policy statement illegal and ordered the FCC to redesignate all comparative renewal hearings to reflect the court's judgment. In a decision written by Judge J. Skelly Wright, a Kennedy appointee, and supported by Judges George E. MacKinnon and Malcolm R. Wilkey, both recent Nixon appointees, the court said that its action "today restores healthy competition by repudiating a Commission policy unreasonably weighted in favor of the licensees it is meant to regulate, to the great detriment of the listening and viewing public." According to Judge Wright, the Commission's suggestion that "it can do without notice and hearing in a policy statement what Congress failed to do when the Pastore bill . . . died in the last Congress is, to say the least, remarkable." The policy statement, Judge Wright observed, in effect administratively enacted the Pastore bill, and in his view the FCC's issuance of the statement without a prior public hearing raised additional serious questions.[46]

Judge Wright further held that "superior performance" should be regarded as "a plus of major significance in renewal proceedings" and that a new applicant had a heavy burden to produce sufficient evidence to displace an incumbent licensee in a comparative proceeding. He suggested that the FCC define both quantitatively and qualitatively what constitutes "superior programming service." Interestingly, the court of appeals decision relied heavily on language contained in the House Investigations Subcommittee staff study and the dissenting opinions of Commissioner Johnson.

The court's decision was unwelcome to the industry. *Broadcasting* editorially condemned it as "a new prescription for anarchy in broadcast regulation," adding: "It is a formula for dismemberment of the system." The decision, *Broadcasting* asserted, "will create infinitely more chaos than prevailed in the year between the FCC's WHDH-TV decision and its adoption of the Policy Statement." The editorial concluded that the remedy must be found in Congress and that "nothing less than survival is at issue."[47] Although most Commissioners believed that the decision could lead to considerable instability in broadcast ownership, they agreed neither to seek a rehearing of the case by the full nine-judge panel of the court of appeals nor to ask for review by the Supreme Court for fear that further judicial review "might make things worse."[48]

Politics of "Relief" Continue

The history of policy in the area of comparative renewal hearings since the *Citizens Communications Center* case is a convoluted one, involving all of the parties to the regulatory process. Almost from the day of the *WHDH* decision, "renewal relief"—usually combining protection from competing applications with other issues of the moment (most prominently, a longer license term)—has been a primary lobbying effort of broadcaster groups, including the National Association of Broadcasters.[49] Congress has struggled unsuccessfully with new legislation in the area, and citizen groups have lobbied in Congress to defeat that legislation.[50] In various ways the issue has been addressed by presidents from Nixon through Reagan.[51] The FCC attempted to formulate policy while at the same time "motor[ing] right along,"[52] deciding comparative renewal cases on a case-by-case basis. The cases have produced long and discursive analyses of the comparative problem by articulate Commissioners such as Nicholas Johnson, Richard Wiley, Glen Robinson, Charles Ferris, Joseph Fogarty, and Tyrone Brown.[53] The courts have had to deal with numerous appeals of these FCC decisions, "laboring valiantly, sweep[ing] up behind," and producing caustic criticisms of the process on their own.[54] As one court succinctly noted, "The administrative practice in Commission comparative renewal proceedings is unsatisfactory."[55]

The most immediate FCC response to the rebuff it received in the *Citizens Communications Center* case was to amend its Docket 19154 proceeding to inquire into the possibility of defining quantitatively the meaning of "superior" performance as called for in the *Citizens* case (although the FCC never did adopt the phrase "superior").[56] The Commission amassed a substantial record, but it would be years before it would do anything with the information and, when it did act, the Commission simply decided not to adopt quantitative, percentage-based renewal standards after all.

Meanwhile broadcasters took their cause to Congress. In 1974, despite vigorous opposing testimony from representatives of the citizen movement, both the House and the Senate overwhelmingly passed slightly different versions of a bill, H.R. 12993, that was regarded as acceptable by most in the broadcast industry. The vote in the House was 379 to 14, and in the Senate 69 to 2. Both versions extended broadcast license terms, a longstanding industry objective, but more importantly from the industry's perspective, both provided for the celebrated two-step renewal process originally proposed in S. 2004. Under the new provisions the FCC would first have to determine that a licensee's operation had failed to meet properly ascertained community needs during the previous license term before accepting competing applications. Essentially, it would have to deny renewal before considering new applicants.

Unfortunately for broadcasters, House Interstate and Foreign Commerce Committee Chairman Staggers was angered when the House voted to increase the broadcast license term from three to five years—which he regarded as a breach of faith by industry lobbyists, whom he thought had agreed to a four-year term. As a result Staggers refused to name House members to the conference committee formed to resolve differences between the House and Senate versions of the bill. Prior to this, some delay in consideration of the bills had resulted from the impeachment investigation of President Nixon. Consequently, the 93rd Congress adjourned without passage of legislation that broadcasters wanted desperately.[57]

Since 1974 broadcast interests have not fared very well in Congress with respect to "renewal relief," although they have gained longer license terms. A major reason has been that Congress, between 1976 and 1980, preferred to focus on broad revisions of the Communications Act of 1934 rather than on narrower, more specific bills such as legislation dealing with broadcast renewal problems (see chapter nine). Most of these "Communications Act rewrites" have addressed the comparative renewal problem—usually by eliminating it through either indefinite license terms or a two-step comparative renewal process—but none has passed. In mid-1979 Congressman Lionel Van Deerlin (D-California), chief proponent of the comprehensive rewrite approach, abandoned that strategy. Van Deerlin himself was defeated for reelection in November 1980. As a result, Congress probably will return to a piecemeal approach to communications legislation. Eventually, one of the pieces may deal with comparative renewal.

Since inaction is the most typical characteristic of Congress, broadcasters have looked to the FCC for possible relief and, at least in specific cases, have found it. Unfortunately for broadcast interests, the courts, in late 1978 and early 1979, stepped back into the picture and overturned a key FCC decision in this area. The result, at least as of early 1982, is continuing ambiguity over the state of comparative renewal policy.

Case-by-Case FCC Policymaking

Since 1969, the FCC has encountered several comparative renewal cases. Many remain in limbo, sometimes because they are still pending at the FCC and in other instances because court review awaits. Three of the most controversial cases are the Commission's 1973 renewal of RKO General's KHJ-TV (Los Angeles) license and consequent rejection of Fidelity Television's competing application;[58] the FCC's 1980 rejection of RKO General's application for renewal of WNAC-TV (Boston);[59] and the Commission's 1976, 1977, and 1981 decisions to renew the license of Cowles Broadcasting's WESH-TV (Daytona Beach-Orlando, Florida).[60] All these decisions were questioned ultimately by the U.S. Court of Appeals for the District of Columbia Circuit.

The 1973 challenge by Fidelity was one of those hard cases that rarely make good or clear law. It was, however, a victory for those who value industry stability over whatever benefits may accrue in replacing an existing "average" broadcaster with an untested competitor. Although the hearing examiner in the case characterized KHJ's past broadcast performance as "poor," he was equally unimpressed with Fidelity and particularly downgraded its plans to integrate ownership with inexperienced management. Nevertheless, he granted the license to Fidelity rather than to the incumbent, RKO General, Inc., then involved in a case alleging antitrust violations by its parent, RKO General Corporation. On appeal to the full FCC, however, the hearing examiner's decision was reversed, with RKO gaining renewal from a divided Commission.[61] In this case there was no doubt that KHJ's performance could not be characterized as "superior" under the *Citizens Communications Center* standard. The best that the Commission could do was to elevate the evaluation of the station from the hearing examiner's "poor" to "average," an elevation that made the difference. Significantly, the FCC conditioned renewal of the KHJ license on whatever might be the outcome of another challenge to RKO—the WNAC-TV proceeding involving RKO's Boston TV station.

The Commission also was plagued, in the Los Angeles case, with the issue of the integration of ownership and management and the question of diversification. The FCC downplayed the latter by finding that KHJ was "one of many media outlets in the market" and noting that nothing on the record indicated any "adverse effect on the flow of information" by virtue of RKO's interest.[62] In essence, the Commission managed to renew an incumbent, faced by a qualified challenger, without finding the past record of the station to be "superior," and it did so in a way that may have altered traditional Commission policy on diversification and integration of ownership with management. Certainly Chief Judge

David Bazelon thought that was what the Commission had accomplished when, a few months later, he wrote a lengthy statement explaining why he voted, without success, to have the decision reviewed by the entire U.S. Court of Appeals for the District of Columbia Circuit.

According to Bazelon the FCC had simply failed to make a real comparison between RKO and Fidelity, opting instead for "pervasive result-oriented reasoning [removing] any veneer of rationality attaching to the comparative licensing decision."[63] He felt that the Commission's determination to renew KHJ-TV led to violation—by the FCC and later by his judicial colleagues—of the standards of the *Citizens Communications Center* case; he also felt that it would set a new precedent on diversification and integration of management and ownership. There can be no doubt that Bazelon viewed the FCC decision, and the court decision affirming it, as totally unfounded.

For several years it appeared as if that would be the end of the KHJ controversy. The U.S. Supreme Court refused to review the court of appeals decision,[64] and it seemed as if RKO had emerged victorious, albeit through a close call. All that changed on June 4, 1980, when the FCC—as usual on a close 4-to-3 vote— concluded that because of illegal business activities by its parent corporation, General Tire and Rubber Co., and because of close business ties between parent and subsidiary, RKO General lacked the "character" to hold the license for WNAC-TV in Boston.[65] Strictly speaking, at this point the *RKO* case ceased to be a comparative renewal case; indeed, the Commission did not decide that the license should go to the challenging applicant who had started the in-depth inquiry into RKO in the first instance. Since, however, grants of renewal of RKO stations in Los Angeles (KHJ-TV) and New York (WOR-TV) had been given, and competing applications denied, with the express condition that those grants were subject to whatever might ultimately happen in the Boston case, the *WNAC-TV* case has a proper place in the history of comparative renewal policy. The potential impact of the case is huge, for in addition to the three television stations directly involved in disputed licensing cases, RKO owns another TV station in Memphis, Tennessee, and twelve radio stations, all of which are open to challenge by the June 1980 decision. Some estimates have placed the potential stakes of the June 1980 decision as high as $400 million to $600 million.[66]

As to comparative renewal policy itself, the key cases involve the contested renewal of Cowles Broadcasting's WESH-TV (Daytona Beach-Orlando, Florida). After Cowles filed for renewal of its WESH-TV license on October 31, 1969, it found itself challenged for the license by a competing group, Central Florida Enterprises, Inc. In June 1979, after more than five years of review, the FCC granted the renewal application of Cowles and denied the application of Central Florida.[67]

The decision was, at first, not particularly controversial, although once again the Commission divided sharply—4 to 3. The majority opinion, written by Commissioner Charlotte T. Reid, who was joined by Commissioners Robert E. Lee, James Quello, and Abbott Washburn, changed Administrative Law Judge Chester Naumowicz's characterization of Cowles's past record from "thoroughly acceptable" to "superior" under the *Citizens Communications Center* standard, gave Cowles the associated "plus of major significance," and renewed Cowles's license.[68]

This decision proved to be too much for the other members of the Commission—Chairman Wiley and Commissioners Robinson and Hooks. Each wrote a dissent. Hooks argued that the majority had not really tried to apply the 1965 policy statement on comparative hearings, as he believed the *Citizens* case required.[69] Wiley's personal inclination was to grant Cowles its renewal, but he simply could not find its record "superior." Grudgingly, he voted to deny renewal, urging Congress at the same time to overhaul, and probably abolish, comparative renewal hearings.[70] Robinson's dissent, the longest of all, was a colorful criticism of the history of the FCC's comparative renewal policy and ended with a plea for changes in the Communications Act to authorize nearly automatic renewal for licensees who had substantially performed under Commission policies and for an auction to decide among competitors for new stations.[71] After recounting the whole tortuous story from the *WHDH* through the *Fidelity* cases, Robinson provided a frank, but discouraging, description of the comparative renewal process as of late 1976:

To the perceptive observer of the history of renewal contests, it will doubtless be apparent by now that there is less to such "contests" than meets the eye, that, in fact, it is not a real contest between two applicants but a pretend game played between the Commission and the public. The outcome of the game is predetermined; the art (and the sport) is to maintain interest until the inevitable outcome is registered. The Commission's role is to look judicious in pursuing a process that yields only one result; from the public the fun is watching the show and trying to anticipate how the Commission will finesse the result in the particular case. It rather resembles a professional wrestling match in which the contestants' grappling, throwing, thumping—with attendant grunts and groans —are mere dramatic conventions having little impact on the final result. Of course, wrestling fans know the result is fixed and generally in whose favor; still they fill the bleachers to see how it is done. So it is in the present case.[72]

In late 1976 the *Cowles* case seemed dormant. Appeals from the losing competitor were probable, but it appeared that the FCC majority had managed to slip Cowles under the broad umbrella of "superior" service as prescribed by the *Citizens Communications Center* case. Indeed, in September 1976 the FCC told Congress that "no new major policy direction was set by the case,"[73] which was true for the time but hardly true in early 1977 when the Commission—on it own and after the departure of Robinson and Reid—decided to "clarify" its earlier *Cowles* decision.

Somehow the Commission had become troubled by its characterization of Cowles's record as "superior." Perhaps it was finally swayed by Chairman Wiley's dissent. In any event the FCC decided that "superior" wasn't quite the right word anymore and that, instead, it would describe Cowles's record—in language reminiscent of the old 1970 policy statement—as "sound, favorable and substantially above a level of mediocre service which might just minimally warrant renewal."[74] Ironically the Commission's judicial support for this shift of language was the court of appeals decision in the *WHDH* decision, which had helped create this policy crisis in the first place.

The change in language was cheered by the broadcast industry. *Broadcasting* magazine editorially praised the Commission for "what could become the basis for a sound renewal policy."[75] The magazine encouraged the Commission to broaden it quickly into a policy statement of general application and wondered if it wasn't "the next best thing to renewal legislation."[76]

The Citizens Communications Center, joined by the National Black Media Coalition and the National Citizens Committee for Broadcasting —almost the same parties that had challenged the 1970 policy statement—quickly filed a petition for reconsideration of the *Cowles* "clarification." Henry Geller, then chairman of the Citizens Communications Center board and a former FCC general counsel, argued that the Commission should conclude its longstanding inquiry on quantitative renewal standards and then use standards established in that inquiry to determine "substantial" performance meriting a renewal plus.[77]

Also troublesome to the citizen groups was language in the FCC "clarification" that reworked the Commission's treatment of diversification of media holdings and integration of ownership and management in the *Cowles* case. The original FCC decision had given the competitor, Central, a "clear preference" over Cowles on the diversification issue because of Cowles's substantial media holdings outside Daytona Beach. The clarification tried to explain why this clear preference had not tipped the scales in favor of Central. In 1977 the Commission found the answer in "the nature and management of Cowles' other mass media interests, the autonomy given local management, and most especially their remoteness from Daytona Beach." The Commission saw "no evidence in the record that the dangers of concentration . . . exist in this case." With that, the preference for Central was relegated to the status of "little decisional significance."[78]

On the integration issue the FCC's clarification stressed that although management was not well integrated with ownership, "Cowles

had accorded WESH-TV's local management team substantial autonomy in its operations." The Commission thought it necessary to "make
it clear . . . that this factor [the autonomy given WESH management]
did serve to further diminish the preference accorded Central."[79] To
support its interpretation of both the integration and diversification
issues, the Commission, not unnaturally, cited the court of appeals decision in the *Fidelity* case, which seemed to accept the FCC's similar
treatment of RKO's Los Angeles media holdings. Geller's petition argued—unsuccessfully, since the FCC eventually rejected it—that the
concepts of "remoteness" and "autonomy" were at odds with Commission and judicial precedent and that they undermined the multiple-
ownership and minority-ownership policies of the FCC. On June 30,
1977, the Commission, by a vote of 4 to 1, rejected Geller's petition for
reconsideration, leaving further action, if any, up to the courts.[80]

Judicial Complications Again

Court action eventually overturned the FCC's "clarified" *WESH* decision, in the process throwing the entire comparative renewal policy
area again into disarray. On September 25, 1978, the U.S. Court of
Appeals for the District of Columbia Circuit, acting on an appeal filed
by the losing competitor—Central Florida—vacated the FCC's decision in favor of Cowles and remanded the case to the FCC "for proceedings consistent with this opinion."[81] From the broadcast industry's point of view, however, the court decision was intolerable, for
the only view consistent with the court's opinion was that comparative renewal applicants should be treated no differently from applicants for new licenses and that their past broadcast records, whatever
they might be, could not be made "decisional" against challengers for
licenses. As *Broadcasting* described it, the decision "set off alarms in
the offices of broadcast licensees," swinging "the door to challenges to
renewal applicants—which had appeared to be closing— . . . wide
open."[82] NAB President Vincent T. Wasilewski called the decision
"the most disturbing from an industry stability viewpoint in a long
time, more than WHDH-TV."[83]

In addition to hinting that renewal and new applicants should be
treated alike in comparative hearings, and that past records could not
be made decisional in favor of incumbents, the court expressed its
inability to understand how the FCC had treated the "standard comparative issues" under the 1965 policy statement. The court noted that
the FCC had favored Central Florida over Cowles on the general comparative issues of diversification, integration of ownership with management, and minority participation and had found against Cowles for an
unauthorized move of the station's studio. It was therefore troubled

when the Commission, based wholly on a noncomparative assessment of Cowles's past performance as "substantial," confirmed the organization's "renewal expectancy." The court had been told by the FCC that this decision was based on "administrative feel," but to the court such "intuitional forms of decision-making, completely opaque to judicial review, fall somewhere on the distant side of arbitrary" and could not be sustained. "Renewal expectancies," said the court, were confined to the likelihood that an incumbent would prevail in the full comparative inquiry. While past "superior" performance might be relevant within such an inquiry, the court insisted that a clear or strong showing by challengers on other comparative factors might overcome this advantage.

In an editorial *Broadcasting* described what it saw as the consequences for the industry of the decision:

Any licensee that owns other media anywhere is vulnerable to challenge by an applicant that is without other media ties and is small enough for its owners to be also on-the-scene managers of their intended prey. The prospects of capturing the occupied facility are enhanced, according to the court's new rules, if the challenger includes blacks or other minorities in its composition.[84]

Apparently unable to conclude whether military siege or fairy tale analogies best fit the situation, the magazine elsewhere sardonically summed up its perception of the entire situation through a headline: "Humpty Falls Again."[85] Editorially the magazine concluded that only Congress, not the courts or the FCC, could put things back together.[86]

A legislative solution was even hinted at by the court of appeals. Footnote 60 of the September 25 decision cautioned that "in light of *Citizens,* the case in which the court had overturned the 1970 policy statement, it is doubtful whether any such distinction between incumbents and challengers would be lawful without an amendment to the hearing provisions of the Communications Act."[87] There was substantial interest in appealing to Congress for relief from the effects of the decision: the National Association of Broadcasters, for example, convened a "war council" of thirty-nine major broadcasters who agreed that they would turn to Congress for help, although they could not agree on precisely what to ask for in new legislation.[88] But there was also increasing interest in attempting to persuade the court to revise some of the language of the September decision. The two parties most interested in this course of action were Cowles Broadcasting and the FCC. Cowles, of course, was now in hot water over its license and wanted a totally different court decision. The FCC was particularly upset by what it saw as a substantial intrusion upon matters normally subject to its discretion and, in effect, policy making by the court of appeals.[89] On November 8, 1978, both Cowles Broadcasting and the

FCC filed petitions with the court of appeals asking for a rehearing *en banc,* that is, by the full court.

Such requests are normally denied, and that was what happened in this case. On January 12, 1979, the three-judge panel denied the requests for a rehearing *en banc* but then took the most extraordinary step of issuing a revision and clarification of its own opinion.[90] It completely eliminated the suggestion in the original footnote 60 that legislation might be required in order to allow different treatment of incumbents in comparative hearings. In its revised decision the court strengthened the importance of past programming performance in comparative renewal cases by substituting the phrase "meritorious service"—language from a U.S. Supreme Court decision involving newspaper-broadcast cross-ownership—for the standard of "superior service" that it had suggested was required to get an advantage in a comparative proceeding. Most important to the broadcast industry, the new opinion suggested that the court's major concern with the FCC's actions was not with their substance but with how they were arrived at; in the revised opinion the court made it clear that it would be possible for the FCC to develop a system under which incumbents who had provided "meritorious" service could have a substantial, indeed perhaps decisive, advantage over challengers.

The court's revision put matters back more squarely in the hands of the FCC and lessened the drive by broadcast industry interests for legislation. Editorially *Broadcasting* observed that "the amendment has undone some of the most destructive potentials of the original decision."[91] Now the problem was what the FCC would do. For more than two years, the answer seemed to be that the Commission might wait and hope the specific *WESH* case, although not the general controversy, would go away. The advantage of waiting is that it would allow the Commission to eventually approach the comparative renewal problem more abstractly and without the *WESH* background or, alternatively, it would allow Congress time to intervene through legislation. Early in June 1979 it seemed as if there might, indeed, be an end coming to the *WESH* dispute. On June 1, Cowles Broadcasting, Central Florida Enterprises, and the FCC asked the court of appeals to approve a bargain struck between Cowles and Central Florida to settle the differences between them. Cowles agreed to pay Central Florida $1.5 million for expenses and to put the president of Central Florida on the Cowles board. The Commission asked the court to continue to let it decide if Cowles, with Central Florida then out of the way, deserved renewal.[92] Late in June, however, the court of appeals rejected the bargain. The Commission now had to deal with the case more directly.[93]

Several ways out of this dilemma were pressed on the Commission by interested parties. One commonly mentioned was to return to an approach abandoned by the FCC in 1977 at a time when it thought the "clarified" *WESH* decision had solved the problem. As has been noted, in 1971 the Commission began to consider the idea of a quantitative measure of "substantial" or "superior" programming. In 1977, shortly after its *Cowles* "clarification," the Commission closed that docket with a decision not to adopt quantitative standards. To the FCC such standards would tend to increase artificially the amount of time stations would devote to FCC preferred program types (news, public affairs, and local programming) but would not necessarily improve the quality of those shows and might diminish it. The Commission concluded that quantitative guidelines would not help the comparative renewal process and that they were, instead, "simplistic, superficial approach[es] to a complex problem."[94] The FCC's decision not to adopt quantitative standards survived a court challenge made by the National Black Media Coalition. Indeed, it was upheld by the same three judges who overturned the FCC's *WESH* decision.[95] The Commission had concluded that while it could adopt qualitative standards for substantial service, it preferred not to do so at this time. The court of appeals left that FCC position intact, ruling that nothing in the Communications Act or the Constitution's First Amendment required the Commission to pursue the quantitative course. Thus the option for quantitative definitions of the kind of service that would almost guarantee renewal remained, although this did not seem to be an attractive option to the FCC or the industry.

Remaining, too, was a proceeding asking the Commission to reconsider the quantitative approach. Shortly after the first court of appeals decision on the *WESH* case, Henry Geller, administrator of the Department of Commerce's National Telecommunications and Information Administration (NTIA), filed a petition with the FCC asking the Commission to return to the quantitative standards approach. Geller, long a proponent of that approach,[96] urged the Commission to adopt a policy statement or open an inquiry aimed at using percentage guidelines for "bedrock . . . local and informational" areas of programming as a definition of meritorious service that would bring with it an expectation of renewal. Geller, in fact, urged the Commission to challenge the court's view, consistent since the *Citizens* case, that a "full comparative hearing" meant that a hearing could not automatically end in favor of the incumbent if it were determined that the incumbent's past service had been meritorious.[97] For a while, Geller's approach had the support of some broadcasters, but that ardor waned after the second court of appeals decision on the WESH contest.[98] The broadcast industry seemed content to wait and see what the FCC might do while, at the same time, keeping up pressure on Congress to solve the problem through amendments to the Communications Act.

The Commission finally produced yet another *WESH* decision on June 16, 1981. Responding to the remand from the court of appeals, the FCC attempted a fuller explanation of how it had compared Cowles with Central Florida and especially how it had handled Cowles's past broadcast record. By a 4-to-1 vote, the Commission again voted in favor of Cowles's renewal and denied Central Florida's competing application.[99] Although admitting that Central Florida was better than Cowles on the issues of integration of ownership with management and diversification of media ownership, the FCC took the position that these issues deserved less weight in a comparative renewal proceeding than in a comparative hearing for a new station. The Commission admitted that Cowles's unauthorized move of its main studio to Orlando from Daytona Beach was a serious problem, but it pointed out that Cowles had continued to maintain its Daytona Beach studios.

On the crucial question of what to do about Cowles's past record, the Commission maintained, once again, that the incumbent should get a substantial—and in this case, decisional—preference for its past service. The FCC's analysis was at least partly quantitative. WESH-TV's percentage of news and public affairs programming—almost 16 percent—exceeded the average amount of such programming presented by network affiliates in the top twenty-five TV markets. The Commission claimed that a strong preference, indeed a renewal expectancy, was necessary in cases like Cowles where "meritorious" service had been provided because:

. . . (1) There is no guarantee that a challenger's paper proposals will, in fact, match the incumbent's proven performance. Thus, not only might replacing an incumbent be entirely gratuitous, but it might even deprive the community of an acceptable service and replace it with an inferior one. (2) Licensees should be encouraged through the likelihood of renewal to make investments to ensure quality service. Comparative renewal proceedings cannot function as a "competitive spur" to licensees if their dedication to the community is not rewarded. (3) Comparing incumbents and challengers as if they were both new applicants could lead to a haphazard restructuring of the broadcast industry especially considering the large number of group owners.[100]

This FCC decision is not likely to be the last word on the controversy. Attorneys for Central Florida Enterprises appealed to the U.S. Court of Appeals for the District of Columbia Circuit.[101] Their appeal could be substantially aided by the thirty-one-page dissent of Commissioner Fogarty, which attacked at length what he called the "majority's latest exercise in insensibility."[102]

Whence Any Solution?

Concurrent with this FCC action, half of the U.S. Congress—the Senate —attempted a legislative solution of the comparative renewal problem. Under one bill passed by the Senate the dilemma would be eliminated for radio by making licenses "termless," that is, permanent. If licenses never had to be renewed, there would be no comparative renewal proceedings for radio stations.[103] Under another proposal, the long-sought, two-step process would be established for television.[104] These contemplated changes to the Communications Act, as well as many others, were eventually incorporated into the Senate's version of the federal budget for fiscal 1982. Senator Robert Packwood (R-Oregon), chairman of the Senate Commerce Committee, was praised for adopting this tactic.[105] Broadcasters hoped it would provide them with a solution to the comparative renewal problem along lines they could support.

Unfortunately for them, however, the House of Representatives, especially Representative Timothy Wirth (D-Colorado), chairman of the House Telecommunications Subcommittee, was not nearly as anxious as the Senate to support these specific solutions to the comparative renewal problem, nor to embrace the tactic of including them in budget legislation. Wirth was upset that such substantial matters of broadcast policy could be folded into consideration of President Reagan's reform of the budget, where they would not get the close attention by his subcommittee that they would normally receive.

After a difficult series of meetings and compromises, the budget emerged from a Senate-House Conference Committee and was ultimately approved by President Reagan, with the comparative renewal problem barely addressed. Although broadcasters got an extension of license terms—from three years for both radio and television to five years for TV and seven for radio—they did not get the termless radio licenses that would have eliminated radio comparative renewal proceedings. Nor was the two-step renewal system adopted for television. In fact, the only part of the budget bill addressing the comparative renewal process was a slight change in the Communications Act intended, according to the conference committee, to discourage the filing of "frivolous application[s] for a station license in order to harass an incumbent which is applying for renewal of its license."[106] The change stipulated that a competing applicant could not agree to withdraw its application in exchange for money or anything else of value without the FCC's approval. The Commission was to approve only if it concluded that the agreement to withdraw was in the public interest or if it found that "no party to the agreement filed its license application for the purpose of reaching or carrying out such agreement."[107] Although it seemed likely that Congress would continue to consider the comparative renewal problem, and other broadcast issues, in further legislation, broadcasters' hopes for a solution to their problem through the budgeting process were dashed.

Two further questions deserve comment: (1) Is the policy area as important as the parties contend. And (2) can any settlement be expected, given the politics of broadcast regulation? As to the first, many nonindustry observers believe broadcast interests overestimate the dangers of losing licenses through comparative renewal hearings. Since the *WHDH* decision, the FCC has not granted a TV license to a challenger when the incumbent had anything like a record of acceptable past service.[108] The industry is correct, however, in arguing that defending (or bringing) competitive applications is an exceedingly costly business. It has been estimated that the challenger to WPIX-TV in New York City spent $2 million just to get through the initial hearing stage, and the incumbent spent an additional $1.5 million to the same point.[109] Court fees further inflate those figures. Such high litigation costs, combined with the low probability of success, doubtless mean that the interests of citizen groups, especially of minority groups that already have difficulty attracting capital, cannot be served by filing competing applications for broadcast stations.

What can citizen groups and broadcasters, both concerned about the outcome in this area of law, do? Geller's proposal for clearer FCC policies, including quantitative guidelines, is certainly one approach. It is not necessarily the one the Commission prefers to pursue. Indeed, in 1976 the FCC took a diametrically opposite approach when it recommended to Congress that the entire comparative renewal process be abolished, a position several FCC members continued to press on Congress through the late 1970s and into the 1980s. The Commission stated that with the regular license renewal process at its disposal plus its ability to use the Fairness Doctrine on a case-by-case basis, the government's grip on broadcasters is so firm that the comparative license renewal process is both unnecessary and counterproductive.[110] The Commission reiterated this request to Congress on September 17, 1981, when it proposed that the Communications Act be amended to create a two-step renewal process under which the licensee would be renewed, without consideration of competing applications, if it had "broadcast programming which responded to significant issues or problems facing the residents of its service area."[111] Recognizing, however, that immediate congressional action on its request was unlikely, the FCC on October 22, 1981, opened an inquiry asking what it should do given the current language of the act and all its interpretations by the courts and the Commission.[112]

It seems as if any lasting solution to the comparative renewal policy dilemma must come from one of the two parties to the regulatory process whose contributions to broadcast regulation are most durable —the courts or Congress. If there truly is a constitutional aspect to ownership policy, as Judge Bazelon argues,[113] then the final word could come from the U.S. Supreme Court. If, on the other hand, constitutional aspects are minimal, then final policy will probably have to come from Congress, which, no doubt, will continue to be buffeted by diverse lobbying interests. It is obvious that no solution to this case study, which of all the cases presented here most closely resembles a policy stalemate, can escape being formed by the politics of broadcast regulation.

NOTES

1. This chapter focuses on recent comparative renewal policy issues from the late 1960s through the early 1980s. The problem, however, goes back to the beginning of the FCC. The first case the Commission argued before the U.S. Court of Appeals for the District of Columbia Circuit was a comparative renewal case. The argument was on December 12, 1934—after the FCC had been in business fewer than six months. The Commission's decision to prefer the incumbent over the challenger, on the ground that past service had been "acceptable" and seemed likely to continue, was supported by the court (*Don Lee Broadcasting System v. FCC*, 76 F.2d 998 [D.C. Cir. 1935]).
2. Although we shall try to restrict this chapter to comparative renewal hearings, it is almost impossible to divorce that subject from other FCC policy areas. Comparative hearings are also held among applicants for unoccupied broadcast channels, using procedures that have been criticized as inefficient (see Dissenting Statement of Commissioner Glen O. Robinson in *Cowles Florida Broadcasting, Inc.*, 60 FCC2d 372, 435–448 [1978]) but are nonetheless clearer than the procedures that are followed when one applicant is an incumbent. Comparative renewal policy is also entangled with media ownership policy and FCC efforts to integrate ownership with management, as will be shown in the *WHDH, Fidelity,* and *Cowles* cases described in this chapter.
3. Separate Statement of Commissioners Benjamin Hooks and Joseph Fogarty in *Broadcasting Renewal Applicant*, 66 FCC2d 419, 433 (1977).
4. *Ashbacker Radio Corp.* v. *FCC*, 326 U.S. 327 (1964).
5. *Johnston Broadcasting Co.* v. *FCC*, 175 F.2d 351, 359 (D.C. Cir. 1949).
6. *Hearst Radio, Inc. (WBAL)*, 15 FCC 1149 (1951).
7. *Policy Statement on Comparative Broadcast Hearings*, 1 FCC2d 393 (1965).
8. *Seven League Productions, Inc.*, 1 FCC2d 1597 (1965).
9. *Wabash Valley Broadcasting Corp. (WTHI-TV)*, 35 FCC 677 (1963).
10. *WHDH, Inc.*, 16 FCC2d 1 (1969).
11. See "The Strange Ch. 5 Decision," *Television Digest*, January 27, 1969, pp. 1, 2.
12. His statement read:

On the first round I voted against WHDH, Inc. On the second round, in light of certain changed circumstances, I cast my vote for WHDH, Inc. This is now the third round and it is no less difficult for me to choose among those competing applicants. In view of my previous participation and finally the fact that my vote is not essential to resolution of the matter, I have simply abstained (*WHDH, Inc.,* 16 FCC2d, at 23–24).

The FCC's decision in the *WHDH* case was affirmed by the courts (*Greater Boston Television Corporation* v. *FCC,* 444 F.2d 841 [D.C. Cir. 1970], *certiorari denied,* 403 U.S. 923 [1971]).

13. *Television Digest,* January 27, 1969, p. 2.
14. 16 FCC2d, at 27.
15. Ibid., at 28. After its successful quest for the Channel 5 license, Boston Broadcasters, Inc., fulfilled the promises of increased locally originated programming that had helped it gain the license. For many years the station led all other network-affiliated VHF stations in that category of service. To the extent, however, that the FCC's decision, and especially Commissioner Johnson's support for it, was based on a desire that Boston have a locally owned network-affiliated station, the decision was undercut in mid-1981 when sale of the station (now WCVB-TV) to Metromedia, Inc., a large group owner, was announced. The price, $220 million, was the highest ever for a TV station. As *Broadcasting* noted, the sale, if approved by the FCC, "represents a windfall for the stockholders of BBI. That company got the ch. 5 allocation essentially for legal fees of about $2 million" ("Metromedia—WCVB-TV—$220 Million," *Broadcasting,* July 27, 1981, p. 27).
16. Louis L. Jaffe, "WHDH: The FCC and Broadcasting License Renewals," *Harvard Law Review,* 82 (1969), 1693, 1700.
17. "$3 Billion in Stations Down the Drain?" *Broadcasting,* February 3, 1969, p. 19.
18. "Boston Stake: $3 Billion" [editorial], *Broadcasting,* February 3, 1969, p. 84.
19. Quoted in "Ironics of TV Spotlighted at NAB," *Television Digest,* March 31, 1969, p. 3.
20. See "The White House Looks into FCC's Future," *Broadcasting,* March 31, 1969, p. 36. Hyde's term expired on June 30, 1969, but President Nixon asked him to continue as Chairman until a successor was confirmed. Commissioner Cox's term expired on June 30, 1970.
21. See "Pastore Submits Antistrike Bill," *Broadcasting,* May 5, 1969, p. 58.
22. William H. Wentz, "The Aftermath of WHDH: Regulation by Competition or Protection of Mediocrity?" *University of Pennsylvania Law Review,* 118 (1970), 368.
23. 17 FCC2d, 872.
24. See "July Hearings on Renewals," *Television Digest,* June 9, 1969, p. 3.
25. Wentz, "The Aftermath of WHDH," p. 395.
26. Reported in Nicholas Johnson, *How to Talk Back to Your Television Set* (New York: Bantam Books, 1970), p. 205.
27. Quoted in "Pastore Hits Renewal-Bill Opposition," *Television Digest,* October 20, 1969, p. 2.
28. Reported in "Picket Lines Due," *Broadcasting,* December 1, 1969, p. 10.
29. Reported in "Pastore and Blacks Clash on 'Racism,' " *Television Digest,* December 8, 1969, p. 2.
30. Ibid., p. 4.

31. The excerpts quoted from the statements of the FCC majority and each of the Commissioners are contained in *Hearings Before the Communications Subcommittee on S. 2004*, 91st Congress, 1st Session, Part 2 (December 1, 2, 3, 4, and 5, 1969), pp. 375–412.

32. "Burch Miracle?" *Broadcasting*, December 29, 1969, p. 5.

33. See "A Return to Order in Renewals," *Broadcasting*, January 12, 1970, p. 36.

34. See "Renewal Protection—Program Performance," *Television Digest*, January 12, 1970, p. 3.

35. 22 FCC2d 430 and 433 (1970). In hearings on S. 3434, before the Subcommittee on Administrative Practice and Procedure, Senate Committee of the Judiciary (July 2, 1970), Johnson claimed that the Commission had worked with White House approval in adopting the policy statement.

36. 21 FCC2d 355 (1970).

37. Ibid., at 357.

38. Quoted in "FCC Renewal Policy Supplants Pastore Bill," *Television Digest*, January 19, 1970, p. 1. The policy statement did in fact discourage competing applications. In 1969, when the *WHDH* decision was announced, eight renewal applicants were challenged. However, during 1970 not one competing renewal application was filed.

39. Ibid., p. 2.

40. 24 FCC2d 383 (1970).

41. Ibid., at 386.

42. Ibid., at 389.

43. Brief of CCC and BEST, Case No. 24,471, p. 5.

44. U.S. House of Representatives, Committee on Interstate and Foreign Commerce, Special Subcommittee on Investigations, *Analysis of FCC's 1970 Policy Statement on Competitive Hearings Involving Regular Renewal Applicants*, 91st Congress, 2nd Session (November 1970).

45. See "FCC Disputes Hill Report on Renewals," *Television Digest*, December 21, 1970, p. 2.

46. *Citizens Communications Center* v. *FCC*, 447 F.2d 1201 (D.C. Cir. 1971). Judge Wright's opinion appears at 1202–1215.

47. "Life or Death?" [editorial], *Broadcasting*, June 21, 1971, p. 108.

48. See "No More Appeal on Renewal Policy," *Broadcasting*, July 5, 1971, p. 44.

49. A rival group, the National Radio Broadcasters Association, has occasionally tried to separate the renewal problems of television stations from the generally less disputed area of radio by proposing and supporting radio-only renewal relief bills.

50. See H.R. 15168, 94th Congress, 2nd Session (1976), introduced by Representative Richard Ottinger (D-New York), which contained a shopping list of citizen group reform issues attached to a license renewal proposal.

51. Under the Nixon administration, Dr. Clay T. Whitehead, then head of the Office of Telecommunications Policy, hinted to broadcasters that administration support for longer license terms and protection against competing applications turned on individual licensees pressuring networks to cease broadcasting anti-Nixon "ideological plugola." See "The Dust Hasn't Settled After Speech by Whitehead," *Broadcasting*, January 1, 1973, p. 18.

52. Statement of Chief Judge David Bazelon in *Fidelity Television, Inc.* v. *FCC*, 515 F.2d 684, 726 (D.C. Cir. 1975).

53. See the dissenting opinion of Commissioner Nicholas Johnson in *Moline*

Television Corp., 31 FCC2d 263, 277–288 (1971); the dissenting statement of Chairman Wiley in *Cowles Florida Broadcasting, Inc.*, 60 FCC2d 372, 430–433 (1976); the dissenting statement of Commissioner Robinson in the same case at 435–448; the dissenting statement of Chairman Ferris and Commissioners Fogarty and Brown in *WPIX, Inc.*, 68 FCC2d 218, 415–455 (1974); and the dissenting statement of Commissioner Fogarty in *Cowles Florida Broadcasting, Inc.*, 86 FCC2d 993, 1024 (1981).

54. See statement of Chief Judge David Bazelon in *Fidelity Television, Inc.* v. *FCC*, 515 F.2d 684, 726 (D.C. Cir. 1975).
55. *Central Florida Enterprises, Inc.* v. *FCC*, 598 F.2d 37, 41 (D.C. Cir. 1978).
56. *Further Notice of Inquiry in Docket No. 19154*, 31 FCC2d 443 (1971).
57. See "Renewal Relief Dies on Hill: What Chance of Reincarnation?" *Broadcasting*, December 16, 1974, pp. 19–20.
58. *RKO General, Inc. (KHJ-TV)*, 44 FCC2d 123 (1973).
59. *RKO General, Inc. (WNAC-TV)*, 78 FCC2d 1 (1980).
60. *Cowles Florida Broadcasting, Inc.*, 60 FCC2d 372 (1976), *clarified* in *Cowles Florida Broadcasting, Inc.*, 62 FCC2d 953 (1977). *Overturned* by *Central Florida Enterprises, Inc.* v. *FCC*, as *amended* January 12, 1979, 598 F.2d 37 (D.C. Cir. 1978); *certiorari dismissed*, May 17, 1974, 441 U.S. 957. *Cowles Florida Broadcasting*, 86 FCC2d 993 (1981).
61. *RKO General, Inc. (KHJ-TV)*, 44 FCC2d 123 (1973). The vote was in essence 3 to 2, nearly as fragmented and incomplete as the *WHDH* decision four years earlier. Commissioners Wiley and Hooks did not participate. Commissioners Robert E. Lee and Charlotte Reid wrote a joint opinion favoring KHJ, although Reid had not participated in the oral argument. Chairman Burch concurred in the result without further statement. Commissioners Johnson and H. Rex Lee dissented, Johnson calling this "the worst decision of this Commission during my term of seven years and five months" (Ibid.).

Nearly two years later Chief Judge David Bazelon agreed with Johnson. See *Fidelity Television, Inc.* v. *FCC*, 515 F.2d 705 (D.C. Cir. 1975).
62. *RKO General, Inc.*, 44 FCC2d 123, 134 (1973).
63. *Fidelity Television, Inc.* v. *FCC*, 515 F.2d 684 (D.C. Cir. 1975).
64. *Certiorari denied*, 423 U.S. 926 (1975).
65. *RKO General, Inc. (WNAC-TV)*, 78 FCC2d 1 (1980). The FCC had actually decided to lift the licenses much earlier, in late January 1980. It took nearly six months to write and approve the order. See "FCC Lifts Three RKO Licenses; 13 Others Are Now in Jeopardy," *Broadcasting*, January 28, 1980, pp. 27–28.
66. For computation of the $400 million estimate, see "FCC Lifts Three RKO Licenses," p. 27. For the $600 million figure see "Reconstituted FCC Votes to Restudy RKO Ruling," *Washington Post*, May 20, 1981, p. D7. In this article it is reported that a five-member FCC, under Chairman Robert E. Lee, voted to ask the U.S. Court of Appeals for the District of Columbia Circuit, to which RKO had appealed, to return the case to the FCC. The strategy had been suggested by RKO's lawyers, obviously hopeful of a different outcome under the Republican-led FCC of 1981. A few weeks later, however, the new general counsel of that FCC notified RKO that the Commission would not, after all, ask the case to be returned; Court review continued, and the FCC started an inquiry into whether character was relevant to licensing. See Gen. Docket 81–500, Policy Regarding Character Qualifications in Broadcasting Licensing, 46 *Federal Register* 40899

(1981). In December 1981, the court affirmed the FCC's decision in the WNAC-TV (Boston) proceedings for further consideration by the Commission. *RKO General, Inc.* v. *FCC,* U.S. Court of Appeals for the District of Columbia Circuit, No. 80–1696 (December 4, 1981). In December 1981 the court upheld the FCC's WNAC-TV (Boston) nonrenewal, but remanded the KHJ-TV (Los Angeles) and WOR-TV (New York) cases to the Commission. *RKO General, Inc., v. FCC,* 50 RR2d 821 (D.C. Cir, 1981).

67. *Cowles Florida Broadcasting, Inc.,* 60 FCC2d 372 (1976).
68. Ibid., at 417–423. Commissioner Robinson acidly commented:

> One might think it important to know what constitutes "superior performance." The answer I derive from the Commission's opinion is that "superior" means whatever the licensee has done, providing the licensee has not seriously misbehaved. . . . This evidently is the Commission's version of the Court of Appeals' "hard look" requirement: it looks hard until it finds what it is after (ibid., at 441–442).

69. Ibid., at 434.
70. Ibid., at 430–433.
71. Ibid., at 442–448.
72. Ibid., at 439. Robinson further called *Fidelity*

> a *tour de force,* accomplishing even more than the Commission had purported to accomplish with its ill-fated 1970 Policy Statement. In 1970, the Commission merely purported to guarantee renewal to an incumbent which demonstrated "substantial" service. In *Fidelity,* it managed to grant renewal to an incumbent who demonstrated "average service," who was actually the weaker candidate on one major comparative criterion, and not materially better on the others (integration and local ownership) (ibid., at 438).

73. *Report of the Federal Communications Commission to the Congress of the United States, Re the Comparative Renewal Process,* November 1976 [mimeo.], p. 40.
74. *Cowles Florida Broadcasting, Inc.,* 62 FCC2d 953, 955 (1977). The 1970 policy statement had provided, in part:

> [The Commission] is not using the term "substantially" in any sense of partial performance in the public interest. On the contrary, as the discussion within makes clear, it is used in the sense of "solid," "strong," etc. . . . performance as contrasted with a service only minimally meeting the needs and interests of the area.

75. "Start of Something Big," *Broadcasting,* January 10, 1977, p. 82.
76. "The Next Best Thing to Renewal Legislation?" *Broadcasting,* January 10, 1977, p. 20.
77. *Petition for Reconsideration,* February 3, 1977, pp. 7–10.
78. *Cowles Florida Broadcasting, Inc.,* 62 FCC2d 953, 956–957 (1977).
79. Ibid., at 956.
80. *Cowles Broadcasting, Inc.,* 40 RR2d 1627 (1977).
81. *Central Florida Enterprises, Inc.* v. *FCC,* 598 F.2d 37 (D.C. Cir. 1978).
82. "Court Upsets FCC's Policy on Renewals," *Broadcasting,* October 2, 1978, p. 28.
83. Quoted in ibid.
84. "Sitting Ducks" [editorial], *Broadcasting,* October 2, 1978, p. 82.
85. "Humpty Falls Again," *Broadcasting,* October 2, 1978, p. 5.
86. There is a suggestion of this in "Sitting Ducks," when the magazine speculated, "There will be a different look [by broadcasters] to the rewrite of the Communications Act now in process at the House Communications

Subcommittee" (*Broadcasting*, October 2, 1978, p. 82). A few weeks later, in another editorial, *Broadcasting* stated: "The guess here is that in the long run broadcasters may find that relief is not spelled 'FCC' but 'Congress' " ("Points of Order" [editorial], *Broadcasting*, November 6, 1978, p. 90).

87. Because subsequent revision of the case deleted this footnote, it has no legal significance and is difficult to locate. When printed in the *Federal Reporter*, the case reflected the revisions made January 12, 1979, and the language does not appear (*Central Florida Enterprises, Inc. v. FCC*, 598 F.2d 37 [D.C. Cir. 1978]). *Pike and Fischer Radio Regulation*, however, did not so revise the case. The original (September 25) decision is found as *Central Florida Enterprises, Inc. v. FCC*, 44 RR2d 345 (1978), with footnote 60 at 360. The instruction to amend the opinion appears as *Central Florida Enterprises, Inc. v. FCC*, 44 RR2d 1567 (1979). The instruction to delete most of footnote 60 is at 1570.

88. See "War Council on WESH," *Broadcasting*, October 30, 1978, p. 27. See also "Where to Turn?" *Broadcasting*, October 9, 1978, p. 1.

89. See "FCC Mobilizes for WESH Fight," *Broadcasting*, October 23, 1978, p. 26; "WESH-TV Remand Lights a Fire under the FCC," *Broadcasting*, October 9, 1978, p. 25; and "Renewal Relief," *Broadcasting*, November 6, 1978, p. 7.

90. As mentioned, see note 87 above. Many of the revisions are incorporated in the published version of the decision in the *Federal Reporter*. Nine new paragraphs added at the end of the original text begin at page 58. See *Central Florida Enterprises, Inc. v. FCC*, 598 F.2d 37, 58–62 (D.C. Cir. 1978).

91. "Second Chance" [editorial], *Broadcasting*, January 22, 1979, p. 90.

92. See *Broadcasting*, June 4, 1979, p. 30; and *Television Digest*, June 4, 1979, p. 3.

93. See *Broadcasting*, June 25, 1979, p. 30; and *Television Digest*, June 25, 1979, p. 3. Another controversial comparative renewal case involving WPIX-TV (New York) was eventually settled by such an agreement. In June 1978 the Commission decided to grant renewal of WPIX-TV and deny a competing application for the station filed by Forum Communications. The Commission's basic concern was that WPIX-TV had engaged in some questionable news practices and had been less than completely forthcoming with the FCC during early stages of the Commission's investigation. By a 4-to-3 vote, WPIX-TV won renewal over the lengthy and passionately argued dissent of Chairman Ferris and Commissioners Fogarty and Brown (*WPIX, Inc.*, 68 FCC 2d 381 [1978]). Their dissent appears at 415–455. The case caused concern in the broadcast industry because WPIX's support was largely among holdover Republican appointees to the Commission, while the dissenters were Carter appointees or, in the case of Fogarty, a Democratic Ford appointee. The broadcasters' concern was that another Carter appointment would allow the views of the dissenters, hardly sympathetic to the broadcasters' desire for stability, to prevail. The case came to an end, however, in early June 1979 when the FCC, WPIX, Inc., and Forum filed a settlement agreement with the U.S. Court of Appeals for the District of Columbia Circuit, to which Forum, the loser at the FCC, had appealed. Under the agreement WPIX purchased Forum for between $9 and $10 million ("Settled At Last," June 11, 1979, pp. 50–51). WPIX's incentive to settle was probably due, in large part, to the fact that its victory at the FCC had been rooted in the language

of the FCC's *WESH* decisions—decisions which, by then, had been questioned or undercut by the U.S. Court of Appeals.

94. *Broadcasting Renewal Applicant,* 66 FCC2d 419 (1977). Some still support quantitative renewal standards in Congress, notably Representative Al Swift (D-Washington).

95. *National Black Media Coalition* v. *FCC,* 589 F.2d 578 (D.C. Cir. 1978).

96. Before joining the NTIA, Geller had been one of the parties seeking to overturn the FCC's decision not to adopt quantitative standards. See note 94.

97. See "Geller Takes Initiative on License Renewal," *Broadcasting,* November 8, 1978, p. 25. See also RM-3236, announced by the FCC on November 15, 1978.

98. See "Line Lengthens Behind NTIA Play for Percentage Guidelines for TV," *Broadcasting,* January 22, 1979, p. 52. Among the supporters were General Electric Broadcasting, Taft, ABC, and McGraw-Hill.

99. *Cowles Broadcasting, Inc.,* 86 FCC2d 993 (1981).

100. Ibid., at 1013.

101. See "Cowles Wins Again in Daytona Beach," *Broadcasting,* June 22, 1981, pp. 24–25.

102. See *Cowles Florida Broadcasting,* 86 FCC2d 993, 1024–1055, at 1055 (1981).

103. S. 270, 97th Congress, 1st Session (1981). This bill would also have put into the Communications Act the FCC's 1981 deregulation of the amounts of commercial and noncommercial, nonentertainment program time adopted by the Commission in its radio deregulation proceeding (see chapter seven) and would have prohibited FCC regulation of radio station formats (see chapter five).

104. S. 601, 97th Congress, 1st Session (1981).

105. Also incorporated into the budget bill were S. 821, a bill that would have allowed the FCC to collect fees to cover the cost of FCC regulation and that converted the FCC from a permanently authorized agency to one that had to be renewed every three years; and S. 720, a bill dealing with the structure and funding of public broadcasting. On the entire process and the complexity of the issues involved, see "Packwood Shifts Deregulation Bills from Slow Freight to Fast Express," *Broadcasting,* June 15, 1981, pp. 29–30.

106. U.S. House of Representatives, *Report No. 97-208, Omnibus Budget Reconciliation Act of 1981, Conference Report,* 97th Congress, 1st Session (July 29, 1981), p. 898. This report, in Title XII, Subpart B, pp. 392–407 and 890–900, reviews all the changes in communications policy that were under consideration during the budgeting process.

107. Ibid., p. 405. The Omnibus Budget Reconciliation Act of 1981 also allowed the FCC the option of using a system of random selection, weighted in favor of "groups or organizations, or members of groups or organizations, which are underrepresented in the ownership of telecommunications facilities or properties" for deciding among competitors for *new* stations (ibid., p. 404). Congress had in mind "minorities, such as blacks and hispanics, as well as . . . women . . . and . . . other underrepresented groups, such as labor unions and community organizations" (ibid., p. 897). See also "Broadcasters Win Big on License Terms," *Broadcasting,* August 3, 1981, pp. 27–28 and "Net Gain" [editorial], *Broadcasting,* August 3, 1981, p. 104. See Random Selection Technique for Choosing Among Mutually

Exclusive Applicants for Telecommunications Licenses, 46 *Federal Register* 58110 (1981).

108. Two possible exceptions should be noted. In *Star Stations of Indiana, Inc.,* 51 FCC2d 95 (1975), Don Burden eventually lost five radio station licenses in a proceeding that began as a comparative renewal hearing. However, the hearing raised serious questions about Burden's character, and he was, personally, eventually determined unfit to continue as a licensee. The U.S. Court of Appeals for the District of Columbia Circuit affirmed the FCC without opinion, and the U.S. Supreme Court denied certiorari. See *Star Stations of Indiana, Inc.,* 59 FCC2d 834 (1976). In the KORK-TV proceeding, Donrey Media lost a license due to fraudulent billing, lack of candor, and misrepresentation. Once again the proceeding began as a comparative renewal hearing, but as in the *RKO General* cases, the competitor, Las Vegas Valley Broadcasting Company, gained the license only after the FCC had disqualified Donrey from further consideration. See *Western Communications, Inc.,* 59 FCC2d 1441 (1976); *affirmed in part, reversed in part, Las Vegas Valley Broadcasting Co.* v. *FCC,* 589 F.2d 594 (D.C. Cir. 1978), *certiorari denied,* 441 U.S. 931 (1979), *rehearing denied,* 442 U.S. 947 (1979).

109. See Dissenting Statement of Commissioner Glen O. Robinson in *Cowles Florida Broadcasting, Inc.,* 60 FCC2d 372, 447, n. 34 (1976).

110. *Report of the Federal Communications Commission . . . Re: The Comparative Renewal Process,* pp. 32 and 41.

111. *FCC Legislative Proposals, Track II,* September 17, 1981 [mimeo.], pp. 15–17. The Commission claimed that its proposed amendment would provide "stability, that is renewal expectancy, to those licensees who are adequately serving the public interest. The amendment would also substantially reduce the Commission workload since the language of this amendment, along with the recently enacted lottery provision, will eliminate most hearings among competing applicants" (ibid., p. 17).

112. Formulation of Policies Relating to the Boardcast [sic] Renewal Applicant, Stemming from the Comparative Hearing Process, 46 *Federal Register* 55279 (1981). The FCC said that the objective of the inquiry was "to set standards for 'meritorious broadcast service' for broadcasters seeking renewal of license. . . . Absent the most compelling circumstances, we believe that only renewal applicants failing to meet the standard of meritorious service should be required to demonstrate comparative superiority" (ibid., at p. 55280). The FCC indicated the inquiry might result in yet another policy statement (ibid., at p. 55281). Concurring Commissioners Fogarty and Rivera both observed, in Rivera's words, that the language of the Notice of Inquiry made it "difficult to envision how . . . a standard [of meritorious service] will be created" (ibid., at p. 55283).

113. Statement of Chief Judge Bazelon in *Fidelity Television, Inc.* v. *FCC,* 515 F.2d 725–726 (D.C. Cir. 1975).

Nine

Starting Over:
Congressional Efforts
to Rewrite the
Communications Act,
1976–1980

Forty-two years after the Communications Act was signed into law, Representative Lionel Van Deerlin (D-California) proposed that it be rewritten "from basement to attic." Such thinking was regarded as heretical on Capitol Hill: it had taken Congress seven years to rewrite the Radio Act of 1927 and fifteen years (1961–1976) to replace the Copyright Act of 1909. Many of Van Deerlin's colleagues likened the quest for a rewrite of the Communications Act to tilting at windmills. A senior member of the House Communications Subcommittee characterized rewrite legislation as "the equivalent of a 20-course meal, one that would be indigestible if the courses were presented too quickly or one that would take 10 years to eat if each course were cooked to perfection by the very capable kitchen staff."[1]

Three years after the rewrite concept was first advanced by Van Deerlin, the goal of comprehensive legislation was abandoned by the House Communications Subcommittee. *Variety,* in an article headlined "Reality Catches up with Van Deerlin," observed that amending the 1934 Communications Act from scratch, and overturning the legal precedent that method entails, obviously will not be bought by Congress, no matter how much technology has antiquated the law.[2] Contrary to *Variety*'s assessment, however, the rewrite process was in many respects a sweeping victory for the proponents of change. As will be shown, numerous fundamental principles underlying the rewrite effort were embodied in landmark FCC policy decisions and set the agenda for a national debate on communications policy. Largely because of Van Deerlin's efforts, communications issues in the late 1970s took on a new acceptance and a higher priority.

Background for the Rewrite Efforts

On April 27, 1976, Van Deerlin was unanimously elected chairman of the Subcommittee on Communications by the Democratic caucus of the House Committee on Interstate and Foreign Commerce. The week before, Representative Torbert H. Macdonald (D-Massachusetts) had resigned as chairman because of poor health and had endorsed Van Deerlin as his successor. Van Deerlin, who credited Macdonald's endorsement for his unanimous selection, announced that all members of Macdonald's subcommittee staff, including its counsel, Harry M. "Chip" Shooshan III, had agreed to stay on.[3] He also promised to continue projects Macdonald had instituted, particularly fifteen days of planned hearings on cable television.[4]

Van Deerlin, in order to chair the communications subcommittee, had to give up the chairmanship of the House Subcommittee on Consumer Protection and Finance. It was not a difficult decision for him; as he observed, he anticipated "being with broadcasters was going to be a lot more fun than being with manufacturing chemists."[5] In a strong campaign for chairman he let his colleagues know he was the "man for the job."[6] His qualifications were indeed unique. He had served on the communications subcommittee during ten of his fourteen years in Congress. Prior to election to his first term in 1962, he had served as a news director and anchorman for KFSD radio and television in San Diego and XETV, Tijuana, Mexico, and as city editor of the *San Diego Journal*. Since Van Deerlin's home town, San Diego, is the site of one of the largest cable systems in the nation, he had followed closely the development of the cable industry.

Three weeks after being elected chairman, Van Deerlin presided at the first of a series of comprehensive oversight hearings on cable television regulation. Perhaps the first public glimmer of the intention of the subcommittee to undertake a much more ambitious mission, a full review of the Communications Act, came at a cable hearing held on July 28, 1976, when Representative Louis Frey, Jr. (R-Florida), the subcommittee's ranking minority member, commented:

For some time I have been echoing what [Representative Van Deerlin has] said about the need to look at this entire Communications Act of 1934 in view of where we are going in the new technology, and it becomes apparent when you push in one place it pops out in some place else, and you put a Band-Aid on it.[7]

Common carrier issues, not cable or broadcasting, were highest on the subcommittee's political agenda during Van Deerlin's first few months as chairman. In a move which *Business Week* characterized as American Telephone & Telegraph's "most daring political power play since the passage of the Communications Act of 1934,"[8] AT&T

launched a multimillion-dollar lobbying effort to obtain passage of the Consumer Communications Reform Act of 1976, commonly known as the "Bell bill." The bill responded to FCC decisions allowing increased competition in the telephone industry. It would have transferred to the states the power to regulate the use of new telephone equipment and would have increased the legal burden that an AT&T competitor had to meet before being licensed by the Commission to offer private line services. Some observers regarded the bill as designed to force Congress to focus on an extreme proposition, thereby assuring that the policy debate would be a reaction to AT&T's agenda rather than follow the FCC's pro-competitive stance on common carrier issues.[9] Nearly 200 senators and representatives sponsored the Bell bill in the 94th Congress, prompting Representative Tim Wirth (D-Colorado), a member of the communications subcommittee, to comment that when "better than 40% of the House cosponsors any bill, it's either a damn good piece of legislation or somebody's exerting an awful lot of pressure."[10]

Van Deerlin opposed the Bell bill, believing that "a lot of people are waking up to the fact that under this bill, many who now have a choice of carrier would be at the mercy of a single service."[11] Lou Frey and several other members of the communications subcommittee shared Van Deerlin's concern. Van Deerlin and Frey decided to express that concern through what would prove to be a most ambitious project. In an action described by Theodore B. Merrill, writing in *Business Week*, as a "bold, strategic move," they instructed the subcommittee staff to examine the Bell bill in the context of a review of the entire Communications Act.[12] If all industry segments were involved, Van Deerlin reasoned, the lobbies would tend to balance each other in hearings and debates.

On August 6, 1976, the day following the last subcommittee hearing on cable, Van Deerlin announced that a prime undertaking in the 95th Congress should be a "basement-to-penthouse revamping of the Communications Act."[13] He said that Frey agreed with the need for such a review of the 1934 act—written when the only mass medium of electronic communications was radio—adding that the idea of revising the nation's basic communications law had been gaining popularity: "Everybody's saying it now." He referred to a speech in June by Jimmy Carter, then the Democratic presidential candidate, calling for a review of the entire act.[14] According to Van Deerlin, he and members of the subcommittee staff had discussed the idea of a possible rewrite after recognizing that there were many contending forces pushing for legislation on a piecemeal basis:

We have so many competing interests in various directions. The urge among broadcasters is for some kind of license-renewal legislation. You have the feeling of the cable industry that it's got to have relief from the 1972 rules. There is the push by the telephone company for legislation that goes right to the heart of what a regulated common carrier should be.

And at the end of every political campaign, you have the push for some reform of equal time and the Fairness Doctrine rules that the Commission evolved from Section 315.

It seems to me, and to Congressman Frey who put it succinctly when he said: "We've just been putting Band-Aid on top of Band-Aid for so long," that maybe it's time to go back and think of it more basically.

[The Communications Act was enacted] at a time before commercial television, before coaxial cable, before satellites, before microwaves or optical fibers or laser beams or any of these things.[15]

Van Deerlin hoped to derail the Bell bill with his rewrite project. He also wanted to achieve four broad substantive goals. First, as a former newsman intensely dedicated to the preservation of journalistic freedom, he sought the repeal of Section 315 (equal opportunity) and the elimination of the Fairness Doctrine and other government restrictions on broadcast programming. "If Thomas Jefferson were writing the Bill of Rights today," Van Deerlin often stated, "he would make clear that the First Amendment applies to broadcast as well as print journalism."[16] Second, spurred by a populist antipathy to bigness and monopoly, he supported open entry and greater economic efficiency in the common carrier industry. Third, as a representative from a district with the nation's highest penetration of cable television, he wanted deregulation of the cable industry. Fourth, he sought deregulation of radio and television accompanied by the creation of new outlets to achieve greater diversity of programming sources. A basic tenet of Van Deerlin's philosophy was that true competition would decrease the need for government regulation and, with respect to the common carrier industry, spur technological innovation and lower costs. In addition, he wanted to bring communications issues into the national political debate and in the process take away the leadership on communications issues from the Senate Communications Subcommittee, where it had been lodged during the twenty-one years John Pastore (D-Rhode Island) served as chairman. Pastore's retirement, which almost coincided with Van Deerlin's selection as subcommittee chairman in the House, opened up this opportunity.

In early September Van Deerlin announced that the subcommittee would hold hearings later that month on the role of competition in the common carrier industry. He said that although he was approaching the hearings with "an open mind," he predicted that in the next Congress, "there'll be a lot fewer people sponsoring [the Bell] bill" as a result of what they learn during the House hearings.[17] The established telephone companies, principally AT&T, were opposed to the rewrite project, believing that the subcommittee should first give its attention to the Bell bill. Said an AT&T spokesman: "We proposed the Consumer Communications Reform Act (. . .) before they proposed the Communications Act revision, and we frankly feel that we have precedence because the competitive field is going its merry way and we have to work under the FCC's competitive edict."[18]

The November 1976 elections had a major impact on the rewrite project. As one Senate Commerce Committee staff aide put it, the fifteen-member Senate Communications Subcommittee was "wiped out": two members retired (John Pastore [long-time subcommittee chairman] and Philip Hart [D-Michigan]) and three were defeated (Vance Hartke [D-Indiana], Frank Moss [D-Utah], and Glenn Beall [R-Maryland]).[19] The defeat of Hartke was of particular significance since he was slated to be the new subcommittee chairman and apparently would have joined Van Deerlin in pushing for a rewrite. Hartke had said that his first undertaking as Chairman would be a series of hearings "across the whole spectrum of communications" designed to determine whether this nation's communications system conforms to the ideals in the act and to look at "new communications technologies coming down the road that no one I know has done a lot of preparation for."[20]

Despite the setbacks for the rewrite in the Senate, Van Deerlin started to gear up in the House. During the fall he hired additional subcommittee staff and started lining up allies. Before year's end, the Office of Telecommunications Policy indicated that it would help Congress "get off the base" by preparing rewrite proposals.[21] The subcommittee, in an effort to obtain the cooperation of broadcasters and citizen groups, formed an advisory panel consisting of eight representatives, four from the industry and four from the citizen movement. Speaking to the Federal Communications Bar Association to muster support for the rewrite efforts, Shooshan, chief counsel for the subcommittee, expressed concern about rumors on Capitol Hill that broadcasters were out to "stonewall" the rewrite project and observed: "If everybody spent more time making input and less time going around Washington complaining about who's making input, we'd all be better off."[22]

The 95th Congress began with renewed evidence that the Senate, after all, might involve itself in the rewrite approach. Senators Warren Magnuson (D-Washington), chairman of the commerce committee, and Senator Ernest "Fritz" Hollings (D-South Carolina), newly elected chairman of the communications subcommittee, both indicated that they planned "a total review" of the Communications Act during the 95th Congress and asked the Office of Technology Assessment (OTA) to conduct a preliminary study reevaluating the assumptions of the act in light of new technologies.[23] On the House side, the commerce committee approved a budget for the communications subcommittee of $498,-000 (nearly twice that of the previous year). Of that amount, $256,000 was earmarked for ten permanent staff members (including the addition of an engineer and a legislative assistant) and $200,000 for consultants.[24]

The *Options Papers*

In April 1977 the subcommittee staff released the *Options Papers,* which outlined possible new directions for the regulation of broadcasting, cable, domestic common carriers, land mobile radio, and international telecommunications. Also included were ways to protect privacy, better manage the spectrum, restructure the FCC, and reorganize public broadcasting. The papers claimed to be "policy neutral," since their purpose was merely to set out "a series of alternative options" for the subcommittee to consider in rewriting the act. For example, the broadcast paper, drafted by Shooshan, listed four options for Congress in regulating radio and television, all of them "mechanisms for extracting the value of the spectrum being used and translating that value into benefits to the public." Those options were:

1. Retention of the current licensing system, with consideration given to the appropriate length of the license term, to staggering renewal dates, and to the types of information to be submitted in license renewal applications
2. A system of leasing, under which the obligations of a broadcaster would be set out as conditions in a lease agreement and which would generate fees based on a percentage of profits that "could be used to accomplish desired public benefits"
3. A public utility approach that would give each broadcaster monopoly control over the frequency, with a rate of return established to create "an incentive to the broadcaster to utilize excess profits for more local programming, expanded news and public affairs, minority training programs, etc."
4. An access or quasi–common carrier approach, under which a broadcaster would be treated like a common carrier for a certain percentage of the broadcast day—the access percentage requirement replacing most of the other, more general content rules or concepts such as the Fairness Doctrine and equal time[25]

The other papers—on topics ranging from cable to spectrum allocations —took a similar approach: that is, they delineated the basic current controversial issues and outlined, without recommendations, numerous alternative approaches that Congress could take.

The *Options Papers* intensified the antagonism of the cable, broadcast, and common carrier industries to the rewrite project.[26] The cable industry, though pleased with options suggesting experiments that would deregulate cable, was alarmed by any discussion of cable systems being treated as common carriers. The NAB said that its deepest regret about the broadcast options paper was that "it seem[ed] to assume that radical change is needed."[27] AT&T warned that radical change in the current common carrier regulatory structure "could jeopardize the continued excellence" of the present system, which has resulted in communications systems in this country that "far surpass those of any other nation."[28] By contrast, such citizen groups as the Office of Communication of the United Church of Christ, the National Black Media Coalition, and the National Citizens Committee for Broadcasting applauded the general tenor of the *Options Papers.*[29]

In a speech before the Iowa Broadcasters Association in June, Vincent Wasilewski, president of the National Association of Broadcasters, called the rewrite project "possibly the most ominous and far-reaching danger we have faced in the industry."[30] He noted that "Chip" Shooshan, the author of the broadcast options paper, had angrily criticized the NAB for using the words "radical and revolutionary" in describing those options but indicated the association would stick with that wording. The NAB president urged broadcasters to fight the rewrite project "with every weapon at our disposal."[31]

In an attempt to calm industry fears of radical change, Van Deerlin attempted to modify the title of his project, an indication of the importance rhetoric often played in its fate. Van Deerlin said his intent was not for a "rewrite" of every sentence of the Communications Act, but rather for a "substantial reappraisal" or "review."[32] He said that the terminology had to change because he sensed "that a lot of people [had] become unnecessarily fearful."[33] In another effort to improve his liaison with the broadcasters, he hired Howard Chernoff, a retired San Diego broadcaster and newspaper executive, to join the subcommittee staff as a part-time consultant. Van Deerlin expressed the hope that "the industry will think well of Chernoff [so] that he can be useful to us in assuaging their fears that we're out to do them harm."[34] Van Deerlin also sought broadcast support by making speeches before various state associations of broadcasters.[35]

Wasilewski was not alone in criticizing Shooshan and other members of the subcommittee staff. Throughout the subcommittee's consideration of the rewrite bill, the staff members, especially Shooshan, played an uncommonly prominent public role and received criticism from the trade press as "an arrogant crew of intellectuals that has alienated every interest group it has dealt with."[36] Van Deerlin was largely responsible for this situation because of the freedom he extended to subcommittee staff members to join the public debate over the rewrite.[37] *Broadcasting* magazine observed that the visibility of Shooshan rivaled that of any of the subcommittee members.[38]

Lou Frey tried to reassure broadcasters: "The staff is not rewriting the Communications Act. If there is going to be a review of the Act, the members are going to be doing the reviewing."[39] He promised to oppose the rewrite if "things get out of control": "Nobody's out to destroy the broadcasting industry or throw any bombs. The world's not coming to an end. Don't jump out any windows."[40] Van Deerlin made a similar speech before the NAB board in June to assure broadcasters that the *Options Papers* were merely points for discussion written by the staff and that the subcommittee itself would produce the actual legislation. He also indicated that no rewrite bill opposed by broadcasters would have any chance of passage. Both Van Deerlin and Frey continued to maintain an active dialogue with broadcasters in order to obtain their support.

During the next few months, the subcommittee held thirty-three days of hearings, primarily consisting of seminar-style panel discussions and involving 484 witnesses on such topics as spectrum management, ownership and industry structure, regulation versus competition, and new technologies.[41] *Variety* commented that the *Options Papers* might as well not have been written for all the consideration they were given during the hearings. A disappointment to Van Deerlin was that most of the witnesses were heard only by him and Lou Frey; other members of the subcommittee dropped in only occasionally because of their involvement on the House floor, where energy bills were under consideration[42], or their perception of the futility of omnibus rewrite legislation. He noted that his frustration was occasioned by recognition of the importance of persuading "members of Congress that we're in the middle of a technological revolution in communications. One that just won't wait. We have to make them realize that, if there's no sweeping revision, there's going to be pandemonium."[43]

The chairman was also having difficulty convincing subcommittee members of his ability to put together a politically viable rewrite bill. A subcommittee member questioned whether Van Deerlin's "ineptness" in finding a consensus on a report on violence on television (see chapter three) threw into question whether the subcommittee could handle a rewrite of the Communications Act.[44] Van Deerlin acknowledged that he had failed to provide firm leadership on the report but noted that it was "much better to have it happen on an issue like the violence report."[45]

During the fall Van Deerlin and Frey met with specially created broadcast and cable advisory groups consisting entirely of industry representatives. "There has been a total change . . . 180 degrees" in the broadcasters' attitude toward the rewrite project, Van Deerlin commented after a five-hour meeting with broadcasters.[46] Buoyed by the favorable reaction they received in a meeting with the National Cable Television Association's rewrite committee, Van Deerlin and Frey said they were now optimistic that the rewrite legislation would pass Congress before 1980.

There was some discussion at the broadcast advisory committee of two possible trade-offs: (1) a form of mandated public access, requiring stations to give time to groups or individuals to express their views in exchange for repeal of the Fairness Doctrine and equal time; and (2) a requirement that broadcasters pay a percentage of their gross revenues to support public broadcasting or to boost minority ownership of stations in exchange for deregulation and longer license terms. A broadcaster attending the meeting said: "The Committee kept talking about trade-offs, asking what we'd be willing to give up. We didn't propose giving up anything."[47]

Two weeks after the meeting, Shooshan told *Broadcasting* that it would "be difficult to get even radio deregulation through the Subcommittee unless there is something that the public and public interest groups see in it for them—a trade-off."[48] He said that as a matter of practical politics a trade-off would be necessary if broadcasters were offered a plus in the rewrite but acknowledged that politics would not permit the imposition of license fees or mandatory access requirements on broadcasters if they did not want them.[49]

Van Deerlin and Frey apparently underestimated, however, the strong negative reaction broadcasters would have to the mention of trade-offs. Responding to Shooshan's tit-for-tat approach and a statement by Van Deerlin indicating that to gain approval of the rewrite broadcasters would have to give ground, the broadcast advisory committee unanimously agreed to refuse Van Deerlin's request for a list of rewrite priorities. In a letter to Van Deerlin, the group expressed disdain for the rewrite approach, observing that "any amendments to the Communications Act should be made with a rifle, not with a shotgun."[50]

Van Deerlin was reported as being "really ticked off" at the broadcast advisory committee for failing to submit a list of priorities: "I could hardly believe it when they decided to tell the Subcommittee 'Just go away. Just leave things as is.' "[51] He noted that appointments made by the Carter administration to key posts (Charles Ferris to the FCC, Henry Geller to the NTIA, and Michael Pertschuk to the FTC) should lead broadcasters toward a closer relationship with a potentially sympathetic Congress. Another way broadcasters could cooperate with the rewrite, Van Deerlin said, would be to seek some common ground with the critics of broadcasting: "When push comes to shove, the broadcasters are going to find out some things about these public interest organizations that they didn't know last year." He left the door open for further discussions with the advisory group: "The candle will remain in the window."[52]

In an attempt to salve the wounds opened by the broadcast advisory committee's action, NAB President Wasilewski sent a conciliatory letter to Van Deerlin stating that his association had cooperated and wanted to continue to cooperate on the rewrite. He expressed hope that "a relatively minor past misunderstanding" can be "wiped off the slate" and noted that the advisory committee had not been empowered to draft legislation or negotiate for the industry.[53] Wasilewski pointed out that the position of the NAB, as set forth in a "statement of principles" adopted by the association's board, was that a dramatic overhaul of the Communications Act "might seriously impair or hamper a system that has successfully fulfilled its mandate to the public."[54] Van Deerlin wrote Wasilewski to say that "the candle would still burn brightly" if the NAB was willing to talk about "trade-offs." He characterized the NAB's "statement of principles" as a document whose message seemed to be: "Keep the gold in Fort Knox." He added: "It reads like the report of a committee project co-chaired by King Midas and Marie Antoinette, with Barbara Fritchie penciling in the rhetoric."[55]

Despite the rhetoric, Van Deerlin and the broadcast advisory committee did meet again in February 1978, although the only tangible result of the meeting was a commitment to give the advisory committee an opportunity to review a draft of the rewrite bill. Broadcasters were assured that the entire rewrite project would continue to be closely supervised by the subcommittee members themselves.[56] The drafting of the bill had become so controversial and the lobbying so intense that Van Deerlin and Frey had their staffs meet in closed drafting sessions at the legislative counsel's office, arguably contrary to promises of close supervision by all members of the subcommittee since neither the other subcommittee members nor their aides were invited to the discussions.[57]

While the subcommittee was considering the *Options Papers,* there were several court decisions that made legislation seem more urgent for some groups and less urgent for others. Most of these decisions favored the cable industry and undermined the interests of broadcasters and AT&T. For example, in March 1977 the U.S. Court of Appeals for the District of Columbia Circuit struck down FCC rules limiting the programming offered by pay-cable systems and designed to prevent the "siphoning" of popular programs from conventional, advertiser-supported television.[58] A series of court decisions continued to erode AT&T's telephone service monopoly. In April 1977 the court of appeals ruled that the FCC had to authorize local interconnection competitors with Bell subscribers unless it specifically determined that the "public interest would be served by creating an AT&T monopoly" in a given area.[59] The ruling effectively legalized specialized common carriers, such as MCI's "Execunet" service, which then competed with AT&T's long-distance telephone service.

The Rewrite Bill (H.R. 13015)

On June 7, 1978, Van Deerlin and Frey held a press conference to unveil H.R. 13015, a 217-page bill that proposed to abolish the FCC, replacing it with a Communications Regulatory Commission, and declaring in its preamble that government intervention in the telecommunications field would be allowed only "to the extent marketplace forces are deficient." Van Deerlin said: "I can't think of any legislation going into the hopper with as much fact-finding and deliberation behind it as this bill."[60] Both Van Deerlin and Frey acknowledged that the bill nevertheless represented only a starting point but once again expressed confidence that rewrite legislation would be approved by both houses of Congress by 1980.

H.R. 13015, described by *Broadcasting* as "a deregulator's dream,"[61] represented an attempt to balance the economic and regulatory interests of the broadcast, cable, and telephone industries by proposing both significant benefits and painful trade-offs for each industry. The main provisions of the bill are summarized in Table 2.

Television Digest commented that the reaction of the broadcast, cable, and common carrier industries to H.R. 13015 was "similar to that of a man kissing his sister: Nice, but not that nice. It offers a juicy carrot to all, at the same time taking something away."[62] Thus the initial comments from leaders in the affected industries typically consisted of praise for the benefits bestowed on them by the bill (usually at the beginning of the press release) followed by a denunciation of any trade-offs. Wasilewski, for example, said that the NAB applauded "much of what the House Communications Subcommittee is attempting to accomplish—less regulation, achievement of greater First Amendment protection, a fair climate for industry growth and increased service to the public" but then noted the NAB's strong opposition to the spectrum fee proposal.[63] Robert Schmidt, president of the National Cable Television Association, applauded the proposed deregulation of cable at the federal level but asked the subcommittee to ensure that "regulations dismantled at the federal level would not be reassembled" by the states.[64] He also expressed concern that the bill would allow AT&T, "the world's largest and most profitable monopoly," to enter the cable business.[65] William Ellinghaus, AT&T vice-chairman, said that AT&T "welcomes provisions of the bill that preclude constraints on the kinds of technology" common carriers can offer their customers and "the bill's declared intent to assure . . . full and fair competition."[66] He cautioned, however, that AT&T would oppose the proposed divestiture of Western Electric, predicting that such action "would slow

Table 2   H. R. 13015 (Van Deerlin)

1. *Radio broadcasting.* Radio stations would be totally deregulated except for technical engineering matters. Licenses would be granted indefinitely subject to revocation only for violations of technical rules.

2. *Television broadcasting.* Television licenses would be granted at first for five years and then granted indefinitely ten years after enactment of the bill. The Fairness Doctrine, abolished in its entirety for radio, would be replaced in television with an "equity principle" requiring stations carrying programs about controversial issues to do so equitably. The equal time requirement, no longer applicable to radio, would be limited for television to candidates for president, vice-president, the U.S. Senate, and other offices for which voting was statewide. Television stations would be required to air locally produced programming "throughout the broadcast day."

3. *Broadcasting multiple ownership.* All existing multiple ownerships would be grandfathered (allowed to continue). Overall limits in the future would be dropped to ten stations—five in television and five in radio. (Owners may now hold up to twenty-one stations—seven television, no more than five of which may be VHF; seven AM; and seven FM stations.) Also, ownership of AM, FM, and television stations would be limited to one station per owner per market.

4. *Cable.* Cable television would be regulated not at the federal level, but at the state or local level. The bill would also repeal a law involving rates charged cable systems for use of telephone poles (commonly known as the "pole attachment bill")—legislation that cable diligently sought in order to eliminate what they considered exorbitant pole attachment fees prior to federal regulation.

5. *Spectrum fees.* The owners of broadcast stations and other users of the electromagnetic spectrum would be required to pay fees based on the value of the spectrum they used. The fees would be phased in over a ten-year period. Proceeds would go to a telecommunications fund to support (a) federal regulation, (b) public broadcast programming, (c) minority ownership of broadcast stations, and (d) the development of telecommunications services in rural areas.

6. *Public broadcasting.* The Corporation for Public Broadcasting would be replaced by a private, nonprofit Public Telecommunications Programming Endowment, the sole purpose of which would be to provide grants for production and acquisition of programming. The bill would eliminate existing restrictions on editorializing and endorsement of political candidates by public broadcasters.

7. *Common carrier.* The bill would remove nearly all restrictions preventing AT&T from entering other telecommunications fields (including cable and computer/data processing services); require the divestiture of Western Electric (Bell's equipment manufacturing subsidiary), and subject the Bell system to increased competition. Of particular importance was the bill's rejection of the approach advocated earlier in the Bell bill to restrict the degree of competition in telephone communications.

8. *Communications Regulatory Commission.* In place of the seven-member FCC, a five-member Communications Regulatory Commission would be created. Commissioners would be appointed for one ten-year term and would be subject to stricter conflict-of-interest rules. An Office of Consumer Assistance would be created within the Commission to serve the role as public ombudsman.

9. *National Telecommunications Agency.* The Commerce Department's National Telecommunications and Information Administration would be abolished and replaced with a National Telecommunications Agency. The agency would have primary responsibility for developing and implementing executive branch policy and would advise the president on telecommunications matters.

technological innovation, increase the cost of facilities and lead eventually to higher rates for services."[67]

The reaction from citizen groups, in contrast to the ambivalent statements of industry leaders, was uniformly hostile; of all the interested parties, they had received the fewest benefits. Everett Parker, director of the United Church of Christ's Office of Communication, called the bill's proposals "a disgrace . . . a bigger give-away of public rights and property than Teapot Dome."[68] Nolan Bowie, executive director of the Citizens Communications Center, complained that "nowhere in this bill is the term 'public interest' used."[69]

The emotional intensity of citizen groups' reaction may be attributed to a feeling of betrayal. They complained that none of the alternatives listed in the *Options Papers* for increased and more effective consumer representation before the FCC was included in H.R. 13015. Nor were any of the reforms suggested by public interest advocates at subcommittee hearings adopted.[70] Andrew Schwartzman, executive director of the Media Access Project, observed that although nobody expected the ultimate bill to have much resemblance to H.R. 13015, it mattered a great deal where the starting point was.[71] Since citizen groups lack the economic and political capital to sustain intensive lobbying campaigns, Schwartzman said, they are "outgunned very much more at the end of the legislative process. So when the bill starts out as one that is essentially unfavorable to the interests we represent, it is only going to get worse."[72]

In hindsight the most perceptive of the initial reactions to H.R. 13015 was that of broadcast historian Eric Barnouw who said

I didn't study it very much because I was sure it wouldn't go through in any form resembling the way it is now. The commercial broadcasters will attack the notion of the fee [on them] to support public broadcasting and the media-access people will attack everything else. They'll probably both succeed in chipping away at it.[73]

One of the most apparent strategies of Van Deerlin and his staff was to weaken the opposition of broadcasters by driving a wedge between radio and television. H.R. 13015 provided greater deregulation for radio than television. Also, the proposed schedule of fees was devised so that VHF television stations (users of the largest portion of the broadcast spectrum) would pay more than 90 percent of the fees assessed broadcasters. A month after H.R. 13015 was introduced, the National Radio Broadcasters Association's board of directors met with Van Deerlin and the subcommittee staff and announced that the NRBA was 100 percent behind the Communications Act rewrite. NRBA President James Gabbert said the association's directors believed that "it's the best thing that ever happened to radio."[74] Van Deerlin, in a speech before the NRBA critical of the NAB, described current FCC regulation of radio as "a situation which is exploited by those who purport to represent you as broadcasters and not as radio broadcasters. This is an important distinction."[75] Lou Frey took a similar stance, urging the NRBA "to put the pressure on the right way and don't get run over by anybody."[76]

During the hearings conducted by the subcommittee during the summer and fall, the broadcast provisions of the bill that attracted the most attention were the omission of the public interest standard and the proposal for a spectrum fee. *Broadcasting* magazine described the Communications Act of 1934 as "the indispensable Linus blanket," with both the regulators and the regulated united in common alarm at the proposed disappearance of the "public interest, convenience and necessity."[77] Four of six FCC Commissioners (Chairman Charles Ferris, Abbott Washburn, Robert E. Lee, and Tyrone Brown) testified in opposition to the substitution of the "marketplace" standard for the "public interest." The testimony of these Commissioners varied in intensity from "mild to outraged" opposition to H.R. 13015, prompting Van Deerlin to complain "in feigned injury that he had been given the mask of Simon Legree."[78] In contrast, Henry Geller, assistant secretary of commerce for communications and information, generally supported H.R. 13015 and agreed with the deletion of the "public interest" standard: "All the public interest standard says is 'We give up. Congress doesn't know [how to regulate communications].'"[79]

Judging from the testimony at the subcommittee's hearings, the disadvantages of H.R. 13015 far outweighed the advantages as industry and public witnesses alike vented their worst fears about the new order —or disorder—the bill would create.[80] Van Deerlin repeatedly assured witnesses that the bill would not be placed before the subcommittee until there was a rewrite of the rewrite. He said the revised bill would be far less painful to both industry and citizen groups because it would have to sound reasonable to 535 members of Congress: "We're not looking to be laughed out of town."[81] Van Deerlin, for example, believed there was only a semantic difference between the "public interest" and the bill's "marketplace" standard but indicated that it would be worth restoring the phrase "public interest, convenience and necessity" if "it's going to save any votes in the House."[82] He assured the cable industry that he would respond to the National Cable Television Association's request for a provision to avoid more regulation by state and local government.[83]

Van Deerlin was willing to make these accommodations in order to produce a bill that would gain the support of his colleagues. Some in Congress viewed omission of the "public interest" standard as a sign of unwillingness to ensure protection for the consumers of communications.[84] However, while Van Deerlin regarded the spectrum fee as the essential *quid pro quo* for deregulating broadcasters, several of the most active members of the subcommittee—Tim Wirth, (D-Colorado), Martin Russo (D-Illinois), and Henry Waxman (D-California)—expressed strong reservations about the concept as well as about where the funds collected from fees would go.[85] Adding to the political uncertainty of the rewrite approach was the departure of Frey, the bill's co-sponsor, who had decided to run for governor of Florida.

Van Deerlin, however, found solace in the October 1978 announcement by Senate Communications Subcommittee Chairman Hollings of plans for a "renovation" of the Communications Act. Hollings observed: "The '34 act should not be packed off to a nursing home. But it must be renovated to meet a new age."[86] Van Deerlin saw Hollings's call for "omnibus amendments" to the act as indicating support for his own rewrite efforts.[87] Another development in the fall of 1978 that encouraged Van Deerlin was the decision of the U.S. Court of Appeals in the *WESH* case (see chapter eight), a decision that made broadcasters believe more urgently than ever in the need for legislative license renewal relief.

Rewrite of the Rewrite (H.R. 3333)

Van Deerlin, in an interview in the January 1, 1979, issue of *Broadcasting,* once again expressed optimism about the passage of a rewrite bill by the end of 1980. Acknowledging his role as a "broker" trying to bring groups together with shared interests, he noted that there had been some encouraging developments. Foremost, he said, was a growing consensus within the telephone industry for rewrite legislation affecting common carriers—an aspect of the bill that in 1979 seemed "more insoluble than broadcasting."[88] Second, he was encouraged by the decision of the NAB board, reversing its previous position, to submit its own legislative proposal. A major reason for NAB's apparent change in attitude, according to Van Deerlin, was the provision in H.R. 13015 for almost total deregulation of radio. Since in terms of the number of stations, radio accounts for more than 80 percent of the industry, the radio deregulation provision, Van Deerlin noted, had "driven a wedge" between radio and television licensees and made it difficult for others to hold the line against the rewrite.[89] He rejected as politically unwise the suggestion that radio deregulation be considered separately from the rest of the rewrite: "You would lose the interest of 8,000 commercial broadcasters. . . . If you want to get a whole package, you'd better keep a single set of strings around it."[90] Van Deerlin said that the ultimate test for the rewrite would be how it stood up in Congress, where communications matters traditionally were not considered major matters, and the key to getting it passed was to produce a measure that "is perceived as being fair and equitable."[91]

With the retirement of Frey, James Collins (R-Texas) became the subcommittee's ranking minority member. This development was viewed by many observers as harming Van Deerlin's chances for a bipartisan joint bill. Collins said initially that he would like to see the rewrite legislation broken into three or four different bills, but subsequently, and surprisingly, he indicated that despite reservations about provisions affecting public broadcasting, the spectrum fee, and other sections of H.R. 13015, he would sponsor a rewrite bill. This statement stunned broadcasters, since he had sent a letter to Texas broadcasters stating that he would not be a rewrite co-sponsor. According to the trade press, Collins agreed to co-sponsor the bill only after Representative James Broyhill (R-North Carolina), a member of the subcommittee, agreed to be a co-sponsor.[92] Another factor that prompted Collins to change his position was the willingness of Van Deerlin to take out "some of the more objectionable features" of the revised bill, such as the link between the proposed spectrum fee and the support of public broadcasting.[93] Collins and Broyhill, it should be noted, said that their co-sponsorship did not necessarily mean a commitment to support all the provisions of any new bill.

On March 12, 1979, Hollings introduced S. 611 (611, coincidentally, being the number of the Bell System's telephone repair service). The measure was co-sponsored by Senate Commerce Committee Chairman Howard Cannon (D-Nevada) and subcommittee member Ted Stevens (R-Alaska). On the same day, Senator Barry Goldwater (R-Arizona), the subcommittee's ranking Republican member, together with Harrison Schmitt (R-New Mexico) and Larry Pressler (R-South Dakota), introduced S. 622. While both bills were considerably less sweeping than H.R. 13015, Van Deerlin said he was very pleased: "The very fact that bills were introduced by both the [Senate] chairman and the ranking member tells us we're a heck of a lot closer to enactment than anyone would have thought possible."[94]

Almost until the moment the Senate bills were introduced, Hollings and Goldwater were talking about joining forces behind a single bill, but their negotiations broke down over the spectrum fee issue.[95] Goldwater, in his statement on the Senate floor introducing S. 622, said: "I found it impossible to support a bill which included license fees based on the scarcity value of the radio frequency spectrum."[96]

As shown in Table 3, S. 611, described by Hollings as a "renovation," left intact much of the existing Communications Act. S. 622, on the other hand, which is shown in Table 4, called for more sweeping change through more substantial broadcast deregulation.

Less than three weeks later Van Deerlin unveiled H.R. 3333, known

Table 3   S. 611 (Hollings).

1. *License terms.* The license terms for radio would be indefinite, but the FCC would "audit" a random sample of all stations annually. The term of television licenses would be increased to five years.

2. *Renewal procedures.* To take away some uncertainty created by the court of appeals' *WESH-TV* decision (see chapter eight), the FCC would be prohibited in comparative renewal proceedings from considering other media interests of the incumbent if the licensee complied with rules on cross-ownership.

3. *Fees.* Users of the spectrum would pay a "public resource" fee, which would generate $80 million a year. Nearly all ($79 million) would be paid by broadcasters, and most of that amount ($77 million) would come from television stations.

4. *Cable.* Restrictions on cable's use of broadcast signals would be permitted only when the broadcaster met the burden of proving the need for such restrictions. The bill would provide for state regulation of cable franchising in general, local access channels, subscriber fees, and other requirements not affecting broadcast transmission. Telephone companies would be permitted to own cable systems operated by others.

5. *Spectrum changes.* A National Commission on Spectrum Management would be created to conduct an eighteen-month study and recommend improvements in the allocation and management of the spectrum.

Table 4   S. 622 (Goldwater).

1. *License terms.* License terms for radio would be made indefinite. For television, the term would be three years for stations in the top twenty-five markets, four years for stations in markets twenty-six through one hundred, five years for stations in markets below the top one hundred.

2. *Renewal procedures.* The FCC would be required to renew a station's license if the licensee "substantially met" community problems, needs, and interests during the preceding term. In comparative renewal situations, the FCC would undertake a two-step process, under which the proceeding could be terminated if the incumbent licensee had met the renewal standard.

3. *Fees.* The FCC would charge a fee based only on the cost of regulation, not as in S. 611 on the basis of spectrum users making profits from a public resource. The Commission, the ultimate recipient of the funds, would determine the size of the fees.

4. *Cable.* Cable and pay television would continue to be regulated at the federal level, but the burden of proof for restricting cable carriage of distant broadcast signals would be shifted to the broadcaster. The FCC would be authorized to adopt antisiphoning rules protecting sports events. The FCC also would be authorized to adopt rules for cable systems covering equal employment opportunity, provision of free or leased channels for community-originated programming (access channels), access for political candidates, equal time, and the Fairness Doctrine. Broadcasters would be allowed to own and operate cable systems, while telephone companies would be permitted to provide cable facilities but not to control program content.

5. *Deregulation.* For radio stations the bill would eliminate guidelines for the presentation of news, public affairs and other nonentertainment programming; community ascertainment; regulation of program formats; the Fairness Doctrine (the equal time requirement and the personal attack rule would be retained); program log requirements; and restrictions on the advertising of products that are legally sold. The FCC would be required to look for ways to cut back on television regulations and to make annual progress reports to Congress. Congress would be given the power to veto any new rule that would increase regulation of television.

as "Rewrite II" or "son of rewrite." The bill differed significantly from his earlier bill, H.R. 13015. He expressed optimism that the revised rewrite bill would be passed in the 96th Congress, possibly by Thanksgiving.[97] Helping the bill's prospects, Van Deerlin believed, was its co-sponsorship by Collins and Broyhill. Van Deerlin perceived that Collins's image as a "self-proclaimed conservative would certainly cast an aura for people I am not able to persuade."[98] Another reason for Van Deerlin's optimism was "new evidence within the last few days of administration support" for the rewrite.[99] He also pointed to a "change in political climate" in the Senate reflected by the introduction of S. 611 and S. 622.[100]

H.R. 3333 was in many ways more radical than H.R. 13015 but provided sweeteners in the form of more freedom and less regulation to attract support from the broadcast, cable, and common carrier industries. *Broadcasting* characterized the bill as an attempt by Van Deerlin to bid "for adjustments that will meet most objections of contending forces without being all things to all comers by compromising his basic philosophies."[101] As shown in Table 5, however, the bill also introduced several new concepts that would be regarded as unacceptable by citizen lobbies and the cable industry.

The most hostile reaction to Van Deerlin's new bill came from citizen groups. The Office of Communication of the United Church of Christ condemned H.R. 3333 as the "Titantic without lifeboats."[102] NCCB Board Chairman Nicholas Johnson labeled the bill "a multibillion dollar giveaway"[103] and proceeded to help form the Coalition for Public Rights in Broadcasting, an umbrella organization to oppose the bill consisting of such diverse groups as the National Organization for Women, Ralph Nader's Congress Watch, the Consumer Federation of America, and the Friends of the Earth. In addition, five labor unions (the National Education Association, the American Federation of State, County and Municipal Employees, the United Steelworkers, the Screen Actors Guild, and the United Auto Workers) and the Coalition of American Public Employees joined together to form an ad hoc committee to oppose H.R. 3333 and the two Senate bills. Van Deerlin reacted angrily to citizen movement opposition: "I am a member of what is probably the oldest public interest group in this country—the Congress. Unlike the Ralph Naders and Nick Johnsons, members of Congress are elected —chosen by the people—to represent them.[104] However, the lobbying served to convince some members of the subcommittee of the need to adopt a narrower approach. Following Nicholas Johnson's testimony, Representative Marc Marks (R-Pennsylvania) said: "There are some of us on this subcommittee who . . . are going to see that this point of view you've just taken is well represented."[105]

The cable industry regarded H.R. 3333 as a measure that jeopardized

Table 5   H. R. 3333 (Van Deerlin).

1. *License terms.* The license term for radio would be indefinite. For television the initial term after passage of the act would be five years, with licenses becoming termless (indefinite) after two renewals.

2. *Renewal procedures.* Comparative renewal proceedings would be abolished. If the Communications Regulatory Commission decided to deny or revoke a television license, the new licensee would be chosen by a lottery among qualified applicants.

3. *Fees.* License fees would be assessed on all commercial users of the spectrum and would be based on the cost of processing a license application and the scarcity value of spectrum space used. The total fees to be collected at the end of a ten-year phase-in period would be about $150 million. (Under H.R. 13015 the fees were expected to generate about $300 million to $400 million annually.) About 80 percent of the fees would come from television. The money would go into the general fund of the U.S. Treasury. (In H.R. 13015, the money was earmarked for public broadcasting and other programs.)

4. *Cable.* The bill would eliminate all current government regulation of cable. As a trade-off, cable systems would no longer be able to carry broadcast programming without permission from either the broadcaster or the program owner. The Department of Justice would decide whether broadcast cross-ownership of cable systems in the same market should be prohibited. Telephone companies would be able to own cable systems; however, if telephone companies began offering services such as pay programming and videotext, they would be required to make the system's facilities available to anyone else wanting to do the same.

5. *Deregulation.* The bill would do away with nearly all but the technical regulation of radio, including the Fairness Doctrine, equal time, equal employment opportunity enforcement, and program format regulation. For television the Commission would continue to enforce the Fairness Doctrine (although only at renewal time), equal employment regulations, and a requirement that if time were sold to one candidate for public office, it had to be sold to all other candidates for that office. To be eligible for renewal, television stations would have to show that they broadcast "local public affairs and local programming" throughout the day. These requirements would be in effect only for two five-year terms; after two terms, all content regulation of television would cease.

6. *Ownership limitations.* Except for a ban on owning more than one AM and one FM station in the same market, there would be no restrictions on the ownership of radio stations. No entity would be allowed to own more than seven television stations nationally, nor more than one television station per market.

7. *Public broadcasting.* Public broadcasting stations would be permitted to carry commercials, clustered in no more than three places during the day and totaling no more than 3 percent of total program time. In addition, public broadcasting would be given a permanent congressional authorization of $1.50 per person per year.

its continued existence. NCTA President Robert Schmidt said that the bill's requirement that cable operators obtain permission from broadcasters or program producers to use their programs would be like putting "the fox in charge of the chicken coop."[106] He also attacked the bill for opening cable to domination by telephone monopolies.[107] Ralph Baruch, chairman and chief executive of Viacom International, predicted the program consent requirement would put cable "out of business," as did Ted Turner, owner of superstation WTBS-TV, Atlanta, who said it would "stop cable dead."[108] Stephen Effros, representing the Community Antenna Television Association, an association of small cable systems, said that the paperwork alone attached to program consent would bankrupt small cable systems.[109] Van Deerlin made a number of appearances before cable groups to gain their support but was unable to convince them that the benefits of cable deregulation outweighed the bill's trade-offs. In exasperation, he told the NCTA: "If the song needed a title it would have to be 'Please Fence Me In.' And each refrain is the same, too. It goes, 'All I Want Is a Fair Advantage.' "[110]

Broadcasters found H.R. 3333 to be considerably more attractive than H.R. 13015. The NAB, the Association for Maximum Service Telecasters, and ABC continued to oppose the rewrite concept, preferring selective amendments to the Communications Act. The NAB generally supported most of the bill but strongly objected to the trade-off of a spectrum fee. Van Deerlin responded by promising that there would not be any legislation without a spectrum fee.[111] Van Deerlin warned broadcasters that if they were uncooperative he would delete the broadcast provisions from the bill. He asserted that broadcasters were not in as strong a bargaining position as they were under H.R. 13015 because of two factors—the "dozen citizen groups looking at the bill" and AT&T's willingness to work with the subcommittee.[112]

Death of the Rewrite

Perhaps the most significant obstacles to passage of the bill were placed by Van Deerlin's colleague in the House, Representative Collins. Moments after Van Deerlin declared the public broadcast provisions of H.R. 3333 to be "an integral and essential part of the whole," Collins told a National Public Radio Conference that public broadcasting should be cut out of the bill.[113] Representative Al Ullman (D-Oregon), chairman of the House Ways and Means Committee, asked the Speaker of the House to refer H.R. 3333 to his committee on the ground that the fees were really a revenue-raising device.[114] The trade press reported that deep divisions were apparent among members of the subcommittee. A major critic and opponent of the bill was subcommittee member Wirth, who was trying to establish himself (ultimately successfully) as the logical successor to Van Deerlin. Several of the younger Democrats on the subcommittee besides Wirth—Al Swift (Washington), Albert Gore (Tennessee), and Edward Markey (Massachusetts)—were opposed to the deregulation of broadcasting proposed in H.R. 3333.[115] During the July 4 recess, members of the subcommittee were visited by broadcasters, cable operators, and members of the newly formed citizen-labor lobby, urging resistance to the rewrite.

When Van Deerlin presided at the first of two sessions on the bill in July, it became apparent to him that his colleagues would not support the basement-to-attic rewrite approach. On Friday, July 13, Van Deerlin, Broyhill, and Collins sent a letter to subcommittee members announcing that the rewrite bill was dead:

First, most members of the Subcommittee feel more comfortable proceeding with the 1934 Act as a vehicle for implementing change. Second, it is clear that telecommunications common carrier issues are the ones on which immediate action is imperative. This is a position shared by the Senate leadership, the administration, the Federal Communications Commission, the private industries involved, and labor and consumer groups.[116]

Variety began its obituary of H.R. 3333 with this observation: "Following two years of debate, 95 days of public hearings and testimony from more than 1,200 witnesses, Rep. Van Deerlin has conceded the obvious—that there is insufficient support in his House Communications Subcommittee to approve the controversial rewrite of the 1934 Communications Act."[117] Van Deerlin blamed his own shortcomings for the defeat of H.R. 3333, saying he had written a bill in which "everybody found something to dislike."[118] He also noted, "I probably didn't lead as strongly as I should have."[119]

Van Deerlin believed that another problem stood in the way of his securing support: members of his subcommittee were "spread thin" and did not have sufficient time to study the issues.[120] He also pointed to the common ground shared by broadcasters and citizen groups in lobbying against the bill: "With the ABC Network coming down on the same side as Ralph Nader, it was hard [for subcommittee members] to buck."[121] He said that he had always considered the provisions relating to the telephone companies as the most important part of the bill, and indeed, on December 13, 1979, following the demise of H.R. 3333, all of the members of the House Subcommittee on Communications co-sponsored H.R. 6121, a bill containing many of the same common carrier provisions as H.R. 3333. Van Deerlin later said that he would have preferred to include in H.R. 6121 a provision aimed at providing rural areas with cable coverage but recognized that "pretty soon we'd be bogged down and we wouldn't get any legislation. We could see that would start the dominoes—Jack Valenti and retransmission consent, then the NAB. Unlike Vietnam, there is no light at the end of that tunnel."[122]

Even after the July 1979 letter to the subcommittee, a resurrection of the rewrite occasionally seemed possible. Van Deerlin, in a speech before the International Radio and Television Society in September 1979, told broadcasters to "cancel the wake" for the rewrite. "I wouldn't be running for re-election next year if I believed the rewrite were dead. Our work will continue."[123] However, in an article he wrote several months later, Van Deerlin conceded, "There is no 'Rewrite III' nor any plans for one."[124] The question of whether Van Deerlin would pursue the rewrite issue, however, was definitively decided by congressional election time in 1980. The rewrite legislation was a factor determining Van Deerlin's fortunes in that election. Voters were said to have felt that he spent too much time on the rewrite at the expense of local needs and perceived him as ineffective because the rewrite efforts had failed.[125] His opponent made a last-minute mailing to voters, suggesting that their telephone bills would increase fivefold if H.R. 6121 were enacted.[126] Whatever the reasons, Van Deerlin lost his House seat in the 1980 Republican sweep, and with his defeat went many of the hopes of those who felt that a fundamental recasting of the nation's basic communications law was required.

While Van Deerlin's rewrite effort ultimately failed as a piece of legislation, the introduction of several measures and the debate they elicited had a significant impact on communications policy decisions. First, there was improved congressional oversight of the FCC's actions. Along these lines FCC Commissioner Glen Robinson observed in 1978:

As part of a studied effort over the last two years to review and revise the entire legislative mandate of the FCC, the Subcommittee on Communications and its staff have shown greater attentiveness to, and more understanding of, important policy issues than has been evident for at least twenty years.[127]

Second, the FCC was spurred to action by rewrite proposals that threatened the very survival of the agency. A former general counsel of the FCC, Robert Bruce, regarded the "rewrite" process as having "an enormous impact" on the development of substantive policies by the Commission: "The Commissioners and staff were asked by Van Deerlin to respond to sweeping across-the-board proposals for overhaul of the Communications Act and had to develop a coherent agency point of view in a very concentrated period of time."[128] By taking actions administratively that implemented the rewrite's legislative goals of deregulation and increased marketplace competition, the Commission took some of the steam out of the drive for legislation and established the agency in a leadership role. The Commission made major decisions on the deregulation of radio, on cable television (eliminating rules governing the importation of distant signals and exclusivity protection for syndicated television programs), and on the licensing of earth stations. It took several bold initiatives in providing for open entry into and deregulation of the common carrier industry. Among those initiatives were extensive deregulation to enhance competition in the international record carrier industry (the companies that transmit hard-copy messages by cable and satellite overseas), deregulation of terminal equipment (from the Princess telephone to teletype terminals), continuation of regulation of such "basic" communications services as traditional transmission and switching but deregulation of "enhanced" services (e.g., the translation of one computer language into another), and reduction of rate regulation of nondominant carriers (e.g., those who resell WATS and private line services on lines leased from the telephone company and those who compete with dominant carriers by means of their own microwave systems).[129]

With respect to the provision of new broadcasting outlets, the FCC proposed the reduction of AM channel spacing from ten to nine kHz, the dropping in of four VHF television channels, the creation of a new, low-power television service, the authorization of a direct-to-the-home satellite broadcast service, and the liberalization of FM allocations rules. Thus, except for repeal of Section 315 and the Fairness Doctrine (actions requiring the passage of legislation), Van Deerlin prodded the FCC into implementing virtually all of the substantive goals discussed earlier in this chapter. In Van Deerlin's eyes and those of many other Washington observers, the FCC's bold actions "would have been impossible without the thunder and lightning sparked by those first two comprehensive bills."[130]

Third, and in the opinion of Van Deerlin most significant,[131] the rewrite process served to derail the Bell bill, a measure sponsored in 1976 by 175 representatives and 17 senators, by refocusing the debate on common carrier issues. By mingling the common carrier issues with broadcasting and cable issues, the legislative process became much more complex and drawn out. Both Van Deerlin and Frey believe that their efforts to rewrite the act had an impact on AT&T's basic approach to communications policy issues.[132] Unlike John deButts, former chairman of AT&T who was adamantly opposed to increased competition in 1976, his successor Charles L. Brown announced that he intended to be guided by "a new realism" that recognizes that "competition is a fact of life in our business."[133]

Largely because of Van Deerlin's efforts, communications issues took on a new importance in Congress and the White House. His bills laid the groundwork for plans to amend the Communications Act that future more conservative Congresses may build upon. Perhaps the true legacy of rewrite was best expressed by Van Deerlin:

The rewrite is generating a new environment in Washington—an environment in which the old laws and established institutions are being challenged by the skepticism of new players in a new era. As a long-time observer and participant, I tell you this: things will never be the same again.[134]

NOTES

1. Statement of Representative John M. Murphy (D-New York), *The Communications Act of 1978, Hearings before the Subcommittee on Communications, House Committee on Interstate and Foreign Commerce on H.R. 13015,* 95th Congress, 2nd Session (1978), Vol. II, Part I, p. 358.
2. *Variety,* July 18, 1979, p. 29.
3. See "Macdonald Retirement Changes the Line-Up," *Broadcasting,* May 3, 1976, p. 42. See also Paul W. McAvoy, ed., *Deregulation of Cable Television* (Washington, D.C.: American Enterprise Institute, 1977).
4. "Macdonald Retirement Changes the Line-Up," Ibid.
5. Quoted in "Van Deerlin: Making a Difference," *Broadcasting,* May 7, 1979, p. 46.
6. See "The Communications Act: Broadcasters' Bogeyman," *Media Decisions,* August 1977, p. 60.
7. U.S. House of Representatives, Committee on Interstate and Foreign Commerce, Subcommittee on Communications, *Hearings, Cable Television Regulation Oversight,* Part 2, 94th Congress, 2nd Session (1976), p. 945. Frey did not attend the first day of hearings (May 17, 1976) but inserted a statement in the official record. After discussing the need to develop a "national cable television policy," his statement noted that "Of course, developing this policy will be a tough job, and it may well be that in order to do so, we may have to think in terms of re-examination of the entire Communications Act." Ibid., p. 2. Torbert Macdonald, a year earlier, had commented that the Communications Act "is the product of a time when telecommunications technology was in a relatively primitive stage." He felt the time was ripe for a reexamination of the entire act. Because of the poor state of his health, he did not try to undertake such an ambitious project. See "Macdonald Wants a Tether on FCC, [and] Some Fat Trimming," *Broadcasting,* June 23, 1975, p. 32. However, the Subcommittee's 1976 budget justification, drafted by Shooshan, contained the following phrase: "The subcommittee intends to undertake the redrafting of the Communications Act of 1934."
8. "AT&T's Bold Bid to Stifle Competitors," *Business Week,* March 15, 1976, p. 82.
9. Louis J. Sirico, "House Trading with Ma Bell: Who Benefits?" in *Telecommunications Policy and the Citizen,* ed. Timothy Haight (New York: Praeger, 1979), p. 225.
10. Quoted in *Telecommunications Reports,* September 20, 1976, p. 3.
11. "NCTA to Oppose Bell Bill," *Television Digest,* September 4, 1976, p. 4.
12. Theodore B. Merrill, Jr., "A Slick, Thoughtful Overhaul of the Communications Industry," *Business Week,* July 10, 1978, p. 86.
13. Quoted in "Rewrite of Communications Act Serious Subject on Hill," *Broadcasting,* August 9, 1976, p. 19. Van Deerlin quickly abandoned the "basement-to-penthouse" phrase in favor of "basement-to-attic."
14. Ibid.

15. Quoted in Earl B. Abrams, "Inside the FCC," *Television/Radio Age,* January 3, 1977, p. 83. According to Representative Tim Wirth (D-Colorado), an early supporter of the rewrite concept, the impetus for review was the inability of the 1934 Act to embrace developments in technology, "new blood" on the House and Senate Communications Subcommittees, and pressure from the cable and telephone industries. See *Television Digest,* September 20, 1976, p. 6.

16. Quoted in "Mass Media Laws, Changes Proposed," *Washington Post,* March 30, 1979, p. D20.

17. Quoted in *Television Digest,* September 6, 1976, p. 4.

18. Richard Cohen, "Communications May Never Be the Same When Congress Gets Done," *National Journal,* February 5, 1977, p. 21.

19. Quoted in "Senate Roles Are in Upheaval After Elections," *Broadcasting,* November 8, 1976, p. 24.

20. Quoted in "Rewrite of Communications Act Serious Subject on Hill," *Broadcasting,* August 9, 1976, p. 19.

21. See "Don't Stonewall—Shooshan," *Television Digest,* December 20, 1976, p. 5. See also American Enterprise Institute, *Telecommunication Law Reform: Legislative Analysis* (Washington, D.C.: American Enterprise Institute, 1977).

22. "What Happens to Broadcasting if Regulatory Act Is Rewritten?" *Broadcasting,* December 20, 1976, p. 26.

23. See "Senate's 'Total Review,' " *Television Digest,* February 14, 1977, p. 3. Van Deerlin and Frey subsequently supported the OTA study and asked to be included in the deliberations.

24. Ibid. Some observers believe that Representative Harley Staggers (D-West Virginia), chairman of the House Interstate and Foreign Commerce Committee, was indirectly responsible for the lack of comprehensive action on communications issues in previous years because of his keeping of only a skeleton staff to cover the hundreds of issues under the full committee's jurisdiction. See "House Panel Considers Major Overhaul of 1934 Communications Act," *Congressional Quarterly,* June 4, 1977, p. 1113. Associate minority counsel George "Toby" Harder described the committee's work in these days as "dabbling" in communications (ibid.). In 1974 this pattern of control by the chairman of the full committee changed when the subcommittee chairmen received more power and separate staffs for majority and minority members (ibid.).

25. U.S. House of Representatives, Committee on Interstate and Foreign Commerce, Subcommittee on Communications, *Options Papers Prepared by the Staff for Use by the Subcommittee on Communications, Committee Print 95-13,* 95th Congress, 1st Session (1977), p. 81. Critical of the staff's failure to defend the existing Communications Act, *Broadcasting* commented in an editorial that the subcommittee had "been presented with staff option papers numbering about 800 more pages than the average Congressman will read and contained in three volumes with a gross weight of six pounds, three ounces" ("Option No. 1," [editorial], *Broadcasting,* May 2, 1970, p. 90).

26. The initial reaction was summarized in a headline in the broadcast trade press: "Options Papers: OK in General, Not So OK in the Particulars" (*Broadcasting,* May 2, 1977, p. 26). Van Deerlin and Frey wanted the *Options Papers* to evoke controversy and thus were

pleased that radical proposals for change were discussed: "We wanted to tell the industries in a dramatic way that the rewrite effort was serious and merited their attention" (interview with Lou Frey, Washington, D.C., July 16, 1981). A lawyer for the Senate Communications Subcommittee, while acknowledging the "laudable" objective of developing policy options, observed that the inclusion of radical and often conflicting proposals proved to be unnecessarily divisive and served only to intensify the antagonism toward the subcommittee of "already apprehensive" industries (interview with Mary Jo Manning, Washington, D.C., July 13, 1981).

27. See *Television Digest*, May 9, 1977, p. 6.
28. See "Rewrite," *Industrial Communications*, July 8, 1977, p. 8.
29. The *Options Papers* included alternatives such as government funding of public participation in FCC hearings, an Agency for Consumer Protection, and an Office of Public Counsel.
30. Quoted in "NAB Won't Give on Rhetoric Over Review of Broadcast Law," *Broadcasting*, June 20, 1977, p. 33.
31. Ibid. Major portions of Wasilewski's speech were reprinted in "Inside the FCC," *Television/Radio Age*, July 4, 1977, pp. 109–110.
32. See "Van Deerlin Calls Communications Act Study 'Review' not a 'Rewrite,' " *Broadcasting*, May 20, 1977, p. 19.
33. Ibid.
34. Quoted in "Government and the Media," *Media Report*, April 11, 1977, p. 3.
35. Van Deerlin said that he traveled to state meetings of broadcasters "so they won't think they are dealing with some far-off, far-out idealists" ("The Communications Act: Broadcasters' Bogeyman," p. 60).
36. "Electronic Puzzle in D.C.: Comedy, Drama or Farce?" *Variety*, September 12, 1979, p. 47. Another commentator inquired: "Why has Shooshan been singled out for the broadcasters' enemy list? Because in recent years, he has been outspoken on a number of subjects that tear at the industry's premises, not to mention its pursestrings" (Earl B. Abrams, "Inside the FCC," *Television/Radio Age*, February 28, 1977, p. 101).
37. See "Van Deerlin: Making a Difference," *Broadcasting*, May 7, 1979, p. 42. Shooshan commented: "I don't do anything or say anything that Van Deerlin doesn't know about or approve. . . . It's a game plan that Van Deerlin controls" (ibid.).
38. Ibid.
39. "Van Deerlin and Frey Defend Rewrite," *Television Digest*, June 27, 1977, p. 3.
40. Ibid.
41. In August NAB President Wasilewski sent a letter to Van Deerlin recommending that a transcript of the hearings be reprinted as soon as possible and commented that the record "would provide an excellent reference" source for subcommittee members and for future research (*Television Digest*, August 15, 1977, p. 4). The panel discussion hearing record was never published because the stenographer, given the free form of the round-table discussions, was unable to follow the discussion or transcribe the tapes.
42. See "Van Deerlin Lowers Curtain on Act One," *Broadcasting*, August 8, 1977, p. 21.

43. Quoted in "The Communications Act: Broadcasters' Bogeyman," p. 60. One observer commented that the biggest legislative obstacle to rewriting the Communications Act was "that most congressmen, as well as most of the public, do not see a need for change in the three industries. Telephones do work. And one can choose from a wide range of radio and television news and entertainment programs" (Merrill, "A Slick, Thoughtful Overhaul of the Communications Industry," p. 86). Frey attributed poor attendance by other members of the subcommittee to the perception by most members of Congress that there was not a "constituency" for communications issues (interview with Lou Frey, Washington, D.C., July 16, 1981).

44. See "Victories on Saccharin, Violence," *Television Digest,* July 26, 1977, p. 2.

45. Ibid.

46. Quoted in "Euphoria about Rewrite in San Diego," *Broadcasting,* November 14, 1977, p. 20.

47. Quoted in "Rewrite Back on Track—Van Deerlin," *Television Digest,* November 14, 1977, p. 1.

48. "Shooshan Sees Little Change for Broadcasting in Act Rewrite," *Broadcasting,* November 21, 1977, p. 22.

49. Ibid. Shooshan also stated that in his view, "the politics of the subcommittee won't permit the outright repeal of the fairness doctrine and equal time" (ibid.).

50. See "Hot Broadcasters Turn Cold Again Over the Rewrite," *Broadcasting,* December 12, 1977, p. 21.

51. Quoted in "Van Deerlin & Rewrite," *Television Digest,* December 19, 1977, p. 4. Van Deerlin was reported to have had a "personal quarrel" with the advisory committee for releasing its letter to the trade press before he had been informed of its contents. See "If There Ever Was a Honeymoon, It's Over," *Broadcasting,* December 19, 1977, p. 22.

52. Quoted in "If There Ever Was a Honeymoon, It's Over." Several days later, the Office of Communication of the United Church of Christ submitted a proposal for the rewrite. Van Deerlin called the proposal "significant, enlightened and well-prepared. . . . It's the only comprehensive proposal for a revision of the act that we've received so far. That is what we've wanted all the interested parties to do" (quoted in "Church Group Drafts Proposals to Update Communications Act," *New York Times,* December 27, 1977, p. 65).

53. See "NAB Says It Isn't So," *Broadcasting,* January 2, 1978, p. 22.

54. Ibid.

55. Quoted in "Van Deerlin Widens the Rift Over the Rewrite," *Broadcasting,* January 9, 1978, p. 24.

56. See "The 'Rewrite': Animal, Vegetable or Mineral?" *Broadcasting,* February 27, 1978, p. 30.

57. Barry Cole and Mal Oettinger, *Reluctant Regulators: The FCC and the Broadcast Audience,* rev. ed. (Reading, Mass.: Addison-Wesley, 1978), p. 311. Edwina Dowell, former subcommittee staff counsel, said that since other members of the subcommittee were not ready to draft a bill, invitations were neither extended nor expected (telephone interview with Edwina Dowell, New York, July 9, 1981).

58. *Home Box Office, Inc.* v. *FCC,* 567 F.2d 9 (D.C. Cir. 1977).

59. *MCI Telecommunications Corp.* v. *FCC,* 561 F.2d 365 (D.C. Cir. 1977),

certiorari denied, 434 U.S. 1040 (1978). The next year, the Second Circuit Court of Appeals affirmed an FCC order that required AT&T to allow customers of its private line services to "share" or "resell" those services in a manner that would use facilities more efficiently and promote competition at the retail service level.

60. Quoted in Irwin B. Arieff, "House Panel Offers Plan to Deregulate Communications," *Congressional Quarterly,* June 17, 1978, p. 1547. Both Van Deerlin and Frey were aware of the pitfalls of the basement-to-attic approach and anticipated the possibility that the broadcast provisions might have to be "broken off" from the common carrier and cable provisions. Contrary to their public posture on this issue, they were prepared to take that step at the appropriate time (interview with Lou Frey, Washington, D.C., July 16, 1981).

61. "And It Is from the Basement to the Attic," *Broadcasting,* June 12, 1978, p. 29.

62. "The Rewrite: It's Here," *Television Digest,* June 12, 1978, p. 1.

63. Ibid.

64. "And It Is from the Basement to the Attic," p. 41. Steve Effros, executive director of the Community Antenna Television Association, commented: "The bill has thrown us out to sea and released a shark—Bell" (quoted in "Rewrite Bill Draws Mixed Reviews from Cable Industry," *VUE,* June 26, 1978, p. 7).

65. See "At First Blush: No Panic in the Industry Street," *Broadcasting,* June 12, 1978, p. 40.

66. Quoted in "Communications Law Overhaul Is Being Proposed," *Wall Street Journal,* June 8, 1978, p. 33.

67. Ibid.

68. Quoted in "Plan Seeks to Lessen F.C.C. Role," *New York Times,* June 8, 1978, p. 61. Dr. Parker's allusion to Teapot Dome, which was prominently mentioned in virtually every newspaper and magazine story on H.R. 13015, irked Van Deerlin: "I must say I feel a little stung now and then by charges that deregulation is gouging at the public interest . . . that it's comparable to Teapot Dome or the railroad land grants" (quoted in "Van Deerlin: Making a Difference," p. 46).

69. Quoted in "House Panel Offers Plan to Deregulate Communications," p. 1547. Van Deerlin explained why the "public interest" standard was omitted:

> We thought the phrase never really meant anything to users of the airwaves and to those who regulate the industry. . . . A lot of games have been played with it, and there have been a lot of empty promises made to serve the public interest. But stations automatically received license renewals no matter what they promised and no matter what the quality of the product (quoted in Les Brown, "Broadcast Regulation: Plan Makes Waves," *New York Times,* June 12, 1978, p. C19).

70. Harvey J. Shulman, "Is Structural and Procedural Change a Better Answer for Consumers Than the 'Reform' of Abolishing the FCC," in *Telecommunications Policy and the Citizen,* pp. 82–83.

71. Mel Friedman, "A New Communications Act: The Debate Begins," *Columbia Journalism Review,* October 1978, p. 41.

72. Quoted in ibid.

73. Quoted in "Reactions," *Washington Post,* June 13, 1978, p. B8.

74. Quoted in "NRBA Lines Up with the Rewrite," *Broadcasting,* July 24, 1978, p. 29.

75. Quoted in "Rewrite & Good Vibes at NRBA," *Television Digest,* September 25, 1978, p. 1.

76. Ibid.

77. See "Square One," *Broadcasting,* July 24, 1978, p. 114.

78. "FCC Consensus Is Against Key Elements of H.R. 13015," *Broadcasting,* July 24, 1978, p. 80. Shooshan was of the view that "Ferris's natural instinct for protecting his turf" resulted in a series of actions designed to undercut the House rewrite effort. For example, in Shooshan's opinion, the Commission's decisions on radio deregulation, cable deregulation, and computer and common carrier deregulation were motivated by Ferris's desire to remove the incentives of various industry groups to support rewrite legislation (interview with Harry Shooshan, Jr., Washington, D.C., June 26, 1981).

79. Quoted in "Geller Wants Full Authority over Allocation of Spectrum Space," *Broadcasting,* July 24, 1978, p. 84.

80. See "Getting in Their Licks on the Rewrite," *Broadcasting,* September 18, 1978, p. 23.

81. Ibid.

82. Quoted in "FCC Consensus Is Against Key Elements of H.R. 13015," *Broadcasting,* July 24, 1978, p. 80.

83. See "Van Deerlin Says Reluctantly That Cable Will Get Some of What It Seeks in Revision of Rewrite," *Broadcasting,* October 2, 1978, pp. 57–58.

84. Van Deerlin subsequently characterized the deletion of the "public interest" standard as a "political error of the first magnitude" (quoted in "Van Deerlin Offers a Look at Rewrite II," *Broadcasting,* March 19, 1979, p. 92).

85. See "House Members' Rewrite Thinking," *Television Digest,* August 21, 1978, p. 1. Wirth later expressed support for the spectrum fee concept at field hearings conducted by the subcommittee in December.

86. Quoted in "Seed of Rewrite May Be Sprouting on Senate Side," *Broadcasting,* October 16, 1978, p. 22.

87. Ibid.

88. See "Now It's the Rewrite of 1980," *Broadcasting,* January 1, 1979, p. 32. Van Deerlin said that the heads of the independent telephone companies are "joining in solutions that didn't seem possible two years ago." He regarded as significant that AT&T Chairman John deButts was taking early retirement; according to Van Deerlin, deButts initially opposed permitting the unrestrained growth of new business carriers but is now of the view that "we have to find ways to accommodate to the new era" (ibid.).

89. Ibid. Other subcommittee members viewed the owners of VHF television stations in the large markets as constituting a more potent political force than small-market radio stations.

90. Ibid. In the fall of 1977, NAB Board Chairman Donald Thurston accused Van Deerlin of trying to "divide NAB's constituency" with his talk of separate treatment of radio and television:

> Yet he does not have a separate radio bill. . . . He says we're different in order to gain political points, but he treats us with one bill because he knows we are one industry. He'd like to seduce the radio industry with false promises in order to do his will on television (quoted in "Thurston Accuses Van Deerlin of Divide-and-Conquer Tactics on Rewrite," *Broadcasting,* October 23, 1978, p. 24).

91. Quoted in "Now It's the Rewrite of 1980," p. 32.
92. See "Collins to Co-Sponsor Rewrite," *Television Digest,* March 26, 1979, p. 6.
93. See "Collins Enlists in Van Deerlin's Rewrite Cause," *Broadcasting,* March 26, 1979, p. 30.
94. Quoted in "Senate Bills 611 & 622," *Television Digest,* March 19, 1979, p. 1.
95. See "Senate Beats Van Deerlin to the Draw on 1934 Law," *Broadcasting,* March 19, 1979, p. 36.
96. Quoted in ibid.
97. See "Rewrite II—The Specifics," *Television Digest,* April 1, 1979 pp. 4–5.
98. Quoted in ibid.
99. Quoted in "Rewrite II More Radical Than Its Predecessor," *Broadcasting,* April 2, 1979, p. 29.
100. Quoted in "Van Deerlin II," *Broadcasting,* April 2, 1979, p. 98.
101. Ibid.
102. See *Television Digest,* May 7, 1979, p. 2.
103. Quoted in "Rewrite II—The Specifics," p. 5.
104. Quoted in "Van Deerlin Eyes Mark-up for H.R. 3333," *Radio & Records,* June 15, 1979, p. 4.
105. Quoted in "Rewrite II: The Jawboning Begins in Earnest," *Broadcasting,* May 21, 1979, p. 32.
106. Quoted in "Rewrite II More Radical Than Its Predecessor," p. 32.
107. Ibid.
108. Quoted in "Rewrite II: The Jawboning Begins in Earnest," p. 32.
109. Ibid.
110. Quoted in "Rewrite on Reef?" *Television Digest,* May 28, 1979, pp. 1–2.
111. See "Van Deerlin to Broadcasters: Get on Board or Be Left Behind," *Broadcasting,* May 21, 1979, p. 33. Citizen groups were also opposed to a spectrum fee as a trade-off for deregulation. Ralph Jennings of the Office of Communication of the United Church of Christ said: "It is difficult to imagine a spectrum use fee large enough to offset the loss of responsive local programming" (quoted in "All This Rewrite Talk," *Broadcasting,* May 28, 1979, pp. 67–68).
112. Ibid., p. 33.
113. See "Contrary Collins," *Broadcasting,* March 28, 1979, p. 70.
114. See "Spectrum Fee Running into Housemanship," *Variety,* May 16, 1979, p. 87.
115. See Pat Gushman, "The End of an Era, Throwing in the Rewrite Towel," *Cablevision,* July 30, 1979, p. 12. Also, some subcommittee members regarded the rewrite effort as essentially a one-man show—Van Deerlin's attempt to establish a "legacy" before he retired from Congress.
116. Quoted in "Rewrite Written Off," *Broadcasting,* July 16, 1979, p. 24.
117. Paul Harris, "Reality Catches Up with Van Deerlin," *Variety,* July 18, 1979, p. 29.
118. Quoted in "Rewrite II Dead—Amendments Next," *Television Digest,* July 16, 1979, p. 1.
119. Quoted in "Rewrite Written Off," p. 24. Van Deerlin, according to some Capitol Hill observers, employed "old school" leadership: support

the bill because I am the chairman. However, many of the Democratic members of the subcommittee were elected in 1974—the so-called Watergate Class—and were unwilling to support the bill simply because of its sponsorship by Van Deerlin.

120. See Judy Sarasohn, "Van Deerlin Drops Plans for Comprehensive Rewrite of 1934 Communications Act," *Congressional Quarterly,* July 21, 1979, p. 1444.
121. Quoted in ibid.
122. Quoted in "Cable Out of House Bill," *Television Digest,* December 17, 1979, p. 5. Jack Valenti is the head of the Motion Picture Association of America, and a frequent testifier before Congress on copyright matters. Retransmission consent is an often-proposed notion that cable television systems should get the consent of copyright holders—including the movie companies Valenti represents—before transmitting copyrighted television broadcast signals. The compulsory license granted cable systems in the 1976 Copyright Revision eliminates the need to obtain such consent. It is considered, however, an imperfect system by many copyright holders, and remains controversial. At this point, Van Deerlin sought to avoid controversy.
123. Quoted in "Van Deerlin Refuses to Say Die," *Broadcasting,* September 17, 1979, p. 27.
124. Lionel Van Deerlin, "Progress Made Via 'Rewrite' Dialog," *Variety,* January 9, 1980, p. 213.
125. See "New Names on Hill," *Television Digest,* November 10, 1980, p. 4. *Television Digest* had carried a story the week before the election stating that "Van Deerlin does not face [a] serious reelection threat" (*Television Digest,* October 27, 1980, p. 4).
126. Ibid.
127. Glen O. Robinson, "The Federal Communications Commission: An Essay on Regulatory Watchdogs," *Virginia Law Review,* 64 (1978), 182.
128. Interview with Robert Bruce, Washington, D.C., July 8, 1981.
129. For a discussion of these common carrier decisions, see Daniel L. Brenner "Communications Regulation in the Eighties: The Vanishing Drawbridge," *Administrative Law Review,* 33 (Spring 1981), 255–268.
130. Van Deerlin, "Progress Made Via 'Rewrite' Dialog," p. 213.
131. Interview with Lionel Van Deerlin, Washington, D.C., July 7, 1981.
132. Ibid.; also interview with Lou Frey, Washington, D.C., July 16, 1981.
133. Quoted in Burt Schorr, "Congress Is Moving to Inject Competition into Long Distance Telecommunications," *Wall Street Journal,* February 5, 1980, p. 48. Unlike deButts who was an advocate of the Bell bill, Brown espoused a new AT&T philosophy accommodating competition and new technology. Although H.R. 6121 reversed the principal elements of the Bell bill, AT&T supported it. Ironically, AT&T's competitors also switched their position. While they had generally supported H.R. 13015, they harshly condemned H.R. 6121, calling it another Bell bill (interview with Charles Jackson, former staff engineer, House Communications Subcommittee, Washington, D.C., July 20, 1981). In January 1982 AT&T and the Justice Department announced settlement of an antitrust case under which AT&T will give up its local operating companies but is freed to enter other areas of telecommunications competitively.
134. Quoted in "Van Deerlin Refuses to Say Die," p. 28.

A Closing Look:
Reflections on
Broadcast Regulation

The case studies in the preceding chapters have gone beyond organization charts and formal descriptions of agency procedures in order to convey some of the flavor and detail of the politics of broadcast regulation. This section summarizes how that process works by integrating the case studies with the model of the broadcast policy-making system developed in chapter four and by showing how the generalizations about that system apply to the case studies. It is important to remember that this model, like many, is not highly predictive. Rather, the model serves as a guide for what to look for (and for what not to overlook) in trying to understand how the system works. It is useful for picking out what is important and for focusing attention on what contributes to the development and resolution of policy disputes, but it cannot predict the long-run outcome of these policy controversies.

The Model Applied to the Case Studies

Chapter four distinguished between narrow, short-term, authoritative policy outputs and broader, long-term policy outcomes that are the product of many related policy outputs. The broadcast policy-making model can aid in understanding both outputs and outcomes, although it is easier to analyze outputs with it than outcomes. This is unfortunate because outcomes have long-run significance transcending specific outputs. Only by analyzing the immediate, however, is it possible to understand the indeterminate.

Consider an example of this crucial distinction between outputs and outcomes derived from the case study in chapter eight on comparative license renewal policies. A classic statement of what to look for in order to understand a political process is Harold Lasswell's emphasis on explaining "who gets what, when and how."[1] Those questions are relatively easy to answer when the "what" is not very broad and the "when" covers only a brief period of time. If broad issues or long periods are involved, the questions are harder to answer. In chapter eight we reviewed the continuing dilemma of how the FCC should handle comparative renewal disputes. There are many points within that saga where someone (a *who*) got something (a *what*) and where it is fairly clear *when* and *how* he got it. It matters greatly, however, where we enter any such chain of events. Suppose, for example, we started in 1970, just after the FCC issued its 1970 policy statement on comparative renewals. We would then say that the broadcast industry got what it wanted (greater assurance of renewal in the face of a challenger) fairly quickly (shortly after the *WHDH* decision) by skillful manipulation of the administrative process of an FCC already predisposed to reduce the uncertainty it had created about renewal standards through the *WHDH* case. In addition, the broadcasters' victory would be explained by saying that the FCC acted partly under pressure from, and partly to do a favor for, members of Congress who wanted to help the industry but were blocked from doing so in Congress by the citizen groups who had injected the issue of racism into the debate.

There are two major problems with such a "winner" or "loser" analysis. First, it is rooted in the moment being analyzed. Victories in the field of broadcasting, however, are not permanent. The next "policy output" may result in a different winner for different reasons influenced by different parties. The second problem, related to the first, is that short-run "wins" are not necessarily cumulative in the long run. Citizen groups learned this when they won repeated battles with the FCC and the industry over format change policy in the U.S. Court of Appeals for the District of Columbia Circuit, only to find those victories wiped out by a single U.S. Supreme Court decision. Applying the model simplistically to just small-scale battles can easily mislead.

The model must be used to understand outcomes as well as outputs. This is a difficult task, for neither we nor anyone else have so far developed a comprehensive theory to explain, in a complex political system, how to link related but still distinct outputs.[2] We can, however, use the model to guide us through the details of the selected case studies, to help us pick out the overall patterns of involvement (or noninvolvement) of the key groups in the broadcast policy-making system, to assist us in identifying important interactions among those major determiners of regulatory policy, to serve as a reminder of things we should not overlook, and to provide the background for opinions about outcomes.

Tables 6 through 10 represent what comes from such a use of the model when applied to the case studies. We have included in the tables four aspects we earlier identified as important in understanding how the system of broadcast regulation works: (1) which groups were in-

Table 6   Format Changes.

Proximate Cause of Controversy: A coalition of citizen groups and the courts forces changes, unsatisfactory to the FCC and the industry, of the way the FCC examines radio station format changes.

Main Participants/ Activities/Inputs	Major Authoritative Outputs	Outcomes/ Comments
FCC: Must face adverse decisions of court of appeals, citizen group petitions to deny. Responds with 1976 policy statement; seeks to preserve status quo.	U.S. Supreme Court supports FCC and industry. Preserves status quo: nonintervention of FCC in format choices.	FCC likely to stay out of format area, but keeps option open for later involvement. U.S. Supreme Court seems to respect that option.
		FCC and industry have increased interest in radio deregulation, reliance on marketplace forces.
Court of appeals: Responds to citizen groups and pushes FCC into involvement it does not want. Says its change is modest, but others see it as radical.		Court of appeals has been warned, for second time recently, that U.S. Supreme Court won't let it be a policy maker: its role is less activist. To extent court of appeals has been valuable to citizen groups as an ally, this reduction in court's role may be crucial to issues beyond format regulation.
Citizen groups: Act as the major stimulant to controversy. File petitions to deny; seek substantial change.		Citizen groups seek new ways to get FCC involved in format regulation.
Industry: Forms major alliance with FCC to preserve status quo. Is active in court cases.		
Congress and White House: Act as spectators only, although aspects of the Communications Act rewrite involve format change issues. Department of Justice supports FCC.		

Table 7   UHF Television.

Proximate Cause of Controversy: The FCC fails to adopt early policies supporting the development of UHF television. Specifically, its 1952 decision to intermix UHF and VHF markets left it with the continuing responsibility to try and make UHF work.

Main Participants/ Activities/Inputs	Major Authoritative Outputs	Outcomes/ Comments
FCC: Cripples UHF at the beginning, under pressure to make the service work. Proposes deintermixture as well as all-channel sets as answer.	FCC gives up deintermixture; Congress provides All-Channel Receiver Act. FCC uses it, plus other congressional support, to provide some continuing assistance to UHF industry through tuner/antenna rules.	UHF seems generally supported, although some other interests (such as land-mobile radio) covet some of its spectrum space. Future policy debates may be over whether to protect UHF from competing new communications technologies. Success of service seems to depend more on entrepreneurial than political skill of UHF interests.
Industry: Generally supports FCC goals of better UHF service but opposes accomplishing that through means disruptive to successful VHF broadcasting. TV manufacturers oppose what they see as regulation of them.		

Main Participants/ Activities/Inputs
(continued)
White House: Has minor role, though shows some recent interest in management of UHF spectrum.

Congress: Is seen as major source of authority to do something about problem. Sees it as related to success of public broadcasting, a service of interest to key members of Congress.

Citizen groups: Have very minor role, although show some interest in UHF potential for minority-owned stations and spectrum management issues.

Courts: Have little role to date; offer only minor interpretations of limits of FCC authority.

Table 8   Commercial Time.

Proximate Cause of Controversy: Members of the public complain to the FCC about the number and length of commercials on radio and television. The FCC appears at times anxious to respond to public requests for regulation.

Main Participants/ Activities/Inputs	Major Authoritative Outputs	Outcomes/ Comments
FCC: Responds to public and industry concerns about commercial time matters. Does 180-degree turn, at least in radio, between 1963 and 1981. Is influenced by change in philosophy, technology, and proliferation of stations.	1963: FCC promises, under pressure from Congress, not to adopt rules on commercial time. Keeps promise formally, but evolves informal standards. 1981: FCC decides to leave ad level in commercial radio up to marketplace forces.	Restoration of ad regulation in radio seems unlikely. Next industry push will be for similar ad deregulation for television. Citizen groups will oppose move at FCC and through courts. If Commission loses in court, pressure likely in Congress for changes in Communications Act to restore what industry had gained.
Industry: Consistently opposes regulation. Becomes FCC supporter of 1980 proposal to eliminate radio commercial time rules, which is truly a joint FCC-industry initiative.		
Citizen groups: Are not active in 1963 fight. By 1980s, are anxious to keep FCC rules but have few allies.		
Congress: Becomes a dependable supporter of the industry on this issue. Opposes FCC in 1963, supports it in 1980–1981.		
Courts: Are little involved in early stages of controversy. Are likely to be involved through citizen group appeals of FCC deregulation.		

Main Participants/ Activities/Inputs

(continued)

White House: Quietly supports industry views.

Table 9 Comparative Renewals.

Proximate Cause of Controversy: Vagueness in Communications Act's standards for comparative renewals leads to an FCC decision that the industry thinks will destroy license stability.

Main Participants/ Activities/Inputs	Major Authoritative Outputs	Outcomes/ Comments
FCC: Becomes embroiled in controversy with *WHDH* decision. Aside from that case, however, sides with industry on need for license stability. Looks for it also in Congress and courts. Tries to create standards that cannot be overturned.	None that have proven durable. In practice, the system has substantially produced license stability.	Unclear. Since, in practice, most parties, except citizen groups, get what they want— and there is relatively easy renewal— pressure is not continuous enough to resolve controversy. If FCC should come up with a solution or decision not acceptable to industry, likelihood is high of industry-Congress alliance to restore high renewal expectancy. Resolution need not necessarily come from Congress, if FCC can come up with solution that survives court review.
Courts: After *WHDH* case, become major perpetuator of the controversy. Overturn, sometimes at citizen group urging, FCC efforts to resolve issue.		
Industry: Has goals similar to FCC: seeks stability and participates in FCC, court, and congressional activities to try and obtain it.		
Congress: Is viewed by FCC and industry as likely source of resolution of controversy. Pressure from citizen groups and politics has blocked resolution to date.		

Main Participants/ Activities/Inputs

(continued)

Citizen groups: Are interested in outcome, although they rarely file competing applications. Want to keep pressure on industry not to regard licenses as guaranteed.

White House: Mostly watches from sidelines.

Table 10:   Communications Act Rewrite.

Proximate Cause of Controversy: Changing communications technologies appear to stretch to the limits the Communications Act of 1934. Some parties, both common carrier and broadcast, are dissatisfied with things the FCC is doing to them under the existing act.

Main Participants/ Activities/Inputs	Major Authoritative Outputs	Outcomes/ Comments
Congress: House Communications Subcommittee, under Rep. Van Deerlin, is major proponent of unified, comprehensive approach to rewrite. Besides Van Deerlin and Frey depth of commitment to it is unclear.	None discernible without inferences about side-effects of the rewrite process. No comprehensive act adopted, although the Bell bill is derailed.	Congressional staff/members claim it did not fail but instead affected FCC decisions on competition in common carrier communications and policies toward cable television and radio deregulation. Such claims are hard to verify empirically. Rewrite attempts set groundwork for future legislative proposals likely to be of less broad scope.
Industry: Is actively involved in entire process. Congress exploits some industry divisions (e.g., radio vs. TV). Must also battle nonbroadcast industries.		

Main Participants/ Activities/Inputs
(continued)

Main Participants/ Activities/Inputs	
FCC: Generally supports rewrite but opposes key provisions and is reluctant to lose flexibility of 1934 act. Testifies, but does not take active role, in Congress. Takes actions that reduce ardor of parties supporting rewrite.	*White House:* Watches process and is generally, but not strongly, supportive.
Citizen groups: Are involved but ineffective, except on those issues and strategies that coincide with industry.	*Courts:* Have little role in rewrite process, except as court decisions make parties unhappy and, therefore, more willing to consider compromises to restore benefits courts had taken away or refused.

volved (arranged, in general, in descending significance of involvement in each table); (2) how those groups interacted; (3) what the major authoritative outputs were—at least as of the time the analyses were conducted; and (4) the likely long-term outcomes associated with the pattern of short-term outputs identified in the case studies.

The usefulness and limitations of such a model are now apparent. This kind of comparative analysis of policy case studies permits identification of patterns of influence and involvement from which insight into the general functioning of the system can emerge. Use of the model enhances the understanding of specific outputs and provides a sense of what contributes to outcomes by providing background. It can also be used to organize data and observations in order to determine whether or not the policy case studies support, contradict, or call for modification of the seven generalizations about the process identified in chapter four.

The Case Studies and Generalizations About the Politics of Broadcast Regulation

Seven generalizations about the operation of the broadcast policy-making process were developed in chapter four. It is instructive to look again at those generalizations in light of the case studies.

1. PARTICIPANTS SEEK CONFLICTING GOALS FROM THE PROCESS

Theorists of regulatory behavior have focused increasingly on participant goals, how they interact—and conflict.[3] In broadcasting, many participants are driven principally by threats or benefits of an economic nature, but for some—citizen groups for example—other values may at times motivate actions. Broadcasters usually seek a profit from their operations. When some other participant introduces a different value, conflict occurs. In the format change cases, citizen groups and the U.S. Court of Appeals attempted to further the social goal of diverse service, which broadcasters perceived as conflicting with their objectives. Broadcasters argued that if their financial goals were pursued, diverse service was as likely to follow as it was from the policies sought by citizen groups and furthered by the court of appeals. Similarly, in the early days of the commercial time limit case study, the FCC attempted to respond to pressures to limit the quantity of commercials, creating automatic conflict with broadcaster goals. The goals of other participants in the process are a bit harder to define than the broadcaster's goal of profitable operation, but the case studies throw at least some light on them. Clearly Congress and the president can be driven by the political goal of reelection; in the rewrite case study some conflict occurred because of the personal political gains sought by individual politicians. Politics also probably played a role in deliberations on the All-Channel Receiver Act. There Congress blocked the FCC's expressed goal of deintermixture because broadcasters and other interest groups convinced members of Congress that the proposal was politically risky—especially for members of Congress from areas slated to lose VHF television. The degree to which participants seek conflicting goals is particularly clear in the rewrite case study, where so many powerful participants, with so many different goals, became involved that reconciling all the conflicts (or even just the major ones) proved impossible. The magnitude of that conflict made legislative action impossible.

2. PARTICIPANTS HAVE LIMITED RESOURCES INSUFFICIENT TO CONTINUALLY DOMINATE THE POLICY-MAKING PROCESS

This generalization simply says that no one of the six major determiners of regulatory policy wins all the time. In such an environment coalitions become important. The proposition is well supported by the case studies. The FCC was able to succeed in passing the All-Channel Receiver Act only because of significant support from other participants, notably the broadcast industry. Similarly, the coalescence of views of the industry and the FCC over format change policy was, eventually, sufficient to overcome the support the U.S. Court of Appeals had from citizen groups on that issue. The industry and Congress, jointly, were able to block the FCC's plans in 1963 to regulate advertising time, but neither it seems could unilaterally dominate the policy-making process on this or other issues. Because the broadcast industry seemed to get a lot of what it wanted in the format change, UHF, and advertising time limit case studies, one might be tempted to conclude that the industry can dominate the process. The comparative renewal case study, however, shows that thus far at least, the industry has been unable to promote a solution there favoring its interests.

Congress probably gets much of what it wants in those few instances when its members can rally around an objective. The members of Congress were not able to unite, however, in favor of Representative Van Deerlin's rewrite proposal, and indeed the project ended amid allegations that it had been a one-man show. The case studies show not only that individual participants lack the resources to dominate the process over the long term but also that no single participant can push through a preferred policy over the objection of all other groups. Things get done because parties pool their limited resources in making policy.

3. PARTICIPANTS HAVE UNEQUAL STRENGTHS IN THE STRUGGLE FOR CONTROL OR INFLUENCE

This statement is clearly related to the previous generalization. If no party can consistently dominate, the incentive is great on any particular issue to look for coalitions and allies. Even the most potent of participants in the system engages in this behavior. The FCC, for example, usually joins with either the industry or Congress. The tendency to look for support of this type is increased if the FCC is divided about its own commitment to a position. The format change controversy is one in which the FCC pooled its strength with that of the industry to take on citizen groups and the U.S. Court of Appeals for the District of Columbia Circuit. The combination of that court with the citizen movement has been a common one in broadcast policy making for the last decade or more. The format change case suggests that the combination may not be a particularly powerful one in the future. Citizen group influence seems currently diminished. It remains to be seen whether the court of appeals will reduce its policy-making role, as the U.S. Supreme Court believes it should.

The court of appeals has been an ally of other participants at other times. In the UHF case study from 1962 through the 1980s, for example, the electronics manufacturing associations have been largely unable to overcome the desire of the FCC and Congress to impose obligations on them such as the All-Channel Receiver Act, but by teaming with the courts in 1980 the manufacturers were able to slow the pace of FCC-imposed technical standards for UHF receiving equipment. The dispute between the U.S. Court of Appeals and the Supreme Court over format policy, however, suggests that courts are uneven in their influence on the system. The court of appeals is frequently involved in cases about broadcast policy, but it has been a particularly weak ally for the citizen movement in the long run since its decisions can be, and have been, brushed aside by the Supreme Court. That very observation, however, suggests that the Supreme Court is, when it enters the scene, one of the most powerful allies one can have.

4. THE COMPONENT SUBGROUPS OF PARTICIPANT GROUPS DO NOT AUTOMATICALLY AGREE ON POLICY OPTIONS

Participant "groups" exist, and can be identified, precisely because they usually have much in common—either as to objectives or available strategies. Power is clearly greatest when a group is united and speaks with a consistent voice. One of the reasons that the FCC was so successful in the format change case was that it remained unified in its refusal to regulate format changes through several years and many changes of Commissioners. It could turn convincingly to the Supreme Court and say that format regulation was not an issue in which the Commission—rather than just one set of Commissioners—wanted to be involved. But such consensus within groups does not arise automatically on every issue. In the case of comparative renewal policy, for example, it is striking that there is such a great degree of variance within the FCC over time. Some Commissioners have supported a two-step renewal policy solution, while others have had different preferences. The format change case is a stark example of how short of consensus the group we have called "the courts" can be. The case study, in fact, can be viewed as the U.S. Supreme Court versus the U.S. Court of Appeals for the District of Columbia Circuit. In the rewrite case study, Congressman Van Deerlin at times attempted to exploit differences between radio and television segments of the broadcast industry—by offering more to radio than to TV—in order to diffuse the influence that united broadcasters might otherwise have had over the outcome of the process.

5. THE PROCESS TENDS TOWARD POLICY PROGRESSION BY SMALL OR INCREMENTAL STEPS RATHER THAN MASSIVE CHANGE

A major qualification of this generalization is that what is "massive" or "incremental" is very much in the eye of the beholder. In the format change case, for example, the court of appeals continually characterized its decisions as modest—an interpretation with which the FCC and the industry took great exception. It remains accurate, however, to assert that the system more often moves slowly in small steps than quickly in large leaps. Sometimes a party will knowingly propose an unrealistically large leap so that a fallback step will seem moderate by comparison; the FCC seems to have done this with the proposal to deintermix VHF and UHF television only to settle for the All-Channel Receiver Act. Similarly, this may have been the grand plan for Van Deerlin's rewrite: he may have hoped that after the implications of massive change contained in the *Options Papers* and the first rewrite bill sank in, parties concerned with the Communications Act would settle for changes that, earlier, would have been declared radical.

Gradual change is also reflected in the kinds of mopping up operations that often follow a major change. Again, the case study on UHF-TV is a good example. After the FCC first harmed UHF through its 1952 allocation system, Congress took a major step through the All-Channel Receiver Act in 1962. Thereafter, both Congress and the FCC have had to return, from time to time, to that issue for minor adjustment. Congress has given the FCC money for further studies; the Commission has, through rules and regulations, gradually become more and more specific about UHF-TV receiver characteristics (if not technical performance standards), and the industry has slowly recovered some of the economic ground lost in 1952.

One of the inevitable consequences of a focus on incrementalism is a tendency to deal with short-range ills and bottlenecks—that is, to deal with the immediate and try to put off the long term, which, of course, only makes the notion of long-term problem self-fulfilling. The comparative renewal problem has been particularly marked by the tendency to go after short-term problems with what is hoped will be a quick fix. The 1970 policy statement was adopted in response to the immediate problem posed by increased filing of comparative applications at renewal time. Confronted with the complex option of formulating standards for comparative renewal proceedings, the Commission chose a simpler policy that would obviate the need for hearings in most such situations. Unfortunately for the FCC, the Court of Appeals disallowed this easy repair. Although the policy statement was designed to discourage the filing of competing applications at renewal time and thereby alleviate the broadcaster concern about the license stability, it did not deal well with the intricacies of the comparative renewal problem as created by deficiencies in the Communications Act. The failure of the rewrite process to lead to a comprehensive revision of the Communications Act of 1934 is, of course, a classic example of the preference for the incremental as opposed to the abrupt.

6. LEGAL AND IDEOLOGICAL SYMBOLS PLAY A SIGNIFICANT ROLE IN THE PROCESS

The case studies again show the degree to which arguments about policy can become mixed with arguments about symbols or rhetoric. Both the format change cases and the UHF-TV cases often turned into discussions of "freedom of choice," but the phrase had multiple meanings. It could mean the freedom of listeners to select particular radio formats—with the government keeping that choice broad by format regulation—or it could mean freedom for broadcasters to decide to offer certain formats. It could mean freedom for a TV set purchaser to decide not to purchase a set with a UHF dial that might be, for the time being, unneeded, or it could mean freedom for the manufacturer to decide what to produce.

Given the vagueness of the Communications Act of 1934, nearly everyone participating in the policy-making system can claim to be acting "in the public interest." Such claims, when they are made by everyone, do not advance discussion very much. But when Congressman Van Deerlin proposed to start anew, however, by dropping the phrase, critics from all sides attacked the elimination of the standard, although they clearly disagreed on what it meant.

7. THE PROCESS IS USUALLY CHARACTERIZED BY MUTUAL ACCOMMODATION AMONG PARTICIPANTS

Of the seven generalizations, this is the one that is least evident in the case studies. There is a good reason for that. The case studies we presented were purposely chosen because they reflect very significant policy controversies over which there has been great difficulty in reaching a quick resolution. There are thousands of examples we could have chosen where parties to the process struck a fast bargain that reasonably accommodated mutual interests. Such examples, however, would be less interesting than the case studies we chose. Even in our case studies, however, there are some efforts at accommodation. For example, the *en banc* decision of the Court of Appeals for the District of Columbia Circuit—in its review of the FCC's 1976 format policy statement, with all of its qualifying language about the Commission's tendency to overread prior court cases—seems to have been seen by the court as a last effort to reach accommodation with the Commission. The UHF case study shows trends toward accommodation as well. There Congress struck a balance with the FCC by passing the All-Channel Receiver Act after the Commission had retreated on deintermixture. Since the passage of that act, development of UHF has proceeded without much controversy except, on occasion, on the part of those who covet some of its spectrum space. Such relative unanimity over the development of UHF is probably easy to achieve since few, if any, economic or political interests are threatened directly by UHF television.

In addition there is a tendency to keep open options for future accommodations. In both the format change and commercial time areas, for example, the FCC expressly kept open the option that it might revisit those policies later, despite its present decisions not to adopt regulations in the area. Such a prospect would not be welcomed by broadcasters, but it at least could be offered to citizen groups. In the meantime, broadcasters, seeking to be accommodating, decided to continue the NAB Radio Code provisions relating to commercial time limits despite the FCC's deregulation of the area.

Some Final Observations

We have seen that the broadcast policy-making system is usually modest in its goals, flexible in policy choices, sensitive to feedback, and prone to dealing with immediate problems through steps and options that are only incrementally different from existing policies. We recognize that a consequence of these characteristics is a reactive rather than an innovative system—sluggish to respond to change in its environment, particularly to technological change that probably will be very rapid in the next decade or so. Clearly there are problems with this kind of policy-making system.

A legitimate question is whether there can be a significantly better system. To that, there can be several responses. One response, more common in the past than in recent years, is to ask, "Why doesn't the FCC regulate the industry more vigorously?" Such a question assumes that things would be improved by more regulation. However, the recent history of some other regulated industries (such as banking or transportation) suggests that stricter government controls may, at least sometimes, be ineffective or counterproductive. During the last few years, talk of nontechnical deregulation has emerged in television broadcasting and the process is almost a reality in radio and cable television. It is important to remember that deregulation will not be implemented in broadcasting from outside the current policy-making system but rather through it. Deregulation seems drastic to citizen groups, but it has gained the support of major segments of the FCC and the Congress. It may be the easiest policy option to support if the traditional justifications for regulation, notably the alleged "scarcity" of broadcast voices, are undercut by technological change. It can also be implemented without massively changing the policy making system. Calls for fundamental modification of the policy-making system, just as calls for massive change in its outputs, do not take into account the highly complex, politically sensitive, and rapidly changing character of broadcast communications and seem unlikely to be implemented. Under the system of policy making we have described, all interested parties are involved in a generally ordered bargaining process. Most parties with significant views get heard, although many will be unable to have their views prevail. Proximate solutions usually can be arrived at. The stake this country has in broadcast communications seems too precious to be subjected to drastic actions that may not allow for gradual modification of the system to deal with new conditions.

A second major question is whether the present system operates "in the public interest." The answer is probably yes, although a system that seems preoccupied with incremental or marginal change may seem less than heroic. Such a modest approach, however, tends to raise the level of competence of policy decisions as the attention of all involved is concentrated on familiar, better-known experiences and questions. It reduces the number and complexity of new factors that must be analyzed. This system is much more than a mechanism whose actions are dictated by the most politically powerful forces. Even the weakest participants in the system have some influence over policy, if not directly through their actions then at least through influencing the actions of others in determining what goes on the policy agenda. These participants interact with others in a policy making process where possibilities and options are continually tested, and alternative means of accomplishing desired ends are constantly debated. The very act of evaluating proposed moderate options may reveal hidden or unknown defects in proposals and lead to consideration of more sweeping alternatives. Attempts to initiate unpopular policy need not be merely an exercise in futility, for they may lead to the eventual establishment of a different, more popular, and more effective policy.

Broadcast regulatory policies that result from this policy-making system are not abstract theories. They are, rather, real-world political decisions allocating material rewards and deprivations—decisions, to use Lasswell's phrase, about who gets what, when, and how. They have important consequences for society. The development of policy in this manner is not easy. Before any proposal can emerge as policy, it must survive trial after trial, test after test of its vitality. The politics that governs broadcast regulation offers no escape from that imperative.

NOTES

1. Harold D. Lasswell, "Politics: Who Gets What, When and How," in *The Political Writings of Harold D. Lasswell* (Glencoe, Ill.: Free Press, 1951), pp. 295, 309.
2. Bruce Owen and Ronald Braeutigam have said the following about the difficulties of grand theories:

   The first step in future research must be to develop more formal models from which . . . hypotheses can be derived and tested. This is an extraordinarily difficult task. It is difficult partly because of the enormous richness and variety of regulatory behavior and partly because of the absence of much significant, repetitive, commensurate behavior conducive to statistical analysis (Bruce Owen and Ronald Braeutigam, *The Regulation Game: Strategic Use of the Administrative Process* [Cambridge, Mass.: Ballinger, 1978], p. 240).

3. See, for example, the work of Michael Porter and Jeffrey Sagansky, "Information, Politics, and Economic Analysis: The Regulatory Decision Process in the Air Freight Case," *Public Policy,* 24 (Spring 1976), 263–307. It is, of course, very difficult to be sure you properly understand goals in the same terms as the participants.

Annotated
Bibliography

General Works on Regulation

Although the literature on independent regulatory commissions is immense, the number of studies dealing with the political aspects of regulation is very limited. Three classic works that provide insights into the politics of regulation are Merle Fainsod's essay, "Some Reflections on the Nature of the Regulatory Process," in Carl J. Friedrich and Edward S. Mason, eds., *Public Policy: 1940* (Cambridge, Mass.: Harvard University Press, 1940), pp. 297–323; the study by Samuel P. Huntington, "The Marasmus of the Interstate Commerce Commission: The Commission, the Railroads, and the Public Interest," *Yale Law Journal,* 61 (April 1952), pp. 467–509; and the work by William W. Boyer, *Bureaucracy on Trial: Policy Making by Government Agencies* (Indianapolis, Ind.: Bobbs-Merrill, 1964). A study by William L. Cary, *Politics and the Regulatory Agencies* (New York: McGraw-Hill, 1967), illuminates many aspects of the regulatory process but only partially defines the political context of the problems he encountered as Chairman of the Securities and Exchange Commission. A fresh and thorough review of the various theories of the origins, practice, and justification of regulation is Barry M. Mitnick's *The Political Economy of Regulation: Creating, Designing and Removing Regulatory Forms* (New York: Columbia University Press, 1980). An essay pointing out the complexities of a broad theory of the politics of regulation, and the different perspectives on the topic of economists and political scientists, is John Q. Wilson's "The Politics of Regulation," in John Q. Wilson, ed., *The Politics of Regulation* (New York: Basic Books, 1980), pp. 357–394.

Valuable background material on independent regulatory commissions may also be found in the crucial studies by Robert E. Cushman, *The Independent Regulatory Commissions* (New York: Oxford University Press, 1941); and Marver H. Bernstein, *Regulating Business by Independent Commission* (Princeton, N.J.: Princeton University Press, 1955; reprinted by Greenwood Press, Westport, Conn., 1977.) A helpful book of readings edited by Samuel Krislov and Lloyd P. Musolf, *The Politics of Regulation* (Boston: Houghton Mifflin, 1964), emphasizes the interrelations of social interests and regulatory outcomes. *A New Regulatory Framework: Report on Selected Independent Regulatory Agencies* (Washington, D.C.: Government Printing Office, 1971) contains recommendations by the President's Advisory Council on Executive Organization for restructuring regulatory agencies as well as a selected bibliography of articles, books, reports, and studies useful for understanding the regulatory process. A thoughtful evaluation of the council's report is Roger G. Noll's *Reforming Regulation* (Washington, D.C.: Brookings Institution, 1971).

On the FCC: The Federal Communications Commission is one of seven agencies whose internal decision making and politics are analyzed by David M. Welborn in *Governance of Federal Regulatory Agencies* (Knoxville: University of Tennessee Press, 1977). A thorough review of theoretical perspectives for examining the FCC is provided in G. Gail Crotts and Lawrence M. Mead's "The FCC as an Institution," in Leonard Lewin, ed., *Telecommunications: An Interdisciplinary Survey* (Dedham, Mass.: Artech House, 1979) pp. 39–119. For a handy, annotated guide to both the agencies and literature of communications regulation, see "A Guide to Government Policy Making Bodies in Communications in the United States and Canada," *Aspen Handbook on the Media: 1977–1979 Edition* (New York: Praeger, 1977), pp. 173–197.

On the FTC: One of the best works on the FTC is Alan Stone's *Economic Regulation and the Public Interest: The Federal Trade Commission in Theory and Practice* (Ithaca, N.Y.: Cornell University Press, 1977). Also important is Kenneth W. Clarkson and Timothy J. Muris, eds., *The Federal Trade Commission Since 1970: Economic Regulation and Bureaucratic Behavior* (Cambridge, England: Cambridge University Press, 1981).

On Regulatory Reform: The regulatory process was the subject of increasing attention by Congress in the mid-1970s. A 749-page study, *Federal Regulation and Regulatory Reform* (the "Moss Report"), by the Subcommittee on Oversight and Investigations, House Committee on Interstate and Foreign Commerce, 94th Congress, 2nd Session (Washington, D.C.: Government Printing Office, 1976), provides a detailed review of the FCC and eight other regulatory agencies. In July 1975 the Senate Committee on Government Operations (later renamed the Committee on Governmental Affairs) was directed to conduct a comprehensive study of federal regulation in order to assess the impact of regulatory programs and the need for change. Following eighteen months of study the committee issued six volumes of its *Study on Federal Regulation:* Volume I, *The Regulatory Appointments Process;* Volume II, *Congressional Oversight of Regulatory Agencies;* Volume III, *Public Participation in Regulatory Agency Proceedings;* Volume IV, *Delay in the Regulatory Process;* Volume V, *Regulatory Organization and Coordination;* and Volume VI, *Framework for Regulation* with a separate appendix volume containing ten case studies, including one on cable television by Bruce Owen (pp. 347–389). All were published by the Government Printing Office in 1977 and 1978. A good general work by Ralph Nader's Congress Project is David E. Price's *The Commerce Committees: A Study of the House and Senate Commerce Committees* (New York: Grossman, 1976). A fascinating study of the manner in which appointments were made to the FCC and the Federal Trade Commission during a twenty-five-year period appears in the work of Washington lawyers James M. Graham and Victor H. Kramer, *Appointments to the Regulatory Agencies: The Federal Communications Commission and the Federal Trade Commission (1949–1974),* published as a Committee Print for the Senate Committee on Commerce, 94th Congress, 2nd Session (Washington, D.C.: Government Printing Office, 1976).

In recent years economists have turned their attention increasingly to the analysis of the regulatory process. A crucial work here is Alfred Kahn's *The Economics of Regulation: Principles and Institutions,* 2 vols. (New York: Wiley, 1971). This rich literature tends to focus on two sets of questions. The first involves the economic effects of regulation—who benefits and who is hurt by regulatory policies. An excellent overview of this topic may be found in Clair Wilcox and William G. Shepherd's *Public Policies Toward Business,* 5th ed. (Homewood, Ill.: Irwin, 1975), especially chapter 16, "Regulation of Communications." The theory that the economic purpose of the regulatory system is to slow down or dampen the effects of market forces and that industries can use regulation to their advantage is developed by Bruce M. Owen and Ronald Braeutigam in *The Regulation Game: Strategic Use of the Administrative Process* (Cambridge, Mass.: Ballinger, 1978). Several chapters deal with communications regulation. Also, many issues of the *Bell Journal of Economics and Management Science* carry articles on the economic effects of regulation. The second type of question economists have tended to ask about the regulatory process concerns why regulators adopt policies that favor some interests (often established) and hurt others. A path-breaking study by George J. Stigler, "The Theory of Economic Regulation," *Bell Journal of Economics and Management Science,* 2 (Spring 1971), pp. 3–21 analyzes how and why economic regulation favors the interests of politically powerful interests in terms of the market forces of supply and demand. This theory has been advanced by economist Richard A. Posner as well in "Theories of Economic Regulation," *Bell Journal of Economics and Management Science,* 5 (Autumn 1974), 335–356 with a bibliography on pp. 356–358. A collection of essays by Professor Stigler is contained in a useful paperback by him entitled *The Citizen and the State: Essays on Regulation* (Chicago: University of Chicago Press, 1975).

A large number of new studies that critically examined the philosophical, political, and economic bases of regulation were published in the late 1970s and early 1980s. Among those of note were works by Timothy B. Clark, Marion H. Kosters, and James C. Miller III, eds., *Reforming Regulation* (Washington, D.C.: American Enterprise Institute for Public Policy Research, 1980); James C. Miller III and Bruce Yandle, eds., *Benefit-Cost Analysis of Social Regulation* (Washington, D.C.: American Enterprise Institute for Public Policy Research, 1979); Peter H. Schuck, *Regulation: Asking the Right Questions* (Washington, D.C.: American Enterprise Institute, 1979); and *Regulating Business: The Search for an Optimum* (San Francisco: Institute for Contemporary Studies, 1978). In addition, many articles critical of regulation appear regularly in *Regulation: AEI Journal on Government and Society,* published bimonthly by the American Enterprise Institute for Public Policy Research, Washington, D.C. A useful bibliographical survey of some of this material is contained in James E. Anderson's "Economic Regulatory Politics: A Selected Bibliography," *Policy Studies Journal,* VII (Summer 1979), 833–844, and the economic literature is summarized in A. Lee Fritschler and Bernard H. Ross's

Business Regulation and Government Decision-Making (Cambridge, Mass.: Winthrop, 1980).

Congressional Quarterly, Washington, D.C., and *The National Journal,* Washington, D.C., have provided valuable analyses of regulation policy changes during the late 1970s and early 1980s. See, for example, Laura B. Weiss's "Reagan, Congress Planning Regulatory Machinery Repair: Administration Takes Sweeping Action," *Congressional Quarterly Weekly Report,* March 7, 1981, pp. 409–414 (which includes an analysis of efforts to apply cost-benefit analysis to regulation, a summary of issues concerning legislative veto of regulations, and a useful review of regulatory reform proposals under President Carter). See also the Schuck monograph cited above, which originally appeared in the *National Journal* on April 28, 1979; and Lawrence Mosher's "The Approaching Boom on the Tube: The Regulatory Boxes No Longer Fit," *The National Journal,* February 23, 1980, pp. 304–310.

Literature on Communications Regulation

No definitive work exists on the political problems of the Federal Communications Commission, although two recent studies offer useful evaluations of the Commission's role in the regulatory process as a controller of technological innovation: Vincent J. Mosco's, *Broadcasting in the United States: Innovative Challenge and Organizational Control* (Norwood, N.J.: Ablex, 1979); and Richard Berner's *Constraints on the Regulatory Process: A Case Study of Regulation of Cable Television* (Cambridge, Mass.: Ballinger, 1976). Also important to understanding cable television regulation are U.S. House of Representatives, Subcommittee on Communications, House Interstate and Foreign Commerce Committee, *Cable Television: Promise versus Regulatory Performance,* 94th Congress, 2nd Session (Washington, D. C.: Government Printing Office, 1976); and Don R. LeDuc, *Cable Television and the FCC: A Crisis in Media Control* (Philadelphia: Temple University Press, 1973). Walter B. Emery's *Broadcasting and Government: Responsibilities and Regulations,* rev. ed. (East Lansing: Michigan State University Press, 1971) offers a comprehensive (albeit dated) study of the legal aspects of broadcast regulation. Emery's study provides useful insights into the backgrounds of Commissioners, the various government agencies concerned with broadcasting, and Commission-congressional relationships.

Considerable material concerning broadcast regulatory policy prior to 1948 is contained in the doctoral dissertation of Murray Edelman entitled *The Licensing of Radio Services in the United States, 1927 to 1947: A Study in Administrative Formulation of Policy* (Urbana: University of Illinois Press, 1950; reprinted by Arno Press, New York, 1980). Also covering the early period is Philip T. Rosen's *The Modern Stentors: Radio Broadcasting and the Federal Government: 1920–1934* (Westport, Conn.: Greenwood Press, 1980). Robert S. McMahon's, *The Regulation of Broadcasting: Half a Century of Government Regulation of Broadcasting and the Need for Further Legislation,* is a detailed account of congressional consideration of laws on broadcast regulation written for the Committee on Interstate and Foreign Commerce, U.S. House of Representatives, 85th Congress, 2nd Session (Washington, D.C.: Government Printing Office, 1958). A supplement to the McMahon study, "A Legislative History of Broadcast Regulation," appears on pp. 93–216 of the *Option Papers* prepared by the staff for use by the Subcommittee on Communications of the House Committee on Interstate and Foreign Commerce, 95th Congress, 1st Session (Washington, D.C.: Government Printing Office, 1977).

A critical appraisal of the effectiveness of several FCC policies is found in the General Accounting Office's June 1979 report, *Selected FCC Regulatory Policies: Their Purpose and Consequences for Commercial Radio and TV,* CED-79-62 (Washington, D.C.: General Accounting Office, 1979). A well-written case study of *ex parte* influences in TV assignments is Victor G. Rosenblum's "How to Get into TV: The Federal Communications Commission and Miami's Channel 10," in Alan F. Westin, ed., *The Uses of Power: 7 Cases in American Politics* (New York: Harcourt Brace Jovanovich, 1962), pp. 173–228. A valuable discussion of the role of Congress during the 1920s and 1930s is contained in the study by Carl J. Friedrich and Evalyn Sternberg, "Congress and the Control of Radio-Broadcasting," *American Political Science Review,* 37 (October, 1943), pp. 797–818. An analysis of the role of Congress in formulating broadcast regulatory policy during the early 1970s appears in an article by Erwin G. Krasnow and Harry Wm. Shooshan III (later counsel to the Subcommittee on Communications, House Interstate and Foreign Commerce Committee), "Congressional Oversight: The Ninety-Second Congress and the Federal Communications Commission," *Harvard Journal on Legislation,* 10 (February 1973), 297–329; reprinted in *Federal Communications Bar Journal,* 26, No. 2 (1973), 81–117.

Participant-oriented material on the FCC can be found in several first-person books. Bernard Schwartz's *The Professor and the Commissions* (New York: Knopf, 1959) is a controversial account of abuses at the FCC by a New York University law professor who was hired by the House Committee on Interstate and Foreign Commerce in 1957 to study the regulatory commissions. Schwartz claimed that he was fired by the committee in 1958 after he proposed to expose violations of the *ex parte* rules and other laws that were politically embarrassing to the FCC, certain members of Congress, and the administration. Another first-person account based on experiences at the FCC, Charles S. Hyneman's *Bureaucracy in a Democracy* (New York: Harper & Brothers, 1950), is a thoughtful examination of government regulation. A collection of Newton Minow's speeches when he was Chairman of the FCC appears in a book edited by Lawrence Laurent entitled *Equal Time: The Private Broadcaster and the Public Interest* (New York: Atheneum, 1964). *How to Talk Back to Your Television Set* (Boston: Little, Brown, 1970; reissued with added bibliography and an index by Bantam Books, New York, 1970) is a lively, readable synopsis by Commissioner Nicholas Johnson of his views on various regulatory issues intended to give practical advice to citizens on how to change television programming. Johnson, along with John Jay

Dystel, has written "A Day in the Life: The Federal Communications Commission," *Yale Law Journal*, 82 (1973) pp. 1575–1634, an effort to describe one day's work of the Commission. A book by Barry G. Cole, a former consultant to the FCC, and Mal Oettinger, who had been a reporter for *Broadcasting* magazine, *The Reluctant Regulators: the FCC and the Broadcast Audience* (Reading, Mass.: Addison-Wesley, 1978), provides a behind-the-scenes account of the Commission's handling of such issues as license renewal and children's television. Former Commissioner Glen O. Robinson, a college professor before his brief FCC stint, has returned to academe and continues to produce thought-provoking analyses on the regulatory process. See, for example, "The Federal Communications Commission: An Essay on Regulatory Watchdogs," *Virginia Law Review*, 64 (March 1978), 169–262. See also Glen O. Robinson, ed. *Communications for Tomorrow: Policy Perspectives for the 1980s* (New York: Praeger, 1978), especially part four, "Government Institutions and Policymaking Processes in Communications," pp. 351–462.

For insights into the theory and application of First Amendment principles to broadcasting, four books merit special attention: Fred W. Friendly's *The Good Guys, the Bad Guys and the First Amendment: Free Speech vs. Fairness in Broadcasting* (New York: Random House, 1976); Benno C. Schmidt, Jr.'s *Freedom of the Press vs. Public Access* (New York: Praeger, 1976); Steven J. Simmon's *The Fairness Doctrine and the Media* (Berkeley: University of California Press, 1978); and Geoffrey Cowan's *See No Evil: The Backstage Battle over Sex and Violence on Television* (New York: Simon and Schuster, 1979). The Cowan book is largely an account of the so-called "Family Viewing" case, mostly from the perspective of those who challenged that NAB Code policy.

In addition to the general regulatory economics books and articles mentioned above, four works are recommended as a starting place for those interested in the economics of broadcasting: Roger G. Noll, Morton J. Peck, and John J. McGowan's *Economic Aspects of Television Regulation* (Washington, D.C.: Brookings Institution, 1973); Bruce M. Owen, Jack H. Beebe, and Willard G. Manning, Jr.'s *Television Economics* (Lexington, Mass.: Lexington Books, 1974); Bruce M. Owen's *Economics and Freedom of Expression: Media Structure and the First Amendment* (Cambridge, Mass.: Ballinger, 1975); and Harvey J. Levin's *Fact and Fancy in Television Regulation: An Economic Study of Policy Alternatives* (New York: Russell Sage Foundation, 1980).

TEXTBOOKS

There are several excellent textbooks that provide background for understanding the historical, economic, technical, sociological, and regulatory aspects of broadcasting. Perhaps the best overall is the work by Sydney W. Head with Christopher H. Sterling, *Broadcasting in America*, 4th ed. (Boston: Houghton Mifflin, 1982). Law textbooks dealing with communications law in general, but with at least some attention to the electronic media, include Donald M. Gillmor and Jerome A. Barron's *Mass Communication Law: Cases and Com-*

ment, 3rd ed. (St. Paul, Minn.: West, 1979); Harold L. Nelson and Dwight Teeter, Jr.'s *The Law of Mass Communications: Freedom and Control of Print and Broadcast Media,* 4th ed. (Mineola, N.Y.: Foundation Press, 1982); Harvey L. Zuckman and Martin J. Gaynes's *Mass Communications Law in a Nutshell* (St. Paul, Minn.: West, 1977); William E. Francois's *Mass Media Law and Regulation,* 2nd ed. (Columbus, Ohio: Grid, 1978); Don R. Pember's *Mass Media Law,* 2nd ed. (Dubuque, Iowa: Brown, 1981); Marc A. Franklin's *Cases and Materials on Mass Media Law,* 2nd ed. ((Mineola, N. Y.: Foundation Press, 1982); and Franklin with Robert Trager's *The First Amendment and the Fourth Estate: Communications Law for Undergraduates,* 2nd ed. (Mineola, N.Y.: Foundation Press, 1981). Texts with a more specific focus on broadcasting and cognate media include William K. Jones's *Cases and Materials on Electronic Mass Media: Radio, Television and Cable,* 2nd ed. (Mineola, N.Y.: Foundation Press, 1979); Douglas H. Ginsburg's *Regulation of Broadcasting: Law and Policy Towards Radio, Television and Cable Communications* (St. Paul, Minn.: West, 1979); and John R. Bittner's *Broadcast Law and Regulation* (Englewood Cliffs, N.J.: Prentice-Hall, 1982).

The Practising Law Institute (PLI), based in New York City, runs continuing education programs for attorneys and related professionals. Several seminars each year focus on communications law topics. Textbooks, including original commentary as well as substantial republication of important documents, are published. Look for texts on communications law in general, copyright, radio and television, cable television, and advertising. The Legal Department of the National Association of Broadcasters has published a *Legal Guide to FCC Broadcast Rules, Regulations and Policies* (Washington, D.C.: National Association of Broadcasters, 1977, with irregular updates). The loose-leaf guide is a management-oriented summary of FCC rules and regulations important to the industry on a day-to-day basis.

HISTORY

A rich and fascinating social history of American broadcasting is provided in the comprehensive three-volume work by Erik Barnouw: *A Tower in Babel: A History of Broadcasting in the United States to 1933; The Golden Web: A History of Broadcasting in the United States, 1933–1953;* and *The Image Empire: A History of Broadcasting from 1953* (New York: Oxford University Press, 1966, 1968, and 1970, respectively). Each volume contains a chronology, the text of major laws relating to broadcasting, and an extensive bibliography. A more recent book by Professor Barnouw, *Tube of Plenty: The Evolution of American Television* (New York: Oxford University Press, 1975), condenses material dealing with television found in the first three volumes and provides about five years of updating. Christopher H. Sterling and John M. Kittross's *Stay Tuned: A Concise History of Broadcasting* (Belmont, Calif.: Wadsworth, 1978) details trends in broadcast regulation in the context of the development of radio and television.

Other useful books on various aspects of the history of broadcasting include works by Llewellyn White, *The American Radio: A Report on the Broadcast-ing Industry in the United States from the Commission on Freedom of the Press* (Chicago: University of Chicago Press, 1947; reissued by Arno Press, New York, 1971); and Sydney W. Head with Christopher H. Sterling, *Broad-casting in America*, cited above.

The FCC's *Annual Reports* constitute excellent background material from the Commission's perspective; reports for the years 1935 through 1955 were reissued by Arno Press, New York, in 1971. A collection of landmark legal documents affecting broadcasting (with helpful introductory notes) is con-tained in Frank I. Kahn, ed., *Documents of American Broadcasting*, 3rd ed. (Englewood Cliffs, N.J.: Prentice-Hall, 1978). Washington communications attorney Victor E. Ferrall, Jr., has compiled an anthology of law review articles on broadcasting published between 1959 and 1978: *Yearbook of Broadcasting Articles* (Washington, D.C.: Federal Publications, 1979). An anthology by Lawrence W. Lichty and Malachi C. Topping, eds., *American Broadcasting: A Sourcebook on the History of Radio and Television* (New York: Hastings House, 1975), includes ninety-three documents and articles on various aspects of broadcasting, ranging from network programming to gov-ernment regulation.

PRIMARY SOURCES

The following publications of the Government Printing Office in Washington, D.C. contain copies of the basic laws, regulations, and decisions pertaining to broadcast regulation: the *United States Code* (all federal laws; the Communi-cations Act of 1934, as amended, appears in Title 47); the *Federal Register* (daily materials on rulemaking proceedings by governmental agencies); the *Code of Federal Regulations* (a compilation revised annually of rules and regulations adopted by such agencies, with the FCC's rules and regulations in the four volumes of Title 47); *FCC Rules and Regulations*, revised regularly by the Government Printing Office; and *Federal Communications Commis-sion Reports* (the decisions, public notices, reports and other documents of the FCC). Many useful documents are brought together in Gilman G. Udell (compiler), *Radio Laws of the United States* (Washington, D.C.: Government Printing Office, 1979). A useful index to *FCC Reports* is *FCC Decisions—Interpreting the Communications Act of 1934: An Index*, 2 vols. (Washington, D.C.: Government Printing Office, 1978).

The standard, privately published, comprehensive reference work in the field of broadcast regulation is *Pike & Fischer Radio Regulation* (Pike and Fischer, Inc., 4550 Montgomery Avenue, Bethesda, Md. 20014). This includes (1) the current text of broadcast laws and regulations; (2) legislative histories of such laws and of rules proposed and adopted by the FCC; (3) decisions, reports, and other rulings of the Commission; and (4) decisions of courts and other government agencies directly affecting radio and television. Another com-mercial publication, *Media Law Reporter*—a weekly loose-leaf service pub-lished by the Bureau of National Affairs—provides the text of court decisions of significance to the electronic and print media.

BIBLIOGRAPHIES AND JOURNALS

An excellent annotated bibliography of major published works dealing with the background, structure, function, content, and effects of the communications media is Eleanor Blum's *Basic Books in the Mass Media: An Annotated, Selected Booklist Covering General Communications, Book Publishing, Broadcasting, Editorial Journalism, Film Magazines, and Advertising,* 2nd ed. (Urbana: University of Illinois Press, 1980). The subtitle accurately describes the bibliography's contents. See also George D. Brightbill's *Communications and the United States Congress: A Selectively Annotated Bibliography of Committee Hearings, 1870–1976* (Washington, D.C.: Broadcast Education Association, 1978); Christopher H. Sterling's *Broadcasting and Mass Communications: A Survey Bibliography,* 9th ed. (Philadelphia: Temple University Press, 1982); and William E. McCavitt's *Radio and Television: A Selected, Annotated Bibliography* (Metuchen, N.J.: Scarecrow Press, 1978). *Broadcasting/Cable Yearbook,* published annually by Broadcasting Publications, Inc., Washington, D.C., includes an annotated booklist of major works. *Mass Media Booknotes,* edited by Professor Sterling, is a monthly review of recent books on broadcasting and other media.

Several scholarly journals *(Journal of Broadcasting, Journal of Communications, Journalism Quarterly, Federal Communications Law Journal, Journal of Law and Economics,* and *Comm/Ent)* regularly publish articles on aspects of broadcast regulation. The major communications journals provide annual and cumulative indexes. Law journals are indexed by two services: *Index to Legal Periodicals* and *Current Law Index.* Important popular journals include *TV Guide* and *Channels of Communication.* Much of the popular literature is indexed by *Reader's Guide to Periodical Literature.* A useful guide to student work is John M. Kittross's *Theses and Dissertations in Broadcasting: 1920–1973* (Washington, D.C.: Broadcast Education Association, 1978).

The Five Case Studies

Surprisingly little useful research has been published concerning the five case studies in chapters five through nine. What literature exists tends to be either impressionistic and one-sided accounts or journalistic reports scattered throughout issues of trade periodicals such as *Broadcasting* and *Television Digest.* The footnotes in chapters five through nine provide citations to the pertinent FCC, judicial, and congressional documents. Detailed contemporaneous accounts of FCC actions in the five cases (as well as other aspects of broadcast regulation) are reported weekly in *Broadcasting.* Although *Broadcasting* is the best known of the trade journals for the broadcast industry, *Television Digest* and *Variety* offer informative accounts of FCC actions each week, frequently from a less industry-oriented perspective. Both *Broadcasting* and *Television Digest* publish annual indexes, although the ones in *Broadcasting* so far cover only 1972 to 1977. For an index to earlier and later issues, use *Business Periodicals Index*. Also useful, and indexed in *Business Periodicals Index*, is a biweekly trade journal, *Television/Radio Age*. Each issue includes an "Inside the FCC" column. Television Digest, Inc. also publishes, *Public Broadcasting Report, Satellite Week, Video Week*, and *Communications Daily*. These, plus another trade publication, *Telcom Highlights*, are useful in following telecommunications issues beyond those of commercial broadcasting. Reports on FCC matters from the perspective of various citizen groups can be found in *access* magazine, published by the National Citizens Committee for Broadcasting.

FORMAT CHANGES

The literature on this topic is mostly found in law reviews and does not focus on the political aspects of the issue. The law reviews contain articles that can be classified into three categories: (1) case notes summarizing one or more of the format change cases (we shall not comment further on these here); (2) articles prescribing what the FCC or the courts should do about format changes; and (3) articles dealing with the political aspects of the dispute (to the extent that they discuss the relative roles of the FCC and the Court of Appeals for the District of Columbia Circuit). Chapter five was written just after the U.S. Supreme Court's 1981 decision, so it is likely that the law review literature will expand with commentaries on that decision. For now, the best articles are Peter del Vecchio's "The Judicial Role in the FCC Decisionmaking Process: A Perspective on the Court-Agency Partnership in the Entertainment Format Cases," *Boston College Law Review*, 21 (1980) 1067–1109. This is an excellent, careful review of the partnership doctrine, and it correctly predicted that the U.S. Supreme Court would overturn the court of appeals on the ground that the latter had substituted its policy judgment for that of the FCC. A straightforward chronology of the format change cases is provided by John H. Pennybacker in "The Format Change Issue: FCC vs. U.S. Court of Appeals," *Journal of Broadcasting*, 22 (Fall 1978) 411–424. The two most interesting "what the law should be" articles are Daniel L. Brenner's "Government Regulation of Radio Program Format Changes," *University of Pennsylvania Law Review*, 127 (1978), 56–110; and Bruce M. Owen, "Regulating Diversity: The Case of Radio Formats," *Journal of Broadcasting*, 21 (Summer 1977) 305–319. The latter is a summary of studies done by Owen for the National Association of Broadcasters that was filed with the FCC as part of its 1976 inquiry and was influential in the Commission's decision not to get involved in format change regulation. Finally there is one important analysis in a trade journal: Mel Friedman's "The Supreme Court Test of Format-Change Issue: FCC's On-Off Switch in Radio Deregulation," *Television/Radio Age*, October 20, 1980, pp. 40–42ff.

UHF TELEVISION

Considering its increasing importance as a medium, and the relatively long period of time UHF policy has been a controversy, it is amazing how little has been written on the subject. The best single source on the current technical situation may be the final report of the FCC's UHF Comparability Task Force: *Comparability for UHF Television: Final Report* (Washington, D.C.: Federal Communications Commission, September 1980). Unfortunately, it is not likely to be widely distributed. Articles of some interest include Alexander Korn's "What the 'UHF Handicap' Really Means in Terms of Audience and Revenue—and Why," *Television/Radio Age*, June 19, 1978, pp. 24–26ff; and Rolla Edward Park's *Cable Television and UHF Broadcasting*, Rand Corporation Report R-689-MF (Santa Monica, Calif.: Rand, 1971). Economists have continually found UHF an object of interest, though they generally have concluded that it was bound to fail. See Harvey J. Levin's *Fact and Fancy in Television Regulation: An Economic Study of Policy Alternatives* (New York: Russell Sage Foundation, 1980); and his earlier work, *The Invisible Resource: Use and Regulation of the Radio Spectrum* (Baltimore: Johns Hopkins Press, 1971). A long analysis of events leading up to the passage of the All-Channel Receiver Act in 1962 is available in "Notes: The Darkened Channels: UHF Television and the FCC," *Harvard Law Review*, 75 (June 1962), 1578–1607. There are two doctoral dissertations on early deintermixture efforts: John Michael Kittross's "Television Frequency Allocation Policy in the United States" (University of Illinois, 1960; reprinted by Arno Press, New York, 1979); and Avard Wellington Brinton's "The Regulation of Broadcasting by the FCC: A Case Study of Regulation by Independent Commission," (Harvard, 1962). Some aspects of the 1962 drive to pass the All-Channel Receiver Act are discussed in chapter six, "All-Channel Television," of Newton N. Minow's *Equal Time*, cited above. Douglas W. Webbink analyzes this legislation in his critique, "The Impact of UHF Promotion: The All-Channel Receiver Law," *Law and Contemporary Problems*, 34 (Summer 1969), 535–561. An earlier version of this chapter by Lawrence D. Longley appeared as "The FCC and the All-Channel Receiver Bill of 1962," *Journal of Broadcasting*, 13 (Summer 1969), 293–303.

COMMERCIALS

The only published material that systematically examines events surrounding the FCC's efforts to adopt the NAB code time standards as its own is an early version of chapter seven, written by Lawrence D. Longley, "The FCC's Attempt to Regulate Commercial Time," *Journal of Broadcasting*, 11 (Winter 1966–1967), 83–89. A criticism of the Commission's 1963 initiative on legal and constitutional grounds was published at the time by Douglas A. Anello and Robert V. Cahill, attorneys with the National Association of Broadcasters, "Legal Authority of the FCC to Place Limits on Broadcast Advertising Time," *Journal of Broadcasting*, 7 (Fall 1963), 285–303. A discussion of the FCC's policies on commercials following the abortive attempt in 1963 is contained in an article by Carl Ramey, "The Federal Communications Commission and Broadcast Advertising: An Analytical View," *Federal Communications Bar Journal*, 20 (1966), 71–116. About the only recent law review article on the same topic is by FCC Commissioner Robert E. Lee, "The Federal Communications Commission's Impact on Product Advertising," *Brooklyn Law Review*, 46 (1980), 463–486. This article is particularly interesting because much of its content, and even its language, was later incorporated in the FCC's 1981 order deciding to deregulate commercial radio advertising practices.

COMPARATIVE RENEWAL POLICY

Like the controversy itself, the literature on this area is extensive and inconclusive. Sterling "Red" Quinlan's *The Hundred Million Dollar Lunch* (Chicago: J. Philip O'Hara, 1974) is a "new journalism" account of the WHDH proceedings. A detailed chronology of events leading to the *WHDH* decision and its aftermath until 1973, plus a listing of significant sources, are contained in Robert R. Smith and Paul T. Prince's "WHDH: The Unconscionable Delay," *Journal of Broadcasting*, 18 (Winter 1973–1974), 85–96. A number of law review and other articles have focused on the controversy since WHDH. Some of the more insightful are Louis Jaffe's "WHDH: The FCC and Broadcasting License Renewals," *Harvard Law Review*, 82 (1969), 1693–1702; "Comment, The Federal Communications Commission and Comparative Broadcast Hearings: WHDH as a Case Study in Changing Standards," *Boston College Industry and Commerce Law Review*, 10 (1969), 943–971; William H. Wentz, "Comment: The Aftermath of WHDH: Regulation by Competition or Protection of Mediocrity?" *University of Pennsylvania Law Review*, 118 (1970), 368–409; Robert A. Anthony's "Towards Simplicity and Rationality in Comparative Broadcast Licensing Proceedings," *Standford Law Review*, 24 (November 1971), 1–115; Rosel Hyde's "FCC Policy and Procedures Relating to Hearings on Broadcast Applicants in Which a New Applicant Seeks to Displace a Licensee Seeking Renewal," *Duke Law Journal*, 1975 (May 1975), 253–278; Henry Geller's "Comparative Renewal Process in Television: Problems and Suggested Solutions," *Virginia Law Review*, 61 (April 1975), 471–514; Robert W. Buck's "FCC Comparative Renewal Hearings: The Role of the Commission and the Role of the Court," *Boston College Law Review*, 21 (January 1980), 421–454; Robert J. Brinkman's "The Policy Paralysis in WESH: A Conflict between Structure and Operations in the FCC Comparative Renewal Process," *Federal Communications Law Journal*, 32 (Winter 1980), 55–104; Andrew Clark's "The Recognition of Legitimate Renewal Expectancies in Broadcast Licensing," *Washington University Law Quarterly*, 58 (Spring 1980), 409–438; John H. Pennybacker's "Comparative Renewal Hearings: Another Dialogue Between Commission and Court," *Journal of Broadcasting*, 24 (Fall 1980), 527–547; and Milan D. Meeske's "Impact of WESH Case on Procedures for Comparative License Renewals," *Journalism Quarterly*, 57 (Autumn 1980), 451–455ff. For its insight and wit, no one should miss Glen Robinson's dissenting statement in *Cowles Florida Broadcasting, Inc.*, 60 FCC2d 372, 453–488 (1976) or Joseph Fogarty's dissent in the same case (five years later), *Cowles Broadcasting, Inc.*, 86 FCC2d 993, 1024–1055 (1981). An analysis of the development of the FCC's comparative renewal policy based on the model in *The Politics of Broadcast Regulation* can be found in the doctoral dissertation of Stanley D. Tickton, *Broadcast Station License Renewals Action and Reaction, 1969 to 1974* (University of Michigan, Ann Arbor: 1974). A study entitled *Licensing of Major Broadcast-*

ing Facilities by the Federal Communications Commission, which was prepared by Professor William K. Jones for the Administrative Conference of the United States, is an excellent volume for background reading on the FCC's processing of renewal applications and its standards in comparative hearings. The study was reprinted in U.S. House of Representatives, Subcommittee No. 6, Select Committee on Small Business, 89th Congress, 2nd Session, *Activities of Regulatory and Enforcement Agencies Relating to Small Business,* Part 1, A103–A112, A165–A174 (Washington, D.C.: Government Printing Office, 1966). For those with real stamina, there are all the Senate and House hearing records on the innumerable "renewal relief" bills introduced between 1966 and 1976 and, after that, comments on the comparative renewal dilemma found in various hearings to rewrite, revise, reform, refurbish, and renovate the Communications Act of 1934 listed in the next section of this bibliography.

COMMUNICATIONS ACT REWRITE

The best materials to date on this controversy are the contemporaneous accounts in the trade press. No record was ever published of the 1977 "panels" conducted by the House Communications Subcommittee prior to the introduction of the first rewrite bill. The subcommittee, however, did publish the staff *Options Papers* that constituted the starting point for the act's proposed revision. See *Options Papers,* Subcommittee on Communications, Committee on Interstate and Foreign Commerce, U.S. House of Representatives, 95th Congress, 1st Session (Washington, D.C.: Government Printing Office, 1977). A citizen group reaction to the *Options Papers* is provided in Timothy R. Haight, ed., *Telecommunications Policy and the Citizen: Public Interest Perspectives on the Communications Act Rewrite* (New York: Praeger, 1979). Both the Senate and House did print hearing records of their rewrite efforts in 1978 and 1979—all published by the Government Printing Office. See *The Communications Act of 1978, Hearings on H.R. 13015,* 5 vols., in 8 parts, Subcommittee on Communications, Committee on Interstate and Foreign Commerce, U.S. House of Representatives, 95th Congress 2nd Session (1979); *The Communications Act of 1979, Hearings on H.R. 3333,* 5 vols., in 7 parts, Subcommittee on Communications, Committee on Interstate and Foreign Commerce, U.S. House of Representatives, 96th Congress, 1st Session (1979); and *Amendments to the Communications Act of 1934, Hearings on S. 611 and S. 622,* 4 vols., Subcommittee on Communications, Committee on Commerce, Science and Transportation, U.S. Senate, 96th Congress, 1st Session (1979). Some caution is advised in approaching this record, which occupies more than two feet of bookshelf. None of the law review or academic communications journal articles published as of late-1981 provides substantial insight into the *politics* of the rewrite process. For an early effort to assess the rewrite, see Manny Lucoff's "The Rise and Fall of the Third Rewrite," *Journal of Communication,* 30 (Summer 1980), 47–53. A very brief summary of some of the rewrite issues is found in chapter twelve, "Reexamining the Communications Act," of John R. Bittner's *Broadcast Law and Regulation* (Englewood Cliffs, N. J.: Prentice-Hall, 1982) pp. 381–394.

Index

DATE DUE

PRINTED IN U.S.A.

HIGHSMITH 45-102

121269